If a Million Fell from the Sky

A memoir

Written by

J International

Manzanita LLC

Table of Contents

Author's Note

Though most events are described as I remember them, some were presented allegorically to examine aspects of my life that required a more elusive reckoning. Certain characters are composites, and some timelines have been condensed for clarity. Above all, this is a story of transformation—a journey toward a newfound perspective.

Part I – Life

"God does not require us to succeed. He only requires that you try."

— Mother Teresa

Chapter 1

My mother gave me a dollar. She explained it was an allowance and would teach me how money works. I handed it to the cashier and pocketed the change from my purchase. I hoped all my lessons would be that simple.

My allowance started at a buck and slowly rose to five. Every Monday, she gave me the full amount, aiming to teach me a second lesson: saving for a rainy day, or at least till the following Monday. But the rain came quickly after riding my rickety bike to 7-Eleven. When faced with blue and red Slurpees spinning in the tank, candy bars, soda bottles, and scrumptious hot dogs begging for a bite, how was I supposed to budget and plan? Besides, if I ran out of money, I could always sneak another dollar or two from my mother's purse when she went directly to bed after work.

Aside from my mother eventually discovering my thievery and moving her billfold to a secure location, inflation—which I understood through the lens of all my favorite sugary and starchy delights rising in price as fast as my allowance—left me with more and less all at once. I had more to learn about money than I thought. With my mother's purse now accompanying her to bed and the rising Slurpee CPI chipping away at my 7-Eleven basket of goods, I didn't understand why I couldn't have ten or twenty dollars a week instead of five. Even as a young boy, I yearned for bigger bills. I knew we weren't rich. My secondhand shoes, our recurring meatloaf dinners, which were questionably fit for consumption, and the tiny Honda Civic Hatchback parked in front of our humble home informed me of that. But I was convinced she could give me more—just a little more. I figured bolstering my stake only required proof of my impressive work ethic, which she might not have noticed.

"Mom, I want to talk to you about raising my allowance."

"Okay," she said while we sat in the living room. A train rumbled along the tracks behind us. Beyond them was a shopping center we walked to on the weekends when she wasn't exhausted from what I later understood is called the Daily Grind.

"So, I've been doing all my homework and washing the dishes without you asking me."

"Yes, but you're only rinsing them in cold water, and I usually have to scrub them again."

"Oh, I'll start using soap and hot water. You won't have to do that next time. They'll be really clean. Can I get another dollar now?"

"You know, at my job, I only get a raise *after* I've done something to impress my boss, not based on promises. But no matter how much money you make, you'll never have enough if you buy a bunch of things you don't need, like those gloves that change color in the cold or the remote-controlled car you saw in the back of that magazine. Where are you getting all those magazines from? Did your father give them to you?"

The answer was yes. He'd given them to me and permission to eat as much sugary cereal as I pleased. After they divorced, the court awarded my mother custody of me, but I saw my father every other weekend. What he didn't give me was money. He promised to double my allowance if I convinced her to let me live with him, but until then, I had to be satisfied with *Apple Jacks* and *Mad* magazine.

I tried to think of another tactic to increase my allowance, but my mother had made up her mind. She had the same unimpressed look she'd given me when I showed her the Rubik's Cube I said I solved by peeling the stickers off and reapplying them with matching colors on each side.

She steered the conversation away from augmenting my income and advised me further on the merits of frugality. "Whenever you buy something, you want to get the best deal. That's why I've shown you little tricks, like how they cut the price of deli food after 7 p.m. at the supermarket."

"But by then, that stuff is gross. The macaroni and cheese looks like plastic, and the chicken tenders are hard as rocks!"

"Well, let's pray the day never comes when you don't have enough money to eat. You'll be begging for those chicken rocks if that happens. I've been interviewing for a teaching job, which might mean we'll have a little extra money soon. Keep doing your homework and chores, and we'll talk again next month."

I did as my mother instructed. She got the job, and my allowance steadily rose to ten dollars. I had a natural gift for math. Although I hadn't taken pre-algebra yet, I could already solve for x and imagine my life once I hit twenty dollars a week. While it had its frustrations, I'd become quite comfortable with my mommy-defined benefit plan in exchange for a couple of chores.

Shortly after I hit the ten-dollar mark, my mother and I chatted at our kitchen table with worn-down expandable wings, which we'd scored from a nearby yard sale. The previous owner patched them up with wallpaper commemorating the Ford Motor Company assembly line. The images of industrious men fastening parts on the Model T were as formative to my childhood as the bland vegetable stew my mother made for dinner.

"Julian, since Henry was kind enough to give you your own room, I'd like you to start working and pitch in more. I've already spoken with a nice man at the *News Journal* who'll show you how to deliver newspapers next week."

She'd broken up with her boyfriend, Max, my father's former best friend, leaving Max for his brother, Henry. It's fair to say Mama's dating pool was small, but she didn't paint her relationships with romantic language. Survival characterized many of her motivations back then.

***

The washing machine dutifully made sloshing sounds while my mother did laundry in the basement of Henry's townhouse. Although I'd soon be delivering newspapers, I wanted to know how the washer and dryer worked. I preferred my cushy setup doing chores at home rather than working for someone I didn't know, even if they were a "Nice Man," as my mother had assured me.

"Mom, why did you and Dad get divorced? He said it was your fault." The washing machine shook its rusty bolts, lurching into the spin cycle.

7

"No, Julian, your father is sick. He's violent and manipulative. That means he tries to control you. He talked about free love and changing the world before we got married. Then he started hitting me! Don't listen to his nonsense. He only has himself to blame."

I'd forgotten many of those moments, like old film reels lost in the attic of my mind. I tried not to linger in its fractured light. I preferred easier recollections of happier times we'd had.

Yet I vividly recall being at the bottom of a staircase, playing war games with toy soldiers the last time we were together. But there'd been another war in the kitchen nearby.

My parents' heated conversation escalated into screaming; something smashed, and my father shouted words he'd told me not to say. I was afraid to look.

Grabbing his jacket and storming out of the house, all I saw was his thin, greasy hair flopping around his ears and bell-bottom jeans. The screen door was stuck. He tried twice to open it, then forced his way out, leaving it scraping the front step.

My mother was on the kitchen floor, her hand on a bruise above her eye, with a blotch of spinach dripping on the wall behind her. What was happening? Spinach shouldn't be on the wall. With a wan smile, she pulled herself up and said, "Everything's fine, Julian. Keep playing with your toys." I went back to my soldiers, but it wasn't fun anymore.

My parents depicted their problems differently, with each claiming they weren't to blame for them. I was so young when they were together that it was hard to say which version captured the whole saga of their separation.

"Look, I never hit her," my father explained at his new place in Wilmington, Delaware, when I confronted him with what I remembered. He'd abandoned his working-class buddies since obtaining a PhD in management. Suits with leather elbow patches replaced his tie-dye shirts and graveyard shifts. My mother called him a yuppie—a very angry yuppie.

"All I did was try to calm her down, but sometimes she'd start screaming with her arms flailing all over the place and hurt herself, so I held her still—gently, Julian. I never tried to hurt her. Not once.

You're old enough to hear this. Your mother isn't well. She might have to be hospitalized someday. I'm worried about her. I really am. The truth is, you should be living with me. You like it here. That park across the street is nice, isn't it? Have you ever seen so many trees? And how about that steak dinner we had last night? Remember how the waiter brought out that big wooden pepper grinder? I bet your mom doesn't take you to places like that. Talk to your mom about it. Tell her it's what you want. You want to live with me."

I looked toward the park, then back at him. "Another thing, Julian. When she tried to take you away, what was I supposed to do? Sit there and let her steal you from me?"

Though my allowance had increased, I still wanted more. With more money, I could buy remote-controlled cars, boats, and airplanes. I'd buy all the things kids at school showed off, like indestructible digital watches that were so strong you could wear them to the bottom of the sea—even though none of us had ever gone to the bottom of the sea. So maybe working for the man wasn't such a bad idea after all. After an exhaustive search, I found my mother's billfold behind a bottle of Jack Daniel's in the top drawer of her nightstand. It had become a matter of matching wits rather than supplementing my income. The fun of pilfering from her purse disappeared after she learned of my avarice.

Chapter 2

The nice man who managed paper routes laid out the routine with a checklist scrawled on a blackboard. I got the gist of it despite being distracted by the periodicals he'd piled up and plastered on the walls. He said something about checking for new customers and promptly reporting any complaints. I was nervous during the meeting but eager to start. I assumed the entire gig would be like the then-popular arcade game *Paperboy*, which involved a series of obstacle courses and rolled-up paper tosses that I'd execute from the comfort of my BMX bike.

It started well enough. While wearing a hooded sweatshirt with a carrier bag slung from my shoulder, my breath billowed in the cold morning air as I rode to the corner where newspaper bundles were fastened with tight yellow ties. If I didn't snip them carefully, they splayed into the grass, glistening with morning dew, turning the pages into pulpy globs unfit for anything more than clogging storm drains. When I began, some customers must've received papers with missing or sopping wet sections. Sunday papers jam-packed with extra ads, comics, and coupons were the worst. I used to like the fat, multicolored pages stacked high on my front stoop. I'd bring the paper inside, locate the comic section, and curl up on the couch to read and chuckle at the ones I understood. But with the added weight, I wasn't laughing anymore.

I initially placed each paper by the front door, but that was no fun. That was not how I'd played *Paperboy*. With a flick of the wrist, I mirrored the game, sending them sailing from my bike to all my customers, speeding things up nicely. Having barely qualified for the minor leagues in my local baseball division, it was no surprise that my pitch was less than perfect, but as long as the paper landed on their property, I moved on to the next house. Perfecting their placement would have left less time to goof around and read magazines when I completed my route. After a month, I lost a few customers but gained some too, so I didn't sweat it. The nice man told me several people had complained about not receiving their daily newspaper. He confirmed that I understood "daily" means "every day."

As the nice man cut my paycheck, he gave me my first performance review.

"How do you think everything is going, Julian?"

"It's going great. I'm getting better at throwing papers from my bike, so I get everything done real quick! Every time I do my route, I get a little faster."

He nodded with a strained smile. "Well, that's good. I'm glad to hear it. Remember, it's important that everyone gets the papers they paid for so they can roll out of bed, grab a cup of coffee, and scoop them up from their front porch. Seeing the paper by the door matters more than getting it there quickly. If they have to pluck them out of the bushes, that's less satisfying, don't you think?" He waved his finger like a conductor while he spoke. The orderly tradition of papers arriving squarely on front porches gave him great pride and satisfaction. People depended on it. A misplaced periodical tugged at the thin fabric holding our community and its decent ways together. He inched forward and continued, "A woman who only gets a paper on Sundays called and said she hadn't received her copy last week. Don't forget to check the list I gave you that says who gets what, when."

"Oh yeah, I check that before I go out, but I haven't been bringing it. I'll start doing that," I acknowledged, knowing the man was right but annoyed that the job was so complicated. Daily deliveries are hard enough. Why would anyone only want a paper on Sunday or any other random assortment of days? That shouldn't be allowed.

"Keep up the good work, Julian, and call me anytime if you need something. Here's another copy of the list. You understand. It shows who gets what, when." He said, Who gets what when with the same enthusiasm every time. He must've liked hearing it, so I repeated the phrase as I took the list.

"Who gets what, when."

The nice man showed me to the door with a friendly, fatherly pat on the back. My family lived in a townhouse fifteen minutes from the *News Journal* office. The houses around his office were grander than ours. Some were three stories tall, with arched doors and cobblestone walkways crisscrossing all manner of shrubbery. I pedaled past their steel gray cars with tinted windows and chrome trim, down narrow side streets, and then into the woods along the creek, where I transcended the architecture and icons of class amongst the trees. Everything was equal there, but when granted access to those stately manors via a classmate or an associate of my mother's, their opulence perplexed me. My mother had the same reaction, so it remained unreconciled. What is the purpose? Why are so many tables and chairs tidily arranged in rooms that no one ever occupies? Statues? Wine cellars? Closets larger than my room? Were two or three families living there? Why else would they need so many things?

My mother beckoned me into the living room a month and a half later. She had a lifeless look as she motioned for me to sit beside her. "Julian, Mr. Reynolds from the *News Journal* called." She bit her lip and paused, wanting to admonish but not discourage me from future labor. "He's letting you go. You lost too many customers. You upset them. Sunday papers missing half the pages, papers in the bushes, papers on the roof! Julian, what were you doing, delivering newspapers to the birds!" she threw her hands up to convey the seriousness of my offense. "I should've asked Henry to go with you the first week, but you know he has to work too. We don't want to cause any trouble. He's been very generous by letting us stay here. You're lucky he gave you your own room."

I doubted any of my friends had these conversations with their parents. They weren't reminded how fortunate they were to have their own room, nor that they might lose it if they upset the owner. In retrospect, this should not have come as a surprise, but at the time, I was shocked. I'd been grounded and berated before, but I'd never been fired. Suburbia itself had expectorated me and my rogue paper deliveries from its holy harmony.

"But it's hard, Mom. You don't understand. Those papers are heavy. How can I carry them all?"

"How can you carry them all? You better figure that out if you want to survive in this world."

I didn't get what my mom was so worried about. She and Henry had jobs, and there had to be something else I could do. But I suspected even if we all made more money, it still wouldn't be enough for me to stop hearing about how I should be grateful for unseaworthy fish sticks and soggy turkey sandwiches after 7:00 p.m. How much did I have to carry to stop worrying Henry might evict me from my bedroom?

***

The next day, my mother made me resume doing chores, including lawn care, as I'd proven unfit for the working world. I'd done these tasks before, but it now required Sisyphean fortitude to push our lawn mower up the comically steep incline of Henry's yard. As I went about my business, I noticed a boy with curly blond hair mowing his yard across the street. However, no sweat formed on his brow because his lawn was small and flat. Like any seasoned executive, absolving myself of responsibility was preferable to accepting it. I walked over to greet him. "Hi, what's your name? I'm Julian."

"Ben."

My mother's mantra was that education would spare me from a future of begging for hardened chicken outside the corner deli, but in addition to my studies, she promoted plumbing as the ideal profession. *"You'll get used to the smell,"* she said. *"Look at your father. Every time he falls in shit, he comes out smelling like roses."*

I didn't want to be a plumber, but I liked to read. Tom Sawyer and his fence-painting antics were already part of my literary canon, whereas Ben was unfamiliar with the story.

"It's fun mowing the lawn, isn't it?" I suggested.

"No, not really."

Ah, just the reaction I wanted. "That's because your lawn is flat; mine has a hill, so I can do stuntman stuff. I've seen the big kids down the street taking out their lawnmowers and doing tricks even when they don't need to cut the grass."

"What stuntman stuff? I didn't see you doing anything cool like that."

"I didn't want to show off, but since we're friends now, I'll show you." Yes, I was already learning tricks of the trade from my old man.

Ben eyed me dubiously.

I crossed the street and made a show of mowing. At the top of the hill, I got the lawnmower to launch high enough to spin around and hop on top, with its blades whirling as it rolled downhill. It serendipitously didn't gather much momentum given that it was in bad shape and not made for such maneuvers, which the manual undoubtedly forbade.

Ben stopped mowing and watched. He crossed the street, acknowledged that I might be onto something, and asked to try it. I told him not to worry if he didn't get the hang of it right away.

"You're doing awesome!" I encouraged him while he stood atop the mower as I sat back, having not even offered to mow Ben's lawn in exchange. But a shriek from his front door cut my otherwise clever ploy short.

"Benjamin, what are you doing!" His mother wailed as she crossed the street and trotted toward us. They had the same curly blond hair, so I needed no introduction.

Although leaping on the mower provided stuntman satisfaction, the spinning blades underfoot were not to be trifled with. The reward was incommensurate with the risk. At that moment, I was aware of this, but it took me a lifetime of folly to appreciate.

"Our grass is flat, but Julian has a hill, so it's more fun," Ben told his mother, using my line of reasoning.

"Hi, I'm Julian," I said, shrugging sheepishly.

"Well, Julian, Ben needs to get back to his chores. And stop jumping on that mower; it'll run over you."

At ten years old, I was already accident-prone. I'd had plenty of tumbles on the playground. I broke my arm when I saw a guy using a zip line in a movie, then made one in our backyard, which snapped midway through my slide. On one occasion, I got a rusty nail stuck in my head when I leaped across a ravine and collided with the bridge above. It wasn't painful, but the sight of blood spurting from my head made me run screaming home to Henry, who took me to the emergency room, where I wailed even louder as they jabbed me with a syringe at the point of perforation in my skull and then vigorously scrubbed the wound. On that day, I wore a *Ghostbusters* shirt, which was all the more ghoulish thanks to the red streaks from my bloodied scalp running down the back.

"Okay, I'll be more careful," I told Ben's mother, disheartened as my newfound pal returned to his tidy square. I finished my task stunt-free.

Two days later, Ben's family, the Greens, invited me to McDonald's. I'd already spent my allowance, and my home had no free lunches. So I borrowed a dollar from my mother, who reminded me I needed to repay it.

"Now assume you'll pay your share, but if they tell you, 'Oh, don't worry about it. It's our treat.' You should say, 'Are you sure?' But don't overdo it. If they insist, then say thanks. You want to be polite, but it never hurts to save a buck." Compartmentalizing a lesson in manners and thrift into a single explanation—that was my good ole ma.

McDonald's was nearby, so we grabbed our food and returned to Ben's house. His family had a brand-new Dodge Caravan with power windows and seats. On the way back, Ben told me what the trim levels signified.

"See, we got the LE. That's the luxury edition. It's way better than all the other cars around here." Ben's older brother, Seth, sat up front. "Show him the compass, Seth!" Seth pressed a button, and a digital "NE" glowed on the dash. "There you go, man, northeast; never get lost in this thing. This is real luxury. The best." He spread his hands across the plush leather arms of his captain's chair and reclined with the touch of a button.

15

"Shut up, Ben. You already said that," Seth chided.

"Well, my car has roll-up windows and a lever for the seat," I said, deflated.

Ben, sensing my mortification, tried to soften the blow. "Okay, but if you drive off a cliff and crash into the water, you can roll down the windows when the power goes out. Yeah, we'd probably die in this thing."

The conversation bothered me. Ben's car was nicer than mine. I knew that without him telling me. But that's the problem: he did tell me. As if being poor isn't bad enough, people wealthier than you want to ensure you're aware of it. Except it was Ben's imagination in this case.

"Mind your manners, Benjamin. Besides, there's an LX model, too, so this one isn't top of the line," Ben's father shot back. He had a beard and dark hair. Ben's older brother, Seth, resembled him.

"But you said that LE's the best? Whatever, I don't care. At least the LE is better than the SE; that one doesn't even have power seats," Ben reassured himself. He grabbed a handful of my fries and remained silent the rest of the way home.

Years later, I discovered there wasn't an LX version of the Caravan and that the LE we rode in was the top-tier model. I belatedly appreciated his old man saving me with a bluff.

Chapter 3

I t's a pachinko machine," my uncle Larry explained as I studied the odd contraption, which resembled a pinball machine but stood upright. We were in Flushing, New York, visiting my grandparents.

The pachinko had a stenciled wood backing with colorful spirals. As my uncle pressed a lever, little metal balls zigzagged between spikes and pockets before descending into a tray at the bottom. Meanwhile, lights flashed, and music played.

"When your mom and I were young, we had one that didn't have all these lights and sound effects. In my opinion, it's better without them. Watch." Larry flipped a switch. My mother and grandfather joined us. The balls tumbled down without lights or other fanfare. It was better with the lights.

"Papa, remember what you used to say about this thing?" my mother asked.

"Of course, Sophia," my grandfather said. He was short with sharp features and, like my uncle, still had a full head of hair. "I told you we're like the little balls cast into the world without choice. Each goes its own way but always ends up in the tray, and that is life— whether hiding in a hole or running around, eventually something gets us all."

My mother laughed, patting him on the back, and said teasingly, "Isn't that a little morbid, Papa?"

"Well, you know, I'm from Czechoslovakia. Oh, there was beauty! Ah, the women and the music. There was style, great food, and stories, but life was difficult, especially with the Nazis ..." He paused to collect himself and chose his words carefully: "... bothering everyone. It was wiser to see things as they were rather than as we wished."

"I'm not as morbid as you, Papa," Larry said. "I just like to play the game. The problem with the pachinko is you can't tilt it like a pinball machine to wrestle with your fate a little."

17

"That's the kind of thing you would think," my mother complained, but Larry didn't care.

"Give it a rest, you two; stop being silly. Let's eat supper, and then I want to show Julian a gift I got him," my grandmother said. But first, my grandfather and I went upstairs to check out his jewelry collection. He kept everything in a box containing a haphazard collection of valuables like watches, bracelets, and diamond necklaces with elaborate festoons. The mother-of-pearl inlay on the box and golden locket he held beneath a lamp with an intricately carved cameo highlighted how handcraftsmanship was more highly valued when they were made. I liked the vintage things my grandparents had: lithographic movie posters, often more captivating than the films they promoted; a working cuckoo clock; the pachinko machine; and a red chaise lounge, though it was missing half its buttons and covered in dog hair.

Later, I sat beside my grandmother, a mild-mannered Hungarian woman. Despite having vision too poor to drive, regrets or complaints never crossed her lips. She smiled and spoke with an elevated pitch, explaining the significance of several documents she'd placed on a table. A few had Hershey's logos, but no chocolate was in sight. I tried to match her delight, but I would have preferred one of those new video game systems kids at school were talking about.

"Julian, listen. I want you to understand that it's possible to grow your money in America in ways we couldn't in Budapest. All we grew were onions and tomatoes!" she smiled, clasping her hands.

"But what are they, and what do I do with them?" I asked, trying not to show my disappointment.

My grandmother pushed her thick glasses higher on her nose, making her eyes appear to float about her face. "What do you do? Nothing! That's the best part. This is a stock certificate," she pointed to one of the papers. "Now you own part of The Hershey Company, so the more products they sell, the more money you'll make."

My home in Newark, Delaware, wasn't far from Hershey, Pennsylvania—a Wonkaville-type town with a cocoa aroma and

Hershey's Kisses atop the lampposts. With this image, I quickly concluded, "Does that mean I should eat more chocolate?"

My grandmother laughed, "Yes, I suppose you could look at it that way, but ask your mother first."

We said goodbye and climbed into my mother's Honda Civic Hatchback. It was a small, round, cream-colored vehicle. It looked like a butterball, and every time we crossed the Brooklyn Bridge in it, I worried we'd blow into the East River. However, its exceptional gas mileage always pleased my mother, which she celebrated by tapping the fuel gauge. "You see that, Julian. It hasn't moved an inch. This car must get a hundred miles per gallon. That really adds up."

Her brother waved and walked to his car as we fastened our seat belts.

"Look at that car. What is he thinking?" she grumbled.

"What's wrong with it? It looks cool."

"It's a BMW. They cost like a million dollars—a total waste of money."

Wow, a million dollars! That sounded good to me.

We followed him out of the neighborhood. "He has no business driving that car. Showing off like that. We were so poor growing up—my mother made us go to bed at 7 p.m. so we wouldn't complain about being hungry. Sometimes, she gave me brandy to make me shut up and go to sleep."

"But Grandpa has so many nice watches and necklaces. Why were you poor?"

"He has all those rings, watches, and things because he couldn't sell them. He was a jeweler; his hands still shake from that." My mother furrowed her brow and added, "My brother has too much debt. He shouldn't live in that big house either. Well, I won't give him any money if he asks for it."

I decided not to ask for a pachinko as we joined the stream of cars leaving New York.

Power lines sparked in the moonless night as we sped past mammoth towers, lighting up factories and processing plants on the way home. I pictured men and women in overalls standing alongside roaring furnaces, swinging sledgehammers against anvils inside.

They were making the guts of skyscrapers: glass, concrete, and steel—the stuff of skylines. They were hard at work like the men immortalized in daguerreotypes pasted on our kitchen table. People in those places are paid to make real things. What do my stock certificates produce? How can pieces of paper my mother will lock in a box make money while I do nothing?

My grandmother was so elated by the concept of stock certificates that she forgot to tell me about the documents beside them: US Savings Bonds. My mother, wary of overfeeding my young capitalist mind, explained their value would double by the time I graduated from college and that I should otherwise forget about them. That was decades from now! I'd be an old man by then. Visions of red leather Thriller jackets, knobby-tired BMX bikes with chrome pegs, and all the fast food I could eat faded.

***

I began checking Hershey's stock quote in the paper's business section. It was much nicer to read than deliver. There were other quotes and statistics in the paragraphs surrounding the latest valuation of my chocolaty slice of commerce, but I didn't bother trying to understand them, the accompanying charts, or the daily flip-flopping monetary policy analysis. I just knew I felt better when a plus sign was printed beside Hershey's latest quote. It often had a plus sign, which I celebrated by grabbing one of their blocky brown and gray bars whenever I went to 7-Eleven. My mother explained that these purchases benefited the dentist far more than the company. Still, whenever the stock rose, I felt rich and ready to splurge, although I'd never sold a share or knew how.

No one in our neighborhood considered themselves wealthy besides Ben, but when times were good, people washed their cars and mowed their lawns. They had picnics and barbecues. A general sense of ease and friendliness filled the air.

Those good vibes proved fleeting when Hershey's stock price didn't have a single plus sign for nearly a month, and it wasn't the only one. I stopped eating chocolate, which was fine because I'd gotten a couple of cavities. I noticed other people having problems, too. Thugs roamed the streets before dawn, smashing car windows and stealing stereos. Restaurants were half-full, then empty.

When Henry and my mom watched TV, newsreels showed people waiting outside old government buildings with the American flag fluttering high on a pole, looking more sanguine than everything else around it. My mother explained that something about oil, the Persian Gulf, and interest rates was causing people to lose their jobs.

"Why doesn't everyone buy a bunch of stuff at the mall and make the stocks go up?" I responded to her unsatisfactory explanation.

Henry, who'd been drafted and served in the Vietnam War, interjected, "Julian, do you know what the Vietnamese call the Vietnam War?"

That seemed like a trick question. I wanted to beat Henry at his own game but had to say, "No."

"The American War."

I stared at him blankly.

"I'm trying to show you that we all see the world through our experiences and perceptions. The stock market is speculative; the same news that makes it go up one day suddenly makes it go down the next. They'll run it up again, so don't spend another minute thinking about which way it's going. A steady paycheck is what matters."

"Listen to Henry. He knows what he's talking about," my mother added.

I still didn't like seeing Hershey's stock go down.

Henry saw I was still thinking about it and clarified, "Julian, when there's war or trouble in the economy, people aren't in the mood to go shopping. The opposite is true: they stay home and stores close. Everyone tries to find a reason, but there isn't one. The one rule you can count on is the survival of the fittest. Life is an endurance contest, and the people with the most money tend to endure the longest."

My mother, aware I was too young to get wrapped up in endurance contests or the economy, said, "Okay, I think we've had enough of our lovely little discussion. You know what, Julian? Let's watch that new movie, *Back to the Future*, this weekend."

"How do you go back to the future?"

"We'll have to watch and find out."

I was about to forget the whole thing when she added, "Julian, you should really be a plumber. People always need their pipes fixed."

My mother and I had a great time at the movies. Afterward, seated beside the five-and-dime store with a pizza and Coke, she explained, "The five-and-dime actually had stuff for a nickel and a dime when I was a kid in the Bronx. That was around the same period Marty traveled to in the movie. But when times were tough, your father and I snuck into church luncheons and signed up for burrito-eating contests. You might not believe it, but I could beat him almost every time!"

She'd flipped to happy tales about my father when they were young and good times with her brother, but they'd divorced, and she claimed her brother abandoned their values. How can she flip back and forth like that? Is one side untrue? I didn't know, but I was sure of one thing: There were people I wouldn't forgive.

Stocks kept falling, and people got a lot less friendly in our neighborhood, but as Henry foretold, the economy came back to life. Upbeat stories replaced news clips about eviction notices and unemployment rates. Schoolchildren sported new clothes, and stock prices had plus signs again. Yet prosperity didn't return to every street—mine in particular. Empty houses with peeling paint and drunken students throwing beer-binging ragers outnumbered the relative calm of families who had lived beside us. Ben and Seth moved to a nicer part of town since their parents had jobs that endured no matter which way the stock market wobbled. My mother kept her teaching job, and Henry weathered a round of layoffs. As a result, we had enough dough for an upgrade, too. I was hoping for a big ole LX house.

***

Henry worked for the phone company and took me to his office once. From the outside, it looked like a gray, blocky building from the Communist Bloc, but inside, it was a wondrous world of switchboards, vacuum tubes, spinning tape reels, and mainframe computers spanning the length of a basketball court. After our tour, we had cookies and milk in the company cafeteria—chocolate for me, of course.

"Julian, one of these days, those monstrosities with their reels and punch cards will fit on a desktop. A new type of machine called an Apple computer already can, but engineers can't make something as powerful as a mainframe that small yet."

"Are computers like the steady hands game we made?"

"Not exactly. That only buzzed when the metal rod touched the ring. A computer can perform a variety of tasks."

I was intrigued but didn't understand the concept beyond what I'd seen in movies, where hackers banged cryptic commands into terminals at lightning speed to shut down the Pentagon, then spent the rest of the film evading multiple federal agencies.

I got a better sense of what Henry was saying after spending more time with him in his workshop, where he kept dozens of tiny electrical components in carefully arranged plastic trays. Henry learned electrical engineering in the Army and had primarily designed our steady hands game. He explained that electronics worked like the brain, with transistors and capacitors instead of axons and dendrites. He didn't mention that the brain is more easily short-circuited. We built machines that counted, clicked, and turned lights on and off. They never amounted to more than toys, but Henry said computers might replace our jobs one day, so learning about them was better than being a plumber, but don't tell your mother.

Taking a cue from the Greens, we moved to a roomier place a mile up the road in the same neighborhood as Ben after my brother Kevin was born. This time, both of our lawns were flat.

***

"Don't let the crocodile bite you. Jump, jump!" I urged Ben as we wiggled our joysticks while playing *Pitfall* in my basement. Ben was a grade below me, but we went to the same school, a short walk from our neighborhood. We left early one day to snag some leftover cookies and cake at my house, but Henry and my mother were already home when we arrived. I froze, sure they'd scold us, but Henry led Ben and me to the basement, pointing to the Atari 2600 he'd purchased and set up on the TV downstairs. Though Kevin was only a few years old, the console's rudimentary sound effects and blocky eight-bit emulations of gold bars and reptilian foes piqued his interest. He watched, enthralled, as I changed cartridges. Henry and my mother were arguing upstairs, but it was a barely audible tit-for-tat, not screaming, accompanied by broken furniture, bruises, and green stains on the wall.

"Okay, who's your favorite singer?" I asked Ben.

"Michael Jackson."

"Oh man, me too!"

"Yeah, Michael's so rad, moonwalking and beatboxing."

"He doesn't beatbox, but I wanna dance like him."

"Have you seen the music video for 'Bad'? MTV started playing it last night," Ben said.

"No, we don't have cable. My mom said all she had were records and board games as a kid, and we don't need it."

"Board games? They're boring. That's why they call them *bored* games. Everybody has cable now. It's the same as having a phone."

"How much does cable cost? Do you know?" I asked.

"Yeah, my mom left the bill on the kitchen table once. We have all the regular channels like MTV and Nickelodeon and shows with animals running around—you know, the ones with a guy talking while hippos lie in the mud. Plus HBO; that's a premium channel. I'm pretty sure it's the best one. Oh, the bill was about twenty bucks, but it'll be half that if you don't get HBO."

"I don't know. I doubt my mom will go for it if it costs more than ninety-nine cents."

"That's too bad," Ben said, pitying me, "but Michael says that bad is cool. Bad is good!" He started dancing, did something

24

resembling a windmill, and then tried to moonwalk, but it looked like he was dragging a wooden foot.

I improvised lyrics, encouraging him: "You're bad, very bad," and performed a robotic dance.

My brother giggled, mirroring my words and dance moves as we tried to reenact a Michael Jackson music video neither of us had seen.

Later, a light rain dampened the street. A heaviness lingered. When it cleared, a double rainbow stretched across the city. I rushed inside to show my mom and Henry. My mom didn't want to come out, but Henry did.

"Look, look, it's a double rainbow. Grab the camera. Let's take a picture."

Henry put his hand on my shoulder. After a long pause, he said, "Ah, let's just look at it, Julian. Some things are only meant for memory." We gazed at it, then he went back inside, and the dull sounds of displeasure resumed.

My mom and Henry divorced later that year. He moved one town over, and I rarely saw him after that. My brother began spending weekends and occasional weekdays with him. It was hard on all of us, but the worst part was that they sold their stylish new Acura Integra. Ben had given me two thumbs up when we drove past his house.

Further up the driveway, my mother's trusty hatchback with roll-up windows awaited. They purchased the Acura a year ago, but she never sold her Honda. Deep down, she must have known we'd be crossing the Brooklyn Bridge in it again.

Chapter 4

I don't want to sit there," I told my stepbrother Gilbert, who I'd become related to through my father's second wife, BB. I was in Modesto, California, where he'd relocated with BB and her children after accepting a management position there. By order of the family court, I went from seeing my father on alternate weekends to spending every school holiday with him out West.

"What are you worried about? It's fun. Allen and I used to play the same games when I was a kid," Gilbert explained. I was ten, he was sixteen, and his eldest brother Allen had moved out a year ago when he turned eighteen.

"All right, I'll do it." I sat under the grand piano as Gilbert instructed. Gil, who'd studied piano, began playing melodiously. It wasn't too bad until the crescendo came—a building demolition of piano keys pounding on my eardrums. I covered my ears and ran for the door. Gil cut me off and slid the lock shut high above the hinge, barring my escape. His black hair, long nose, and bushy brows made his V-shaped grin look devilish. Why is the devil always smiling? Gil seemed to know.

My mother and father were short. Henry—still married to my mother at the time—was tall. That, and his other positive traits, made me wish he were my father. To Gil's delight, no amount of chocolate milk cartons would have added enough inches for me to reach the lock. He ushered me back under the piano by the bench.

"Maybe it's better if you sit here while I play," I proposed as Gil massaged his fingers in preparation for the next few bars of his racket.

"No, you don't get it. You have to sit there and listen to me. That's what I did, and that's what you'll do. If my mom and your dad have a little retard like you, you can play for them."

He resumed his violent hammering. My ears rang, and I instantly had a headache. Tears burned down my face while I blocked my ears the best I could as he added lyrics to his ear-busting ballad.

"SOAP ON A ROPE, I'M LOVIN' WHEN I'M SCRUBBIN' EVERY FRIDAY NIGHT, YEAH, IN THE SHOWER OR THE TUB, I'M RUBBIN' ALL THE SUDS!" he yelled maniacally, though he'd eased up on the keys, likely due to his fingertips throbbing. I kept thinking something in me would break any second, but that moment had already passed.

Unlike my mother, my father had cable TV, and I watched the nature channel Ben mentioned while I was there. In a recent episode, gazelles lazily ate grass and bounded happily by a lake. As one drank from its shallow edge, I observed that its long, elegant antlers must be a lethal form of defense. A lion crouched nearby. I was sure with one lion against a herd of gazelles, he'd be no match for the phalanx they'd form to fight him off with those mighty spears protruding from their heads. However, as the lion crept toward the gazelles, they scattered across the African plain, kicking up a massive plume of dust, with stragglers trailing in the rear. The beast leaped toward its target and struck it to the ground with extended claws as the rest fled. The gazelle twisted, trying to stay upright as its skinny, sticklike legs wobbled and gave out. It straightened its forelegs, but its hindlimbs refused to cooperate. A glimmer of hope remained as it swung its antlers wildly, but it soon lay motionless, even though it had the strength to strike again. By then, those long antlers were no more than decorations. All that remained was for the lion to complete the kill. I wondered why the gazelle hadn't fought to the last breath until then when I learned what it's like for your soul to depart before death.

"OH, BABY, THEN SALLY CAME ALONG AND WAS SCRUBBING ME TOO!"

I recognized the song, but the lyrics were wrong. Everything was wrong. I wanted to leave my body behind, float through the ceiling, and drop into another house—anywhere—without someone assaulting me with a piano and demonic verses.

"STOP! STOP!" I yelled. The plea came from a primal part of myself that didn't want to die. Someone banged on the door and the racket stopped. Gil kneeled beside me and spoke as I curled myself into a ball.

"Stop crying, wipe your face, and don't say anything, or I'll put you inside the piano."

I willed my trembling away and followed Gil as he unlocked the door, staring me down like a hellhound in a flaming pit.

"What the fuck was all that noise, dipshit?" Allen barked, punching Gil in the shoulder. Allen was Gil's half-brother. The father they didn't share must've given him his broad chest and handsome features. Allen had long blond hair, an earring, and tattoos. I'd met other demons from the BB clan, but only BB and Gil wore dark formal attire as if they were going to the opera every evening.

Allen waved me over. "Hey, Julian. I want to show you something." As I passed, Gil squeezed my hand until my bones cracked and scampered off.

My father had married BB five years ago while living in Delaware, and my visits were limited to alternating weekends. Gil did little more than kick my shins under the table back then. When they moved to Modesto two years ago, Gil exploited my extended stays by finding new ways to torment me, such as making me guzzle soda until I puked and locking me in closets where time stretched into infinity. The bolted door stood sentinel, the blackness pressing on me as fear flooded in like a broken gasoline pump—long after my release.

I enjoyed seeing the long rows of almond trees, grapes, apricots, and lizards sunning themselves on rocks out west—in contrast to the East Coast's gray winters and cookie-cutter housing tracts—but these were small consolations compared to the years of agony I endured to see them.

Later, Allen and I sat in the backyard by the pool. Allen pulled a wad of crumpled letters from his pocket. He'd taped one together.

"Here, little man, your mom sent these. You can read them here. It's okay."

My mother embarked on letter-writing campaigns while I was in California, sending them every few days. BB or my father usually intercepted them. My father did me the courtesy of burying her letters beneath wilted lettuce and chicken bones in the garbage. However, BB made a show of ripping them up around dinnertime.

Their kitchen had a full suite of appliances: a food processor, a dishwasher, and a trash compactor. I became terrified of that domestic device and refused to use it after imagining myself shut inside with its metal walls contracting. At first, there'd be pressure on my skin, and then my bones would break. The compactor wouldn't yield until it pulverized me. I looped through this short snuff film years and years after Gil stuffed me under the piano to even out whatever bad shit had happened to him.

"Another one, Julian? It's not right. How long are you here for, two weeks?" BB asked, wearing a gown with vampiric lace while holding an envelope from my mother between her crimson-colored fingernails. "You need to tell her to stop this. It's disruptive and tiring," she complained, brushing back her long black hair. I'd never seen her outside before. Isn't there something about garlic cloves or holy water that could rid me of these vermin?

My father peppered the letter-ripping ritual with fairy tales about the wonderful life I'd have if I told my mentally ill mother that living with him was what I wanted. It was best for everyone.

"They have a great private school here, Julian. You don't need to go back to Delaware. I've already spoken with them, and it's fine for you to finish the year here. You know, it's not like a school at all. It's more like a sports club. They have horses you can ride, a gym with big mats, and a trampoline. Can you imagine taking a class where all you do is bounce on a trampoline? A few kids from our neighborhood go there. After dinner, you can meet one of them. I know their parents. They said to tell Julian to stop by anytime."

Stepmommy Dearest drew the procession to a close, tearing the unopened letter in half, then adjourned to the living room where she listened to Bach while eating olives, blue cheese, and drinking children's blood in her black-laced gown. As she dined on yummy nibbles, I thought of the scene in *The Dark Crystal* when the Skeksis feasted on the loins of smaller beasts.

I sat beside Allen, reading letters from my mother. They expressed how much she missed me and hoped I was having a good time. The first one was postmarked before my departure, timed to arrive when I touched down, which meant she missed me before I left. She then listed all the fun things we'd do when I returned, many of which we were unlikely to do, but I still liked the list. My mother played the same game of winning my affection as my father, but I preferred living with her. She always included comics about us drawn as mice or cats—doing something unremarkable but endearing in animal form. The animals and imaginary list of good times were easier to digest than the abuse I suffered nearby.

I'd never asked Allen to retrieve the letters; we rarely spoke other than those times by the pool. I don't know why Allen was cruel to Gilbert but kind to me, nor what had been passed down in their toxic lineage, but I wanted no part of it.

Amid Gil's malice, I'd gathered the courage to tell my father what had been happening. Fearing Gil's retribution, I provided partial details, hoping he'd fill in the rest.

"Dad, Gil's been playing these weird games with me. Sometimes they make me sick. We took off our clothes, and it was ... I don't know what we were doing. He was touching me. I don't like him. He's mean to me." I took a deep breath, proud of my bravery. Yes, this will be the end of it.

"Julian, Gil loves you. He told me that. I'm sure he's only horsing around. All boys do this kind of crap. Try to toughen up. You'll face bullies your whole life; the sooner you learn to stick up for yourself, the better. Gil would never hurt you, so you don't need to worry. All these things will work out once you come live with us. I know Gil's excited about that, too."

Ten months after that conversation, my father died of pancreatic cancer. After that, I never saw any of them again, but I kept worrying about Gil anyway.

Shortly after my father died, I told my mother about Gil's wicked games with the same veiled approach I'd used with my pusillanimous papa. Unlike him, she got the drift and embraced me, sobbing while repeatedly saying how sorry she was that any of this had happened. She felt she should have stopped it, even though she hadn't known what Gil was doing. I was comforted and glad I'd told her but soon regretted it. Something between us and within her broke that day. She started crying and apologizing, perseverating over fears that I'd never get a job, marry, or have lasting friendships due solely to her parental negligence. She repeatedly recounted how she'd been pressured to marry my father, whom she'd met in Europe. He was sweet, charming, and considerate, but she wasn't ready for marriage. Yet their parents pushed them into it, and by the time she saw his true colors, it was too late.

Chapter 5

Isaac and I started Hebrew school within a week of each other. Five years later, we were both thirteen and ready to celebrate the conclusion of our curriculum, which had whittled away hours I longed to spend with my friends instead of attending its thrice-weekly classes.

Isaac's father drove a Porsche 928. Over the years, Pops pulled up in kickass rides that were the stuff of *Car and Driver* magazine covers. The 928 was his most impressive car yet. When I was thirteen, I finally got to ride along. I was at the age when I had posters of cars like that, but I hadn't seen one in person. When Pops arrived in the Porsche to pick up Isaac, its falcon doors rose, and he got in. Is it a car or a spaceship? The Porsche had rounded edges, wide, aggressive wheels, and a rear fin. Can it go underwater? His father spotted me eyeing it and told me to hop in. Isaac folded his seat forward, and I shimmied into the back. Before I could buckle up, his father hit the gas. Our classmates narrowly evaded the speedy coupe, clutching Hebrew lessons and hymns as their carefully placed yarmulkes and bobby pins flew asunder.

"So, Julian, my man, your Bar Mitzvah's coming up. Are your parents going to throw you a big ole shindig or what? What're you getting?" His dad turned and faced me, speaking in a rolling shout with an unblinking gallon-of-coffee stare without decelerating. Isaac was more sedate.

"I asked for Nike Airs with orange laces and a camcorder. I'm sure they'll get me a bunch of other stuff, too. The party ... um, everyone in my family is gonna be there. My grandma will get the food. I like this cake they make in New York, so she'll bring one of those, or, actually, I bet she'll get a few different ones, so there's enough for everyone. We'll play music and ..." I paused before adding, "... and we're going to Action Park."

"Action Park?" he scoffed.

"It's an amusement park with a wave pool and a cannonball slide that's super scary. It goes upside down in a loop," Isaac explained.

"I know what it is. But so many other people will be there. That sounds exhausting. Aren't you going to take pictures? Why don't you go somewhere a little more private? Like Taryn. Her family rented a hotel in Cape May. It had a huge deck with plenty of room for everyone, and they got great shots by the water."

"I don't think we're gonna do that, but I want to go on that cannonball slide."

Mr. Espresso was back at it. "Oooh, is your grandma going on that upside-down slide? I'd love to see that! Well, those are real nice gifts, buddy. You've earned them! Nothing wrong with keeping it in the family. But I'm sure you'll have a blast at Isaac's Bar Mitzvah next week, right? We've got live bands, fireworks, and we're giving away a bunch of cool gear by the pool! I mean, that's a party, right!" He nodded vigorously, apparently answering his own question and delighted he'd asked it.

During the bar mitzvah phase of our tutelage, some of my classmates flaunted their social class with parties at wineries and waterfront hotels. Others, like Isaac, had them at their palatial estates. However, incidents making my low station unmistakably clear were already weighing on me beyond the synagogue walls.

***

A team of attendants in orange vests directed guests arriving at Isaac's Bar Mitzvah celebration toward a parking lot outside the tall gate guarding his estate. Thankfully, my mother dropped me off farther up the road, so no one saw me exiting her gas-sipping butterball. Beyond the entrance, a stone walkway encircled a house that looked like a hotel, with sweeping stairways, balconies, and chimneys at various points along the rooftop. Ben didn't know anyone there, but I wished he'd come along. He'd get a kick out of the LX stuff going down like the vintage Ferrari GTO Isaac's dad had parked out front, which kids lined up for photos. Another set of staff led us around the sprawling abode toward a large pool beside a tennis court, surrounded by smaller residences and outbuildings.

I was disappointed we didn't tour Isaac's mansion. I would have preferred to spend the evening there than with most of my classmates, though the less affluent kids who'd arrived in jalopies like mine weren't half bad. An emcee welcomed us amid balloons, banners, and spotlights, encouraging us to have fun before introducing a live band. Later, elaborate pyrotechnics exploded above everyone splashing in the pool. There had been a prize giveaway moments ago. I'd won an INXS record.

Several of my classmates were getting cozy in a hot tub, which interested me more than the Huey Lewis and the News cover band performing. Wait a second, is that the actual band? I walked over to the tub. I'd begun appreciating my female counterparts' contours and feminine wiles, so I used this opportunity to practice flirting. Nice bikini you've got there, Lizzy Hoffman. I didn't bring a bathing suit, but it was a summer night, and my shorts would dry quickly, so I slid off my underwear and hid them in the INXS record jacket. I still wasn't sure if I wanted to get wet, but after Allison Cohen slid in with her precociously large cups, I joined the bubbly fun. Girls in the tub were mildly receptive to my advances, and one scooted next to me for a little snuggle, but I didn't get far for reasons beyond my appearance.

The problem was my last name, Weiner, pronounced "whiner," which I didn't like but was better than the alternative. Julian Lawrence Weiner is my full name. My first and middle names were slick, but then my last name had to come along and ruin the virtuous trio I almost had going.

"Wee-ner, wee-ner, wee-ner!" At least one kid in every class gleefully repeated, accompanied by a roomful of snickers, whenever the teacher chose the more embarrassing pronunciation during roll call.

"John Warner ... Emily Watson ..."

Like a coin toss, it could go either way, but it usually went like this: "Julian wuh, wuh ... Julian WEENER. Is Julian Weener here? Please raise your hand." (And make a fool of yourself.)

34

"Weener is a hot dog!" they dimly observed.

"Remember how Curly from *The Three Stooges* had hardly any hair? If your last name is Weener, that means you have a little dick," they deduced.

"Weenie, weenie, Weener," kids from traditionally incompatible cliques cast aside their differences to collectively sing, often accompanied by synchronized dance moves. Yep, good times all around.

The Weenster felt the low-voltage rush of bare teenage thighs brushing against his in the tub, but he failed to round any bases. In fact, he wasn't even called from the dugout, so I got out of the tub, dried off, and retrieved my underwear from the record jacket. After I slid them on, Isaac spotted me and mentioned that his father thought I might want to try on some clothes they kept in a wing of their estate, which was, of course, larger and better furnished than my house. While Isaac rummaged through a closet, I stood beside a bay window overlooking a sculpted garden. He stepped out and placed a pile of clothes on his bed.

"My father said you can have these shirts and pants since he's sure I'll have plenty of new ones after my grandparents take me shopping. I mean, if you want them." Isaac said, softening the potential indignity of receiving hand-me-downs. But I attended a public school miles away from his private academy, so no one would know the clothes were his.

"Sure, I'll take them. Hey, it looks like our feet are about the same size. Do you have any Nike Airs you don't want? With the little window, you know, down here," I said, pointing toward the sole of my shoe.

"I thought you were getting a pair of those after your Bar Mitzvah."

"Oh yeah, that's right, ha. I can't believe I forgot about that! Yeah, I don't need any of those."

"You're not really getting them, are you?" Isaac said.

"Well, I asked for a pair, but I might not get them, so I thought I'd check if you had some just in case."

"Sorry, no Nikes, but I have some Polo shirts. They're nice; they look good."

"Polos?" I knew about the sport of polo but not the brand.

"Yeah, like this one, Ralph Lauren, you know, the little guy riding a horse with a polo stick," Isaac explained, pointing at the iconic logo on a blue dress shirt he'd pulled out from the pile.

"I know that. See, I always call them Ralph Lawrence shirts, like me, Julian Lawrence. I don't call them Polos. That's why I wasn't sure what you were talking about, but I'll take them. I like Ralph Lawrence shirts." Isaac politely ignored my bullshit and gave me some shirts plus a pair of khaki pants to go with them, which I tossed beside the INXS album after saying, "Thanks."

He shook his head and put everything into a paper bag with braided handles and shiny calligraphic script. The bag looked suave; I considered carrying my books to class with it. I was about to go back outside, but I wanted to know why his dad had been so dismissive when I told him I was going to Action Park. What was up with that?

"Why did your dad say that stuff about hotels and Action Park? I don't know. It seemed like he was making fun of me."

"He was probably trying to be funny. I love my dad, but he embarrasses me sometimes. He's a complicated guy. He changed a lot after my mom died."

"My dad changed after my parents got divorced, too. He was always a dick. But it's gotta be awesome driving around in your dad's cars and living here."

"I like his cars, but a lot of the people he hangs out with are super judgmental. Kids at my school are like that, too."

"Like what?"

Isaac sat on the bed. "After her funeral, my dad bought a Porsche. I guess that's how he dealt with it. Pete saw me when my dad dropped me off and said the car was cool. At lunch, I told him about my Bar Mitzvah because I was going to invite him. But then he said his uncle told him Jews only care about money, and my dad probably evicted an old lady to buy it. He laughed—I don't think he understood the history behind people saying things like that. I told

36

him what he'd said didn't make sense—my dad's a chemical engineer, not some hotshot investor—and he dropped it. After school, I saw Pete get picked up in a Mercedes twice as expensive as the Porsche. So he definitely wasn't jealous. But it's wack that he thinks it's fine for his family to buy a nice car, but when mine does, we're greedy. That's what I mean by judgmental."

I sat beside Isaac and caught sight of kids outside partying and eating cake. "My mom's kinda uptight about money. A couple of people have teased me about that, but she only acts that way because my parents used to have these crazy fights, and she grew up really poor, so saving money helps her feel more secure. She's really generous, though. One of her former students went to jail, and she writes postcards to him every month. She always stays late to help anyone struggling with their homework, too."

I frowned and continued, "One time in woodworking class, a kid beside me started drawing swastikas on the wings of his balsa wood plane. He said Hitler was a hero because he saved Germany after the Jews messed up its economy and signed a treaty that made them lose World War I. He told me the Jews didn't want anyone to find out, so they made up a big lie about the Holocaust. Then he said they did that because they aren't human. They have goat's feet and pray to the devil every night. I thought he was joking, but he said he'd seen it himself. He didn't know I was Jewish. I should've shown him my feet."

"Yeah, it's called a scapegoat, but it has nothing to do with people having goat's feet. Germany lost World War I and signed the Treaty of Versailles for a lot of reasons, like their military strategy sucked, and all the strongest countries in the world stepped in to kick their ass. But spending so much money on a war they lost would've made them look like dopes, so they blamed the Jews instead, and well, you know the rest. Scapegoat comes from the Torah, remember? We learned about that and what happened during World War I in class."

"Maybe I didn't go to class that day. Do I need to know any of that for my bar mitzvah?"

"No, don't worry, all you need to do is read the haftarah. There's no quiz at the end. People like that kid will probably never change. My great-grandfather could show him his tattoo from Auschwitz, and he'd still say the Holocaust was a lie because believing crap like that makes them feel important. Like they know this big secret that you don't, and you're a fool for believing it. Don't ever let them see you cry, though. That only makes them feel good, and don't ever call them antisemitic, either; they'll say, 'Why should Jews have their own word for hate unless they've got something to hide.'"

"My mom said racism is dumb because if we don't try to understand each other's differences, we won't learn from our mistakes."

"My dad told me something like that. He said, 'No one has a monopoly on good taste.' Your mom's cool. My dad said she's hot."

"What! That's my mom! I don't think about her like that."

"Yeah, but it's still true."

"Alright, if your dad gives me his Porsche, I'll put in a good word for him."

After enjoying the exquisite grub they served for dinner while watching girls getting in and out of the hot tub, I grabbed my fancy paper bag and waited about thirty feet from the main gate for my mom to pick me up. I still didn't want anyone to see me getting into that old car. As I tallied up my secondhand score that evening, I noticed one of the Polo shirts Isaac gave me had something wrong with the logo. The horse had some irregular stitching, and the jockey looked like he was riding a Clydesdale instead of a racehorse. I considered asking my mom to give it to Goodwill but then imagined people laughing at the jockey riding that chubby horse, so I kept it with my already unimpressive wardrobe, waiting for the day Isaac's dad took me and my mom to gallivant around a huge deck in Cape May.

My Bar Mitzvah was two weeks later. The party afterward was a modest affair held in my living room with a plate of cold cuts, cheese, and fancy crackers arranged to make everything look nice. My uncle gave me a few video games. Someone else handed me twenty dollars while congratulating me on becoming a man. But there were no camcorders, Nike Airs, or amusement park tickets because I didn't ask for what I knew we couldn't afford. I wanted to turn the tables someday, but for now, I knew where I stood. Ben, Seth, and a couple kids from my soccer team were there. The atrocities Isaac and I discussed had faded from my mind until I noticed my buddy Fred had a new pair of sneakers with the fat laces I liked. I told him they were rad, but my teammate Derrick had a different take.

"Those shoes are trashy," he told Fred.

"No, they're not. They cost like seventy bucks," Fred shot back.

"So what? My older brother said, only White people trying to act Black or Mexican wear shoes like that."

"What's wrong with being Black or Mexican? I don't know any Mexican people, but half the kids in my school are Black. I see them every day—same classes, same lunch. They're cool with me," I said.

Derrick shrugged.

"How can you tell which one they're trying to be? When you look at a White person ... they look White. So how can you tell which one they're trying to be?" Fred asked.

Derrick huffed and said, "Look, it doesn't matter whether they're trying to be Black or Mexican. My brother has Black friends, and I think one of them is Mexican, so he's not racist or anything. But he said it's not worth his time to find the good ones when most of them would rather shoot someone and steal their shoes than get a job and buy them. The problem is people like that will always be poor, even if they have seventy-dollar shoes."

I shared what my mother had told me about the self-defeating nature of racism.

"I know that. My brother would agree with her. He doesn't care about race. I told you he has friends who aren't White. He's smart; he got accepted to Princeton. He just avoids poor people."

"Well, shouldn't rich people try to help poor people?" I asked.

"Don't be a sucker," Derrick said, huffing again. "You can't help them. You'll never lift them up. They'll only bring you down. So if you want to wear the same loser shoes as them, go ahead, but I won't."

Chapter 6

A year later, midway through eighth grade, my body and mind were striding toward new horizons. I hadn't advanced my cause financially but had managed to elevate my social standing. I persuaded my peers to call me Weens instead of any other surname abomination. It was a phonetic ruse, but in the often brutal campaigns of teenage humiliation, one I deemed successful. Girls were on my mind, and new hair was appearing on my chest, chin, and below my belt. Being cool mattered more than ever. Sitting at a particular lunch table earned you respect, protection, or ridicule.

It was the end of the Eighties, but we still had electric dreams. We kept floppy disks in the little pockets of our bookbags to load a few bytes into the digital devices that were now standard in every classroom. Rogue computer programs had anthropomorphized into anarchists racing light cycles across the silver screen; Synthwave set the mood, and Max Headroom wasn't strange to me at all. No decade has matched its music, movies, or style. The much less impressive Nineties were nearly here. However, I had no futurist ambitions on the eve of that era. I was admiring Wendy's backside at a school dance while the DJ played Experience Unlimited's hit, "Da Butt."

Wendy shimmied, spun, and shook her tail, much to my delight—until she slid over to another guy, and I lost sight of her fine behind.

***

My mother's anxieties started easing. I wasn't sure why until one fateful day ...

"Julian, would you mind turning off my ceiling fan?" she faintly requested from her bedroom about an hour after coming home from work. I entered the dimly lit room and found her in bed, eyes half-open, facing the ceiling.

"Are you okay, Mom?"

"Yes, I'm fine; just tired. Please turn off the fan."

I looked up at the ceiling. The blades were idle because it wasn't on. A half-empty bottle of Jack Daniel's was at the foot of her bed.

"Uh, okay, Mom, I turned the fan off. Why don't you rest for a while?"

"Thank you. I love you, Julian." She closed her eyes and rolled onto her side. I shut the door and went to my brother's room, where he speedily clicked on a Gameboy.

"What game are you playing, Kevin?"

"*Super Mario Land*. Wanna try?" he handed it to me.

As I guided Mario past palm trees and pyramids while collecting coins, I noticed that Kevin's Gameboy had an illuminated display.

"Where'd you get this?"

"Toys 'R' Us."

"Yeah, but I've never seen a Gameboy with a light. They don't usually work in the dark."

"Oh, my dad helped me add that. It's cool, isn't it? You don't need to keep a light on to play."

"Very cool." I handed it back to him. "Hey, Kev."

"Yeah?"

"Did you ever talk to Henry about why he and Mom divorced?"

"No, he doesn't like to talk about it."

"Oh, okay." I stepped toward the door.

"But I heard them fighting about it once."

I turned back, and he continued, "They were in the kitchen, and Mom was crying. Dad looked sad, but he wasn't crying. They didn't see me, though. I was at the top of the basement stairs, listening. Mom said something about Dad trying to control her. Then she said she needed more space. Maybe she wanted a bigger house; I dunno. Then Dad said, 'How much space? It's not normal for married people to need more space.' That's all I heard. Was she mad about our house being too small? I like it. I don't want to move."

"I like it too, Kev, but maybe they disagreed. Sometimes adults argue about stupid things."

"Yeah."

41

"Besides, do you honestly believe Mom's going to splurge on a bigger house?"

"No way," he said, laughing. Henry and my mother weren't arguing about the house, but I didn't want to share that with Kevin. I tousled his hair and returned to my room, which had cutouts from the latest *Sports Illustrated* Swimsuit Issue tacked to the walls beside posters of movies, musicians, and random things I'd grabbed at yard sales.

Although my mother's drinking worried me, it seemed to improve our relationship. There were fewer tears over my father or perceived lapses in her parenting and no questions if I came home late.

Hazel Lane and I had the same gym class and started hanging out after school. At fourteen, she was already shapely from doing gymnastics and being plain old fine. Hazel could do a quick series of handsprings, finishing with a backflip, her wavy brown hair trailing in an arc. She had freckles, a button nose, and heart-shaped lips that made me lose track of what she was saying. One smile from her, and I might not touch the ground for hours.

She lived nearby, so I often grabbed my backpack and got off the bus at her stop.

"How do I find the hypotenuse?" she asked, looking at me and then her geometry homework as we lay on her living room floor.

"Sometimes it doesn't want to be found, and you have to sneak up on it," I replied, poking her.

"Shut up, Weens. Show me," she said, poking me back.

I recalled the equation in a flash and helped Hazel with her homework. She had an awesome place with big wooden beams and skylights. As we closed our books, the surrounding trees made the sun cast viridescent streaks around us.

"So, Jamie's having a party on Friday. There's gonna be a lot of people there, and he said his parents always leave their liquor cabinet unlocked," Hazel said. "Do you think you can make it?"

"For sure, but don't go crazy, Hazel. You don't want Frank to lick you if you pass out. Remember, he tried to do that last time."

"I'm not gonna get drunk, dummy!"

Julian Weiner wouldn't have been hanging out with Hazel, flirting on the floor. He wouldn't have had access to the coolest parties. But Weens did. Weens could do these things. I was self-assured, smooth with the ladies, and no longer ridiculed by my peers.

My skill on the wrestling mat further bolstered my street cred. I was short but strong. Furthermore, if I imagined my opponent was Gilbert, he'd be out on the three-count seconds later.

"No, let me help you. Don't do it, Weens. Don't do it."

"Don't worry. I've been practicing for a while. I can do it."

The day before the party, we were in Hazel's front yard. She'd shown me how to do handsprings, but I'd never done a backflip without her helping me rotate. She didn't understand that Weens could do a backflip if he wanted. He could probably do a double backflip. I gestured for her to step back. After two handsprings, I had a good rotation going, but could Weens do a backflip? Doubts crept in right before I committed to it. I'd done backflips off diving boards, but the truth is, they all ended with a belly flop and the lifeguard telling me to cut it out.

Just do it. Just do it. She'll think you're so cool.

I launched myself backward, tried to tuck into a ball, and then ...

... I felt disoriented. Ugh. What was that popping sound?

"Are you all right, Weens? You landed on your head! Can you move?"

Oh God, I had a splitting headache. I couldn't even blink.

Hazel leaned over me, her wavy brown hair brushing my face. Man, she looked good. Her hair tickled my nose.

I can feel my nose!

I can feel my feet!

I got up!

"You're okay! Weens, don't do that again."

She squeezed my hand, and we held them together for a moment. After brushing myself off, we chatted a little more before I walked home. We did head rolls and lifted weights at wrestling practice to strengthen our necks. Despite only pretending to do push-ups while keeping my knees on the mat by the back wall, now I knew I was invincible.

***

My mother's new boyfriend, Bob, drove a rumbling Chevy Nova. He had big muscles, sang, and loved Elvis. Bob let me drive it on a dusty backroad once, even though I could barely see beyond the hood. I turned the key, and the car rolled forward.

"Now press the brake, Julian. That's the square one on your left. Go on now, show this hunk of steel who's boss." I slammed the brakes, and we were thrown forward, thankfully restrained by our seat belts.

"Alright, you're getting the hang of it, but a little easier next time. That's it. Move your foot to the right and press the gas gently."

The big hunk of steel bucked and roared.

"Whoa! You don't gotta floor it. Easy, Julian, easy."

I adjusted my pedal pressure, and we bumped along the dusty road without being tossed from our seats. Bob leaned back and sang "Viva Las Vegas" well enough for me to see those blazing desert lights shining from the Strip.

A man of Bob's talents demanded an audience. On Friday, he and my mother went to a local Elvis impersonator contest. I usually watched my brother when she went out, but he was with Henry that week. I pulled my bike out of the shed and pedaled to Jamie's house for the party. On the way, some of my classmates rocketed past me in their newly acquired cars, doing triple the speed limit on the narrow suburban street.

I'd heard guys and girls take off their clothes at these parties. Ben's older brother Seth told me he had sex at a house party, or at least he might have. He wasn't sure if he "put it all the way in." I heard a thump, thump, thump as I approached Jamie's house. It was loud, but not too loud. We kept the noise down and avoided puking in the front yard so that the cops didn't come.

"Weens, what's up, bro? Welcome," Jamie said as I entered. He was tall, but I didn't feel small. All was equal inside, as bodies

44

swayed in time to the sound as the top jam shook the floor. Kids were raising glasses, laughing, talking, and kissing on the couch as the long days of school and the forgettable hours when we had nothing to do faded. Everything was good again. I shook Jamie's hand and shouldered through the crowd. I didn't want to drink but didn't mind who else did. I wanted to laugh and fit in, too, but all I needed was the music, my friends, and the energy of the night.

Thirty minutes later, we stumbled upstairs and started playing Spin the Bottle with boys and girls in a semicircle. When the bottle stopped spinning, wherever the front and back pointed determined who did the smooching. Among the participants were Hazel and me. We pretended not to notice each other as the bottle spun in the center. The first spin landed on two girls. Despite gleeful prodding from the boys, they refused to kiss. And then, because it was that special kind of night, the second spin aligned with Hazel and me. Nothing we'd done before that point went beyond flirting or me nearly breaking my neck. I thought she'd laugh and wave me away, but she sprang up and headed for a closet reserved for the smooching stage of the game. I followed, and someone shut the door. I liked her jeans, her shirt, and the freckles on her nose, which I hadn't noticed because we'd never been this close before.

"Hi," she said.

"Hi."

Closer, closer, closer. The split second before our lips met was unbearable—an eternity before our tongues touched. We pressed together, and I felt fire on my lips, fingertips, toes, and other places, too. I shut my eyes and saw the ocean, her long hair flowing in the blue as we drifted, drifted down. Gravity was gone.

Alone, listening to my stereo, I imagined this kiss. I dreamed of it when I held her hand. After sending each other smiles in the hall. On the bus, in class, after class, at lunch, and by the field where we walked after school. It could have been anyone, anywhere, but it was in that house, upstairs—Hazel and me.

"All right, all right, you two ... Next contestants! Let's go, get out of there." A Laotian girl holding a cup of beer instructed us after opening the door.

Later, Hazel and I made out on the couch, ignoring other partygoers flinging potato chips at the television, smoking cigarettes, and locking lips like us. She pulled away, her hair falling before her face, and slurred, "Oh, I'm so drunk." This was true, though it also absolved her of any romantic obligation if her feelings faded when she sobered up.

Three days later, Jamie stopped me in the hall between classes.

"So, have you asked Hazel yet?"

We hadn't spoken since the party because I couldn't bear it if that feeling had only lasted one night. Is that why she hadn't called me? But she blushed when I passed her. She waved. She smiled. What is going on?

"Ask her what?"

"Megan told me Hazel wants you to ask her to the formal. She totally digs you, Weens!"

The formal was a lightweight prom for eighth graders, where we danced beneath a disco ball wearing spiffy clothes. It was corny as hell, but it was also all I could think about. Plus, there was a decent chance they'd play "Da Butt."

That night, Hazel giddily agreed to be my date. I hung up the phone and attempted to moonwalk, though not much better than Ben had.

"She's such a nice girl. I'm so proud of you, Julian. Would you like me to drive you two to the dance?"

My mother's rusting hatchback, which had also started backfiring, made that a hard no.

"We can work that out later, Mom."

"I'm so proud of you."

"I think you said that already."

"Because I am proud of you. I'm sure meeting a girl like Hazel, with your father's influences, was challenging for you." She paused, trying to fine-tune whatever inadvertently insulting thing she was trying to tell me. "There are many ways to meet nice girls other than your appearance ... um, though, of course, there's no specific reason I mentioned that. Anyhow, you know, Bob—well, frankly, he's funny-looking, but he has his own plumbing business."

46

"Uh-huh. Can you help me pay for a tuxedo? I need a flower thing for Hazel, too."

My mother considered my proposal and said, "How about fifty-fifty?"

"Okay."

I'd recently found a job setting up tables and chairs at the University of Delaware Convention Center. My mother covered food and lodging, and my labors funded the rest. But on the rare occasions when she transformed into a doting mother, I'd try to get a beloved son's bonus. It was a modest score, but fifty-fifty was better than nothing.

I had no illusions my appearance would make anyone swoon, but the theme of my mother impressing this upon me stemmed from my growing resemblance to my father. Pops was short, bald, and fat when he died, though he looked all right in old photos, but once evil manifests, the devil is all you see.

I secured my formal attire, and Bob agreed to chauffeur Hazel and me to the formal, though I couldn't get a firm agreement for him not to sing. Seth gave me a condom so I didn't accidentally 'make little Weens.'

***

"Damn, man! You almost shot me. Watch where you're pointing that thing!" Ben snapped.

It was eight days before the formal. I'd fired an air-powered BB gun from my basement toward the back door upstairs, where Ben stood. It made a small hole in the Plexiglas window a few inches to his right. Henry had left the gun behind, tucked in a cabinet beneath the jigsaw that had been idle since he left.

"Sorry, man, I didn't know it was loaded."

Ben gave me the middle finger and left. He'd shot me in the leg before, so I didn't feel bad about it. I fixed the window using scraps I found in a cabinet before my mom got home and avoided a lecture covering the multiple ways I'd misbehaved.

I'd become fascinated by guns and sneaked peeks at magazines about them whenever I could. Though I'd buffed up from lifting weights and wrestling, even the mightiest movie stars used firearms to defeat the baddest of the bad guys. Packing heat was Weens' next step to go beyond social butterfly to action hero. I'd asked my mother if I could have a .22 caliber long rifle like my friends had. It had been six years since Christmas Story came out, so she joked I'd "shoot my eye out" and said she'd think about it. She didn't know about the BB gun Henry left, which tided me over in the meantime.

The following week, my friend Zeke and I were on our way to his house to watch a Mike Tyson fight and shoot targets in the woods when something ominous occurred. I'd made a makeshift holster for my BB gun, which was black and, to my delight, resembled a more powerful pistol. I'd considered making a bandolier, but it would have looked stupid with a string of BBs. Zeke slung his .22 over his shoulder, and we sauntered down the street. Halfway there, a man in a truck stopped, leaned out his window, and said, "Boys, boys, come here." He looked about forty.

"My mama said don't talk to strangers," Zeke snarked.

"You boys have to be careful with those guns. They aren't toys."

I considered shooting his tires to show him who should be careful.

"I'm an ambulance driver. I've seen people's lives forever changed, fooling around with weapons like you two."

"Yeah, okay ... not a toy. I got it. We know how to use them, so don't worry about it, alright?" I said impertinently.

"Where are your fathers? You shouldn't be brandishing those things like little punks," he scolded, then drove off.

"My dad is boning your old lady, so get the fuck out of here!" Zeke yelled, raising his rifle over his head.

We chuckled at the dumb old man. "What a pussy."

We got caught up in the Tyson fight and didn't do much shooting that day, even though he won in three rounds.

On April 24, 1989, five days before the formal, Zeke called, sounding jazzed. He wanted me to come over and check out the cool thing he got in the mail.

"My .22 is out of ammo, but we can use these in my air rifle," Zeke said, showing me the pellets he'd mail-ordered with sharp tips when I got to his house.

"They're almost as good as shooting bullets out of the .22. I shot one through my phone book with my ten-pump rifle. My dad's not gonna like that," he chuckled.

Zeke was going through an awkward stage. His voice was changing, and he had a lot of acne. He didn't have a fine babe like Hazel to hang out with, so he was even more into guns than I was, but that didn't mean he wasn't interested in girls.

"Weens, do you think you're gonna have sex with Hazel?" Zeke asked.

"I dunno. I mean, I kinda hope so, but it's okay if we don't. I like her. I'm not a pervert like you."

"I'm not saying you gotta take pictures. A few details, that's all. Like if it's any different than you know," Zeke said, pumping his hand up and down near his dick, making the international hand sign for jerking off.

"It's gotta feel different. My friend Seth said hand jobs don't feel like that, so there's no way sex is gonna feel like, well, you know." I mimicked his hand gesture, though there was no doubt about what we were discussing.

We dropped the topic, and I held up the bag of pellets he'd procured and took one out. I tapped the tip with my forefinger. It almost made my finger bleed.

"Zeke, you wanna go out back and shoot a couple of cans? I gotta be home in an hour. I'm supposed to watch my brother."

"You've got plenty of time. Relax; let's stop by Jonathan's house first. He wants to check out these pellets. Then you can go play nanny while the big boys go hunting."

Jonathan lived two doors down. I'd seen him hanging out with Zeke but had never met him. He was sixteen and had his own car, but was pudgy, with arms and legs that looked like buns fresh from the oven. I doubted he had any experiences that could address Zeke's carnal curiosity either. I figured he could drive me home after checking out the pellets, and I'd make it on time.

Zeke introduced us. As a teenager always ready to eat, I was happy to see a box of brand-new Ritz Bits crackers with peanut butter beside him.

"Hey, Jonathan, can I snag some of those crackers?"

"Yeah, go ahead. I don't like them that much."

Music to my ears. Perhaps I could eat the whole box. Jonathan lived in a raised ranch house with a short flight of stairs leading to his living room. I went downstairs and watched *The People's Court*, which was already playing on his TV. I overheard Zeke and Jonathan discussing his mail-ordered ammo, but the crackers and TV had my attention. A man was suing a woman because she didn't want the flowers he'd given her. I laughed and shoved a handful of crackers into my mouth.

Zeke's air rifle was fun, but even with the pointed pellets, ten pumps didn't produce much firing power. However, it had a malfunction that let you pump it as many times as you wanted, but after ten pumps, the trigger jammed. Unjamming the rifle required rapidly pulling the trigger until it fired with far more power than the manufacturer intended.

I was vaguely aware of Jonathan fooling with the gun at the top of the stairs, trying to unjam it, but I was focused on Judge Wapner's verdict.

My hand sprang to my right temple, where the pain was. I figured a flying pest had zapped me. I was wrong. I felt a large protrusion. When I brought my hand to my face, my palm was red. An unceasing dull tone sounded, and a chill spread through me.

"You shot him!" Zeke shouted, which I hadn't grasped until he said it. I looked around warily, unsure where Jonathan was, then spotted him holding the rifle by the stairs, recoiling in horror. Blood. My hand was bleeding. No, my head was bleeding, and every time I touched it, my hand was redder. Blood. I tasted it in the back of my throat. Blood with a hideous hot metal taste. My head was pounding. My entire arm was red when I drew my hand away from my temple. Zeke and Jonathan were panicking. Jonathan examined my wound and then rushed toward the stairs, tripping over an ottoman like a rambunctious little boy. Zeke collapsed onto the floor, hyperventilating.

"I'm gonna call my mom," I said, clambering up the stairs, relying heavily on the banister. Zeke regained his composure, went to the bathroom, and returned with two aspirin. I swallowed them, but this was as futile as treating stomach cancer with a pack of Alka-Seltzer tablets.

"Julian, where are you? You're supposed to be watching your brother," she asked.

"Mom, I got shot in the head." I held the phone to my ear with one hand on my temple. The bump had grown larger. "I think I need a doctor. Can you pick me up?"

"What do you mean you got shot in the head? Who shot you? Are you okay?"

"I'm not sure. This guy, Jonathan, shot me with a pellet gun. I think it's stuck behind my ear. I feel so cold. Can you grab my electric blanket on your way out?"

"I'm not going to—I can't do that. Where are you? Tell me exactly where you are!"

"Okay, Mom, I'm going to lie down. Zeke will tell you."

In hindsight, an ambulance would've been the proper mode of transport, but my mother sped over to Jonathan's house as fast as she could. Zeke and Jonathan hoisted me into her car. A neighbor was watching my brother, so it was just us.

"I'm freezing. Can you get the electric blanket out of the back? Plug it in and lay it on top of me," I requested, moving in and out of consciousness. "When we get there, I'm going to take a bath. You can tell them to make me a bath."

My teeth chattered as my body shook. I'd never felt so cold—that was because I was bleeding to death.

Though we should have gone to the hospital, amid the blood, panic, and uncertainty, my mother took me to the doctor's office as I'd requested. She and a random guy in the parking lot dragged me to the reception area. They propped me up against an upholstered seat in the clinic's sunlit atrium, which made it look more like I was sleeping than suffering from a gunshot wound.

My mother pleaded with the receptionist. "Please, my son has been shot. He needs a doctor!"

"Yes, I heard you, ma'am, but a few others are ahead of you. I've notified our internal medicine specialist. Please have a seat."

Just as my future looked grim, a young neurosurgeon who'd recently emigrated from India walked by.

"Madam, may I examine your son? Kindly hold his head upright," he requested.

Unlike the receptionist, who was preoccupied with filing her nails, the doctor quickly spotted the blood. He opened my eyelids and shone a light into them. I looked on vacantly, my mouth agape and pupils filling my irises. He then noticed the protrusion on my right temple and then looked at my mother—also in shock as the reality of the situation set in. She explained, "He got shot in the head."

The doctor spun on his heels and barked at the robotic attendant behind the counter. "Get a stretcher! Call an ambulance and tell them we urgently need a CT scan of a young man with a severe subdural hematoma!"

The Experience

I was alone in a vast expanse, as faint starlight showed I was falling. A low hum vibrated throughout it. With everything around me unfamiliar, I assumed I was no longer living. The hum harmonized into a melody, accompanied by pulsars and swirling nebulae that flared in sympathy with the sound. Their radiant bodies converged into beams of light that amplified into lasers, etching walls, windows, and rooftops, forming a shimmering city of light.

"Above the sky is another sky, existing before the beginning and after the end, where all shapes drift into each other. Through my grace and glory, I give form to the formless and make the unknown known." As I searched for who was speaking, I saw that I had no limbs; I had no body at all. The city splintered into a sea of dying light before toppling onto its side, revealing a desert that stretched beneath a sunless sky with a blue-green glow, peeling from the windswept sand like skin. The sky scrolled endlessly, rumbling with thunder as I soared below it at blinding speed. The sky blended into infinity until a sun emerged within it, one of a multitude. There were suns within the sun. I'd dreamed of other worlds, but never as vividly as this one.

"Examine the universe within yourself. Is it as vast as the one around you?" a voice asked.

My phantom heart beat furiously—I could not resolve the question in my disembodied state.

"If time is eternal, will I see you again?" a man asked, his voice the same as the unseen one I had heard before. Aged and tanned, he sat at the edge of a cave, surrounded by acacia trees high above the desert, holding a cane carved from the gnarled wood in his withered hand.

"Who ..." "... are you?" he said, finishing my question. "Who is the one that made the words?" he asked, confounding me.

"Where am I?" "Where am I?" I asked as he mirrored me. I began to take shape, jiggly like a blob of green Jell-O. Odd, but better than not having a body. Other blobs jiggled nearby, and some raced past in a green blur along circuitry woven around me. I sensed the blobs and I were made of the same thing.

The man and I reached an impasse, falling into silence. Then, with frightening contortions, he transformed into different figures. They were made of fire, and the fire had many flames. They coalesced into a tree with blazing leaves and branches—but they did not resign to ash.

"Can you stay still? I'm confused. You were an old man, and now you're a burning tree? Who are you?"

Within the flames, I heard a voice that spoke in a way that broke the world: "I Am What Will Always Be." A flood of light rushed from the cave, engulfing everything in white. The minor comfort of being a green blob vanished. I plunged through darkness, descending until I saw another sun shining above the sands I'd fallen upon in a cloud-swept sky. A diaphanous woman with silver fur, catlike paws, whiskers, and a tail dragging between her feline footprints approached.

"Do you know my name?" she inquired, then placed her right paw before her eyes. Her face shifted into a glittering green and purple bird mask. She drew back her paw, but the mask remained.

"Am I like the God you knew in Hebrew school?" the chimera teased.

"Well, we never talked about what you look like in Hebrew school, but if you're God, you look a lot different in movies. I remember reading about you testing people's faith, but if I were Abraham, I wouldn't want to kill my son. I know a guy named Isaac, and he's nice. So, I'd act like I was gonna do it and move super slow until you said I'd proven myself and let us leave. Maybe that's not how it works. I don't know. I should've studied harder. I never really learned Hebrew. I had to transliterate the Haftarah portion I read for my Bar Mitzvah. I hope you're not mad about that. Why do you keep changing? I thought there was only one of you."

"I have many masks and am known by many names. That difference may divide you, but when you know my face, we will become one."

I looked up and realized I was naked, prostrate on the rolling sands, pinned down by a force that had quadrupled gravity.

She brought her hand to her face, and the mask melded with it. When she pulled her hand away, she dissolved into the desert. The sand lay still, then stirred, rising toward the distending clouds until they converged across the horizon. A man emerged from their union—his tanned skin resembled the old man's, though he was younger, timeless. His name had been seldom spoken in my life, but I recognized Jesus Christ. Divine. Immaculate. A halo crowned his long dark hair, which framed his bearded face. He radiated warmth and affection—the burning tree alive within him. The power of his presence transcended religion.

"Do you know my name?" he asked with a bright, expansive timbre.

I was too overwhelmed to speak but nodded affirmatively.

He sat upon a throne made of the sky, wearing a seamless robe the color of the sand. "I am the one you seek, but my essence is unseen. You must overcome your hatred and pain for me to reveal it." His voice reverberated in my skull; everything darkened, and I found myself in a small space, cold and claustrophobic.

"Please don't shut me in here. Don't leave me here. Don't leave me."

"Our kindness or cruelty shapes the space around us."

"Okay, I'll be kind. I promise."

"Kindness is created when we are one body. Cruelty empties the good in us if the bond is broken."

Light emanated from my hand, illuminating a path out of the small space, which I followed. "You may sit," Jesus instructed from his celestial throne as I approached. A fallen fruit-bearing tree, rooted in an eternal oasis, lay beside him—he gestured toward it. The light spread from my hand until it lit the entire world, no longer cast from within me. I wore white knee-length shorts and an army-green T-shirt reminiscent of the one my mother bought at Kmart. It was nice to have a body and not be nude, but I would have liked to be luminous like Jesus.

"Do not mistake the light as your own creation; it is the wonder and glory of God. This is a Holy Place that shall never be diminished. You have the will to find your way here, in your life, and for those who succeed you."

"I won't forget, God created the light, I swear. How long can I stay here? I like sitting with you." I thought of my mother, my brother, and everyone I loved who wasn't with me, but Christ's words were soothing, a rapturous song. If his Kingdom is eternal, I would see them again.

"Your soul must be risen to remain in my Kingdom."

I wept, unsure why. "How do I raise my soul?"

"Angels will guide you to the light, but only if you are ready to receive them. Demons will mislead you; some falsify my name and cloak their wickedness with it. If you delight in their temptations, you will descend into endless catacombs of darkness where madness reigns. Learn to love and live without hate, and you will not be deceived. I am the Lord, and this is the law. I am the way into the Kingdom for eternity. That is all you need to know."

Chapter 7

Thirsty. Thirsty. I was very thirsty. My lips, cracked like sunbaked rocks, ached as I licked them. A blurry figure emerged; she was reading a magazine. It was Mrs. Green, Ben's mother.

"Julian, you're awake! You're alive. I'll get a nurse and be right back."

The sterile, white walls of Christiana Hospital's intensive care unit gradually came into focus. I heard beeping sounds, and when I turned my head, I saw machines, monitors, and IV bags with tubes going everywhere, but one struck me in particular. It ran down my hospital gown toward my waist. I traced it to its point of origin, and my heart raced. No, it can't be. Not there! The tube had been inserted into the tip of my penis. I'd discovered a catheter evacuating urine from my bladder. I didn't want it there, so I tried to pull it out. "Argh!" I groaned in pain.

Mrs. Green and the nurse returned.

"No, Julian, you can't pull that out. You've been in a coma. Try to relax. Let me get a doctor, and we'll remove your catheter as soon as possible," the nurse explained.

I wanted to ask for water but couldn't because another tube, which went down my throat and into my trachea, was blowing air into my lungs. I felt a wave of panic, like I was suffocating, even though it was a ventilator helping me breathe. Fortunately, I was still groggy, and someone extubated me before I became agitated and tried to remove it like the catheter. Once free of the ventilator, I wearily asked for water.

"You can't have water yet since you've been asleep for so long, but I'll get a sponge to wet your lips," the nurse explained.

She moistened a sponge on a stick and wet my lips. I grabbed it and sucked on the sponge: one drop, two drops, a clear mountain spring. More, more, give me a river, give me a glacier. Unquenchable thirst. She yanked the sponge out of my mouth.

"Julian, stop it. You have to wait. Sit tight. I'll get a doctor."

Mrs. Green stood by the bed. "How are you feeling, Julian? We weren't sure if you were going to make it. You had a very high fever. They put you in a tub of ice."

"I'm okay, but I don't remember anything after we got in the car except that my head was bleeding and I felt so cold. We were driving to the doctor's office, and then ... I don't know. Do you know what happened after that?" I said weakly. My vocal cords were sore from the intubation.

"I'm sure your mother will tell you all about it. You should rest now."

Fragmented memories of the shooting returned: my bloodred hand, Zeke and Jonathan's panicked faces. Shivering in the car as my mother wiped away tears. Was that me? This same life? And where did the pellet go? Was it stuck in the side of my head? I must have missed the formal. Did Hazel dance with someone else? I wanted to go back in time for the first of many similar moments. It didn't seem too late to undo what had happened. Everything will go back to the way it was once I've recovered. I've been hurt before, but I always bounced back. How much could things have changed?

"Welcome back, young man. Let's remove some of those tubes and get you a cup of water," a doctor said, interrupting my introspection.

Though some tubes remained, the catheter was removed, much to my relief. I gritted my teeth as the doctor withdrew it, then placed a cup of water in my hand.

Welcome back. Yes, I'm back—but where was I? I pictured the desert with its long bands of striated sand and shimmering lights along the edges of a city high above it all. Had God spoken to me? Could he fix this?

I had an intense, total-body thirst, but the water irritated my trachea, so I sipped it slowly as I rubbed my throat. Even though the ventilator tube had been removed, I felt it—a sensation that stayed with me for a long time. In those first few days, I awoke terrified, thinking it and all the other machines were still pumping food and oxygen into me against my will.

Shortly after Mrs. Green left, my mother arrived. She rushed into the room and embraced me. Only two weeks had passed since I'd last seen her, but those weeks contained centuries. "You're alive! You're alive! It's so good to see you sitting there with your eyes open. I had to sign something because they thought you were going to die. Oh God, that neurosurgeon! Dr. Roshan, he saved your life."

My mind wandered as she spoke, returning to Jesus, the cat woman, and the shimmering city of light. Was any of that real, or had I mistaken surgeons leaning over me for those jiggling green blobs? It might have started that way, but it led to something bigger, much bigger. Now I'm here, propped up against a couple of pillows with a machine monitoring my heart rate, trying to make sense of it all. So many questions swirled in my young, discombobulated brain. Should I tell my mom about it? Maybe later. There was a more immediate concern. I had to seize this rare, blessed moment when I knew she'd listen.

"Mom?"

"Yes, Julian," she said, stroking my face.

"Mom, can we get cable TV now? They have different packages. We don't have to get the most expensive one."

She smiled and laughed, as did everyone else. "Yes, Julian, you can have cable TV."

***

Three days later, a team of physicians, including my neurosurgeon, Dr. Roshan, stood before a series of brain scans and anatomical diagrams to explain the surgical course required to remove the "cool thing" Zeke had mail-ordered from my head and the probable ramifications of my injury to my mother and me. It was shocking to learn that the pellet had pierced my skull and sliced through my brain. Dr. Roshan and his team operated for hours to remove it, alleviate swelling, and transfuse blood to replace what I'd lost. Then, they placed me in a pentobarbital-induced coma to control intracranial pressure.

59

"As the CT scan indicates, the projectile perforated Julian's right temple, fragmenting his skull at the point of impact. The projectile continued through the temporal and parietal lobes, lodging in the occipital lobe, severely damaging thirty percent of his brain. We performed a right frontoparietal craniotomy to address cerebral edema, retrieve the projectile, and remove any remaining fragments. The bone flap has been cryopreserved for cranioplasty upon resolution of his edema in two to three months."

While listening to them, I had the vague impression they were talking about someone other than me. The medications they gave me to reduce inflammation and suppress neural activity intensified this notion. The latter intended to reduce the risk of seizures common with traumatic brain injuries like mine. It was all too sudden to believe. A few weeks ago, I was preoccupied with removing Hazel's bra, playing video games, and hanging out with my friends. How can those scans be of my brain? Why have they drafted surgical summaries and a postoperative plan for me?

My mother sighed, shifting in her seat as they continued.

"Based on our surgical findings, established neuroanatomy, and constellation of his injuries, we've determined that Julian has permanently lost his left visual field, a condition known as complete homonymous hemianopia. Visual field analysis confirms that this includes half of the macula and his entire left periphery. Julian will require a comprehensive therapy regimen and specialized schooling to manage this and other impairments that have resulted from his injury."

"But didn't you say the damage was limited to the right side of his brain? Did the bullet damage his optic nerve?" my mother interjected.

Dr. Roshan stepped forward. "Sophia, kindly be assured that Julian's optic nerve was not affected. I expect his visual field loss, though extensive, is unlikely to expand. The brain's visual pathways cross at the optic chiasm, causing the two halves of the visual field to originate from opposing sides of the occipital lobe in the brain's posterior. He made an X with his fingers to illustrate the structure. "There is a crossing of currents. Damage to the right occipital lobe typically results in vision loss on the left, with an inverse outcome when the other side is injured. This occurs most often with a stroke. However, patients like Julian, with traumatic brain injuries, may suffer similar losses."

"So, his optic nerve is okay," she repeated.

"It is unblemished."

The team continued discussing my injury, presenting a bullet-point list of expected outcomes and recommendations projected alongside the scans:

- Difficulty with coordination, memory, planning, and associated executive functions
- Reduced oral and written comprehension, also known as aphasia
- Deficient cognitive reasoning and spatial neglect
- Increased susceptibility to anxiety, compulsiveness, and related mood disorders
- Elevated risk of mortality due to the aforementioned comorbidities

"Julian must exercise added caution, avoiding substance abuse and potentially concussive activities, which could prove fatal in conjunction with his existing head trauma. We'll monitor for additional complications that may arise over time."

These did not sound like the result of a gunshot wound to me. They were the adjudication of my thoughts and actions up to that moment, for which the stiffest possible sentence was imposed. Unfortunately, my mother concomitantly determined that my neural sentencing was a shared imposition of her sins, producing an impressive range of neurotic and passive-aggressive disorders over time.

I could hardly follow their exposition, but I had the general impression they were saying, "He's going to be stupid now." I didn't understand what they'd said about my vision. It sounded like "Hominy Hubbity" and may have been related to a game I played a few days prior. While peering into an egg-shaped machine, a doctor instructed me to press a button whenever a light appeared. The game lasted ten minutes, and I might have gotten the high score by clicking faster than anyone else.

I raised my hand as if I were in class.

"Yes, Julian," Dr. Roshan said, smiling.

"What is Hominy Hubbity?" I asked, gesturing toward my eyes.

"Julian, in your case, homonymous hemianopia means you have a total visual field loss on your left side."

"But I can see you. My vision was blurry before, but it's clear now."

He walked over and stood in front of me. "Let's do a simple test to demonstrate how your vision has changed. Look at me and tell me when you can no longer see my finger." Dr. Roshan slowly swept his finger from my right periphery to the left. As it crossed into my left field of view, my eyes saccaded and followed it.

"Let's try this again. This time, don't move your eyes," he patiently instructed, noting that I may not have noticed I had. "I'll hold one finger in front of you. Focus on that, and tell me when you can no longer see my other finger as it moves across your face." He repeated the test as I remained focused on his stationary finger. I informed him that I couldn't see his finger once it passed beyond the left side of my nose, but why were we doing this? What's the problem? Then Dr. Roshan stood on my right. "Can you see me?"

"Yes."

He stood on my left. "Can you see me?"

"No."

I then understood something terrible had happened. My left field of view wasn't filled in with black, highlighting its absence. It wasn't there at all, and I hadn't noticed until now. The egg machine wasn't a game. It was a test to determine the extent of my vision loss.

My mother sobbed a few times, then calmed herself. With a raised finger, I performed visual sweeps across my face with one eye closed and the other open with identical outcomes. I only had ninety degrees of vision in both eyes now.

Another week went by as I recovered at Christiana Hospital. I could still tie my shoes and hold a conversation, but I'd certainly changed. Aside from chronically bumping into walls, doors, and people on my left side where I could no longer see, I struggled to think clearly. My visual field *and* ability to mentally visualize were like a road atlas missing pages. This left me frustrated and disoriented as perceptual cues were hidden, and every route had unfamiliar forks, requiring detours throughout the ordinary course of cognition.

My attending physician moved me from intensive care into shared accommodations for the remainder of my stay. My roommate Greg was recovering from gastrointestinal surgery. The efficacy of his operation wasn't apparent, but his persistent flatulence certainly was. His groans and gaseous emanations interrupted gatherings at my bedside to celebrate my survival. I was in a reasonably positive frame of mind, but the repercussions of my injury did get me down at times. Greg's apologies after his frequent farts offered welcome comic relief, though I couldn't say the same for the odors.

My mother replayed a tape Hazel and her friend Megan made for me, which she'd first played while I was comatose. It consisted of them singing and sending me well wishes for a speedy recovery. I thought of Hazel every day since I'd emerged from my coma and couldn't wait to get out of the hospital and hang out with her again.

Though I could walk, my stride was stiff from being bedridden, and I spent the first few weeks in a wheelchair. After my mother replayed the tape, I spoke to Hazel while lying in bed, having not yet regained full mobility. I thought of funny things to say before calling her so she'd know nothing had changed and we'd be smooching again in no time.

"Weens! Oh my God. I'm so happy you're alive. Everyone at school was talking about you. Some people said you were playing Russian roulette. Were you trying to kill yourself? That's not true, is it? You know I care about you. You've got to talk to me about stuff like that!"

"No, no way. Some guy you don't know shot me by accident. Hazel, I'm sorry I missed the formal. Did you go?"

It felt so good to hear her voice and say her name—Hazel. Hazel. It reminded me of how my heart felt like it would fly out of my chest when her tongue touched mine and how I couldn't stop smiling when I saw her wearing the flannel shirt she borrowed from me.

"I went, but I was totally crying the whole time. Are you okay?"

"Yeah, don't worry, and don't be sad. I'm gonna be fine. I've mostly been lying in bed since I got here, which is dumb. I didn't need to, but they keep telling me to rest. I really liked the tape you and Megan made for me. My mom played it when I was in a coma. That might be why I woke up." We both giggled. "I've been getting around in a wheelchair. It's annoying, but it beats lying in bed. I can have visitors if you want to come sometime."

"Maybe my mom can—"

Greg let one rip.

"Weens, what was that?"

"Oh, the guy next to me keeps farting. I've been doing that more, too, after being in bed for so long. It's kind of funny."

She laughed nervously.

"So, you're coming back to school, right? There's another girl here; she's in a wheelchair, and they let her use the elevator. I'm sure they'll let you use it, too. You got shot in the head. Of course they will! There's a special bus for her and a couple of other kids. It's the one with the little elevator on the side. But you're not gonna have to be on that bus, right? That's for the handicapped kids. You don't have to ride that one, right?"

"No, I can walk. I can walk fine. I don't need the wheelchair. I'll be through with it in a couple of days, but I probably won't make it back this year. They removed part of my skull and put it in a freezer. It's not a big deal. They're gonna replace it in a few months. Wouldn't it be funny if it was in the freezer at my house and my mom accidentally microwaved it? Hey, check this out. If I reach up and touch where they removed it, I think I can feel my brain!"

"You can? Well, don't hurt yourself. Just get better, okay?"

Oh yeah, real smooth. Next time, say the opposite of what you're thinking, you idiot! Microwave my skull! I can feel my brain! What were you thinking?

The phone call ended moments later. That was the last time I spoke with Hazel or let anyone call me Weens.

64

At the end of the week, I learned I was being transferred to Nemours Children's Hospital in Wilmington, Delaware, for the remainder of my rehabilitation.

"They have a pool, a bowling alley, and you can even finish eighth grade at the school there," a nurse explained when I told her I didn't want to go. I'd gotten used to the hospital's layout and didn't feel ready to learn my way around another one yet. The pleasing list of amenities she rattled off reminded me of my father's tactics, but I knew she wasn't trying to pull a child custody con like the old man had, so I softened up. Actually, it sounded cool, aside from going to school. I doubted I'd be calculating hypotenuses any time soon.

The day before I bid my flatulent roommate adieu and was set to transfer, I was rolling down the hall in my wheelchair. I'd learned to stop the wheels quickly, which made high-speed turns and pop-a-wheelies possible. While practicing these moves, a boy called out, "Show me how to do that, Julian."

It was Joey, a classmate from school. He was also in a wheelchair with a cast covering his leg. "I got hit by a car," he explained. They'd bandaged my entire head, so we made a fine pair.

While showing him wheelchair tricks, we noticed the hall had cleared.

"Race ya?" he said.

"Smell ya later," I yelled, hitting several things I couldn't see on my left as I shot down the hall, made a hard right at the corner, and nearly collided with an orderly carrying a bedpan, who struggled not to spill its contents as he pirouetted around me. Joey, hot on my heels, almost hit him from behind.

The orderly shouted, "Watch out! The boy with the broken leg is racing the boy with the broken head!"

Chapter 8

I continued grappling with how my life had changed at the children's hospital. Cognitively, I struggled with abilities like telling left from right and sometimes forgot what I'd done an hour ago or even in the middle of whatever I was doing. Spatially, the missing parts of my mental map confounded me. However, a conundrum arose as I tried to reconcile my previously unimpaired state of mind with my newly altered one. I felt different but wasn't sure why. My narrowed field of vision was most evident, but other things were broken, too, like a traffic light blinking during a power outage. It still functioned, but not as intended. It was pointless to wonder if I'd do things differently if I hadn't been shot—but I still did.

***

"Julian, this is Mateo. He's come from Uruguay for physical therapy here," a representative at the children's hospital explained, introducing me to my new roommate.

As Mateo stood, I noticed he had sculpted shoulders and biceps. However, his legs were weak. He drew closer to me on his metal crutches. Though I no longer needed a wheelchair, as I'd regrettably told Hazel, a quarter of my skull remained in a freezer while my brain healed. In the meantime, I had to wear a form-fitting helmet that looked like a half-moon strapped to the right side of my head. We exchanged inquisitive glances, each wanting to ask the same question: What the hell is wrong with you?

"I have cerebral palsy," Mateo said.

"I got shot in the head."

"I believe it's a tie," he said. "Neither of us wants to be the other, so we have to accept the way we are."

We both laughed and became fast friends.

My addled brain and high antiepileptic dosages made me sluggish when I was first admitted to the children's hospital. My mother and brother visited, but we didn't talk much. Kevin gave me a backlit Gameboy, which I kept in a drawer. I stared out the window for hours, detached. However, they lowered my dosages soon after my admission, and my cognition improved.

"What's that?" I asked Mateo as he stirred a cup of dried green leaves in hot water.

"A drink called maté. It's popular in South America. Wanna try it?"

"Yeah."

He handed me the maté. The metal spoon he used to mix the drink doubled as a straw. I didn't like the smell but enjoyed the taste. I slurped down the whole cup.

"Whoa, slow down. You should only drink it a little at a time."

"I'll be fine," I reassured him.

That night, I lay wide awake at 2:00 a.m., unblinking with clenched teeth. I figured it was because of the maté and wished I'd drunk less. I pulled out my Gameboy and played a game. The first level was fun, but the second wasn't because villains attacked from the left, where I couldn't see them coming. I soon realized this problem extended beyond the game, as it had in the cafeteria, where I regularly knocked food off the left side of my plate due to my limited vision. I'd remember I couldn't see the whole plate and stop knocking food off it, but I'd forget and have to remind myself again. Another problem was that everything on the plate looked upside-down. Even when I spun it around, it still seemed wrong, though I knew there was no reason for carrots to be above peas or vice versa.

"Fuck this game!" I declared. "It's a stupid piece of shit!" I felt like a hotshot spewing expletives.

Mateo sat up, rubbed his eyes, and said, "*Callate Boludo!*"

"Oh, sorry, Mateo. I didn't mean to wake you up. I can't even play this stupid game anymore. There's something wrong with my eyes and how I see; I can't see on my left side, and my brain is ... not normal now. It makes me so mad. It's not fair."

We sat quietly, then he spoke. "A group of missionaries arranged for me to come here. When I was born, my father saw my legs and left. I guess he wanted me to be a football player or at least walk like a normal guy. My family never could've brought me here without them."

"Shit," I said in sympathy.

"There you go again."

"You didn't miss anything. I mean with soccer. I played before. It's not that fun. People are always kicking you, and it hurts when the ball hits you in the face."

Mateo smiled, then continued, "Well, the missionaries were super excited about me believing in Jesus, the gospel, whatever, and praying with them. Religion never meant too much to me, but I wanted to come here, so I prayed with them and made a show of it. Most of the missionaries liked quoting Bible verses that had little to do with what we were talking about, and then they'd be pleased with themselves like they should win a prize. Elder Timothy was different. He said things that sounded like Bible verses, but he thought of them. Timothy was smart. He probably read the Bible once and could explain it already. Sometimes, he'd see me getting down about my legs." Mateo pointed at his scrawny legs, chuckled bitterly, and shifted the conversation.

"I'm seventeen, Julian. All my friends got these sexy *mamis*. When I see them running on the beach or kissing in the park, I don't know. I want that to be me, you know? There was this one girl, Adriana. I thought she could, uh, how do I say it? See me for me, not as some crippled person. I bought her stuff, and we hung out a couple of times. I was sure she'd be my girlfriend, but when I tried to kiss her, she said, 'Mateo, honey, you're *muy guapo*, but I think it's better if we're friends," Mateo sneered.

"*Muy guapo*?" I asked.

"It means handsome, very handsome. I told Timothy about her, and he said, 'God helps those who help themselves.' Because what's the point of being alive if he does everything for us?'"

"Do you believe that?" I asked.

68

"I agree we should try to help ourselves, but if that doesn't work, those Bible guys will say you didn't try hard enough for God to help you. So, is God really there, or is it a trick to stop you from quitting?"

"I met Jesus when I was in a coma. He told me to learn to love and not hate so demons didn't put me in a dungeon, but I might have imagined that because I was connected to a bunch of machines and bleeding a lot."

"Wow! I've heard about people seeing Jesus and dead people when they almost die, but I never believed it. What else did he say?"

"Jesus also said to remember that God created the light if I wanted to hang out with him again. Oh! Before that, a cat lady who might've been an angel appeared who was upset that I didn't pay more attention in Hebrew school."

Mateo pondered the profound yet puzzling nature of my experience.

"Why was she upset about that?"

"I don't know, Mateo. I told my mom about it, but she was so relieved I didn't die; she didn't have much to say other than I should talk to a Rabbi. I didn't mention what Jesus said since we're Jewish, and she wouldn't understand it any more than I did, but now that I think about it, maybe God was testing me? I told the cat lady I wasn't a good student and didn't know much about God except what I saw in movies where a guy with long hair and a big beard pretended to be him. But then, I think God wanted to prove he wasn't who I thought he was because the cat lady put on a bird mask, did some stuff in the sand, and then became Jesus himself, but learning to love and not hate people seemed to be the most important."

"That makes sense. Whenever I'm angry, it doesn't help much. It's better to be nice even if people don't deserve it. That makes life a little easier. So, do you think it was God or the machines making you dream?"

"The machines and being in a coma must've been part of why I had the experience, but I think it was God, too. Because I don't usually think that way unless I overheard that stuff in my sleep or saw it on TV and don't remember."

"If I meet God, I'll ask him why he didn't give me better legs. Do you think God speaks Spanish?"

"I'm sure he speaks every language. Hey, what does *Karate Boluti* mean?"

"That's a lesson for another time, Julian," he smiled, and we went back to bed.

Mateo and I spoke frequently but had independent routines. I went to physical and occupational therapy on alternate days, school every day, and I attended group therapy sessions with other children on Fridays. Most people are familiar with physical therapy, which involves activities like aquatics and weightlifting to rebuild strength after an injury. My issues were primarily mental, so I typically did as I pleased in physical therapy. Though I'd lost muscle mass while I was comatose, I was already fit from wrestling and benched above my weight in no time. Sometimes, Mateo and I worked out together; he could bench much more than me. The type of Cerebral Palsy he had only affected his legs. When Ben came to see me, he said I looked buff. He suggested I talk to my mom about getting another car like the Acura because her old Honda was messing with my reputation. I smiled when he said that, though I knew she wouldn't upgrade our ride anytime soon. Sometimes, people's imperfections are the best thing about them.

Occupational therapy doesn't involve career training, despite its name. It helps patients relearn tasks that may no longer be intuitive after an injury. It was helpful, but even simple tasks, like grocery shopping, remained challenging. Besides crashing into things on my left, making decisions was difficult. I'd stand frozen in the aisle, facing the colorful characters decorating the cereal boxes of Rice Krispies and Cocoa Puffs. Aside from my mother preferring I eat shredded wheat, why I'd choose one box over another was beyond my shredded cognition. As I stepped through flowcharts of ideation, sections were missing along the way. To compensate, I created random sorting rules, like picking Cocoa Puffs because C and P are in alphabetical order, whereas R and K are not.

The bowling alley was available by request. My family used it occasionally.

"How do you like it here, Julian?" my mother asked, then rolled a gutter ball. My brother knocked down a few pins.

"It's nice. Sometimes I forget it's a hospital. It's more like the club where Francine had her Bat Mitzvah. We should eat at the cafeteria later."

"Do they have ice cream?" my brother asked.

"Oh yeah, you can even make your own sundaes."

He gave me a thumbs-up.

"Next month, there'll be a criminal hearing for Jonathan," my mother told me in the cafeteria as I placed the lima beans that had fallen off the left side back on my plate. "He's been charged with third-degree assault. That stupid boy—I'll never understand what he was thinking or that mother of his claiming he didn't mean to shoot you. But don't worry about that. Just say what you remember, and I'll bring you back here."

"Okay, Mom. I'm not worried." Actually, I was worried, but not about that. I'd been at the children's hospital for over a month and grown accustomed to the inpatient lifestyle. Nurses checked on me throughout the day. Doctors reviewed my charts and concluded, "You're doing great, young man, exceeding all expectations." I liked the snacks everyone got before bed and the occasional Spanish lessons from Mateo. *Tengo dolor de cabeza*, which means "I have a headache," got a laugh and an offer for Tylenol when I said it to a nurse from Mexico. Her shoes were terrific, by the way. I sometimes caught myself thinking, I should've gotten shot in the head a long time ago. The prospect of never leaving was a sweet dream since field trips outside the hospital didn't always go well for me.

Everyone sat near the front when we saw *Indiana Jones and the Last Crusade*. It was hard to explain that I had to sit in the last row because I could only see half of the movie.

"But it just started?" a chaperone asked.

"No, I can only see half of the screen because of my vision ... I can't see the left side up close."

Then there was the jackass waiter who served a group of us at a bustling local restaurant.

71

"How's everyone doing this afternoon? Are you all from the Special Olympics?" He'd surmised upon seeing the group's crutches, wheelchairs, braces, and my half-moon helmet with its dorky-looking chin strap. On our way out, he grabbed my arm and led me toward a microphone intended to notify patrons their table was ready.

"And here we have one of our gold medalists wearing a fashionable accessory that will soon sweep the nation. A round of applause, please." A few people clapped uneasily, and the hospital staff ushered us out. I knew he was making fun of me but couldn't understand why. It's hard enough being disabled without imbeciles ridiculing those least able to defend themselves.

Worries over ill-treatment in a world unwilling to accept us after we were shepherded away from our catered meals and doting hospital staff were a common concern that children at the hospital discussed in our group therapy sessions on Fridays, which everyone called Psych Group.

"I don't know if I can ever ride in a car again. My mom picked me up for a dentist appointment yesterday. I tried breathing slowly like we talked about, but it felt like everything was happening too fast, so I got out of the car and ran back to the hospital. Then my mom was mad, so I got mad at her, but it made me sad because we never used to fight like that," Julie, another patient, explained to Ann, the counselor who led our group discussions. Ann, a recent graduate in her early twenties, had short, dirty blonde hair and round glasses that made her look like a librarian. I found concentrating on what Ann was saying difficult because she was cute ... and I had massive brain damage.

"Julie, I'm sure your mother isn't mad at you. She's concerned. She wants you to be like you were before your accident, but there will be new ways you interact with each other and the world. She'll adjust to it, and so will you," Ann explained.

"I know, but she wasn't in the car with me. I still remember that big smashing sound and all the glass. I can't stop thinking about it sometimes."

"Well, I had it worse. At least you weren't in the back seat with one of those lap belts. The stupid thing cut into my stomach really hard. Everything got all messed up inside. Now I'm gonna have this stupid scar forever," Nicole, the girl beside her, complained, lifting her shirt to show us the vertical scar below her navel. It didn't look that bad, but I understood how she felt. I had a stupid scar now, too.

Ann stopped what always seemed to happen: kids competing to prove that they had the most trauma from their injuries. I tried not to get involved and acted like nothing bothered me, thinking that would impress her. "Okay, everyone, please. We're here to help each other adapt to the changes we've all experienced. Let's do some calming exercises. Concentrate on your breathing and sitting comfortably in your chair."

We did as she suggested.

Although I agreed with Ann, my chair wasn't comfortable. I wanted to lie on a chaise lounge like the one I saw at my grandparents' place and in old movies, where a monocle-wearing shrink studies someone's dreams.

"Julian, you've been quiet the entire time. Do you have anything you'd like to share with the group?"

My response was delayed because I was daydreaming about living in a log cabin with Ann beneath fluffy white clouds reflected in a still pond beside us. Despite my lowered dosages, I still zoned out sometimes. I snapped out of it and said, "I don't know. I'm not afraid of cars or anything like that. A kid shot me while I was watching TV, and I didn't see him do it, so I wasn't scared. After that, all I could think about was my electric blanket because I was cold, but I'm fine now."

"Julian, we don't all need to have the same problems to understand each other. Why don't you share how you're feeling now? Has anything been bothering you since your injury?"

Her lips are rose-colored. I should buy Ann some flowers. Flowers are nice ...

"Bueller, Bueller!" A large boy named Paul repeated while punching me in the shoulder. I jolted back to our conversation.

"Paul, we talked about this! This is a safe place. There's no fighting allowed. Apologize to Julian."

"No, it's okay. I don't mind; it's good practice," I said, striking Paul back. Ann didn't know we had a prior agreement that we could hit each other in the shoulder anytime to perfect our punch. Paul was bigger and older than the rest of us. I'm sure he didn't give it all he's got when he punched me, or I would have been looking up at the ceiling every time. I liked talking to Paul because he was tough, rock-solid. He never complained about having half his face burned in a fire.

"Well, the other day, something did bother me. I have a court case coming up with the kid who shot me, Jonathan. He called to apologize last week. I'm not sure what happened or why he shot me because I didn't see him do it, but I don't think he's sorry. I'm sure his mom made him call because after we talked, she got on and said, 'Julian, Jonathan would never shoot anyone. He didn't understand how the gun worked. Everyone knows it was an accident.' Then she said something about it being illegal to lie and that I'd get in trouble if I didn't say it exactly the way she explained."

"Hell no! Do you want me to go to that courthouse and beat them both up?" Paul proposed.

"Paul, that is not how we talk! That will accomplish nothing. One more outburst, and I'll have them shut off your TV."

"Ah, man, don't do that. I just don't want anyone messing with Julian."

Ann smiled and returned her attention to me as I continued.

"When she said that, my leg started shaking, and then, about an hour later, I started thinking about when Jonathan shot me," I explained, turning off the fantasy of Ann and me walking beneath a waterfall with giant butterflies and unicorns. "Maybe this sounds freaky, but it felt like someone was holding my head and forcing me to watch a movie about being shot, even though it was nothing like what really happened."

Ann paused, looking more serious than I'd ever seen her. "Jonathan's mother should not have said that, and I will ensure she doesn't speak to you again. Tell them what you remember during the trial, not what anyone else wants you to say. And when you're no longer a patient, if something upsets you, remember to stay calm and manage each situation as we've discussed."

Yes, I will be calm after we marry in the field beside our house, surrounded by cornfields, lambs, horses, and our five children.

Anxiety made my legs shake, but it wasn't the only reason. Dr. Roshan called the tremors clonus and explained they're common as the brain heals. He reassured me my antiepileptic medication, Tegretol, which I took twice daily, along with the healing process, should stop the tremors within a year.

Jonathan's mother's subtle threats enraged my mom, but the angrier she became, the more I pitied Jonathan and his mother.

"But, Mom, what would you have done if I'd shot Jonathan?" I asked when we discussed it on the phone that evening. "Remember when I broke April's glasses, and then you called her mother and said she was partly to blame because she was kicking me?"

"That's different, Julian! I'm not going to think about what I'd do because you never would have shot him. Jonathan should have to go to jail for being cruel and selfish."

I wanted to tell her I'd been reckless with guns, too, and the ambulance driver warned me, but I didn't listen, and now a third of my brain was gone.

The academic part of my routine was particularly challenging. The shooting accident occurred two months before I finished eighth grade, so not much was required for me to graduate. Still, my once facile mind that could ace reading, writing, and arithmetic while I spent most of my time playing video games was now a jumble of misfiring neurons that no longer supported such inattentive efforts.

I slogged through literature, history, and science, but math, as they say, was Greek to me. Henry and I once broke down a computer in the basement—they'd shrunk much sooner than he'd expected. He explained that a black box with silver legs resembling a mechanical cockroach clinging to the motherboard was a math coprocessor essential for speedy computation. The computer could function without it, but too slowly to be useful. This mirrored my own situation. I'd retained the ability to reason. However, the gun blast destroyed ancillary components that had facilitated quick thinking and replaced them with faulty wiring. My Japanese math teacher's thick accent exacerbated the problem. The limited geometry my hobbled circuits could still compute made every class a foreboding window into the challenges awaiting me.

"Rite yua ansah hia," he said, indicating where to write my answers.

"You must measuru the pointo on the rine."

Because the instructor's name was Ataru, I called him Atari, widening our communication barrier further. None of this would have mattered if I didn't need to pass geometry to graduate, but the day came when he placed the final exam on my desk.

Ataru saw me looking forlorn at the rows of unselected multiple-choice equations, and our gloomy faces needed no translation. But then he brightened and said, "You hold-a pensuru no righteo."

"No, I hold-a pen-zoo-roo righteo, Atari," I said, mocking him out of frustration. I gathered he was talking about the crisply sharpened pencil I held.

There were only fifteen questions, but innumerable ways to get them wrong. I was about to employ the same quasi-rational logic I'd begun using when I couldn't make a selection and wade my way through it, but then he spoke again.

He insisted I knew the answers but wasn't using the pencil correctly. We debated this until he took the pencil from my hand and laid it on the paper.

"Uh, okay," I said as I picked it up and was about to circle C when he repeated his rebuke.

"I show you ko-rek-tu."

I then noticed he'd placed the pencil down, pointing at B.

I circled B and quietly confirmed, "Correcto?"

He looked around the room and said, "Ko-rek-tu."

After that, I kept one eye on Ataru, who subtly gestured to let me know which answer to circle as I moved the pencil from question to question. And with that, eighth grade was over. Next up was high school.

I spent three months at the children's hospital, but I wasn't awarded a green band until the last two weeks. A trio of colored wristbands dictated mobility around the hospital. New patients received a red wristband, confining them to their floor. You received a yellow band after proving your capacity to use elevators and escalators while maneuvering around your ward. Only after passing the final test of adroit navigation throughout the hospital grounds and receiving a green band were the library, cafeteria, bowling alley, and other amenities accessible without supervision. The yellow band remained fastened to my wrist longer than most patients. A boy I met, blinded by his injury, advanced to the green band faster than me. My mother and the medical staff reassured me that my specific neural deficits made my progression more challenging, but it was still frustrating.

"You have to try," Mateo implored me as I lay moping after failing to qualify for a green band again. I'd obtained the yellow band a month ago, but my progress had since stalled.

"I disagree. Why don't you slip off yours and give it to me?"

Mateo got a green band ten days after his arrival, given that his burdens were unrelated to spatial reasoning.

"No, then you won't have the satisfaction of doing it yourself."

"What if I can't? It was easy for you, but it's impossible for me."

He ignored my wallowing as he propped himself up, grabbed his crutches, and made his way to my bed.

"Watch this," Mateo said, lifting his emaciated lower limbs into the air and performing several swings back and forth on his crutches. I was impressed, but its coolness was tainted by my recollection of the man in the restaurant using the Special Olympics to ridicule us.

"That's cool," I said, managing a smile.

"Yes, it is cool, but that's the easy part. Now watch this." Then, with the crutches pressed to his sides, using a combination of upper-body strength and his legs as ballast to remain upright, he returned to his bed without touching the ground. "You try it," he said, propping his crutches against the wall.

I grabbed his crutches, expecting to show him a few new tricks. I'd mastered wheelchair wheelies and was buffed up, so I was sure this would be easy. However, I couldn't take even a single step and collapsed in a heap, the crutches falling on top of me as if to further mock my effort.

Mateo shook his head.

After multiple failed attempts, I managed to swing back and forth. However, unlike Mateo, I couldn't use the crutches to take more than a single step. I placed them against the wall, then sat down to catch my breath.

"You might be surprised, but I didn't learn that to impress girls in my neighborhood."

"It's harder than it looks. Adriana should've at least let you slip her the tongue," I said, still out of breath.

Mateo laughed and said, "Back home, the drains on my street aren't very good. After it rains, there are big puddles around for hours. I got sick of waiting for one of my brothers to help me, so I learned to do that high-walking—Julian, what do you call that? When people use the big sticks to walk?"

"Stilt-walking."

"*Gracias*. I can't do that stilt-walking stuff for long or lift myself very high, but it's enough to get back some independence. I thought it was impossible at first, especially lifting my legs, but I knew I had to try. That's all you have to do. You have to try, maybe over and over."

"And God will do the rest?"

"Maybe, but at least you saw him turn into a cat."

***

Go down the hall and turn right at the water fountain. The elevator is coming up on the left. Remember to turn your head. Think of the Tin Man from *The Wizard of Oz* with a stiff neck riding in the elevator. When you round the corner, it'll look the same as the hallway you just passed, but pay attention; there's a fire alarm. Pretend the Scarecrow is with him, and he's on fire. That's all you need to do to find your way around the hospital.

I ran through the course repeatedly, as Mateo suggested. It felt like I'd made no progress for days. Then, the map began filling in, not with the original lay of the land but with symbols and stories, such as the elevator scene with the characters from *Oz*, which compensated for the missing portions of my mental map they encapsulated. I navigated using mnemonics and algebraic reasoning, leveraging the parts of my mind functioning properly to solve for those that weren't. With repetition and willpower, I advanced to the green band.

***

My fellow patients offered encouragement. Mateo said I should focus on how good it would feel to be free of the half-moon helmet strapped to my head for months. My mother and brother shared similar sentiments, though she was disappointed I couldn't have the surgery after attending Jonathan's court hearing with my lunar prosthesis attached "to show the judge what he'd done." But as they wheeled me into the operating room to replace my frozen bone flap, I simply felt afraid. The odds of surviving this surgery were far better than the brain surgery I'd already endured, so in a sense, the worst was over. But it wasn't over. What if they messed up the anesthesia? What if I could feel them slicing my head open but couldn't so much as shed a tear to let them know? I thought about Gil's sick and twisted torment. A voice led me through a curated tour of my worst experiences, deliberately ignoring any pleasant memories.

Remember the time you got a nail stuck in your head?

You'll be locked in the dark! Alone forever.

Even death won't end your agony!

I was breathing heavily and on the verge of asking for my cranioplasty to be postponed, even though I knew that my clunky half-moon helmet would remain strapped to my head until I went through with it. Do you really want to keep wearing that stupid thing? I focused on my skull being whole again, imagining the strange and soothing sounds I'd heard in the Holy Place, and soon enough, my mother was standing by my bed, telling me the surgery had gone well. I touched my skull, relieved to find a solid chunk of bone beneath my fingertips, but my joy was short-lived. Under my gown, I found another catheter. I left it alone this time.

The surgical team only shaved the half of my head where they'd replaced my skull, eliciting good-natured ribbing from kids in the hospital, which I also found comical given I knew that my hair would regrow, but the scar, which began at my right temple, ran along the side of my head and descended down the back, was not a source of mirth. Scars were common in the hospital; most of us had them. Puffy keloid scars along the abdomen and across the face. Pink and white ones where arms had been. These were only the scars you could see and served as a shared memento that our lives had forever changed.

***

After a short drive from the far more welcoming children's hospital, the courthouse loomed before us. My mother and I entered the solemn-looking structure with a broad pediment supported by a series of Corinthian columns framing the front door. Once inside, the metal detector thankfully ignored the titanium wiring in my skull. I'd never been in this building before, though I'd been in the family courthouse around the corner when I was younger. I'd felt the same confusion playing under the judge's desk and studying her varicose veins as I did now, trying to piece the space around me together. We proceeded to the courtroom, and the case got underway. Everyone remained silent, sitting in suits and dresses, while the judge explained Jonathan's offense and a stenographer transcribed the proceedings. I was in awe of how our judicial system resolved matters of raw emotion and chaos in such an orderly fashion.

I almost dozed off as Jonathan's lawyer droned on. My mother had retained a lawyer on my behalf, but his services weren't needed that day despite Jonathan's mother suggesting otherwise.

In the social studies portion of my hospital schooling, we learned about Martin Luther King Jr. and Gandhi. I was already familiar with both men, but their pacifist philosophies resonated more deeply with me after my injury and the hard-knock stories I heard around the hospital. Mateo shared his thoughts when I asked him what he thought about them in the days leading up to Jonathan's trial.

"In Uruguay, we don't learn much about those guys, but another man I'm more familiar with might have influenced them. His name is Jesus. I believe you two are already acquainted." I smiled but didn't want to make a habit of joking about things I knew men had crossed oceans and burned each other alive to crusade over.

For reasons as profound as Jesus's teachings and as mundane as the fact we were all being reckless, I told the judge the shooting was accidental, and Jonathan didn't know how the gun worked. Upon further questioning, I conceded I wasn't sure if Jonathan had pointed the gun at me because I was distracted by *The People's Court*. The judge smiled when I said testifying about that show during a trial was funny. My testimony was probably incidental. Jonathan was charged with third-degree assault, and I never saw him again. I wasn't happy with the guy, but I forgave him.

When I was discharged from the hospital a few days later, a doctor reiterated that I should avoid drugs and contact sports. "Have fun, but don't land on your head," he joked as he led us out. Since arriving at the hospital, I'd dreaded leaving its safety, cleanliness, and structured routine. But now that they had put Humpty Dumpty back together again, I was determined to move on with my life. Like most young men, I felt immortal and lived fearlessly. Now, I knew death was all around me, and fear would become my greatest adversary if I didn't learn to control it.

Chapter 9

As the train we clung to rumbled across an intersection, James hollered, "Chugga-chugga-choo-choo!"

"I think I can. I think I can," I sang with him, waving to people waiting in their cars. As we cleared the intersection, I saw a guy in a Buick with a mismatched hood shaking his head from the corner of my right eye.

"Delaware Rowdy Boys!" Sam shouted, clinging to the hopper car behind us.

We jumped off the train using similar but individually modified techniques to avoid falling onto the rocks, then hurried through the woods in case anyone had alerted the rail police to our mischievousness. "Where's that from? A children's story?" Sam asked.

"*The Little Engine That Could*, my boy. Got any smokes?" James replied.

"Yeah, but we oughta get some cigars too." Sam smiled as he dusted himself off, pulled out a pack of Marlboro Reds, and handed one to James. He hadn't mastered disembarking yet and had taken a tumble. He was a bit chunky but a sturdy boy, and other than a few scratches, he was fine. I pulled out a pack of Newport Lights from my shirt pocket and lit one. A lot had changed since I left the hospital two years ago, so let me go back a bit.

***

"What are you doing, Julian?" Ben's mom asked as I sprinted down their narrow hallway.

"I want to see how the world looks when I run," I explained.

"Please stop doing that. I don't want you to hit your head."

This became a common refrain from everyone I knew.

"Don't get too close, Julian. I don't want the ball to hit your head."

"Be careful stepping down from that ladder. One of those boxes could tip over and fall on your head."

"No, I can't let you go waterskiing. I know your friends are going, but it's not safe for you."

My survival and the speed of my recovery after the shooting were miraculous, but once I was home, people spoke to me as if I were five years old, English wasn't my first language, and I was made of glass. This hindered my progress, as I could only rise to the diminished version of myself they'd boxed me into. One unfortunate incident reinforcing this perception occurred while my family held a late-summer barbecue in our backyard as the nights were getting cooler. Kevin and I took turns flipping burgers and hot dogs for a group of our acquaintances. I was having a good time until ...

"Stop shooting me! Don't do that!" I cried out. A neighborhood boy ignored my pleas and continued soaking me with his pump-action water gun. It was clear plastic with bright yellow molding. My mother rushed to my aid and scolded the boy. "Julian doesn't like that. Stop it!"

"But it's a water gun. It's just water," the boy protested as she led him away.

He'd sprayed other people at the party, and I hardly noticed, but when he blasted me, what I'd seen as water squirting from a harmless chunk of plastic became an unrelenting fusillade from an assault rifle slicing through me. I stayed in the house for the rest of the party, taking shallow breaths while listening to guests talk about me until they tired of the topic, then debated which of Delaware's tax-free shopping malls offered the best back-to-school-specials.

My mother vacillated between coddling me and treating me like my former fit self. She limited my activities but still trusted I could watch my brother when she went out with her friends. I didn't like being stuck at home, but she'd gotten me my promised cable TV, so I usually zoned out to old movies and MTV until she came home. One night, however, I couldn't remember if I'd taken the second daily dose of my antiepileptic pills. I'd never had a seizure, but as the quick cuts from Madonna's music video "Express Yourself" flashed on the screen, my leg started tapping and my shoulder twitched.

As Dr. Roshan assured me, the neural issues causing involuntary movements had stopped. Thus, the return of these spasms meant that my growing fear of having a seizure might soon be realized. Cell phones were uncommon then, so I couldn't call my mom to get her reassurance that I wasn't about to go over the borderline.

"Kevin, something's wrong with me. See how my leg is shaking?"

My brother looked up from his bowl of ice cream topped with generously applied chocolate syrup and Cool Whip. "It looks like you're making it shake. Why don't you take a bath?"

"No, I could drown if I have a seizure in the tub. I'm gonna call 911 before it's too late."

"Can I finish my ice cream first?"

"Hello, 911."

"I need help. I'm about to have a seizure!"

"Slow down. Tell me what's going on."

"I forgot to take one of my pills. My leg's shaking, and my shoulder twitched."

"Are you doing drugs? What pills are you talking about?"

"I have a prescription for Tegretol to prevent seizures, but I forgot to take it tonight. That's why I'm going to have one!"

"Okay, stay calm, sir. What's your name?"

"Julian."

"Are you sure you're having a seizure? People usually can't talk if they're having one."

"No, I didn't have one yet, but it's starting! I forgot to take my medicine. Please, I'm scared. My leg is shaking. I want to go to the hospital."

"All right, I'll send someone over to help you."

I sat on the floor, feeling vertiginous like I was doing backflips. Then I thought of Hazel Lane and wondered what she was doing. Would I be thinking about her if I were having a seizure? Maybe I'm not? Should I take another pill? But what if I take too many? Oh

God, it's coming. It's happening now. I'd better lie down. Spinning, falling, fear.

An ambulance and police car arrived, flashing their lights and blaring a siren. My neighbors raised their window shades, and the more curious ones sat on their front stoops, watching with folded arms. A paramedic and police officer pounded on my front door. I let them in.

"Who's having a seizure?" the police officer asked.

My brother pointed at me.

"Is this a prank? You're not having a seizure."

"I didn't say I was having a seizure. I said I was about to have one. My leg tapped a few times, and then my shoulder twitched—"

The officer rolled his eyes, then spoke in a low voice to the ambulance driver, who returned to his vehicle, switched off its siren and lights, but remained parked in front of my house. One of my neighbors shut their front door, but the rest were undeterred, eagerly awaiting the next scene. *"Guns! Dogs! Dead people? Ellen, quit chopping those onions and check this out!"*

"Where are your parents?"

"My mom's not home right now. I'm watching my brother. I got shot in the head and forgot to take my medicine. I take it twice a day. I never forget. Never! I don't know, maybe I took it, but I don't think so." I slumped down, covered my face, and cried. I felt shaky, sweating. Something terrible was coming. I was sure of it. Why couldn't I have gotten up for a glass of water instead of being shot? If I'd moved five freakin inches from where I was sitting, I wouldn't have to know how it feels to be so broken.

"Why are you crying, Julian?" Kevin asked.

"I'm going to have a seizure. My brain—something's wrong with it, okay? I don't have time to explain. I need to go to the hospital. Why are we waiting? Let's go! Why did that guy get back in the ambulance? Don't you believe me?"

"I heard you, but let's talk a little first. What was your name again?" The cop eased onto the couch. I got up and sat across from him on a recliner.

"Julian," I said through sniffles.

85

"Julian, my name is Officer Elias. If it's necessary, we'll take you to the hospital, but I think you'll be okay. I remember reading about you. You're lucky to be alive."

"Yeah, I guess so."

My brother noticed Officer Elias's holstered weapon.

"Is that a real gun?"

"Yes, but that's for the bad guys. You and your brother are good guys. It's nice of him to be here watching you."

I was glad he didn't unholster his gun, though his friendly demeanor kept me from freaking out about it. My brother and I spoke with him for another five minutes. He convinced me I wasn't having a seizure and said my mother could call the station if she had any questions when she returned. Before leaving, he stopped in the doorway, turned around, and said, "Hey Julian, I'm glad you and your brother are okay. I thought this was going to be another drug overdose call. We've had far too many of them lately. I hate nothing more than seeing kids throw their lives away over drugs, throwing away all that potential. It's not just their lives; it breaks the hearts of everyone around them. I've seen it too many times. I'd love to put every one of those scumbag drug dealers in jail," he said, patting his gun, then left.

My mother returned minutes later, intoxicated, which made explaining what happened earlier less embarrassing. She called the police station and heard Officer Elias's summary of the evening's suburban reality show. Afterward, she said I'd done the right thing by calling 911 if I was worried. No one was mad at me, but it was irrational to think that missing a single dose of Tegretol would make me have a seizure. While she was on the phone, I peeked out front. Everyone had gone back inside except my neighbor to the left, a hot-tempered middle-aged man with three daughters who liked to slick back his thin gray hair. He'd pulled out a folding chair to ensure he caught the whole show. "Why were that ambulance and cop here?" he asked, straddling his doorway. "Are you one of those druggies?"

"No, I forgot to take my medicine. I thought I was going to have a seizure, but I was wrong. I'm okay now."

He stood, clenching his jaw, then slammed his door shut. I'd emerged from the hospital empathetic, ready to give the world a big hug, but now I wondered how many people wanted to embrace the boy with the broken head.

I went back inside, relieved my mother hadn't seen our brief exchange, though she found out about it later. That was a pity. I wanted to avoid anything that might send her back to the bottom of the bottle.

***

Sam Drummond lived one street over from me. He was a pudgy, freckle-faced boy with wild, uncombable brown hair. Over the years, he'd tried to hang out with Ben, Seth, and me, but we'd never let him into our tight-knit crew. Ben's mother had seen him smoking and labeled him a bad boy. She deemed him off-limits to them, so I didn't interact with him much either. My mom thought his father was creepy because he liked chatting with her whenever she walked by their house and waved to her from his car. Still, she had no issue with Sam other than repeating the refrain, "There's something odd about that boy," which was validated when he dressed up as Freddy Krueger for Halloween and wore the same costume, replete with knife-fingered gloves for the rest of the week.

"I heard you called the police on yourself when you were smoking crack!" Sam gleefully shared when he saw me parking my bike and taking off my helmet at 7-Eleven, demonstrating both the speed of local gossip and the unwelcome fact that my panic attack remained my neighbors' favorite topic. Ben also asked me about the incident. I explained my pill quandary, and he was glad I was okay. Still, we both knew what had happened: the old Julian was gone, and a new, traumatized one had taken his place.

My bike riding privileges were hard-won after weeks of riding around the neighborhood with my mother and eventually to Main Street, where shops dotted the center of town and locals mingled with college kids. We passed through our old neighborhood on the way there. I scanned the broken sidewalks, barred windows, and surly blokes sitting on lawn furniture, eyeing my mother and me like hungry lions as we sped up without saying a word. I was struck by how differently people lived less than a mile apart.

Sam was a year younger than me, and crack cocaine wasn't something we'd likely ever encounter. However, all the anti-drug campaigns of the day, which insisted that crack and other illegal substances would fry our brains, inevitably elicited jokes and disses among the kids they targeted.

"Your mom smokes crack."

"You're a crack baby."

"What are you, on crack?"

"No, that's not why I called them," I told Sam. "Who said that? Why are people so dumb?"

"Bill Jones, the guy who lives next to you, was whining about it to my dad. They both work at the auto plant under the highway by the state line."

Sam saw me looking toward the ground.

"Don't sweat that guy, Julian. My dad doesn't even like him; he called him a jackass. You want some jawbreakers?"

I opened my palm, and Sam poured a generous amount of hard candy balls into my hand. I used to buy jawbreakers when my allowance was a dollar. They were cheap, and I could suck on them the whole way home from 7-Eleven, but my favorite thing was going to specialty candy shops and buying the giant ones. I don't know how anyone fits them in their mouth, and I never tried. I'd stop atop the bridge near 7-Eleven and throw them at boxcars rumbling by. If you hit one in the right spot, you'd get a satisfying "bang" sound paired with a rainbow confetti blast as it blew to bits.

Across the street was a Friendly's restaurant, formerly owned by the Hershey Foods Corporation. I remember having a slice of ice cream cake there for my birthday shortly after my grandma gave me stock certificates. I'd asked my mom, "Since this place is owned by Hershey's, do we get free ice cream?"

She laughed. "No, but that would be nice, wouldn't it? It's more like you own one of those tiles on the floor." That was much less appealing than free ice cream, but I always liked looking at the tiles after that.

"You want to come to my place and play some Nintendo?" Sam asked. I said I did, and we started walking back with our bikes, sucking on the jawbreakers until they were safe to bite and be rewarded with a flavor blast as you hit the sweet candy core.

We'd also bought a pair of Big Gulps, filling the giant cups with sodas, tea, and syrupy juices. The sugary cocktail was much more appealing in concept than reality.

Sam tossed his drink off the bridge. I took a sip, "Yuck," and did the same. With no train below, our cups exploded on the tracks. We laughed and made our way to his place. After playing Nintendo, we horsed around for a while in his room. It was fun, but mostly, I was grateful he didn't warn me about hitting my head the whole time we hung out.

That weekend, Sam and I raked leaves in his backyard. He'd persuaded me to help, much like I'd encouraged Ben to mow my lawn, but I got a kick out of the way Sam raked, so I didn't mind. He'd scoop up the biggest pile of leaves possible, then launch them over his fence into the neighbor's yard.

"Looks like double duty for them!" Sam cheered, launching a pile over the fence in a single, smooth arc. I smiled, imagining their befuddlement when they saw an unnaturally large mound of leaves behind their house. Next, we did it in tandem, spinning in sync as we launched more leaves over the fence, which had us falling down laughing.

"What the hell are you doing, boys? Don't do that," Sam's dad admonished, arms raised, as he strode through unraked leaves with a cigarette hanging out of his mouth. He was lanky and wore wire-rimmed glasses. I was worried about what he'd do next, but he looked cool. We both stopped in our tracks, holding the rakes in flagrante delicto.

"Boys, you might think that's funny, but it's not. A man buys a house in a nice place like this and expects a certain level of respect from his neighbors. When he pulls into his driveway, he lets out a big sigh," his dad said, demonstrating the sigh. "Because this is what it's all about. His home, his sanctuary. Where he's free from the Daily Grind. Then he sits out back with a smoke, a beer, or coffee—whatever's his pleasure—and takes back the time he still can. It's not everything he dreamed of, but enough to stay sane. What he doesn't want is for even one little thing to make his life more stressful, like those leaves you dumped in his yard. A special type of rage takes over a man when he sees something like that. I wouldn't want you boys seeing that at your young, impressionable age. Now go over there and scoop them up before he gets home."

"Sorry, Dad," Sam said.

"Sorry, Mr. Drummond," I echoed, and we did as he asked.

"I guess he's right," Sam said, "except an old couple lives there. I've never seen them tilting a bottle back to cool out."

I knew Sam's dad was right, even if it didn't apply to this neighbor. I'd raked plenty of leaves and wouldn't want anyone doubling my work. Still, I didn't get what he meant by the Daily Grind and why everything had to be cozy when the day was done, or you might go berserk. I remembered the man at the *News Journal* speaking proudly about people receiving their daily papers on time. *"You do understand that daily means every day?"* The daily paper must've helped with the Daily Grind, whatever it was.

***

Going back to school was bizarre. Would it have felt that way if I hadn't been shot, nearly died, and spent months in the hospital learning to live with a brain injury? High school is vastly different from junior high, but I was sure my injury made it even stranger. I was happy to see so many unfamiliar faces, which meant fewer people pinning me to the old Julian. Who I could no longer be. My scholastic abilities had changed the most. I used to breeze through school with minimal effort, but now I could barely keep up, no matter how much I applied myself.

My curriculum had previously been a mix of regular and advanced courses. When I still had a full tank of brains, classmates leaned over my shoulder to copy answers to quizzes and tests. In the

90

same spirit as Ataru, I'd coolly lift my exam, pretending to review it so others could pass. Desmond, who everyone called Minty, was one such student. He got the name from a teacher who'd pronounced his name Dez-Mint. Unlike me, he liked the alteration. I often ate lunch with Minty and other kids from Wilmington. They were mainly Black and had a unique style and culture I liked. Some of my peers busted on me for my choice of dining companions, but I didn't care about their cliques or coordinated wardrobes. I'd told Minty about Derrick and his trashy older brother, and he shared a story with me. He'd been riding the bus. The driver was Black; when a White lady cut him off, he said, "All those White folks think they own the road." A couple months later, when the driver was White, an Asian guy cut him off, and he said, "Look at that man. Those people come to this country and think they own the road." That may have never really happened, but it was a good lesson.

"Don't do it exactly the same, or we're going to get caught, Minty," I'd warned him when I let him copy my homework back in the day.

"I know, I know. Actually, I can do all this stuff myself. But I don't have time after class. I've got to prioritize. Some of the ladies round my way got me real busy."

"I guess I'm lucky. I've never had that problem. I always have time to study."

"You're funny as hell, bro. We're legit. I got your back anytime. Just lemme know when you need me."

When Minty saw me in the lunch line on the first day of our freshman year, he slapped me on the back and asked if I was all right. He'd cut his hair short, nearly to the skin. Unlike the cuts he used to have with lines clipped into them like Kid 'n Play.

"What happened, Weens? You get into a gunfight? You ought to come round my way. I'll show you how to dodge bullets."

"No, nothing like that," I laughed. "But I'm glad you don't think I tried to kill myself. Most people think they know more about what happened to me than I do. A stupidass kid accidentally shot me, but I'm all right."

Minty nodded solemnly. "Damn. That's a raw deal, Weens, but I'm glad you pulled through. You're strong, man!" He paused and looked at something behind me. "That's amazing."

"Yeah, that's what my doctor said too."

He faced me and burst out laughing. "Not you, homie. Nah, Nah. Here, turn your head. Look over there."

"And what should I be looking at? My vision is a little uneven now, so you might need to point it out."

"I don't want to be pointing. But let me break it down for you, and I think you'll see fine." I scanned the cafeteria for whatever he was going on about. He grabbed me by the shoulders to show me.

"Now, Weens, this particular scenario is the kind of thing you might only peep once every four years. It's something real special. You see that girl over there?"

"What girl?"

"The one wearing a Beastie Boys shirt and tight jeans. Damn, she's about to win the Sexy Mama Olympics."

Like he said, she looked fine, and I looked forward to getting to know more of my new classmates. I turned back to Minty. "I see what you mean. That girl is gold. It makes me proud to be American."

Minty let out a succession of quick chuckles and said, "You're alright, Weens, still funny as hell."

"Word, Minty, but I think I'm gonna go by J now. Weens is kind of the old life."

"Ah, all right, all right. I see. All grown up now. Well, still Minty for me. You know, the ladies like that, and you gotta keep 'em satisfied. Lemme know if you ever need something. I still got your back."

We took our trays back to Minty's table, and I had lunch with his crew, though it wasn't as cool as it used to be. They mostly joked with each other and didn't talk to me much. That was the last time we sat together, but Minty kept his word. We switched roles, and he tilted his exams so I could copy them, which got me through those first few months. Some of my fellow students were now the size of full-grown men. Fights in the bathroom or behind the bleachers

92

could've been fatal for a guy with a busted skull like me. Having Minty and his associates in my social sphere gave me a critical advantage. We had great conversations about everything happening in the world, and we learned a lot from each other, but they also had beatdown skills that convinced most bullies not to bother me. I got slapped a few times in the hallway but was always glad to see whoever dared in a sling after an unplanned absence from school by the end of the week.

***

Every student had a guidance counselor whose primary function was to advise them on classes and extracurricular activities. My guidance counselor, Tamika, also acted as a mental health coach.

"Julian, right here, over here. Look at me. You've got to look people in the eye, or they'll think you're not listening. That's the kind of thing people expect from a man. Look 'em in the eye."

I struggled to 'look her in the eye' because I couldn't see her whole face. I'd learned to splice what I could see together, but it makes people look like the lopsided lines of a cubist painting, whom I tended to view with a grimace and cockeyed glance until I became more familiar with them.

After I explained my limited field of vision, we moved on to what was bothering me. It was my sophomore year, and my antiepileptic drug dosage had been reduced to the point I was nearly done with it.

"I've been taking these antiepileptic pills for two years, Tamika. I'm scared I'll have a seizure when I stop, even though I'm down to two a week, and there have been no problems."

"Let me get this straight, Julian. You're scared of quitting some pills you're just about done with? You know damn well that ain't worth sweatin' over. What you've got to do is breathe and slow down. You can't hang on to every tiny little thing. You gotta get outside your head. I know it's hard sometimes, but whenever I have a problem, I don't sit around all day fussing about it. I talk to people I trust or chill out to a couple of tracks. You're not the only one with troubles, Julian. You ought to listen to Billie Holiday, then you'll know what hard times are really about."

That aligned with Ann's advice, minus the comfortable chair, so I trusted Tamika. I just needed to hear the words again. I breathed in and let my worries go.

"That's it. Breathe in God's good grace and relax." She closed her eyes, and the golden cross hung around her neck, rose, and fell as she breathed with me. Tamika was a full-figured woman; as a teenage boy now minimally encumbered by central nervous system depressants, I took a moment to appreciate her ample bosom beneath it, then quickly looked away before she opened her eyes. I doubted she'd believe such observations were also a product of my altered line of sight.

***

"This is a smooth, steady ride. American-made. Yeah, it uses a lot of gas, but you can't even feel the road," Sam's father said as he drove us in his station wagon to visit his father in Philadelphia that weekend. Sam's mom sat up front, his two younger brothers were behind them, and Sam and I were in the rear-facing bench seat of the steady rider, facing oncoming traffic. Our slow speed created an ebb and flow of cars behind us. A few, mostly middle-aged men, came up close ... realized tailgating us was a lost cause, then blasted past us, honking their horns and hurling insults we couldn't hear over the old-time tunes playing on the radio. Whenever their displeasure became evident to Sam and me, we gave them the middle finger, hoping to further enrage them. At one point, traffic came to a standstill. A well-built guy wearing a Gold's Gym tank top, whose muscles looked like they had muscles, exited his convertible and approached us, ready to rip our fingers off. Sam and I saw his bulging veins as he prepared to punch through the glass, but then the wagon started rolling, and he reluctantly returned to his ride. We stopped extending our offensive appendages after that.

Sam's grandfather had recently moved into an assisted living community.

"This place is swank," Sam's mom said as we entered its Greek-themed grounds, which had white stucco walls, red terra-cotta rooftops, and street names like Corfu and Patras.

"What does swank mean, Mom?" One of Sam's younger brothers asked.

"Lots of classy decorations, like you see here," Mr. Drummond answered, pointing to a spiral staircase adorned with clay pots and marmalade-colored hibiscus leading to a bubbly fountain below.

"How are you doing, Dad?" Mr. Drummond asked as we joined Gramps for iced tea on the patio of his villa, facing an artificial lake where geese alighted upon its still water.

"Oh, it's nice here, Teddy. I wish your mom was still with us, but I'm doing fine. I appreciate you and Donna helping me with the move and settling in. It's been easy living riding around in my golf cart," he explained, glancing at the idle cart in his garage.

"What do you do all day, Grandpa?" Sam asked.

"I watch a little Johnny Carson and play Bridge on the weekends. You know, old farts like me don't need to play video games every minute or listen to loud music on those; what do you call them, with the big speakers?"

"They're called boomboxes, but they're not popular anymore," Sam replied.

"That's it! Boom box, boom boom boom!" he said, rocking in his chair, which cracked us up.

"How's everything going at the auto plant, Teddy?" Gramps asked, adding, "I heard they're thinking about taking away the pension or making you chip in half. Something boneheaded like that! It's not right. They can't expect you to give them all that time, all those years—without some security when you're old. By Golly, I'll tell you what. If I was still there, I'd take one of those bigwigs by the collar and give them a piece of my mind!"

"I'm hanging in there, Dad, but they've got machines doing more work now. It takes fewer people and less time. Even with the union, they've laid off a quarter of the department, but don't worry about that. We're here to see you, not fret about the economy."

Sam and I tried to convince them to let us take the golf cart for a spin. Gramps was okay with it, but his dad said, "Sorry boys, this ain't Disneyland. I'm not about to let you run over one of these grandmas and get sued. I've got enough problems already."

On our way out, we spotted a merry band of oldtimers in Hawaiian shirts driving around the clubhouse in golf carts across from the security gate. They all happily honked their squeaky horns as they rode in circles.

"That looks like fun. I want to live here," Sam said.

"Are you kidding me, Sam? You don't want to live here. It looks fun, but these are old folks. They're nearing the end of their lives. Think of all the pills they have to take and what a pain it is to get out of bed. You've still got so much ahead of you. A career, a wife, and maybe some kids. Focus on your grades and getting into college. I don't want you to end up like me, slaving away at an auto plant about to slash your benefits just to cut bigger checks for the executives."

"Really, Dad? Not this again. I don't even need to go to college. I'm gonna study film and make movies. I want to learn how to do the special effects."

Sam's dad had drifted somewhere else and didn't bother responding to Sam. He took a long look at the oldtimers circling the clubhouse, then drove through the security gate. We stopped on South Street in downtown Philly to get cheesesteaks and sat along the docks eating them before going home.

"Do you really want to live in that place?" I asked Sam after we finished grubbing on the deliciously greasy, gooey, heart-stopping sandwiches.

"Yeah. I wouldn't even mind being around all those grannies as long as I could bring chicks back to my crib. My dad's always stressed out when he comes home from work, and then he complains to my mom about the credit card bill being too high and that we've got to do something; we've got to cut back. He usually snaps out of it by dinnertime and starts busting on me and my brothers again."

"Sam, when's the last time you brought a chick back to your place?"

"Well, not just yet, but it's like my dad said, I've got my whole life ahead of me to master the game."

"My mom doesn't like working much, either. Sometimes, I hear crying in her room after she gets home."

"All right, don't tell anyone I told you this, J, but my dad likes to smoke weed after work. Yo! That shit cools him out. Okay, sometimes I smoke it, too. It's fun, man. You gotta try it."

"Oh, no, the doctors told me if I do any drugs, my brain will blow up or I'll have a seizure. I could die. No way. No, my brain will explode."

"They're lying to you. *Scared Straight* or some bullshit. I'll bet you a thousand dollars that you'll be fine if you smoke weed or do pretty much anything they told you that you can't."

"But how will I collect my money if I die and you're wrong?"

"I guess you won't, and I've saved myself a thousand dollars."

We both laughed. Is Sam right? Have all those doctors, with their clipboards and condescending pronouncements, turned me into a chicken over nothing? They never expected me to be anything more than a dopey kid taking antiepileptic pills.

"Don't get down on yourself if something you never thought about, like riding a bike or reading a book, doesn't come as naturally to you as it did before," they'd said. "You can't expect to pick up right where you left off. You'll need to adapt. Learn what you can and can't do anymore. That's expected. It's all part of the process of living with a disability."

Yeah, fuck them and fuck that. They'd tricked me and made me get all worked up over nothing.

"Maybe a million dollars will fall from the sky, and I'll ride in one of those golf carts before my dad. I'll ride it down Main Street while he's hard at work. That sure would piss him off!" Sam said, chuckling. He looked toward the sky as if it might happen right then, and we returned to the station wagon. I understood what Sam was saying. There had to be a way to skip the whole Daily Grind thing and go straight to those golf carts instead of clinging to my sanity with a beer on the back porch. I would've liked a million dollars to fall from the sky, too, but I didn't expect it ever would happen.

However, a quarter million dollars had already dropped into my bank account.

I was closer to those golf carts than Sam but kept it to myself because I didn't want him to think I had it easy. The money hardly compensated for what I'd been through. I'd gladly give it back to have never been shot. My lawyer filed a claim against Jonathan's parents' homeowners insurance policy while I was in the hospital. We settled for a quarter of a million dollars out of court. Early on, my lawyer investigated suing the gun manufacturer in a separate lawsuit. The severity of my injury was due to the flaw in Zeke's rifle, which made it fire much more forcefully than it should have. The same malfunction had killed and injured others. However, my lawyer advised us against pursuing the case because of the low probability of winning and the high cost of litigation, so we dropped it. I figured that lawsuit could have been worth millions, but I had no idea what to do with a thousand dollars, let alone millions—which is why my mother arranged for Mr. Michelson to manage the funds from my settlement that would be held in a trust until I was twenty-five.

"Julian, I appreciate the opportunity to put this money to work for you. Your mother explained the hardship you've endured to merit this compensation, and I want you to know I'll be personally involved in growing your wealth every step of the way," Mr. Michelson explained when I met him at his wealth management firm in Wilmington. "My goal is to assure that by the time you graduate college, you'll have what my wife, who's an English professor, refers to as 'the Requirements of the Imagination.' That's a quote from Henry James, meaning there are clear advantages to having a little extra money to realize our potential—money to start your own business, buy a car, a house, or take a dream vacation. I'm confident we'll easily meet these requirements if we stay the course and allow the market to work its magic."

Although I knew little about fashion, I could tell Mr. Michelson's clothes were of the finest quality. He wore a Polo shirt, a tailor-made suit, and an impeccable tie, unlike the fraying black thing my mother had made me wear—though at least it wasn't embroidered with

98

another person's initials like some of my other clothes. Aside from a few gray streaks, Mr. Michelson looked youthful, with only a few wrinkles on his brow. I liked him. He had lots of energy and didn't talk down to me, even though I didn't understand any of the pie charts or line graphs in the aggressive growth mutual fund brochure he placed before me. The pictures in a separate pamphlet were easier to understand. It tracked a person's financial journey through life. First, there was a baby in a crib with a 529 plan set up by their parents. Later, they'd graduated from college and were working toward paying off their student debt. Next, you saw them leaning over a desk with a stack of papers as they built up their 401(k). Then, it showed a happy couple signing the mortgage for a new home. Finally, they were walking together on a beach, old as hell, living off their loot and Social Security with big grins.

The requirements to blithely stroll along that beach were daunting. I pictured the oldtimers driving around in their golf carts, spinning like a mobile made of money above my head, but I was glad to meet Mr. Michelson and sit in his office. I felt like I was in one of those perplexing homes with innumerable rooms, but this time, I had someone to explain everything. I liked his tufted high-back chair and matching leather-topped desk with golden pens, tidy piles of paper, and a calculator with dozens of symbols I'd never seen. I imagined stacks of hundred-dollar bills filling every drawer. I especially liked the wide window behind him, offering a panoramic view of the city lights as far as the eye could see, as if he owned them all. I was sure that Mr. Michelson and everyone else in his office felt the same way I did being there—successful. It wasn't a bragging contest between kids. It was a way of life. They drove LX cars that never broke down and ate whatever they wanted whenever they wanted. They didn't have to curl up with a bottle every night to blot out the burdens in their lives. Yes, those golf carts were a nice reward for taking the road required to ride them, but what about men like Mr. Michelson, who owned the sky above it all? I wanted to be like them.

Chapter 10

Two years after starting the big pink antiepileptic pills with TEGRETOL printed in all caps on each capsule, I was finally finished with them. Combined with adolescent neuroplasticity, this led to an abrupt awakening. For the past two years, I'd spent much of the school day staring out the window, drawn to the warm white light. My teachers' voices rose until they got my attention as my classmates giggled. A few months after stopping the medication, I transitioned from remedial to standard courses, though I tested higher in English and enrolled in an advanced placement course. In front of the entire student body, the other Students of the Month and I received awards. Mine was for Most Improved. It had a shiny sun-shaped sticker in the corner and my name in cursive writing, though I wouldn't have minded if they omitted my last name. That, however, marked the pinnacle of my academic achievements. I began experimenting with marijuana and other mind-altering substances, which drew me back to the bright lights shining through the window as my teachers tried to reach me.

***

It was the dead of winter, and it felt good to be in Sam's room with the heat blasting, which his father would undoubtedly bemoan when the next heating bill arrived. Sam had affixed various horror movie posters to his walls. In one, Freddy Krueger, Sam's favorite, grinned in a fedora cap while extending his fingertip blades against a smoky black background. Another poster displayed the iconic blood-stained hockey mask from *Friday the 13th* with a knife through the eyehole. A *Halloween* movie poster with a pumpkin-colored fist gripping a pointed cleaver was among other images, some of which Sam had drawn himself.

"None of these flicks are even scary. Everyone knows they aren't real. Seeing people die in *Faces of Death* grossed me out, but that had to be fake. I don't know why they always rate them R. It's not like I'm gonna watch one, then grab a knife and go psycho on my dog. It's just for fun, like going to a haunted house," Sam said. He made the macabre observation after taking a long drag of marijuana from an apple concoction he'd explained to me fifteen minutes prior.

Sam had deftly poked holes through the top and side of the apple with a long blade, similar to the ones wielded by the creepy characters glowering at us from posters on the walls. He whittled away a little more near the stem before inserting a piece of tinfoil into the cavity, then connected the holes in the center so smoke flowed freely.

"When you smoke weed, you gotta grub down. It makes you hella hungry. That's why this pipe is perfect. We can eat it after we're done smoking. The first time I made one, I accidentally set it on fire after smoking half the bud. It was snowing, so I tossed it out the window." Sam explained, pointing to the window that faced his backyard. "But then my dog, Cruiser, found the burnt apple and ate it. I think he got stoned, like Scooby-Doo, you know?" He smiled and took a lighter to the big green bud he'd carefully placed in the indentation atop the apple as if it were an emerald set in a ring. As he inhaled, it glowed and made a crackling sound. Sam repeatedly assured me I could smoke weed and do all the other things I'd been forbidden to do, which I appreciated. However, I still weighed the terror of what might happen if he was wrong against the equally terrifying prospect of how boring the rest of my life would be if I didn't stop worrying about bumping my head or allowing psychotropic substances to cross the blood-brain barrier.

The room was getting smoky. "Shit, open that window," Sam said, taking another hit and pointing to the same window he'd thrown the flaming apple out. He encouraged me to examine the bud before lighting it. I'd thought marijuana was nothing more than the leaves I'd seen on T-shirts, tattoos, and grade school propaganda reminding us to *Just Say No*. The bud looked regurgitated yet beautiful, with shades of orange and green, traces of purple, and glistening white speckles. It was stinky yet alluring. A beautiful stink that became increasingly aromatic as I took my first hit. A smell befitting how I felt in the following minutes. Sam did most of the toking, as I only dared take a few pulls. After we finished the weed, he placed the still-smoking apple on his desk and popped a CD into the stereo beside it.

"This is Parliament. Now, these guys understand weed," Sam explained as Seventies funk swam into our ears.

We toked up fifteen minutes before the music started. The beat, lyrics, and bass bumping from the stereo made me want to get down with sounds transcending the known world. The music transported me on an interplanetary funkrific ride as vapors curled through the black spaces in my brain, weaving enigmatic sensations together. I sang along after hearing the chorus of "Mothership Connection" a few times.

"Aw, yeah, you feelin' it now!" Sam hooted, then took a bite of the apple. I took three bites after him as it had become the most delicious thing I'd ever eaten. The color, crunch, and juice running down my chin. Yum, yum, yum. The effects intensified, and unfamiliar thoughts trickled through my mind as I funked out.

"Okay, so this apple is red and tastes good, but how do I know that you're seeing the same color as me or that it tastes the same way?" I asked Sam.

"Gimme another bite of that, and I'll tell you." I handed him what was left of the apple.

"For real, though, we're both listening to this song, but do we feel the same way as the people who recorded it? How did they want us to feel? What if we're alone, even though we think we're all connected?" I pondered.

Sam sang along to another track, "Give Up the Funk," and ignored my questions as he stood on his bed boogying with his uncombable hair matching the mood as it bobbed back and forth. Even Freddy Krueger seemed to groove when I glanced at him. The high intensified. Am I exhaling too often? How many times should I breathe per minute? My hands look funny. Do I usually sit with them clenched or open? I sat quietly, debating whether I should claim my thousand dollars from Sam before my head exploded as I'd been warned it would.

I'm blinking too much. Stop blinking. No, if you stop blinking, your eyes will dry out. Keep blinking.

Another song played, making me want to bust a move, so I swung my hips and forgot about my head exploding. I rode Puff the Magic Dragon around the room until I reached a higher level. Once you've arrived, it's as if you were always there. Sam was still boogying on the bed. I stopped resisting the weed and let the tempo take me where it wanted.

"Sometimes I swear I'm psychic. I can hear other people's thoughts and put words in their heads without even talking to them. We don't need to say a thing. People seeing the same colors and hearing the same sounds is like that. If you think it's real, then it is. It's faith. All you gotta do is believe," Sam said, sounding more philosophical than I ever thought he would.

Fortunately, the weed's effects were waning, and I didn't bug out about the oddity of what he said about being psychic. I turned and faced one of Sam's drawings. It was peaceful in contrast to the violent icons of horror fandom adorning his walls. He'd drawn a brilliant sun surrounded by rays in a purple sky stretching over rolling hills. I hadn't noticed it during my cursory inspection earlier. There was also a flying saucer with a horned alien peering out, and the music played. The hook, pitch, and tempo were perfect—unbreakable.

***

I received my driver's license when I turned sixteen, thanks to a chance encounter. My mother hadn't let me enroll in driver's education, citing my visual and spatial deficits as insurmountable obstacles. Even though I'd proven I could do many things I'd been told I couldn't, I wasn't sure if sheer willpower was enough to change lanes, merge into traffic, or drive down Main Street flanked by pedestrians and cyclists capably, so I didn't challenge her decision. To console myself, I reasoned that if I couldn't drive, I could fly a plane—unencumbered by the busy streets below in the clouds. Alas, this comfort faded after acknowledging there was no way to land planes in my neighborhood or flirt with anyone hovering over a field in a Cessna.

My mother played clarinet in the Newark community band. It was a good way for her to manage the stress of being a teacher, which she sometimes confided in me.

"Some of those children are so wild. They run around shouting and fighting with each other the whole time I'm trying to teach them. Then their parents complain when little Sammy Chung fails geography because he was too busy kung-fu fighting with Billy Chin to open his book and let me even pretend he deserves to pass."

"That sounds a little bit frightening."

"Well, it'd be worse if everybody was kung-fu fighting. At least you and your brother never got less than a D. Straight A's are nice, but D is for diploma. Do you know what they call the doctor who graduates last in medical school?"

"What?"

"Doctor."

A dragon mother, she was not, and as long as I got a D, she was satisfied. Perhaps I was even on my way to medical school.

The band was an escape from work and sobriety since several of her bandmates drank as much as she did.

"Don't you think you're drinking too much?" I asked when she went straight to the toilet and vomited after putting her clarinet in the closet.

"I'm sorry. I did have too much tonight. I'll ease up on it, okay?" my mother said as she slid into bed.

"Why don't you do something else to relax? Something that doesn't make you sick?"

She shot upright and replied defensively, now in greater control of her faculties after voiding the contents of her stomach.

"I told you my mother gave me brandy every time I was upset or couldn't sleep, but she never did that with my brother, just me. Because, in her mind, women aren't equal to men. Women should be comforted, not reasoned with. They should stay home and clean, not go to college, and poor, helpless Sophia had to marry your sicko father because she had sex with him once. So if you've got a problem with me having a couple drinks, why don't you call your grandma, okay? Sweet old Granny and her stock certificates. Don't act like I am not taking care of you and your brother. I'm a good mother!"

"No, it's not that. You're a great mom. I always tell my friends I have the coolest mom, but maybe you should drink a little less. Anyway, Grandma's old now. Don't worry about her."

She passed out before I finished talking, so I closed her door and went to bed. My mom must've heard some of what I said because the next few times she came home from band practice, she was clear-eyed and sober—not only sober but elated with exciting news.

"Julian, there's another man just like you."

For a moment, I thought I had a long-lost older brother.

"I met him tonight, and I think you should, too. He's married to one of the ladies in the band. He's sixty-eight and had a stroke two years ago. It left him with vision loss like yours, but his is on the right side."

It seemed okay to meet him, but I wasn't sure what some old dog with a stroke could teach me about my vision that I hadn't already figured out.

"He can drive," she continued.

"Oh, that's interesting."

"Yes, he can drive a car and thinks you can, too. That's why you should meet him."

Now I'm feeling the funk! Going for a double dunk! Yes, sir. Distinguished and disreputable guests, with my golden Mr. Michelson bucks, soon I'll be cruising along the seashore in a convertible, where waves crash against the cliffs, rising to impossible heights in plumes of white and blue, suspended for a moment—that everlasting moment—before surrendering back to the sea. I'll ride through the desert with only a single star and a coyote howling to mark the distance traveled. I'll find new Hazel Lanes stuck in suburban enclaves, dreaming of the day a dude like me braves those quiet streets with endless rows of houses sharing the same four floor plans to take them coast to coast and show them the world they'd been waiting for. Best of all, no more riding the bus to school crammed along narrow bench seats with freshmen and everyone else without wheels.

My mom told me on a Friday, and we met the man and his wife that weekend. In addition to the vision loss we shared, although on opposite sides, the right side of his mouth drooped down, and his speech was slurred. But the message was clear: he could drive. No problems at all, except he'd run into the right side of his garage once, but that was only once, and he was an old man, so a young buck like me could definitely get the hang of it.

"This means I can drive, right?" I confirmed as we drove home.

"I'd better check with a doctor and make sure it's okay."

"Doctor? A doctor won't be driving with me. If that guy can do it, so can I."

"But he drove before his stroke and lost his vision on the right side. You lost yours on the left, and you never drove before."

I was prepared for this. My mother agonized over everything but eventually came around.

The following day at the pet store, while shopping for her cat Phoebe in an aisle with baskets of squeaky toys piled high, I continued articulating why I should have a license: "Look, Mom, it's legal for me to drive. I checked. Those doctors said I wouldn't be able to keep up with my classmates or remember what I did two days ago. They said I couldn't do all kinds of things and were wrong. Whatever you decide, I want you to decide for yourself. We don't need doctors involved."

"Okay, okay," she said after placing a bag of unappetizing pellets on the counter. They still looked better than the fossilized clam chowder we'd eaten the night before. I knew this for a fact because I'd dumped my uneaten helping in Phoebe's bowl; she took one whiff and walked away.

Like a lawyer trying a case, I had to be selective with the Julian Can Drive jury pool, which I wanted to limit to one person: her. There was no reason for any biased viewpoints to alter the outcome.

My mother's sober streak ended when she returned from band practice the following week, slurring like the man who'd had a stroke and went straight to bed. This wasn't unexpected, nor was it my primary concern. Could I take driver's ed or not? That was on my mind, and as she pulled a blanket up to her chin, I found out.

"I need to sign up for driver's ed soon. It's okay, right?"

She shook her head without answering. What the hell? She looked like a stupid baby. Baby Sophia, do you need a bottle of brandy to help you go to sleep?

"Julian, you can't. I can't let anything happen to you. I'm your mother. I have to protect you. You might not like it, but this is the right thing to do." She started dozing off.

"I never complain about watching Kevin or when you hang out with losers with nothing better to do than get drunk. I never ask you for anything. I even have my own money now. You're a dumb bitch. How can you take this from me?"

That hit her like a shot of wake-up juice. She leapt out of bed and dashed to the bathroom. I heard her fumbling around. Yeah, I showed that bitch. Go ahead and puke, you dumb bitch.

I went to the living room and sat on a rocking chair. I rocked back and forth, pleased with what I'd said to her. There's no way I'm snatching defeat from the jaws of victory. I didn't come this far for that. I've earned this. The way I was seated with my left side facing the hallway meant I didn't see her sprinting toward me, and it wasn't because she wanted to see how the world looked when she ran. All of a sudden, I had a bar of soap in my mouth, and she violently scrubbed my teeth.

"Bitch! Bitch! Who's a bitch? I take care of you. I'm a good mother. Don't ever call me a bitch!"

The look on her face was ... insane. By the time I realized what was happening, she'd withdrawn the soapy block and gone back to bed. The taste was thoroughly revolting, lingering even after I rinsed my mouth.

After the shock wore off, I went to her room. She was clutching her blanket and gave me a look—both regretful and unapologetic.

"I guess I don't need to brush my teeth tonight," I said.

She tried to stay mad, but her lips crept into a smile.

"Okay, okay, you can enroll in driver's ed. But don't ever call me that again."

***

"Julian, we put that money to work at the perfect time. We couldn't have asked for a better entry point. It looks like a new bull market is beginning. I can't say I'd advise most clients to pull money out of the market right now, but a man has to have wheels, right?" Mr. Michelson explained to my mother and me when we stopped by to discuss withdrawing money from my head injury trust fund to buy a car. Until I was twenty-five, I couldn't touch it without her permission. I could have sold the Hershey's stock my grandma gave me to buy a car, but I didn't want to. I still liked knowing that every time I saw a Hershey's bar, I owned a square of it. Mr. Michelson showed me a device called a Bloomberg terminal that he used for stock research. It resembled the IBM PC I had at home but had a quirky keyboard with different colored keys and numbers constantly flashing on the screen. The numbers looked agitated, jiggling up and down as if they had an itch they couldn't scratch.

"This is where you are today compared to when we started two years ago," Mr. Michelson said, pointing to a series of market values he'd printed, which looked like a cross between a multiplication table and the state lottery results. I observed the numbers on the right were larger than those on the left. "With the power of compounding, you're already up over $35,000. I can't promise that your balance will be higher every time you visit me. But, throughout history, if you can hang in there, the stock market always rewards you for your patience. So, now and then, I'll put a little money here and a little there, but for the most part, we'll let the market work its magic, and you'll be set. You're fortunate to be investing at such a young age; there's plenty of time to compound your gains."

He'd said 'compound' so casually that I assumed it was common knowledge and didn't ask what it meant. I sat there smiling, knowing even a dollar gain was good. One of my math teachers might have mentioned compounding before my injury. I may have deduced that it's when money makes money through reinvestment in itself, like a snowball growing as it rolls down a snowy hill. But now, all I could think of was when one of the doctors at the children's hospital said a fellow patient needed a new compound, which I'd learned was a mix of medications. Mr. Michelson explained that he'd put a little money here and there. Despite a nagging suspicion that mathematical and pharmacological compounding were different, I clung to the notion they were the same.

Chapter 11

I'd purchased a Toyota truck with a camper shell. Winter was almost over, but it was still cold enough for the windshield to freeze. I was running late for school, so I poured warm water on the glass to deice it, then turned the key. I would have liked to let the engine run longer to warm up the interior, but there wasn't time.

When I first got my license, I picked up Ben on the way to school. However, one day, after spotting his luxury minivan—which didn't look so luxurious anymore as it slumped in the front and the paint had faded—I kept driving and never gave him a ride again. After I started hanging out with Sam, I gravitated toward misfits, punk rockers, and skateboarders. So we weren't best pals anymore anyway. My eyes burned when I saw Ben's mother looking at me curiously from their front porch as I headed to school without him. She'd seemed angelic, sitting by my bedside when I came out of my coma. But these were people from my old life who saw me as a shadow of my former self, so I hit the gas and skidded around the corner.

On my way to school, a blanket was tossed about in the back, and my heart froze like the stiff blades of grass along the road. Is someone back there? I thought about the horror movies Sam insisted we watch, where this scenario always resulted in the characters' violent deaths. I pulled over. Maybe something had come loose. It wouldn't be the first time I freaked out over nothing. I stopped at the same park where I got a nail stuck in my head years ago. The thought of running home with blood spurting from my head fit the moment uncomfortably well.

"None of these flicks are even scary," Sam insisted. I was scared now.

I begrudgingly stepped out into the frosty morning air and lowered the tailgate. Someone was sleeping there. I yelped and jumped back. He rolled onto his side and said, "Close that door. It's cold. I can feel it in my bones." It was a young man's voice. When he turned, I saw he had a punk rock hairstyle, shaved on the sides and spiky on top. I recognized him.

"Who's that?"

"Bond, James Bond."

I laughed. It was James Styles, with whom I was familiar.

"Man, you almost gave me a heart attack. What are you doing back there? Come sit up front."

I'd begun skateboarding the year before. I liked how it unlocks a layer of the cityscape underutilized by the average person. Given my challenges with spatial perception, it aided my recovery. A skateboarder develops a unique mode of vision, similar to how falcons see distinct spectrums of light and shadow, which are key to their survival. We assessed every curb for its ollie or nose slide potential and evaluated every fountain's suitability for doing kick-flips along one of its lower ledges rimming the water.

When I was a kid, Newark was largely farmland. Fields of corn and wheat decorated one-lane roads. The city's rapid development, especially the neoclassic stairwells, walkways, and newly constructed buildings comprising the University of Delaware campus, had usurped the bucolic harmony of our hometown. As a result, skateboarding represented the reclamation of campus grounds and any other structure in the adjoining city that invaded our domain. We conquered every slice of a world urbanized against our will, to the dismay of campus police and passersby, alarmed by the distinct click-clack sound of a 360 shove-it landing successfully at the bottom of a flight of stairs.

Riding alongside me and other miscreants on our freedom rides throughout the city was none other than James Styles.

I'd already missed my first class, so James and I went to Jimmy's Diner on Main Street, where he explained himself. It was a classic fifties retro joint. The checkered floor and padded leather seats—circular at the counter and fitted to the long benches along the walls—evoked a bygone era. Every table had a jukebox. Bacon, eggs, sandwiches, and bottomless cups of watered-down coffee were served twenty-four hours a day. Nothing particularly unique about it, but Jimmy's was an excellent place to kill time because it existed outside of time.

"My mom sent me to a teen rehab place called Rockbridge when she caught me sippin' steady on a flask of vodka in bed. I was sippin' so steady, boy. You'd think a good mama would respect her boy sippin' steady like that," James told me while we waited for our food.

With his tattered black coat, navy slacks, and hard-luck loafers with holes in them, James looked like he'd stepped out of *Oliver Twist*. His skin was tan; I wasn't sure if he was White, but he otherwise looked European, so I assumed he was. Aside from his large aquiline nose, James was pretty good-looking. But his hair—his hair was outstanding. It needed several hours of shampooing, but those inky black strands could've made him a handsome rake if he'd stopped sippin' long enough to go out with some girls.

"What the hell are you talking about?" I asked.

"Don't mind me. I'm mentally ill, even considered subhuman by some well-mannered folks. This is something you must understand if you want to pal around. I realize it was ill-advised, but how else can a young man ease his worries if he can't set foot in a bar and have a chug of Ripple? Ever since my old man OD'd on cocaine, my mother's been less tolerant of my eccentricities."

"When did your dad die?"

"Let's save the sob stories for another time. Right now, I've got eating to do."

"Alright, then, what is Ripple?"

"You don't know what Ripple is? That's an affront to decency! Haven't you seen *Sanford and Son*? 'You big dummy!' *Dun dun dunna, dun dun dunna dunna dun!*"

James had an impressive vocabulary and manner of speaking for a fourteen-year-old who apparently skipped school more than he attended.

"Oh yeah," I said, recognizing the theme song he hummed as I leaned back against the plush booth seat, grinning. I'd seen clips of the show on the news after Redd Foxx, who starred in it, had recently died.

"Tell me about this Rockbridge place. How'd they get you there?"

"A van pulled up around 10:00 p.m. as I tilted back my flask and read *The Stranger*. I saw it in the library and liked the first line: 'Mother died today. Or maybe it was yesterday; I can't be sure.' Four men in white coats marched into my room while my mother and sister looked on. By the way, my sister's hot. She's got pendulous breasts, like my mom. You might like her," James noted, extending his hands out from his chest to emphasize their plenitude. I shook my head, and he continued.

"They each grabbed a limb and lifted me off the bed. I started squirming, trying to break free, even though I knew it was futile. Then my mom said, 'James, these men are from a clinic that will help you get well. They're here to help you. For God's sake, sneaking vodka into your room and staying out all hours of the night! Ever since your father died, you know I have tried. But I just don't know who you are anymore.'

"Then my sister said, 'Open your heart to Jesus, James. Let him in! Mom's trying to help. I'll pray for you.' One of the men jabbed me with this sleepy stuff in a syringe, and I woke up in Rockbridge with a big old headache, though the vodka may have been to blame."

It was noon. Men in hard hats hammered at concrete across the street with a piledriver. I hadn't noticed them until a waitress interrupted James's farfetched story to place our food on the table. I'd ordered a tuna fish sandwich. James ordered steak, eggs, and a chocolate milkshake. I'd hoped he'd select more frugal fare, but he insisted that such nourishment was essential, considering he was still a growing boy. After finishing his steak in a few bites, James continued recounting his stint in rehab while sipping his milkshake.

"In Rockbridge, everyone wore hospital gowns like something out of a Ken Kesey caper. Speakers cycled through hypnotic music with flutes, harps, and a vocal track that seemed to be reversed. Heavenly posters plastered everywhere had preachy lines like, 'Our faith can move mountains.' The funny thing about that one is there was a picture of a placid lake. I wasn't sure if it was a mistake or if they were implying that faith had already moved the mountains.

113

When they carted me off to lunch, I tried opening a door, but it was locked. They sat me next to a girl with cigarette burns on her arms, who asked if I'd confessed my sins to Father Richard, then started rambling about how good it felt when she did. I said I was looking forward to doing that and asked if she had any cigarettes. She started crying, then screamed. Okay, maybe that was a little inconsiderate, but I thought she might have some with the burn marks and all."

"What? Did you really think she'd have cigarettes? Didn't you think there was a decent chance that would upset her?"

"Well, you never can be sure; she could've had some, but I wanted to mess with her, too. I know—not cool. I have at least a minor case of Tourette's, so I can't help it. The next thing I knew, they'd locked me in my room. After sitting around picking broccoli from my teeth, I noticed a wire in my braces was loose. I unlocked my window with it and busted out of there."

His upper braces had no wire, so at least part of the story was true. James removed the rest of his braces a short time later.

"Fortunately, the place is one story. They don't want kids leaping to their deaths to avoid confessing to Father Richard. It was the middle of the day, so I bolted through the woods to a train yard where rail workers were linking boxcars and hoppers. Some bum must've been there before me because that's where I found these clothes."

"Hoppers ... Are they really called that?"

"Yeah, they are. My dad liked trainspotting. He must've had a train set when he was younger because he knew what all the different cars were called. Hoppers have ladders and holes on each side. You can climb aboard and hide in the hole, so I hopped on the hopper."

James reluctantly put down the menu he was still perusing while I paid the bill, and we got back into my truck. While I drove, he recounted that a bend in the tracks caused the train to slow enough for him to leap off a half mile from my house. At one point, pursued by men with hound dogs and rock salt guns, James waded through waist-deep water to evade them, unsure if he'd survive the cold and fast-moving current. He got a lucky break when the hounds started howling in agony as they lost his scent, and the shadowy lot of them disappeared into the night. James surfaced around my neighborhood, creeping along the dark avenues with ice in his hair until he saw my truck, which he recognized by the Bones Brigade sticker on the rear quarter panel—the one with the skeleton peeking through a hole in the wall. Sam had picked it out for me at Switch Skate and Snow on Main Street. Much to James's delight, I'd failed to lock the rear gate, so he settled in for the night.

"Okay, the first thing we've got to get straight is how much of this jailbreak story is true," I declared, feeling wired from the multiple cups of coffee I'd consumed as we motored past the century-old Victorian houses on West Main Street. Going to class was a lost cause.

James turned away from the yellow balusters he'd been studying and said, "Well, the truth of a story isn't paramount. The entertainment value is what matters most."

***

My truck had two ignition keys and a third one that only unlocked the camper shell. I made a copy of that one and gave it to James so he could crash in the back whenever he wanted. I suspected that if I gave him an ignition key, it would be the last time I saw my truck.

Since Sam and I attended different high schools, I mostly saw him on the weekends. The next time we met, I told him James had stowed away in the back of my truck. Sam had also taken up skateboarding and already knew James. However, his chunky frame and general lack of dexterity limited him to grinding curbs and rolling back and forth on his board. We sometimes brought James food or cash, which he appreciated, though he had other means of support. I vacillated between finding humor in his occupancy and fearing what might happen if my mother discovered he lived in the truck.

I often snuck out to talk with James but was never sure if he'd be in the back with the interior illuminated, reading a book, or somewhere else. The truck served as one of his shelters for a year. His itinerant occupancy was facilitated by securing several lodging options among those of us who sympathized with and even envied his unconventional way of living or, at the very least, enjoyed his dubious tales.

***

It was spring break. Sam, James, and I were sitting in my truck outside one of James's alternate pieds-à-terre in an apartment complex mainly rented by college-age kids near Henry's old townhouse. Most units were empty, as the occupants had jetted off to Cancun and West Palm Beach.

"The devil you say!" James exclaimed when Sam asked why his mom hadn't come looking for him.

"I think she's torn between not wanting to be arrested for abandoning me and feeling glad I'm gone. The 'glad I'm gone' part is winning." James took a bite of the fried chicken Sam had scored for him.

"Why would your mother be glad you're gone?" Sam asked.

"She was born after her time, the kind of person who wants everything to be golden and bright as if life were a laundry detergent commercial. She'd have been better off living on a quiet street in the fifties, popping a Valium, and pleasuring herself with kitchen utensils while watching bleached white sheets billowing on the line. I didn't fit into that fantasy."

"You said your dad died from a cocaine overdose?" I asked. I hadn't brought it up since he'd mentioned it at the diner. I didn't want to know which kitchen utensils he had in mind.

"Yeah, he was a real go-getter, a strictly legit hombre who always wore a suit to work. My parents were aiming for the same structured, wholesome lifestyle their parents had before them. Then my dad started coming home late, visiting prostitutes, and using drugs. Something in him flipped, man." James paused and sighed. "My mom found him dead in the garage with a line of coke half-

116

sniffed. She didn't notice until late at night because she'd been waiting for him to come home from work."

James's eyes grew glassy, and he wiped them with his sleeve.

"Man, that's rough. I'm sorry," Sam said.

I didn't know what to think.

"Ah, it wasn't all bad. At first, I liked it when my old man was loosening up. There was a stretch before he spiraled out of control when he transitioned from getting a boner over remodeling the kitchen to playing "Purple Haze" full blast in the living room and telling us to dig it, much to my mother's chagrin.

"I just read *The Fall* by Albert Camus. That's where the line 'The devil you say!' comes from. It made me think of my mom because she's more comfortable sending people off to crazy camp than considering whether she's the one who made them crazy. You'd understand if you read it. Camus also wrote *The Stranger*. You guys might like him. We ought to start a book club. There are lots of books like *The Fall* you won't hear about in high school."

"Man, I already have too much homework. I gotta write an essay about the Babylonian Empire tonight. I ain't about to double up my reading assignments," Sam protested.

I could probably read faster than the average half-blind, brain-damaged person. But going twice as fast over half the distance is still slow since I can only see half the page and have to scan it like an old typewriter with a broken spring. Still, I wanted to help James launch the club if he was serious for reasons that predated our acquaintance.

Not long after a parade of medical professionals clad in lab coats presented my neural impairments to my mother and me as if they were nothing more than another case study they'd coauthored with their credentialed names adorning the cover, I started resenting what they said and wanted to prove them wrong. Throughout my hospital stay, my aptitude was measured through a battery of tests they claimed forecast, within a standard margin of error, what should be expected of me based on the severity of my impairments and where others with similar disabilities fell on a scatter plot of known probabilities.

Amassing an unabridged collection of words was my first act of neurological defiance. After being discharged, I spent countless hours thumbing through the pages of my mother's hefty *Oxford Dictionary* on our living room floor to fatten up my vocabulary. However, halfway through the letter A, I abandoned the pursuit— not because I couldn't retain what I was reading. Because it was boring, I realized I didn't need to know *every* definition. Books were a better way to build my vocabulary because they're written with words that have a purpose in people's lives, and that led me to what I should value most.

"What's *The Fall* about?" I asked James as he ate a spoonful of the matzo ball soup I'd brought him. It was Passover, so that's all I could snag.

He bit into one of the balls, grimaced, and spit it out the window. The half-eaten dumpling rolled into the adjacent parking spot, looking as sad as his family history.

"What is this Jew ball shit? Look, I've been studying the Kabbalah a little, and I like you Jews. In fact, I plan to become a rabbi one day, but I have certain dietary requirements that are unmet by this mushy matzo monstrosity. You know, you Jews should've given those to the Pharaoh. After one bite, he'd have let you go without God having to go through all the trouble of splitting the Red Sea."

I didn't have a quick comeback, so I stared out the windshield, trying to think of one as Sam chuckled at James' preposterous biblical revision.

"Hold on, let me get a good look at that ugly mug." James forcibly turned my face toward him with his palm against my cheek, studied my visage, and said, "That's what I thought. Those Hebrew locks are looking limp. You need a boost to offset your unflattering features. You better ascend Mount Sinai before it's too late. Heston was rocking a real pompadour after he heard the Good Word."

I slapped his hand away. "What's wrong with you? How do you come up with that crap?" He reminded me of his unofficial Tourette's diagnosis and shrugged.

I regretted telling James I was Jewish, but was curious how he knew about the Kabbalah and so many other things I never knew existed. I pondered the paradox of dropping out of school to spend more time studying the things I cared about. Even with my fully functioning brain, I could never absorb as many stories and the incredible places they take you as quickly as he could. Where did that leave me? Although weed heightened my appreciation for funk and made even matzo ball soup savory, I only smoked with Sam a few more times because it brought me to an odd intersection of anxiety and lethargy, leaving me unable to relax or accomplish anything. I'd already blown up my brain. I'd already wasted too much time. Why hadn't I died? What must I accomplish with the life I have left? I refused to consume anything intoxicating unless it helped me solve this mystery. Yes, the Mystery—I considered it:

The hair stood on my neck. I closed my eyes, waiting for the wind to ferry me over the ocean to untrampled islands with groves of luscious fruit and lost manuscripts I'd read lying in my palm leaf hammock, searching for answers to questions I didn't know how to ask. Did I alone believe that solving the riddles of our existence was above all other pursuits? I doubted that, but even if I were the only one, I knew following the trail wherever it went was the only way to claim all the prizes people wanted but would never have unless they were willing to wander in the dark sometimes. Rising, rising— this Earth—no, I was never meant to return. I was heading higher now. Almost home ... But then there was a smacking sound. James was smacking his lips as if he were still hungry. He'd already had three pieces of fried chicken and half a matzo ball.

"Hmm, now that I've digested the soup, a calm has come over me, as if the Lord has rewarded me for the agony of swallowing it. I was wrong to spit that ball out. I was wrong to ridicule your limp locks. I need another bowlful, my Jewish brother, but with a little horseradish sauce this time. Isn't that the way of the Chosen People?" James paused, looked forlornly out the window, then continued, "Where do they sell that soup? We have to get some more. The hour is upon us! I hope I haven't acted too impiously to receive The Holy Father's full matzo ball blessing. My impulsiveness always gets the best of me!"

"I'm not sure. I think you make matzo from a mix. There's a company called Manischewitz that sells it. You should be their spokesman. We could've used a guy like you to get us hyped up on eating kosher grub in Hebrew school," I answered, still wanting to know more about *The Fall*.

"You went to Hebrew school, yet you're clueless about this sacred Jewish culinary delight! Didn't you have a Bar Mitzvah? Didn't you learn anything at all? You should be ashamed of yourself! I'll be accelerating my rabbinical studies just to excommunicate you!."

"I don't think Jewish people can be excommunicated, plus too many people already think we hoard all the wealth and power in the world—which somehow skipped my family, yet I'm still despised for it—so it's better if we don't start attacking each other, too. Okay, back to the book. Tell me about *The Fall*, and then we'll work on getting you horseradish sauce to garnish your blessed balls."

"The protagonist's name is Jean-Baptiste Clamence, which I believe is a French play on words for clemency, which is ironic because—" James noticed he was losing Sam and me. Sam's mouth hung open as if what he was hearing was too heavy for his ears alone, and inhaling might help it reach his brain.

James then provided a simplified summary for his less literary companions: "Clamence is well-mannered, helps others, and people like him, but his nobility is a ploy to make men loyal and win the affection of women."

"Wasn't there a line like that in *Conan the Barbarian*?" Sam interrupted.

James ignored him and continued. "Clamence claims he's a phony, like the boys at Pencey Prep, but as we read his confession of insincere virtue to absolve himself, you realize he's actually exposing our sins."

"A fall from grace," Sam aptly concluded. James and I were taken aback; maybe there was something to his slack-jawed method of observation.

120

Chapter 12

It's a bong. Just fire up the herb and inhale. Water and gravity will do the rest," Temple explained with his hypnotic green eyes fixed on me when I asked about the bulbous glass water pipe on his living room table. "After chilling in the truck, James suggested we check out Temple's pad, right around the corner from where I'd parked. I learned his unique name after he told me about the bong. Tribal-looking squiggles drawn around the bong made it appear to grow out of the table, but the half-smoked joints, ninety-nine-cent science fiction pulp with the covers ripped off, the lamp with a pink panty for a shade, and beer bottles strewn about the mottled furnishings made the place look more like a dumpster. Especially since most of its furnishings were found in a dumpster. I knew that was common in this apartment complex because Ben and I used to ride our bikes through it, spending hours searching for treasure in the massive bins behind every building.

A shirtless guy in leather pants and a pear-shaped woman with unnaturally bright red hair emerged from the rear bedroom and plunked down on a duct-taped leather sofa near the sliding glass door. The guy fiddled with his lip piercing.

"Hey, kids, how are you doing?" Temple asked though they all looked about the same age as him.

"What time is it?" she asked.

Sam glanced at his watch and replied, "A little after noon," then continued looking around, unsure what to make of the place, like me.

"Oh God, I'm going to be late for work. You got a nug for me, Danny? I can't be waiting tables all day unless I'm at least a little stoned."

Dan dug into his front pocket, but his pants were too tight, so he stood up and pulled out a dime bag with a decent-sized bud. He handed it to the woman, who grabbed the bong and lit the bud. The bong gurgled as smoke rose into its chamber when she inhaled. Now that I knew how the contraption worked, I wondered when its murky water was last changed. However, this didn't deter the red-haired woman or Dan, who kept it gurgling.

"You guys want any of this?" he offered after a few hard coughs.

"Yeah, guys, we're all family here. Enjoy!" Temple prodded from the kitchen while he fried something on an electric burner. Sam perked up and said, "Sure, I'll have some," then sucked on the pipe as debris oscillated in its nasty water. I'd thought James was beside me, but he wasn't. This happened to me frequently. I'd be walking and talking with someone, only to look over to my left and realize they weren't there because I hadn't seen them go.

Having lost interest in weed, I joined Temple in the kitchen.

"Do you live here alone?" I asked.

"Nah, my door's always open. If people wanna come here, get high, trip, or trance out for a while, that's fine with me. We don't need to live by the rules of society. Turn on, tune in, drop out—like Leary said. You sure you don't want some of that weed?"

"No, weed makes me a little nervous, but I don't mind if other people smoke it."

"Cool, cool, not your thing. I dig that. All these drugs, man, some people don't want to do meth or LSD. They say it's chemical. It ain't real. But you know, man is a scientist. He assembles what God gives him. We can't step outside of God's universe. Even the atomic bomb is natural. A house doesn't grow out of the ground, just like a bomb ain't made of mud, but it's still natural because its origin is the earth. Some people want to smoke weed, and some people want to sniff glue. Everyone's on their own trip. I know people who are high on life. There are shamans in the hills of Africa. You try to get them to drop acid, and they say, 'So what? I'm already there, man.' Oh, I gotta check on something in the back. Can you keep this grill going? We gotta keep the fire lit, right?"

Temple was grilling potatoes with garlic, onions, and thyme on the stove. They looked good, and I was hungry, but the skillet and unwashed dishes in the sink beside it were as filthy as the bong water, so I moved the skillet around without taking a bite. My question regarding his living situation was whether he had

122

roommates, but he'd gone so far off-topic that it wasn't worth bringing up again. I rested my hand on the sink as I grilled his savory snack. A jolt of electricity surged through me, lighting me up like the weed they were still smoking behind me. I'd been shocked by touching plugs in sockets before, but this was much stronger. Fortunately, the skillet fell from my hand, and I was freed from the electric charge running through the counter. No one noticed I'd dropped the skillet, so I grabbed a spoon from the sink, scooped the potatoes back into it, and quickly put it back on the stovetop. As soon as I finished wiping the floor, Temple returned.

"Ah, looks killer, man!" Temple rinsed one of the plates, which only seemed to make it dirtier, and slid the potatoes onto it.

"Want some?" he mumbled, his mouth half-full.

"Oh no, man, it looks delicious, but I just ate."

"I gotta get one of these bongs, dude. Using apples is cool and all, but it's smoother with the bong. That water effect is dope," Sam said as he rose from the floor where he'd been toking.

"Yeah, it looks nice and bubbly," I replied. "Hey, let's go find James."

It was a two-bedroom apartment. We found James in the rear bedroom.

Tie-dyed tapestries, mandalas, and fantasy paintings of gleaming ice castles and scantily clad warrior princesses covered the room. The kaleidoscope of designs and images was mesmerizing. A clove-scented incense stick burned on the windowsill. A girl about James's age with bleach-blonde hair lay zonked out on a bed by the window, wearing an Operation Ivy T-shirt and frayed denim shorts. She was petite, with very soft-looking skin. A purple streak stained the pillow by her mouth. I had the sudden urge to take her to the children's hospital, but there wasn't much they could do for a zonked-out chick, so I ditched the idea.

"What are you doing back here? Is something wrong with that girl? Is she alright?" I asked James, who was sitting at a foldout table nearby, stuffing powders, pills, and pre-rolled joints into little bags.

"Her name's Eva. She's spending some time away from her folks, like me. Don't worry about her. She got tanked at Skidfest. I don't let her do the heavy shit."

"Is Temple a drug dealer?" Sam asked in a low voice.

"No, it's not like that. If you wanted to score something, I'm sure he'd sell it to you on the cheap, but that's not his thing. Temple comes from a wealthy family and likes to party with different people, that's all. Sometimes I help him get set up with these little goody bags. He kicks me back some change and lets me crash here. It's all good."

It seemed odd that a wealthy guy would dumpster dive for his furnishings, but I didn't dwell on it. I was more interested in how much James told me that he believed.

***

The forbidden allure of rail riding appealed to Sam and me. So, the following afternoon, James showed us where the train slowed, and he claimed to evade hounds and men with guns until he reached my house. I doubted his foxhunting story but believed the train-hopping part. If the train slowed enough for James to leap off, we should be able to board one in the same spot. We didn't know where the train would take us, so we filled backpacks with essentials like cigarettes, beef jerky, and Mountain Dew in case we got stranded. All that mattered now was getting on board.

James showed us the location, and a sharp bend in the tracks supported his story. But after waiting thirty minutes, with every train shooting by too fast to board, we started eating our beef jerky and were about to give up. About halfway through our bags, another train approached, rolling as fast as the others until one of the hooded lights beside us turned red, and it decelerated enough for us to board. We stuffed the remaining jerky in our bags and were on our feet. Up close, the rumbling locomotive looked gigantic. I was afraid but, at the same time, alive, unchained. It was madness, but we needed that madness to keep the chains off.

After hearing James's story, I researched trains at the library and learned that hopper cars, especially ones with large openings, were best suited for the journey. We spotted a line of hoppers approaching. Each had a ladder on either end, which was our ticket to ride. We trotted alongside them with our backpacks bouncing, all thinking the same thing. This is nuts. Are we really going to do this? This is not a train; these are stampeding rhinos that don't look remotely accommodating to three young jackasses trying to hitch a ride. Then, in one decisive motion, James grabbed a ladder, hoisted himself up, and all barriers were broken; he'd gotten on board. Sam and I knew we had to get on that train, live or die. But it was the dying part that was nagging me.

"What are you waiting for? Hop on. It's easy!" James yelled, hanging one-armed from a ladder.

I'm going to slip under the train. I'm going to lose my legs. Can I do this? Yes! Nothing holds you back. Nothing stops this train. As it was speeding up, I hoisted myself onto a ladder with a hard yank. I couldn't see Sam but assumed he'd gotten on. Once on board, I realized I had to get into the hole, or it would be like hanging onto the back of a tractor-trailer jamming down the freeway. I twisted around the ladder, but the hole where I stood was sealed. I surveyed the trailing car and saw its hole wasn't sealed. The train passed through a forest, alive with happy, chirping birds living the life nature intended, unlike me, fumbling on the train below.

I peeked alongside the train and saw the tracks ran straight for another mile. Okay, jump! My heart pounded as I leaped to the other platform and climbed into the hole. I wasn't sure where Sam or James were—hopping onto different cars wasn't part of the plan.

There was no plan beyond boarding the train, so the situation was no better or worse than we'd anticipated. It was a jumble of terror and exhilaration speeding through small towns as the horn blew and the steel wheels rolled rhythmically beneath me. I ate my beef jerky and soda, watching the world go by.

"Yo, yo! Julian! Sam!" I heard James yelling. I climbed out and saw him waving me up. The train was running at full speed, which didn't matter as long as it maintained its momentum, but what if it stopped? What if it brakes even slightly? Damn it! Are we riding these rails or not? I climbed to the top of the train, where James was clinging to a hatch between the walkways rimming the roof. The view up top was dizzying as we crossed a long trestle bordered by farmland stretching into the horizon.

"Did you see where Sam got on?" James asked after I pulled myself up, and we precariously held on to the same hatch. Despite the grand view, I wanted to get off the roof as soon as possible. I pointed toward the rear, shouting over the whistling wind, "I'm not sure. I think we gotta go back until we find him."

I started crawling, but James stood up and said, "No, that'll take too long. We gotta use the walkways and jump from car to car. It's not too bad; it's more like a step. Just lean forward the whole way!"

My pulse quickened. James threw his backpack off the train, and I did the same. I didn't have much in it, but I regretted not taking my cigarettes out first. However, I'd rather stay alive than risk my life with that thing flopping on my back.

We yelled, 'Sam! Sam!' as we moved from roof to roof, which was significantly more nauseating than leaping across the wiggling hooks below. Four cars back, Sam responded.

"Yo, I'm down here!" He called out. We descended the ladder and spotted him. Sam looked scared but grinned when he saw us. The hopper he boarded had a hole big enough for two, so I joined him, and James sat in the one across from us.

"This is wild!" I cheered.

"You want a smoke?" Sam asked, pulling out a pack of menthols. I took one.

James saw the cherry on our cigarettes burning in the shadows of our hideout and yelled, "Good idea!" then lit one up as it hung from his lips.

I took a drag and chuckled, thinking about how our bags had probably landed in a field near a couple of bewildered cows. We sat puffing happily. Sam and I spontaneously shook hands. I liked that menthol cigarette. It didn't hurt my throat like other blends that irritated my trachea—where the ventilator tube had been.

We flicked our spent cigarettes away and pondered how to get off the train. Waiting until it crossed another trestle and leaping into the water below was one possibility among several unenticing options. Fortunately, the train slowed, offering a better choice. As it decelerated, I considered a cinematic leap, ending with a roll, but James had a better idea. Clinging to the ladder with one hand, he tapped the rushing ground with his feet, gauging how wide his stride should be.

He released the ladder when his pace was right, pivoting to avoid being crushed by the sixty-ton freight inches from his ass. His rapid deceleration augmented his steps, requiring him to leap ten feet at a time—until he came to a stop, still standing. I copied James, letting go of the ladder when my timing felt right. Phew! It's good to be off that train. I'm alright. I'm alright. I'm flying! Wait. I'm falling. I'm falling, going down ... I tumbled into the grass, did an unintentional front flip, and landed on my back, largely unscathed.

The train was speeding up. Sam had to make his move or risk dying if he leaped off once it got any faster. "Fuck it!" he shouted, letting go of the ladder as his rate of deceleration forced him to take four giant strides—executed with his arms straight up in the air for some unknown reason—resulting in a rough but survivable tumble into the grass with his backpack still on, unlike James and me. He lay there, moaning, before getting up.

We reached the main road in Philadelphia near where Sam and I had visited his grandfather. Collectively, we had enough money for bus tickets back to Newark, and we exchanged knowing smiles the whole way home. It was one day, one ride, but another step toward freeing ourselves from the yoke that binds people to dull, inauthentic lives. Looking out the bus window, I felt reverse culture shock. The city thrummed at a comfortable cadence. Contented shoppers strolled in and out of stores, swiping credit cards and gently closing car doors, unaware of our untamed ride through another world without walls, borders, or rules only a moment ago. It was already calling me back.

Chapter 13

We called ourselves the Delaware Rowdy Boys and continued hopping trains where they slowed at the bend but generally not as far as the first time. It was better to take commuter rides about two miles down the tracks to the railroad switch, where trains slowed enough to hop off near Newark High School. Sometimes, I left my truck at home and rode the train to school. If it didn't slow down, I had to find excuses to explain my absence the following day, which typically wasn't well received. However, the primary deterrent to free-riding to school on freight trains was the thick, tar-like substance we called war paint that got all over our hands and clothes. Though most of my friends rebelled against societal norms—ironically, by following predefined rules of rebellion—they found the war paint ridiculous and began calling me Hobo J. I resumed driving to class, and after a few more months, we bid farewell to rail riding in search of new thrills. Temple's apartment was one such resource, but skateboarding remained another.

***

"It doesn't look that steep," I said as Sam, James, and I wolfed down the sodas and snacks we'd purchased at Nutter's Sandwich Shoppe, the sole place of commerce located across the hill from us on Wedgewood Road. Our destination was a vertical ramp nearby that our buddy had built. I'd ridden smaller halfpipes and wasn't concerned with the ramp, but I had a bad feeling about the hill we were about to barrel down. It didn't look steep, but tiny skateboard wheels fastened to a piece of plywood left little room for error. A legion of medical professionals had advised me to live more cautiously. They claimed I'd struggle to learn and confuse tables with chairs. Drugs and blows to the head were strictly forbidden lest I damage my brain beyond repair. What was the cost of not listening? Possibly my life. I'd defied them by smoking weed, hopping trains, and busting out bone-rattling tricks on my skateboard, but that didn't mean I wanted to bang up my brain more than it already was. I brought a helmet in case I did a faceplant on the ramp, and strapping it on before going down the hill showed I knew I shouldn't ignore them entirely.

James went first, carving broad, sweeping turns to control his speed. Sam, rolling close behind him, glanced at me with the same pained expression he'd made the first time he hopped off a train. I sincerely thought he was going to cry. We descended toward our destiny at the base of the hill.

James was halfway down, doing tailslides to throttle his speed. Looking good, my man. Sam was stiff, his arms fixed, rolling straight down and picking up tremendous speed. He shot past James, but this was not a race. It was a matter of survival.

I was determined to mimic James's steady, sinuous descent. Yes, that was happening in my mind, but I shot down the hill with the same rigidity and unwanted acceleration as Sam.

Even from a distance, I could see Sam's board wobbling. When that happens, you have to decelerate quickly, or you'll be summarily dismissed from your skateboard and left to try your luck with gravity.

Oh no. God no. I bit my lip. Sam launched from his board after exceeding all permissible speed and tensile strength limits. His arms extended as he twisted mid-air. It was a wonder to behold until his portly frame, ill-suited for such maneuvers, swiftly descended toward the unforgiving Earth. Now fifteen feet behind Sam, James had plenty of time to steer around him. I was bound to share in the fate of one of them. Who, I'd soon find out.

Sam's elbow hit the ground first. He rolled several times before launching into the air again as his shirt blew back and his big belly flopped in the open air. He landed on his backside and tumbled along the asphalt. My skateboard started wobbling. Okay, this has happened before, and you steadied yourself, but not on such a steep hill! Try to slow down. It's not too late. I crouched, widening my turns, but it didn't help. Wobble, wobble. It is too late. Aim for the grass. Try to make it to the grass!

"Fuck!" "Ow!" "Fuck!"

I never knew the ground could feel so hard.

James stepped off his board once he reached the base of the hill and smiled, observing Sam in a bloody heap and me sliding toward the grass I'd unsuccessfully aimed for. My head ached, having struck the ground several times. I should've listened to those doctors, but at least I wore a helmet.

Sam and I had numerous cuts and weeping wounds. We considered returning to Nutter's to get bandages and antiseptic solution. However, the horror of the hill was still too fresh for us to retrace our steps. When we arrived at the ramp, we had little desire to do anything other than nurse our wounds.

James turned and declared, "Well, my least accomplished sons, your piss-poor performance has brought shame to our family. My good looks and agility must have skipped a generation, but what matters most is that you're having a good time. Even if you'll never be as great as me, I want you both to enjoy yourselves." Sam spat out a long stream of blood, which said it all.

***

"Yeah, man, I was surfing on the North Shore. I'm talking about Hawaii, bro. Huge twenty-foot waves were breaking. You could hear them crashing from miles away. But, bro, I channeled the Kahuna spirit and knew I had nothing to fear," Temple chronicled for us while Sam, James, and I attended one of his parties.

"Oh my god, that's so cool! You're, like, really deep," said a skinny Indian girl wearing an Eye of Horus pendant who was high on something. I recognized her. Her name was Misha. I'd seen her in one of my classes.

Temple's hair had grown to shoulder length, but he always wore a hat, likely hiding his thinning hair, which I noticed since I had my own ways of dealing with limp locks. Spring break was over, and keg parties were popping up around the complex. However, Temple held a special place in the hearts and minds of the community, as a dreadlocked White boy with saucer-sized pupils had gushed,

130

"Temple has the kookiest shit!" Temple continued chronicling his endless summer in Hawaii.

"The insane force of the wave shot me through the tube. Dude, the waves were so huge they could have crushed houses. I mean dudes and dudettes," Temple winked at Misha, whose pupils were big as moons. "Everyone was treading water, desperate to get back to shore. Some people died that day, man. But I told her, 'No, Mother Wave, you will not defeat me. We ride as one.' So I kneel—yeah, real low—and cut back to the top of the wave. I must have been going fifty miles per hour when I hit the crest. I don't know how I did it, but I was raging and did a full fucking flip—and then I dropped down, way underwater, but the ocean knew I was not afraid. The ocean ... the ocean carried me unharmed back to shore." Temple spread his arms like the sand he'd returned to after his bodacious bout with Mother Wave.

"What happened to your surfboard?" A guy from another apartment dressed in less eclectic digs than most of Temple's admirers asked. He'd crashed the party, but that was no issue with Temple as long as the dude-to-dudette ratio didn't tilt too far in the dude direction.

Temple started nodding his head, probably buying time to cook up a conclusion to his tale, then repeated, "What happened to the board?"

The party crasher smirked.

"The board broke in half, man, but moments like that show you what's important, what matters. It was worth it."

"So worth it," Misha repeated.

Temple expanded Misha's knowledge of the Kahuna spirit minutes later when they made out on one of the sofas. Later, I found her sitting on a beanbag, applying glow-in-the-dark paint to another girl's face.

"Hey, isn't your name Misha? You were in my world history class last year." She looked up at me, wearing the same face paint she was applying to her companion. The luminescent colors concentrated on Misha's cheeks and eyes reminded me of the beings

I'd seen during my near-death experience, but there was nothing holy about this place.

Still looking dazed, Misha said, "Uh-huh, that's right. I remember you. Your name is ...?"

"I'm Julian."

"Cool. Hey, you want me to do your face after I'm done with Linda, Julian?"

"Oh, ha, ha. No, I'm good. I was just wondering, how do you know Temple?"

Linda turned toward me. The way Misha had applied her face paint made her look like a skeleton. Red and yellow neon rings surrounded her eyes and nose, and the green lines on her lips created skull teeth. I immediately wanted to introduce her to Sam.

"We met him at a football game. He was smoking weed with some other kids behind the bleachers, so we had a couple of hits since we were losing anyway. I know he's probably a lot older than us, which would usually be so lame, you know? But Temple's way cool. He's, like, beyond age." Linda explained.

"Beyond what?"

"Age," Misha repeated. "It's a super interesting way to think about time. He said people should be able to do stuff like smoking weed or having sex based on their *real* age, which includes experiences we've had from all the lives we've lived, not just this one. He can see auras, so he knows everyone's *real* age. Ask him how old you really are; it's wild!"

"Hmm, okay. I've always wanted to know my *real* age. I'll be sure to ask Temple how old I am. I'll see you around."

"Right on, Julian. Have a great night."

At Temple's apartment, multiple bongs and glass pipes adorned table tops, armrests, and beanbag chairs. I found bags of powder and pills between seat cushions, too. A neighbor occasionally strolled in with a bottle of beer or rum and Coke sloshing around in a plastic cup, but if they stuck around long enough, they tended to leave with the kooky stuff. I doubted Temple's generosity was the reason for that. There were freebies, for sure, but plenty of money was exchanged for a range of illicit substances, including heroin, which had become more prevalent around town. Most partygoers were older than me, but high school kids, mainly girls like Misha and Linda, were also in attendance. I made out with a few of them, as did Sam and James, but the nature of the place didn't foster lasting relationships. By the next day, they were loving it up with another dude, raging at the top of the wave.

Even though we had plenty of good times, I was always uneasy there. My alter ego, Weens, was never shy or self-conscious at parties, but after my injury, my guts tumbled whenever I was in a crowd, and the world strobed like a music video. However, my discomfort wasn't due to social anxiety at Temple's place, given that most people were too high on ecstasy, ketamine, and whatever they were smoking in a glass pipe beside the foam-spewing leather sofa to notice me. That's what made me worry. How many laws was I breaking by simply being in the same room as all those drugs and paraphernalia? But what were the alternatives? Most parties in Newark featured a group of frat guys binge drinking in kiddie pools and lip-syncing to hip-hop on their front lawn. I had two main concerns: how long could this go on before the police showed up, and what was the quickest way out of there if they did? The front door sufficed for now, so I closed it behind me and headed toward the parking lot.

Slipping away from the drugs and bonkers behavior was like a drug itself, as my stomach settled down the moment I stepped outside.

While debating whether or not to blow this joint, I came across an old off-roader with jacked-up suspension and faded yellow paint parked in the same spot it'd been for the past month. It had seen better days but was built tough. I'd camped in fields and parking lots in the back of my truck, which taught me the value of these rugged rides. Many of its components were missing. It must've been abandoned. Circling the vehicle, I saw "International Scout" written on the tailgate, though it wasn't fit for scouting anymore. Unsurprisingly, its doors were unlocked. I climbed in and sat behind the steering wheel. There was a brown bench seat in the back, a different color from the green leather on the seats up front.

The dash was unremarkable, but the paneling and round gauges had an old-school style that was still fresh. The whole thing was so ugly that it was beautiful. It seemed familiar. I might've seen it as a kid, rolling down that road I often wanted to go down—about halfway back—and start over again. I locked the doors and reclined in my time machine. I took the whiskey away from my mom, aced every exam, dodged the bullet in '89, and pulled Hazel close in my tuxedo as slow jams spun. I recalled Gil and the grand piano. A wave of panic hit me. It all fit snugly along my timeline. Was it even possible to change anything? Which events had to remain to rearrange my life the way I wanted in this thought experiment?

As I reconstructed my timeline in the front seat of the Scout, a girl walking out of the apartment complex spotted me and approached. It was Eva, whom I'd seen passed out months ago, drooling on a pillow in the back room of Temple's apartment. She and James had an on-and-off relationship.

"What are you doing in there?" Eva asked as she came abreast of the Scout. It was chilly outside. She wore a knit cap and a thin sweater accentuating her svelte figure. Even the way she breathed was elegant, as wispy breaths formed before her face. I straightened my seat and rolled down the window.

"Time traveling," I replied.

"Where are you going?"

"Back to the eighties."

"But the Nineties just started?"

"It's never too soon to right a wrong."

"Well, if it's warmer in the eighties, I'm going with you. Open the door. It's cold out here."

I unlocked the passenger door. She climbed in and closed the door.

"So why don't you like the Nineties?"

"The music isn't the same. Eighties tunes were so good that E.T. came to Earth because even aliens knew no one in the universe could rock it better than us. R'n'B from those days is so smooth your speakers slid off the table whenever you popped in a tape." I started singing "Oh Sheila," swapping "Sheila" for "Eva." Her reaction

134

mirrored my own when my father tried to convince me a dead bird was sleeping. I stopped after two verses.

"Now you're just being silly. There's still amazing music being made."

"Yeah, there are a couple of good songs, but most of them make you feel like you've drunk flat soda. Movies aren't as good, either. You leave one nowadays and start worrying if people at your dinner party don't like the flower stenciling on your dishware. In the Eighties, you left the theater ready to ride a riverboat through the jungle and take on guerrilla warriors with a handful of blow darts and a gallon of gasoline. I liked the purple and green leotards, which were fashionable for women, and a select group of guys that were required to wear matching headbands and tube socks to be fashionable. Every light was shining, and our dreams burned bright. Now that era's over, and things will never be the same. Even though I lived through the Eighties, I feel like they passed me by."

"It was pretty cool back then, but I bet the next generation will say the same thing about the Nineties. By the way, what has James been saying about me? Do you think he wants a girlfriend? I mean, I don't want to be his girlfriend, but you know, if you heard anything, I'm just curious."

"I don't know if he's looking for a serious relationship or capable of being serious. He hasn't really said anything."

"What do you mean 'really'? That means he said something!"

"Okay! James said you're cool. He likes you because you're similar. I mean, you're both, um … emancipated. You both ran away, but he's not looking for a wife yet."

"Whatever, I'm not looking for a husband either. James is a dummy; he doesn't know what he wants. He's so weird. I've never met someone who likes books as much as him. He thinks it makes him smart, but sometimes he forgets he's not living in a fairy tale. James started calling me Frau Eva because that's the name of a character in a book he likes. But at the same time, he seems old … like a hundred years old. Actually, James told me that once. He said, 'I'm the oldest man I know.' What does that even mean? But I didn't run away. I still go home, but my parents never ask where I've been, so it doesn't matter. They're so boring. All they do is sit around drinking beer and watch TV. It's way more fun here."

"How old are you?"

"I'm fifteen, but I'm almost sixteen. Well, in five months, I'll be sixteen. How about you?"

"I'm seventeen, but in five months, I'll be going back to the eighties."

"I don't know if James told you, but Temple has some shrooms. I did them last week. Have you ever done anything like that? It was cool. They, you know, opened my mind. I saw colors and swirly things and even talked to my plants for a little while."

"How did they talk? Were they flapping their petals around?"

That made her laugh so hard her face turned pink. Then she said, "No, I touched the flowers on my windowsill, and I don't know how, but we had a conversation about why they smell so good and how to find beauty even when the world seems ugly. I know it sounds impossible."

"No, it doesn't. I've never done shrooms, but I had an experience like that once."

"You've smoked weed before, right?"

"Oh, yeah. Definitely. I like how it makes music sound, and it's fun to dance when you're high, but it also makes me self-conscious, like I start thinking that I'm blinking too much. You know what I mean?"

"I know what you mean, but if you've smoked weed, you kinda know what shrooms are like. It's trippy. If you try them, you'll see."

I'd seen *The Doors* and watched 1960s counterculture documentaries. They explored ways to transcend our perceptual limits bound by societal constraints and ego. Temple spoke of alternate realities, but mostly to hear himself talk. I knew there was more to life than the mundane activities that occupy most people's time. I'd barely glimpsed those boundless deserts and cities sculpted in light, where holy spirits bestowed sacred wisdom upon me while I was comatose. Yet I cherished that experience more than a lifetime in the ordinary world. Why was I shot, and how did I survive? Why am I alive? It was all part of the Mystery I was working on. Could psychedelics help me solve these riddles?

"How long did it last? Was it scary?" I asked Eva.

"It lasted about six hours. I did the shrooms at my parents' house and stayed in my room the whole time. The first three hours were the most intense. The music I listened to sounded incredible, Julian. It was like alien music! And I know this sounds funny, but I thought my bed turned into water. It was way different than I expected, but it wasn't scary. My parents are so whacked out that even if I had talked to them, I doubt they would've noticed I was on something."

Six hours? I could hang out in my room and learn the higher truths all those hippies and professors talked about in the sixties. What's it like to hallucinate? Would it be like a hologram or a 3D cartoon projected around me? Groovy.

"Yeah, I'm going to try them," I said.

"Okay, International Scout."

I scrunched my forehead, confused. "What?"

"You said you want to time travel, but since you're sitting here, doing it in this old thing, that's what I'm gonna call you so you'll remember what planet you're on."

"I like that. International Scout. But you'd think a guy with that name would've traveled more than me. I went to Tijuana with my grandparents out West once. I got a switchblade and snuck it through customs, but it broke when I got home. That's all the international travel I've done."

"Before my parents became so boring, they took my sister and me to Amsterdam. All those canals were fun to walk around. We went to the Van Gogh Museum. Up close, his paintings are magical. They jump out of the frame and spin inside of you. He probably did mushrooms or LSD."

"LSD wasn't around then. Van Gogh was in an asylum when he painted *Starry Night*. Insanity was enough for him to swirl the sky with all those penumbras riding around the stars."

We sat for a moment, looking out the windshield. Eva was on my right. She looked over at me a few times. Did she want to kiss me—what about her and James?

137

We faced each other. Eva tilted her head and brushed back her hair.

"Your skin looks so soft. Can I touch your cheek?" I asked. It was unusual to say, but our conversation had put me in a funny mood, so why not?

"Sure, if that's your thing. Maybe I'll touch yours, too."

I caressed Eva's cheek, tracing her jawline and ruby lips. She closed her eyes for more than a moment, breathing hard, then gazed into mine when she opened them. Her hand glided across my face, down to my collarbone. I shivered.

Eva's long eyelashes fluttered. More than just soft skin, everything about her was beautiful.

We pulled our hands away.

"That was nice," she said.

I was fighting back tears.

"You should grow a beard. You've already got one started, and it looks pretty good."

"I dunno, that would make me look too much like my dad, which bugs me out. Maybe I'll sport a goatee instead," I said, still catching my breath.

Climbing into the back seat with her crossed my mind. There was the minor issue of James, but as attractive as she was, she seemed more like a kid sister than someone I should get frisky with. So, it went no further than sharing a tender touch.

"Did you get the shrooms from James? I don't want to ask Temple and have to listen to one of his guru speeches first."

"Yeah, from James, but I wish he'd stop dealing drugs. Temple's parties are fun and all, but whatever James has been doing with him seems shady. Don't tell James I told you that."

***

"The mushies are thirty bucks, but you'll need one of them 'psych evals' first. For the low cost of ten additional dollars, I will oblige in your time of need," James said as he sat behind a foldout table in the back room. He looked like a bookie, with a cigarette behind his ear and wads of cash stacked alongside various substances, one of which was the psilocybin mushrooms I sought.

"Well, I reckon that's a real good bargain, but how about waiving the fee since I've never charged you for crashing in my truck, even when members of your small but loyal harem tag along."

James made a pained expression and said, "Ah, an interesting point you make, one only raised by a gentleman of your high esteem and mental stability. Looks like you'll be getting these mushrooms at cost. At cost, my boy. Surely, you won't mention any of that to Frau Eva, who's still young and unacquainted with the ways of men like Jubal and I who require ... variety."

Thus, I avoided a guru speech and psych eval, securing the shrooms. James had slipped in allusions to *Demian* and *Stranger in a Strange Land*, which was lost on most of our peers, who only read what they were instructed to read because they'd already traded their sense of wonder for the comforts of their routines. A golf cart ready to ride around in circles will be waiting for them fifty years from now.

Chapter 14

James gave me a sly grin when I asked, "What if someone sees us?"

"Defiance requires more than words to have meaning," he replied after I shared my concern about creating our own slogan for the Newark High School marquee, as he'd suggested.

We went through with it at 3 a.m. the following morning. I crept out of my bedroom, stepping lightly on any boards that might creak, opened the back door, and found myself alone in the dark. I felt small, standing beneath the mass of stars washed out by the faint glow of streetlights aligned in the same tidy order that governed all things in suburbia. I imagined astronauts looking down at me from the other end of their telescope. "One giant leap for mankind," I said, waving to them in their spacesuits. I walked to my truck, unlocked the door, and climbed in. Even though we'd planned to modify the marquee, I wasn't sure if James would be there. He often crashed at Temple's or with girls from his parties. A group my neighbor would call "Goddamn druggies." Young, old, smart, dumb—James was all these things but also handsome.

Sliding the rear window open, I asked, "You ready?" He grumbled awake.

"Uh, we gotta take care of something else first. Do you have any extra underwear you can grab before we go?"

I turned on the interior light. A dark stain had spread across the blanket and his crotch. I detected the faint smell of urine.

"Does this happen a lot?"

James frowned. I wish I'd been more sympathetic, but I was surprised. His audacity often belied his vulnerabilities.

"Sometimes, I have nightmares where the police have me in the back of a squad car. Then, my mom leaps out of the dark, looking all witchy and shit. 'Take him away,' she says, then they roll into the woods with me locked in the back and leave me there. I wake up with a nice little puddle after those sorts of dreams. It doesn't happen that often, but I pissed my pants in a girl's dorm room once. I dipped out of there before she noticed. I've never told anyone about it until now."

"All right, don't worry about it, but you should spend less time at Temple's place so that stuff with the cops doesn't really happen. I'll go back in and get you another pair."

I begrudgingly returned to my room and got him a fresh pair of boxer shorts from my limited supply. While in the hallway, my mother emerged from her bedroom. She was barely coherent before dawn; it had nothing to do with alcohol. She was a veritable somnambulist. All I had to do was play along, and she'd go back to bed.

'Is it time for school, Julian? Shouldn't you be at school?' she asked, one eye half open.

"I'm going right now, Mom. That's why I'm up."

"You have to finish school so you can go to college and get a good job. Are you doing your homework? It's a terrible feeling when you can't find work and you need—" She stopped midsentence, yawned, and returned to her room. I could still sneak out, but it was less appealing once she'd seen me. The magic of slipping out unseen was gone; now I was an ordinary prankster. However, these minor subversions kept the chains of conformity off us, and it would be daylight soon, so we headed out.

"Hey man, how about rolling up that window? It's chilly in here," James said after trying to use the controls on the passenger side. I had the parental lock on, so his clicking was in vain.

"I told you, listening to traffic helps me drive. Remember, I can't see on the left side."

"Oh, I forgot; I'm riding with Batman."

"Yes, and I'm riding with the Joker."

I always kept the window cracked as road sounds and the height of my truck augmented my field of view, allowing me to avoid incidents behind the wheel I sometimes had while walking around.

We parked a block away and proceeded to where the marquee was. A small oak tree provided the optimal avenue for ascent. We scaled it and reached the flat roof right beneath the marquee. As we

141

expected, a pile of clip-on letters lay beneath it, allowing us to avoid a *Scrabble*-like challenge in our alterations. We'd already decided to spell out "I saw the best minds of my generation destroyed by madness" from Allen Ginsberg's poem *Howl*.

A police car pulled into the high school parking lot after we'd affixed the first five words. Then there was another.

"What are those cops doing here!" I fretted.

"Shut up."

My mom was right. Even while sleepwalking, she knew I was destined for failure. I was not going to graduate. Soon, James and I would be pissing in the back seat of a police car, and his mother would torment us further deep in the woods. One of the police officers swept the grounds with his Maglite, leaving deep footprints in the grass. He looked far more intimidating than Officer Elias. Time moved slowly.

The police searched the area, dissatisfied, certain we were hiding somewhere, maybe under a car or behind a tree. They came close enough for us to hear them breathing, but fortunately, they did not look below the marquee. They returned to their vehicles and left.

"Let's go. Let's get out of here right now," I urged James.

"Just a few more letters, my Jewish brother. Think about how proud old Ginsberg will be."

I reluctantly helped him finish. James stood and admired our work.

"Get down, get down! What are you doing?" Predawn light streaked above us. I pictured ten police cars imminently arriving.

James nodded, satisfied. I was about to prod him again when I caught sight of our subversive message, ready to greet the morning rush of students and admired it with him instead. Yes, Ginsberg would approve. We climbed down the tree, and my bowels staged their own rebellion.

"I gotta take a dump," I said.

"Go ahead."

"No, let's get out of here."

"This is the best place. The police were just here; they ain't comin' back."

My wailing intestines agreed. I sought relief behind a bush near a chain-link fence, tore a flyer for an upcoming pep rally off a pole and finished the task.

"We have to go back," I said on the way to my house.

"What, why?"

"They're going to find my poop and analyze it. It'll have my DNA, and they'll arrest me."

James shook his head.

I pulled over to think.

"Does shit even have DNA in it?" James asked.

"Everything from our body has DNA in it."

"Well, one thing is clear, my boy. You're receiving a quality education. I should go back to school.

I've been missing out."

"They're gonna find that poop and figure out it was me. I gotta hide it somewhere else."

"Yeah, you're right. If the cops find it, we'll be in deep shit."

"Shut up. I'm going back. I'll be quick."

"The devil always rides in the direction you travel."

"Is that Camus?"

"No, I heard it somewhere. It means you often run into whatever you're trying to avoid."

We returned to Newark High. It wasn't daybreak yet, but the horizon was brightening. I dashed to the place where I'd pooped. It was already covered in flies. I grabbed the flyer to scoop it up, then had a moment of doubt. Why am I worrying about this stupid shit? I laughed, realizing it was the sanest thing I'd thought all day. I dropped the flyer and ran back to my ride.

I rolled to a quiet stop in front of my house. My bed was calling me, but the truck still smelled like urine.

"Let's go inside and stick everything in the washing machine."

"Don't you think we should wait until your mom leaves?"

"It'll be fine. If she sees us, I'll tell her I needed to wash a couple of things before school, and she won't care."

My mother had seen James when he, Sam, and I played video games in the basement. She'd blasted us for leaving our skateboards

143

lying around, but they'd never had a conversation otherwise. I wasn't sure what she'd think if they ever spoke. My mom liked Sam, but he was more domesticated than James.

We went to the unfinished side of the basement. I threw the blanket and James's soiled garments into the washing machine then we waited on a trundle bed beside the wood-burning stove on the finished side. I always liked that little black stove; it made me feel like I was living in an old wood cabin, just as I'd imagined living happily with Ann from the children's hospital. Soon after I started the wash, my mother and brother awoke, and she got him ready for school. It would have been preferable if they left without seeing us. However, when they came down moments later, that happy possibility vanished. Did she remember our sleepy conversation from that morning?

"Julian, why are you doing laundry so early?" my mother asked, descending the stairs. Midway, she spotted James.

"Oh, your friend is here."

"Uh yeah, this is James. Remember, he's been here with Sam and me before. I'm washing a blanket that's been in my truck for a while. Some of James's clothes were wet, so I threw them in too. It won't be long. We'll be out of here soon." After explaining what we were doing, I realized I'd opened multiple avenues for interrogation and general displeasure, but I had to stick with the story now.

"Why are his clothes wet?" she asked as she and my brother descended the last few stairs.

"I spilled lemon soda on them," James answered.

"And you don't have a washing machine at your house?"

"The detergent my mother uses displeases me. It smells like peaches and irritates my sensitive skin. By the way, do you know how to make matzo ball soup?"

"What?" my mother asked incredulously.

This would've been a good time for James to tone down his tics.

"Are you the one who lives in Julian's truck?" my brother asked James.

"What are you talking about, Kevin? He only rides with me to school," I snapped, knowing I was already busted.

144

"Oh, I saw him climbing into it when you weren't around. I thought he lived there."

"Julian, please come upstairs," my mother said.

James stood up, likely wishing to beat a hasty retreat.

"Why is James wearing your underwear, Julian?"

"I told you. His clothes got wet from the soda. It spilled all over the place."

James sat down, dejected that his peach detergent story had failed the sniff test and that he wouldn't be receiving step-by-step instructions from my mother on making matzo ball soup. The situation was unraveling fast.

Upstairs, my mother unleashed, "Is that boy living in your truck? Why is he wearing your underwear? Why are you washing his clothes? And why does he want to learn how to make matzo ball soup? I want him out of here!"

"Are you going to let me answer?"

"Yes!"

"James doesn't live in my truck. He takes naps there sometimes because his house is all the way out in Wilmington. He spilled some soda in the back, and now we're washing everything that got wet. I'll get my boxers back after his clothes are dry. Matzo ball soup? That's harder to explain. I gave him some, and he had an epiphany after biting into a ball. Now he has rabbinical aspirations. It makes more sense once you get to know him."

"I want to look in your truck."

"Why?"

"Now."

Since all my James-related secrets had spilled out, I saw no harm in letting her look and had no further objections. We went outside, and I opened it up. Eva was sitting in the back, smiling. How long had she been there? Had she overheard my poop conversation with James? I hoped not.

"Oh, hey, do you know where James is? I want to tell him—" Eva noticed my mom and stopped talking.

"Who are you? How many people live in this truck? What is this, Camp Matzo Ball?" Exasperated, my mother turned away from Eva and faced me. "This has to stop. If you don't finish high school, you'll spend all your money and never make enough to provide for yourself." My mother tried to calm herself, apparently recalling our early morning conversation, but her concern was unfounded. I had a steady C average, which was equal to an A, given I skipped half my classes and didn't do much homework.

"No, ma'am, I don't live here. I was looking for James. He gave me a key. I didn't break in or anything." Despite hanging out in the back of my urine-soaked truck, Eva looked and smelled lovely. I regretted not kissing her. But had she wanted to kiss me?

"Don't call me ma'am. My name is Sophia, but don't call me Sophia either! Call me Mrs. Simmons. Are you comfortable in there? Do you want me to start mail delivery for you?"

"Oh no, Mrs. Sophia, ma'am, there's no need for that. I'd better get going."

Eva scampered off, and my mom yelled, "You come on back if you need to do some laundry, sweetie!"

Mr. Jones peeked through his half-closed blinds, furrowing his brow before snapping them shut. Camp Matzo Ball? I tried not to laugh, but I snorted a little.

"Listen, Julian. I know you have a good heart. Ever since you were in the hospital, you've worried about the hurt and less fortunate—the victims of the world. Something from your childhood might've triggered it. I don't know. Maybe I'm not a good mother."

"Please stop. Let's go inside," I said, observing that my mother, brother, and I each had different last names since she'd reclaimed her maiden name, Simmons. Henry had the last name, Wallace, so I bore the burden of my awkward surname alone. That bothered me more than the random things she was claiming complicity for once we were inside.

"All those kids living in your truck. What other mischief have you been getting into? It's my fault. I should've given you a more stable home." She started tearing up, but James dropped something downstairs, and anger overcame her guilt. "You cannot care for every stray boy and girl you meet! Every generation has kids looking for a cause, 'victims in search of offense,' is what your father called them. That was one smart thing that son of a bitch taught me. We don't need to save the world. The world will be fine without us. You've got to take care of yourself first! You can't help anyone if you're broke. Get that boy out of the basement. Where are his parents? I don't know. He seems like trouble." I began formulating a line of humor, asking my mother if I, too, was a son of a bitch like my father, but being wary of another block of soap in my mouth, I wisely kept it to myself.

After we returned to the rustic lower level, my brother asked, "Mom, did George Washington used to live here?"

"What? No," my mother replied.

"James said he did."

"No, no, my dear boy. I said George Washington probably had a similar bed and stove in his house."

I was sure my brother's account was accurate, but thankfully he didn't argue.

"Can I live in Julian's truck too?" Kevin asked.

***

Two days later, I was in Sam's room, showing him the shrooms I took out of hiding after the Camp Matzo Ball incident blew over. They were dried and crooked-shaped.

"Damn, hoss! I've been wanting to try these. It's so dull here, J; I'm tired of always seeing the same thing on Main Street. You know what I mean? Maybe one day I'll move to New York. What about you? Do you think you'll be here for life?" Sam asked, his mood rising as he contemplated escaping to the Big Apple.

"I like Newark. You can get a plate of food at a fair price and sit undisturbed for a while. I like roaming around campus, and there's a rhythm to the creek and all the trains crossing some old bridge that keeps me calm. A place with big buildings and lots of people won't be like that."

"But don't you want to hang out with new people sometimes? Someone who's traveled and speaks another language. My parents have lived here their whole lives. They haven't seen anything other than what's on the road they take to work every day."

"Yeah, I ought to travel more. You know Eva, right? That girl who hangs out at Temple's. She started calling me International Scout. I can't stay here forever with a name like that."

"International Scout? Like that big four-by-four thing?"

"Ha, yeah. You know the one that's broken down in the parking lot? Eva saw me hanging out in it and started calling me that. I definitely get bored living here sometimes. That's why we've gotta kick down some doors. You wanna take the shrooms tonight?"

"Word. Those are gonna be dope. I'll be jamming to the funk for sure. I gotta do something. I was so bored last night I huffed a whole can of butane in the shower. I probably have less brain cells than you do now."

We exchanged an awkward glance, but I knew he didn't mean any offense. Then he asked, "Yo, can I have half the bag?"

"I dunno. James said I should take all of them. I was gonna give you two or three to try it out."

"It's better if you give me half. Then we'll have the same experience."

I was planning to take the shrooms alone in my room, so I wasn't sure if a fifty-fifty split would bring about transcendent equality between us, but James could be a punk. I doubted I needed to take the whole bag. Sam was right; weed hadn't fried my brain, but what about shrooms? James said they were only a little stronger than weed—like smoking two joints at once.

Two joints ... Would that be like watching a movie or more like my near-death experience? I wasn't drawn to psychedelics out of boredom, though life could be dull in Delaware. I'd read that we only use a small portion of our brains. Could shrooms help me tap into one of my neural reserve tanks? What will that be like? Fun? ... Scary? ... Revitalizing? Sam's right: splitting the bag is perfect.

"All right, I'll give you half of the shrooms. You got another bag I can stick them in?"

"Nah, I gotta go downstairs and get one." We headed downstairs.

148

Sam's parents were seated at their dining room table. His dad's glass of gin sloshed as they talked.

"What are we going to do, Ted? Can your father give us any money?" Sam's mom asked.

"Donna, my father has Alzheimer's. Don't you remember the last time we visited him? He can't do shit but stare out the window now. This is on me. I'll figure it out."

I'd gone with Sam the last time they visited his grandfather. It had been nearly three years since I first saw him and his buddies in the golf carts. Things had sure changed. They had to spoon-feed him and put him in a suit with a zipper in the back because they didn't want him undressing himself. He still managed clips of conversations and recognized Sam's dad. But as for the rest of us, not a glimmer in those old gray eyes.

"Sam, your father lost his job."

Ted shot up, still holding his drink. "Look, I got laid off. They let the whole department go. It had absolutely nothing to do with me. I've been there for almost two decades, and now they've replaced us with machines and foreign workers who they'll pay jack-shit wages, and we have to train."

"Don't do it, Dad; don't train them," one of Sam's younger brothers pleaded from the living room, where he was supposed to be watching *Sesame Street*.

Ted shook his head. "Son, I can't do that. I need that last paycheck, and I'll get unemployment for a while. They're in control, boy. They're the ones in charge. I'm lucky I got off the assembly line and went into inventory. On the line, people skip bathroom breaks out of fear of losing their jobs. Some guys even keep bottles around to piss in! It's inhuman. It was different when my father worked at the auto plant. They had culture. You gave them your time, and they took care of you your whole damn life. It was still like that for the first decade I was there. Oh, they still care. They care about shareholder returns and efficiency. Every time they lay people off, the stock pops. This ain't the USA, I remember." He took a hard swig and continued, speaking more to himself than to us. "They won't defeat me. As long as I can walk, I will feed this family. You've got to get out there. You can't let them knock you down. That's what they want—for me to roll over and die. Make room for the machines."

"I could go back to my accounting job at Macy's," Sam's mom offered.

"Donna, they're not using calculators anymore. They've got software that can run it all without you now."

"What are you saying? That I'm only fit to sit around on my ass? I can get a job, too. I'll call them up tomorrow."

"All right, baby, whatever you say."

Sam grabbed a plastic bag from under the kitchen sink while they agonized over their employment options. I wanted to say something comforting to Sam's dad but thought whatever I said would sound insulting, so I kept my head down and followed Sam to his room.

"Damn, Sam, do you think your dad will be okay?"

"He'll be fine. He's always worrying about getting laid off. Now he doesn't have to worry about it anymore. Okay, I've got a bag. Hook me up, J." Sam held the bag open and looked at me like a hungry chick, ready for the mama bird to spit a chewed-up worm into its mouth. I divvied up the shrooms and gave him half.

"The Mothership Connection," he said, then slid the bag into a drawer beneath his socks.

It was the middle of the week. We decided to wait until Friday to trip in case we needed a couple days to get our heads straight afterward. While kids in class blew spitballs and complained about spaghetti being served for lunch again the following day, I kept going back and forth about the shrooms like I had since I got them.

Why are you doing this? Leave the untapped regions of your brain alone. Flush those crooked mushrooms down the toilet. It's too dangerous. But what is this—what is this world? Something is locked inside me. That's what drove me to psychedelics, and that is still true. Perhaps by damage or design—I'll never know—but life, as it is, isn't enough. There are limitless sources of inspiration I can unlock with the right tools. I sensed them in the lines of poetry I read and the movies I watched.

What happened to Sam's father hit me hard. His job wouldn't have existed without the Industrial Age, but that train kept coming—faster and sleeker until it crushed the men who'd laid down its tracks. Computers were in every house. Simple wiring had evolved into integrated circuits, creating a silicon world mad for speed and data. Equations that took Euclid a lifetime to contemplate now could be solved with a button click. I remember when the recession gutted my old neighborhood.

Henry sat tensely watching the news as experts pointed to peaks and valleys on graphs. A parade of them trying to outdo each other with predictions about how severe the economic damage would be. If this particular line sloped down, history showed it was inevitable. Jobs would be lost. Then they'd cut to a commercial and return with celebrity gossip. The people sitting on broken furniture in my old neighborhood were dots on the line to the newscasters, bankers, and global conglomerates. No matter how fast we cranked the wheel, we were expendable.

What my mom said was true. The world doesn't need me to save it. I have to save myself. The world is constantly changing, and I already have less than I was born with to find my place in it. No one is waiting for me to catch up to whoever I need to be and leave a legacy before my time's up. Something as simple as a bag of shriveled mushrooms might be the way.

***

The knock on my bedroom door startled me. I thought I'd only have to contend with my four walls until tomorrow morning.

"We're having pizza for dinner. It'll be here in about twenty minutes."

"Okay, Mom."

Friday. I'd eaten the mushrooms ten minutes ago. They were bland and crunchy, like my mother's fiber cereal. I didn't feel anything yet, which I attributed to their dull taste. I must've kept them in my drawer too long, and now all their trippy powers were gone. I'd be more optimistic if they tasted like Frosted Flakes. Is it a

151

bad batch, was Eva bullshitting me? But what if they work? We visited the EPCOT Center at Disney World when Henry and my mom were still together and watched Captain EO in 3D. Asteroids and friendly elephantine beings orbited around us while Michael Jackson piloted a spaceship through the cosmos. I can handle something like that if it starts during dinner.

"Okay, guys, pizza's here."

I reached to open my bedroom door, and the wood grain was ... moving? It's starting. It's starting! My heart rate shot up, but it tapered off when I sat down and smelled the pizza, still sizzling in its cardboard box. That was your imagination. This isn't going to work. Enjoy the pizza. My brother sat across from me with a bright smile. Then, the images of men toiling in the Ford factory on the table started wiggling; their machines spun to life but in stop-motion. They turned their wrenches back and forth like a flipbook with two pages.

"Julian, don't you want any?" my mom asked.

I was transfixed by the pizza and its glowing mushroom toppings. Are the mushrooms trying to communicate with me? Why can't they wait until I wolf down a couple of slices? This is bad; they're going to figure out I'm tripping. It might help if you eat something. I grabbed a slice, and the glowing stopped.

The pizza was intensely delicious—deep double yum. I was sitting in a keelless boat, floating down a Venetian canal. Who is that clutching a bouquet of roses atop the Ponte di Rialto? Is that you, Roberto? Did you make this pizza? *"Roberto, la pizza è deliziosa!"* I blew him kisses, which he returned in kind as he stood beneath a large stone archway. *"Perfetto! Perfetto!"* I sang. My brother was staring at me. I'd folded the slice into a little boat, moving it in semicircles. Kevin's face was bulbous, and his lips were cherry red. Cut it out! You don't know Italian, and you're not in Italy! You've never been to Italy. Is Kevin wearing lipstick? Does he always look like that? The cheese and sauce on the remaining slices swirled. They were not food; they were the Milky Way. I felt bad for my mom. She got the pizza to help us escape the worries of the world, but this shit was about to go down, and I had to get back to my room before it did.

"Mom, the pizza is great, but I have a bit of an upset stomach. I'm going to lie down for a little while."

"Can I have the rest, Mom?" my brother asked, already helping himself to another slice.

"Okay, I hope you feel better," she said as I stood up. The floor undulated like it had water running through it. I hurried back to my room.

Lying on my bed with closed eyes, I saw unknown and familiar shapes filling the darkness—morphing into honeycombs and celestial bodies. Every line, point, and angle was perfectly formed, mocking our rudimentary measurements and calculations. Did they originate from my geometry books or represent a greater truth for reasons beyond ordinary cognition? It occurred to me that everything already exists—out there—in a constant state of evolution. That's how God makes the unknown known and gives the formless form. I thought about my near-death experience. I knew very little about Christianity. Yet it was an ecclesiastical vision. I must have seen those Christian icons somewhere; the unconscious mind is keeping a tally, too.

The shapes transformed like origami folding into fractals. A whooshing sound accompanied them, its origin unknown.

I calmed myself with the notion that the mushrooms were organic and that whatever was happening to me was natural. I watched Liquid Television on MTV. *Æon Flux*, a cartoon series, played. The first scene featured a woman cavorting down a hallway in a purple G-string. Next, I saw telephoto shots of mouths and eyeballs. There were boats, planes, and machine guns. Then she leapt from a tall building, performing graceful acrobatics all the way down.

The images in the animation evoked meaning and interpretations beyond what appeared on the screen. It was a new, hidden language. Flipping through channels, I came across a familiar episode of *Leave It to Beaver*, where Beaver climbs onto a billboard and falls into a cup of soup attached to it. The simpler times it evoked were comforting, yet I began questioning things I hadn't before.

Had they shrunken Beaver to make him fit into the cup of soup? Where are the people I hear laughing? Are all those scenes still happening in the past? I turned off the TV. The whooshing sound returned, or the TV may have muffled it. Why am I having these thoughts? I don't like them very much; you've got to stop fighting it. Open your eyes: four-dimensional patterns, lost civilizations, magnetic fields, bioluminescent creatures—I should have been a pair of ragged claws scuttling across the floors of silent seas... No, too much, too much. The more fearful I felt, the louder the whooshing became. I put my hand on my neck and felt my pulse. Every whoosh was synchronized with it. The sound was my heartbeat. I fell back on my bed, relieved. A whooshing sound thumped and echoed. Where is that coming from? How long have I been hearing it? I put my hand on my neck. Ah, it's my heartbeat. I lay back down, relieved. Wait a second. Didn't I just have these same thoughts? Has time stopped? I better check.

The red numbers on my clock radio were menacing. I focused: 8:45 p.m. When did I take those shrooms? I don't know. I'd planned to note the time, but I forgot. I estimated two hours had passed based on when we usually ate dinner. Eva tripped for six hours, but I don't know how much she took. It might be longer for me—far longer. With my brain, this could drag on for days! When did I watch that cartoon? What was it about?

Æon Flux. Why did they write the 'a' and 'e' that way? Stuck together. Were they once a single letter? Aesthetics, aerodynamics, aerosol. Holy shit, I've cracked the code! I thrust my arms up victoriously. A and E fit... inside ... the Parthenon. Oh, those clever Greeks. You rascals! Yes! I understand it all now! I will write a book about this soon. That book will advance humanity to the next phase of our existence ... Wait. How exactly am I going to do that? I quit thinking about Greek letters and called Sam from the phone in my room.

"Hello, is Sam there?"

"You want to talk to Sam?" his mom asked. Why did she ask that? Isn't that what I just said?

"Yeah, just for a minute. Real quick."

"Sam is doing his homework."

"Can you tell him to call me? It's Julian."

"I know. I will."

Does she know I'm tripping? Is she going to call my mom? No, that doesn't make sense. She's never spoken to my mom, but I doubt she'll tell Sam to call me back. Shit. Who else can understand what I'm going through? Hold on a second. Where am I? I looked around the little room. What's dangling over my head? I yanked down a pair of pants. Why am I sitting in my closet? How did I get here? What else have I done that I don't recall?

I found myself on the ceiling, looking down at myself. The immensity of the experience was so overwhelming that I didn't question why it was happening but knew it should not be. The other Julian stared back at me, reminding me of the many horror movies I'd seen with Sam where people were possessed, their heads spun in circles, and green goo poured from their mouths. I tried to talk to him but couldn't speak. I couldn't move at all.

"Can you hear me?" I asked myself telepathically.

"Yes," he replied.

"Can we switch places? I don't want to be up here."

"Not right now, but I'll flip over so you can see below me."

He faced the floor, and I saw beyond what had been obscured. Infinite Julians lay face-first on their beds beneath him. Are there more Julians above me? I looked up and saw Julians stretching into the distance. I looked left and right. There were Julians as far as I could see. I discovered I could change perspective and be myself from any angle. All these selves invoked a lifetime far removed from mine. Ceiling or floor? It didn't matter anymore. Aboard a ship crossing the Atlantic, I saw whitecaps crash against the hull from a porthole in my cabin. A tin plate lay on the floor at the foot of my cot. A rat scurried into a hole, but I didn't mind. "Everything is everything," I said as prisms dispersed from within myself and the objects around me.

Despite the noise on deck and kitchen clatter, I was grateful to be on board. Several weeks at sea are better than fighting in the war. All those tanks and ear-piercing sirens. The stench of dead bodies, corpses putrefying in the flooded gutters of a nation that's lost its way. How could we be so cruel? I opened my eyes as I lay in bed. Was I ever on that ship? No, but why is it so familiar? Not my lifetime. Another. Who I was and will become—but I still don't want to talk to Temple about my *real* age.

I then recalled playing with another boy in a meadow full of knee-high grass and dandelions. Our mothers chatted behind a swing set. One swing was broken, but kids found ways to entertain themselves with its single chain hanging from the frame. Over the hill, power lines ran in and out of a transformer, audibly buzzing from where we stood. I wanted to unsheathe the cables and feel their sparks surge, but the boy distracted me.

"Let's pretend we're monkeys like we saw in the movie," he suggested. We ululated unconvincingly and brachiated on the jungle gym's bars.

The boy ... Who was he? What movie did we watch? I don't know. Where did the rest of that memory go? It remains, but are the edges of its absence enough to guide me back to it? I've got to mark the days with meaning so I don't forget the past. Then I remembered I had a picture of the boy and me playing. I was overjoyed when I found the photo of us lying among a dozen other photos at the bottom of a drawer. I held it level with my eyes and saw the paradox of time—fleeting and eternal—captured in that single snapshot. I turned MTV on again and listened to songs, absorbed in the sounds. Though lyrics may have many meanings, we feel the same beat in the music box of our hearts, whose melody is the blood pulsing through us. The sights and sounds of cinema are similar, spanning time and space. Scenes captured in celluloid transcend the past. They seem to change, even though we're the ones who aren't the same.

The telephone rang. What time is it? All the digits danced fuzzily on the clock. The shrooms hadn't worn off yet. How will I know when it's over? Perhaps it will never end.

156

"Hello, Sam?"

"Yeah."

"Sam, everything is so weird."

"So weird," he repeated, sounding a little sad.

"Are you alright, man?"

"I don't know. They're trying to turn me into a monkey."

"Who is?"

"The people my parents are talking to. I heard them whispering on the phone."

"How are they going to turn you into a monkey?"

"Look, I don't know, Julian! There's probably a machine that can do it, and they're gonna test it on me!"

"Sam, calm down. There's no way that'll happen. It's not possible. I was thinking about being a monkey, too, but no one's going to turn me into one. It's gotta be the shrooms messing with your mind." The knots on my hardwood floor spun like pinwheels.

"Are you seeing things?" I asked.

"Yeah, different colors and stuff is moving around. Hey, I've got to go—my parents are coming. I'm going to try to act normal, then they won't turn me into a monkey."

"Sam, what's all that noise? Keep it down in there!"

"Sorry, Mom. I was just talking to Julian. I'm gonna get back to my homework now." He hung up.

Was it a mistake to give Sam half the shrooms? He'd mentioned hearing things and mind-reading, but I never gave it much thought. We were all a bit skewed. That's why my mother's always apologizing for being a lousy parent, even though she isn't. The guilt: How can you get rid of it? If you can't find a way, it grows all around you until you lose yourself in regrets. I've gotta find a way to explain that she should never feel that way. I'll do that some other time. If I tell her right now, I might start talking about monkey machines and out-of-body experiences.

Forty minutes later, I saw it was 1 a.m. The floor had stopped moving, and time resumed its usual tempo. There was a new dimension, now a part of me, I saw in a parallax view. We gather around the small space we understand, but if we embrace the

157

unknown, we can find the forms we've never seen. What no one knows is our most mystical connection.

I caught sight of myself in the mirror on the back of my bedroom door and then looked up. How many of the evening's optical illusions resulted from my remodeled mind? Could those alterations trick me in other ways? How will I know what is true? At the trip's peak, I felt like a conveyor belt was winding through my mind, filled with nonsensical ideas. Too many numbers pushed me past the answers, but at a slower pace, I could solve equations.

Around 2 a.m., the shrooms' effects had receded enough for me to shut my eyes, free of random images and sounds. While I saw some far-out stuff, the absence of spinning shapes and multilayered semiotics had the greatest impact on me. The quiet of my mind was no longer something to escape. It was something to appreciate, and this was the ultimate lesson. There is goodness in the world, but so much of it is lost in the busy shuffle of our lives.

Dawn broke, delivering the world from darkness. I walked behind my house to a tall elm tree, placed my hand on it, and admired its Shiva-like limbs reaching for the sun. It was autumn, and half the leaves were red—beautiful in the breaking light of day. I'd seen the tree cycle through seasons but never considered its longevity, persisting beyond my lifetime. *'Before the beginning and after the end.'*

***

"Did you really think your parents were trying to turn you into a monkey?" I asked Sam as we sat in his room the next day. He'd removed all his horror movie posters, and his walls were free of any media other than his drawings. They had expressive shapes and a good use of color. I liked them. When I asked Sam why he took the posters down, he said he'd outgrown them, but it was apparent they were also creeping him out.

"Did I say that? Turning into a monkey? No way, man." Sam laughed half-heartedly.

"Yes, Sam, you did. I was worried about you, but I get it, man. Those shrooms were way more intense than I expected."

"Nah, you're bugging out over nothing, J. I was too damn high when I said that monkey shit, which I don't remember saying. I had a joint to chill me out when the shrooms hit. Next time, I won't smoke weed while I'm tripping."

"Next time? I'm not doing anything like that for a while. I felt like I wasn't coming back until the trip was almost over. I'll stick to reality for now."

"Okay, you say that, but Temple has some acid. That's the real deal. It's way cooler than shrooms. You know Ethan, right? The guy who lives in the big yellow house at the end of my street?"

"Yeah, his sister Stacy is in my biology class. She's cute, but we've never talked about anything besides cell division and homeostasis. Have you ever talked to her?"

"A long time ago, but don't bother. We used to go to the same church. She'll ramble about the Twelve Apostles for months before you get in her pants. But Ethan dropped acid, and he was telling me that when he listens to music or watches movies, it's at a new level now, like it woke him up."

"I don't know. I don't think I'll do it. You should take it easy, too. I don't want you to get stuck in that monkey state of mind."

"I told you that was nothing. It was the weed talking. I'm fine now."

I glanced at his mostly barren bedroom walls, and then we went downstairs. His mom and dad were poring over bills piled high on their kitchen table. It reminded me of the final scene in countless family films: a moment of worry, praying for the stingy bankers to be merciful. What are we going to do? Where are we going to live? Then, Pow! Out of the blue, a surprise oil well inheritance saves the day. Pop rips up the half-signed deed and tells the debt collector they're not going anywhere, and the credits roll.

"Don't they have installment plans, Ted? Can't we consolidate our debt and pay a lower rate?" Sam's mom suggested.

"Donna, that'll keep them off our backs for a few months, but they always win. You pay more in interest and only prolong the pain.

Don't worry. It ain't over yet. I'll be pounding the pavement tomorrow—whatever it takes."

Donna shut her eyes and did a facepalm.

Chapter 15

It took several days to feel normal again. The drug's effects had worn off, but the presence of new modes of consciousness intrigued and terrified me until they wove into the fabric of the world I knew. A world reborn.

Walking out to my ride soon after the trip, I smelled a garbage truck approaching. Men hopped off, tossing bags and dumping trashcans into the belly of it. Wait ... is that who I think it is?

"Hi Julian, Good morning." It was Sam's dad. He was working in sync with two bigger, brawnier men, wearing the same gray overalls as him, emptying trash cans at adjacent houses. He scooted over to me.

"Hey, Julian, do you know what's up with Sam? He's been quiet and gets confused lately. Do you know if he's been doing drugs?"

"Hustle up, Ted!" one of the brawny guys shouted as the truck started rolling.

"No, I don't think so. Sam never said anything about that to me," I lied. He looked at me, on the verge of saying more, then gave me a quick nod and hurried down the street.

***

"Don't you want to see the real world, Julian? LSD unlocks colors, chakras, and states of mind exclusive to those who've passed through the doors of perception. Once you cut all the lies away, you won't need their toys and two-week vacations. You can sit by a tree and be satisfied," Temple proselytized, motioning toward a sheet of acid he'd cut up into individual tabs atop a splintering wooden desk he'd recently added to his collection. Then he swiveled, paired with kicks and punches that resembled jujitsu. He liked to do that when attractive females were around, like the three teens who'd stopped by to get some weed. I called his version nitwitsu.

161

What he said wasn't lost on me. I still yearned to see more of the other side he spoke about, but the fear of overloading my mind made me hesitate. "I dunno. I think those mushrooms were enough for now. I felt like I was racing toward a point I'd never return from. I've heard about people on permatrips wandering around and talking to themselves."

"That's not from drugs," Sam countered, flashing a grin at the girls. "If that happens, they're already crazy. That's the kind of thing they tell you in those big assembly halls at school. They want everyone to think the same way so we're easier to control." It had been over a month since our shroom trip. He'd been increasingly paranoid but had begun acting more like his old self.

"I've done it twice; it's fun," James encouraged me after retreating to a couch with two of the girls. They were the same age as him and Eva, who wasn't around.

I started leaning towards dropping acid with them. The shrooms tested my resolve, but I got through the trip. This time, I'd be better equipped. If there is a sky above the sky and worlds beyond the one I know, how can I reach them without drugs such as LSD?

"I'll tell you what, Julian, why don't you try one of those sugar cubes I dosed? There's less acid in them. One of those will take you on a trip that lasts only a few hours." Temple motioned again toward the desk, where a cup half-filled with sugar cubes sat alongside the squares he'd cut from the blotter paper.

The tabs beside the cubes were orange, each imprinted with a smiling sun. I studied them, picturing one dissolving on my tongue, transporting me into a lucid realm where the humming could be heard, and the Mystery was solved. But they also reminded me of a story I'd heard at a high school assembly, similar to those Sam had criticized. A police officer told us about a girl who went blind from staring at the sun while tripping on LSD. Her retinas burned out when she mistook it for a friendly ball of fire dancing in the clouds.

The sun peeked through the buildings across the courtyard. I looked at it, then shut my eyes, concentrating on the negative image that remained. If I drop LSD now, how soon will I lose my reason? What if I end up like the girl? I'm already half-blind; I don't want to lose what's left. I recalled the man who warned me not to play with guns and how I wished I'd listened to him. Even if the policeman's warnings were lies, I didn't want to risk it.

"Nah, I'll just hang with you guys. Make sure you don't jump off a bridge or something."

"Suit yourself, J, but it's time for me to fly," Sam said, grabbing the cup and tossing several cubes into his mouth. I thought he should abstain, but a short trip would be better if he insisted on taking LSD. How much acid could be in those cubes, anyway?

"My man!" James gave Sam a high-five, followed by cheers from Temple as he stroked the Fu Manchu he was growing. James stuck two smiling suns on his tongue, extended it to show me, and then swallowed them.

"I was trying to free you from the chains, bro. You don't see them, but they're there. I guess not everyone's meant to be free." Temple said. Oh well. Fuck him and his broken surfboard.

Temple didn't partake in the trip. He waxed poetic about riding moonbeams and communing with shamans, but I'd only seen him take a courtesy hit when someone handed him a bong with smoke rippling out the top, and even then, I was sure he didn't inhale it.

After James kissed all three girls goodbye, we left Temple's pad and walked toward the University campus. Sam shared his thoughts about his dad's new job as a trashman, which motivated him to toss back the sugar cubes.

"I don't want to be hauling trash like my dad. I respect he's no slouch, but I ain't about to live a life of boredom with a couple of kids in the same town I grew up in like him. That's why I did shrooms with you and took the cubes. You gotta take chances to live the life you want. I don't know if I'll feel anything, but I'm cool with however it goes. I've been thinking that I should be an artist. I've always been into movies and music, and I'm pretty good at drawing, don't you think?"

"Really good. I like your drawings. They're a little far out, though. What are you thinking about when you draw them?"

"Ha, are you bugging out about those little green and gray guys? I gotta take all those pictures and make a movie with them someday.

This will sound crazy, but sometimes I can communicate with aliens and tap into other worlds. It's gonna make me famous; you'll see."

It sounded pretty crazy.

"Maybe your dad understands more than you think. What if he's actually a philosopher?" James observed, rubbing his chin.

"Dude, he's a trashman. You don't have to think; all you gotta do is toss shit in the truck."

"Didn't you watch *Fraggle Rock*? Remember that wise old trash heap? He was kicking all kinds of knowledge."

"I forgot about the Fraggles! I used to watch that and *The Smurfs* every Saturday morning. Remember all those spells Papa Smurf cast and their mushroom houses? You gotta be tripping to come up with a cartoon like that. But I quit watching them and got into horror flicks a long-ass time ago," Sam said.

"I remember those shows. I ain't gonna lie; I peeped the *Care Bears*, too, but those were the dark days before I had cable, and there was nothing else on TV. I think that trash heap in *Fraggle Rock* was a lady, though," I recalled.

"It was a dude!" James insisted.

"No, her name was Marjory. She hung out with two rats—Philo and Gunge," Temple corrected, surprisingly well-versed in Fraggle lore.

"I ain't talking to no trash heap, but if I was a Fraggle, I'd be that old guy with the Indiana Jones hat who sends postcards from outer space," Sam asserted, then looked around curiously. I sensed his famous green and gray friends were about to communicate with him.

While we walked, I remembered the Fraggle with the fedora was Uncle Traveling Matt, and he called the world beyond Fraggle Rock outer space. Similar to how Sam saw aliens and spaceships in the same place where I lived an ordinary life. Am I missing out on something? Should I have tripped with them? ... No, I've already been somewhere far beyond what I saw on shrooms while my brain reassembled. How many live to tell that tale? It's better to sit by a tree and be satisfied for now.

***

"How long have I been talking? Time keeps stopping and starting," Sam asked about thirty minutes later.

"Oh, you haven't been talking that long. Only a minute or two. Don't worry." I was certain Sam would be sending postcards from outer space now.

"Whoa, it's so cool. I see trails," Sam said, waving his hands in circles in front of his face as we continued past Friendly's, where I owned one of the tiles.

"Woo, yeah, yeah." James copied him, waving his hands in big circles like he was spinning fire poi.

"What do you see?" I asked James.

"Yo, you shoulda dropped if you want to know that."

"I'll do it next time. Tell me."

"It's like someone left the camera shutter open. All the light streaks and stretches."

As night fell, drivers turned on their headlights. Temple and James crossed the street toward the long, grassy mall in the center of campus. As we got closer, students and townsfolk eyed us suspiciously. Sam stood motionless on the sidewalk.

"Yo, J, can you walk across the street with me? I can't tell where one car begins and the other ends. It's like one long light."

"Okay, grab my arm and we'll cross." Sam held on to me with both hands, swiveling his head while we walked.

"Are those people talking about me?"

"No, they're talking about a movie," I lied as Sam gripped my arm and jerked his head around, following real and imaginary lights and who knows what else.

"Lazarus rose from his tomb because he was *righteous*. Our beloved Earth remembers him and all of them. Even that tree. Look at that tree—can you see how it carries the world and cradles the sky? The tree has seeds, and those seeds will become trees with more seeds." James exclaimed with gestures that probably had great meaning for him but no one else. We walked among throngs of students, enjoying the evening as shadows lengthened across campus until nothing but lampposts and a smattering of fluorescent

165

lights shining out of classroom windows illuminated the evening. Temple stayed quiet, following close behind.

Three hours later, I found Sam muttering in the middle of a flight of stairs.

"What is it, Sam? What are you talking about?" I knelt, reaching eye level with him.

"Julian, I shouldn't have done so much acid. All of it was a lot. I might've taken ten hits. I'm swimming inside myself. I feel like there are oceans inside of me. I'll never do drugs again. This is the last time. Julian, don't let me do any drugs again."

"Do you want to go home?" I asked.

"No, no. My dad's already been asking me too many questions. 'What people? Where? Why are you spending so much time in your room?' They'll send me away."

"Okay. Try to relax. Focus on me. I'll stay with you until it's over. I don't think you'll be tripping much longer."

We walked among the thickening crowd. Temple rested his hand on Sam's shoulder, startling him.

"You feeling okay, man? You sure took a big dose with those cubes. I don't know if I ever took that much."

Meanwhile, James trotted around students with his arms spread like a five-year-old pretending to be an airplane. About ten stopped to watch him, but he was having a good time, so I shifted my attention to Sam and whatever creepy thing Temple was doing.

"Yeah, but I'll be okay if I sit here for a bit," Sam replied.

"He's doing alright, but I'm going to take him back to my place soon. He'll be better off with fewer people around," I told Temple.

"That won't help. It's better to distract Sam. That'll calm him down," Temple said.

James's make-believe plane landed, and he came over, drooling but still in high spirits.

"Hey Sam, I don't mean to upset you, but you just shit your pants," Temple informed him. "You took a big old dump, and everyone's laughing at you."

"Really? I don't feel anything."

Temple nodded as he tried not to laugh.

166

Sam patted his rear end frantically. "My pants are dry. I don't think I shit myself. Are you sure?"

"Yeah, man. Can't you smell that? Damn, what did you eat? You better go to the bathroom and clean yourself up."

Sam reached down his pants with both hands, felt around, and declared, "I did not shit my pants!" Then he dropped them to his ankles and pointed at his bare white ass. "See? There's nothing there. So shut the fuck up!"

Temple trembled with laughter.

"What is he doing? Why did he take his pants off?" James asked, bug-eyed, in awe of Sam's bare buttocks.

"Sam, pull up your pants!" I demanded, "You did not shit your pants." He yanked them up. Several people laughed and pointed, but most hadn't noticed.

"Cut it out, Temple. You're making him feel worse. How much acid was in those cubes?"

"Not much. Two or three drippy drops, but that's nothing, man. People took ten times that much in the sixties."

Had he also added "drippy drops" to the shrooms? That would explain a few things.

"Well, I'm taking him home," I told Temple. I was worried about Sam and bugged out because it could have been me tripping on a megadose of LSD.

"He'll be fine, Julian. You can't overdose on acid; he won't even remember this. It's like a tribal initiation. The first time I dropped, people were messing with me, too. After it was over, we all laughed. Chill, bro."

I wanted to ditch Temple, but he was having too much fun to shake him. The three of them made me feel like I was tripping, too. We moved off-campus to 7-Eleven, where Sam had teased me for calling the cops on myself.

Watching Tweedledee and Tweedledum reduced to babbling lunatics as Temple scavenged the meat from their bones reminded me of all the times I'd felt vulnerable. I never wanted to feel that way again. I remembered when my mother raised my allowance and how happy I was when I could buy more things at the same store we were at now. I didn't need acid, weed, or far-out places. I needed more money. A quarter of a million was a good start, but money isn't just for the Requirements of the Imagination. Money is required for everything.

"Do you know where you are right now?" Temple asked Sam, facing him with a hand planted on each shoulder.

"7-Eleven?" Sam replied, arching his eyebrow.

"No. You're in your living room. You've been sitting there for years. Your mom is crying because you haven't moved in days. You live in your mind now. Everything is only in your mind."

"Yo, is what he's saying to Sam true?" James grabbed my arm and asked.

Stop messing with him, Temple! He can't handle it. Sam, none of that is true. Let's go back to my place."

Temple raised his hands in mock surrender, palms open. Without another word, I led Sam away. I wouldn't have minded if James had tagged along, but I didn't want to add a battle with my mother to the already troublesome evening.

"I'm freaking out, J. What year is it? How long have I been tripping? Where are you taking me? You can't let them lock me up," Sam sobbed. I consoled him as best I could, and we made it back to my house after what felt like forever. My mom and brother were home.

"Mom, Sam's staying here tonight, okay?"

"Okay, Julian."

I ushered him to the basement.

"There are eyes all over the walls. They're blinking and moving around. Are the men upstairs? Are they outside? Where are they?" Sam said.

I grabbed some leftover Xanax tablets from the medicine cabinet, along with a glass of water. When I returned, I found Sam gazing into the starry night while something more like madness than magic spun inside him.

"I saw men riding seahorses between the stars. Now I see two big elephants," Sam said, wide-eyed. I led him away from the window.

"Elephants are noble beasts. You have no reason to fear them. Take these pills; they'll help you," I said, handing Sam the Xanax.

"I don't want any more drugs! I want this to stop." Sam may have needed more help than I could provide, but if he could sleep it off, it had to be better than facing an inquisition at home. "Remember the first time we hopped a train. I ran across the roof to find you, and then we all jumped off together?" I reminded him.

"Oh, yeah," he laughed.

"Why would I do that if I wasn't your friend? You have to trust me. These pills will help you sleep and stop tripping. Take them and drink this water."

Sam looked at me, unsure of everything. Yet I could reach him because I wasn't a creepy drug dealer taunting him. We'd shared dreams of fame and fortune fueled by late-night horror movie marathons. I was the guy who spent hours in his room spinning old records, searching for that perfect track we could play again and again. I was the one who made plans with him to pick up chicks that never worked out. I was his friend. He took the pills.

Chapter 16

I was in the same grade as Betsy Jones, one of my next-door neighbor's three daughters and the black sheep of their family. She had strawberry-blonde hair, high cheekbones, and pillowy lips. She was well-proportioned, which was unusual considering the rest of her family was … less photogenic. She often waved to me and had a nose piercing, which her father must've thought was inappropriate, but good looks grant wishes that leave the rest of us staring into the well.

Betsy asked me for a ride home after school. She was cute, but so were plenty of other girls that didn't have hot-tempered fathers who'd eyed me suspiciously for years. Still, it was a short drive, and then she could tell Papa Jones what a nice guy I was.

"Did you really overdose on cocaine when the police came to your house?" Betsy asked.

"No, it was crack. Didn't your dad tell you?" I said, pulling out of the parking lot.

"What! Where do you get that? Do you sell it at school?"

"Betsy, I'm joking. I had a panic attack. You know I got shot in the head, right?"

"Yeah, I heard about that. Are you okay?"

"You're not the first to ask, and the answer is probably no, but when the cops came that day, it was because of this dumb thing related to my injury and the medicine I had to take. No cocaine or crack pipes were involved."

"Are you sure? My dad said you're a drug dealer. Do you know where I can get some weed? You don't have to hide that from me. It's okay. I just want to try it once! My dad's way too uptight about that sort of stuff. It's lame. I know he's lame sometimes, okay?"

I started wishing I hadn't given Betsy a ride, even though I enjoyed sneaking peeks at her skirt and bare legs dangling from the seat.

"No. No drug dealing. No drugs. They're bad for you; forget about them. You know that guy Sam who lives a street over from us?"

"Yeah, my dad said he deals drugs too and that he's crazy."

"He doesn't deal drugs either, but he lost his mind using them. You don't need weed. You should join a sports team or the school band. Imagine how much fun you could have with an oboe."

"Now you sound like my dad. Sorry about your friend Sam, though. Okay, if you don't deal drugs, do you know where I can buy some weed? Wanna share a joint with me? I gotta try it at least once. I won't tell anyone. I swear, Julian."

Smoke weed with her? No thanks. I'd rather wear that half-moon helmet again.

"You realize your dad would slide a steak knife into my gut for even thinking about that, right? What's he like? Is he always angry?"

"Ha, ha, no. He's a good guy. I love him to death, but he's overprotective—especially with me since guys are a little more into me than my sisters."

I glanced at her and said, "Well, that's understandable. You do look ... nice."

"You too, Julian. You looked cute when you dyed your hair blond and spiked it up."

"Uh-huh, thank you. That's fabulous."

I had that dye job when I was fourteen—before I got shot. Betsy was still angling for weed.

"Fabulous? Um, okay. I don't hear many people say that anymore."

"Yep, I still like that old-time stuff." We arrived. Betsy thanked me for the ride and stepped out, swinging her hips as she ascended her stairs. I gripped the wheel and chuckled, recalling my conversation with Minty in the school cafeteria. "Sexy Mama Olympics." I was no expert in these matters, but I was confident Betsy was qualified to be on the team. Ah, shit. Why did she have to have such a dickhead dad?

Later that evening, while doing my homework, a police car pulled up in front of my house. He put on a little show with flashing lights but spared everyone the annoyance of his siren. As he pulled up, Betsy's father greeted him, and they approached my house. Mr. Jones clasped his hands and looked toward the heavens with a gesture that was both giddy and pious. The officer rapped hard on my door, and I knew a bunch of bullshit was about to go down.

Soon enough, the officer, Mr. Jones, my mother, and I were all seated in the living room. The cop started questioning me about transporting a minor off school grounds.

"But I'm also a minor," I protested. Betsy and I were both seventeen.

My mother shook her head.

"You can be tried as an adult. This is serious," the officer warned.

"Betsy asked Julian for a ride home. How is that his fault? Shouldn't you be having this conversation with your daughter, Bill?" my mother protested. My brother peeked out of his room and then slipped out of sight.

Ignoring the plain truth of the matter, Bill reignited his quixotic take on the time I freaked out about my anticonvulsant pills.

"I don't want your drug-addicted son selling my daughter any of that crap people like him stick up their noses. I'm doing you a favor by even coming here. Boy, keep your distance from Betsy and my family, understand?"

Boy? He sounded like he was reading from a bad movie script. Why did this man spend so much time hating me when I never gave him a second thought? It infuriated me and demanded a response.

"I didn't give anything to your daughter other than the ride she requested. I'm not a drug addict, dope dealer, or whoever you think I am. That night, when the police came to my house, I thought I was having a seizure. It'd had nothing to do with whatever drugs you think I'm pushing. Why else would they leave without arresting me? Which one of us has brain damage, huh?"

"You watch your mouth, boy!"

"You watch your mouth, boy! I haven't done anything wrong. Your problem is your overactive imagination. If you want me out of your life, then close your blinds. It's that simple."

The officer patted the air with his palms and said, "Let's all calm down. Julian, you steer clear of Betsy and the Joneses, and I'll let you off with a warning. All right, everyone agree with that?"

Bill sneered and slicked back his hair. "Yeah, we'll let it go for now. But I'll be watching you, Julian. Waiting for you to fuck up. Next time, I'll make sure you get locked up. So don't even think about doping up with my daughter."

As I'd told Betsy, even my thoughts were felonious, according to Daddy Jones.

We all stood up. Bill and the officer left without another word. "Be careful around that family. I'm glad you stood up for yourself, but now just avoid them," my mother advised.

"Why's Betsy so much better looking than her sisters? Was she adopted?"

"Don't concern yourself with that. Enough about the Joneses. How about you get back to your books so you can get a good job and prove that idiot Bill wrong."

"Okay, Mom."

I tried to finish my schoolwork but was too worked up. Sometimes, I wished we were still in our old neighborhood. Things had slipped, but people didn't rat you out over their delusions there. Maybe you couldn't lift them up, but they didn't bring you down. Goddamn suburbia. Goddamn Betsy. I hope that sexy mama does get hooked on drugs. Who will Bill blame then? What a bunch of motherfuckers!

***

"Looks like you grew some balls, didn't you, boy?"

"Is that your Bill Jones impression?"

"No, not necessarily. Men of my ... elevated stature naturally address men of your ... lower station ... as, boy," James replied as we sat in the International Scout outside Temple's apartment.

"Well, I showed him what's up. He hasn't raised those blinds since I broke him down with my street logic."

"Street logic? You've never left Merriweather Lane."

"Whatever. Jackass Jones can die for all I care. I hate that motherfucker."

"I see. But didn't you say we should learn to love and not hate?"

"No, that was Jesus, God, or some imaginary being that spoke to me while I was comatose. There's no way Jesus wants us to love him. Why should we even try with people like that?"

"Have you considered that Bill Jones might be exactly the type of person Jesus wants you to love? It's easy to love people who love you back. The ones who hate you need the most compassion."

For a moment, I thought I was talking to Mateo. Then I recalled James had similar Christian influences, though they got him kicked out of his house. Yes, it's easy to love people who love you. It's easy to say we should choose love over hate, but what about the roaring masses filled with impenetrable animosity—the ones who hate you from the day you were born? You can't just stand there and take it if they come out swinging. You have to defend yourself. That's not about love or hate. It's survival.

"Have you seen Sam lately?" James asked.

"I saw him a week ago. They've got him on lithium, and he's not talking about aliens and the FBI anymore. I'm sure he's still thinking about that stuff, but he suppresses it better. He was always different, you know? He loved watching horror movies and drawing things that made me wonder what was cooking in his mind. Still, I never thought a couple of trips would unlock whatever madness was inside him."

"A lot of that sort of thinking ought to stay in the back of our heads. Society couldn't function if we were all hallucinating, hearing voices, and feasting on each other's flesh. Although, I sometimes wonder why there are so many zombie movies. But what some call madness is genius; what some call insanity might be the cure for cancer or the creation of atomic energy. You never know where your twisted thoughts will take you. Madness calls to many of us, but only a few can wrangle it into something useful," James argued, abruptly tilting back the passenger seat. The seats were rusted and jerked back whenever you reclined. I sat upright, thinking about what he said.

Temple continued luring young girls to his drug-fueled festivals, even targeting girls from the junior high school I'd attended. How did he get away with it? It was baffling, but he occupied the only place in town where anything was happening, so we headed back inside.

"What's up with that Sam kid who used to come around here, Julian? Doesn't he like to party anymore?" Temple asked, ignoring his part in Sam's unsociable state.

"Sam hasn't been the same since that sugar cube trip. He mostly keeps to himself, walking his dog around the neighborhood. I still talk to him, but he doesn't always recognize me at first."

"That's too bad," Temple said, only partially interested in the conversation, as he grinned at a pair of girls snorting cocaine on a glass table to the right of us. Without facing me, he said, "I liked that guy; he was funny, but the universe is a big place. Not everyone is meant to explore it."

Temple had decorated his walk-in closet with posters and paint, which glowed when he flicked on a black light. It had pillows along the periphery and a wooden stool partially obscured by an empty bookshelf. Under the influence of various substances, his closet became quite the funhouse.

"Temple's a bit of a perv," James said as he saw me trying to see what was happening behind the bookshelf a little later. I craned my neck and saw Temple with his pants down, encouraging a doped-up junior high chick with purple hair and heavy glitter on her eyelids to fellate him.

"He likes getting his dick sucked on that stool, but he never shuts the door. He's an exhibitionist."

I was both horrified and captivated. Like a car crash you can't look away from, you wonder, What if that were me?

"Sure, take a peek, but don't go in there. Lots of sticky spots," James warned as I lingered on the voyeuristic end of the equation, and he faded into the crowd.

"Suck it, baby; don't just put it in your mouth. Mmm, yeah. It's called a blow job, but you gotta suck. That's it, baby; treat it like a lollipop."

175

Now I had a clear shot of the waifish girl bobbing back and forth as Temple thrust his hips in an unyielding, peristaltic rhythm. I gazed beyond the walls. I may have only been half-blind, but what else hadn't I seen ...

***

"No, I can't do it. It'll hurt."

"Jules ... come on, do it. We're having fun. It's just a game. After this, you can ask me to do something crazy."

Gil had free rein to play increasingly fucked up games while my father was away working on a new business venture.

It started when Gil suggested running around the house with our clothes off. "It'll be like playing in the woods ... like camping. We can make a tent under some blankets, too. That'll be easier than setting up a real one!" he said. I didn't want him to see my dick dangling around, but he'd been nice to me since I woke up, so I went along with it.

Years ago, when my father first relocated to California, I was afraid of the pine tree outside my bedroom with branches that tapped against my window. I lay unable to sleep, watching its disorderly limbs transform into monsters. However, I started talking to the spooky tree and soon became convinced we were friends. Sitting naked on the floor next to Gil was a chance to form a similar alliance.

But once our clothes were off, there was no frolicking in an imaginary forest or playing under makeshift tents. Gil pointed to the mouth of a soda bottle and prodded me to "stick it in there."

"You run on that treadmill first," I instructed him, not wanting to play but not having much choice.

"Sounds fun, all right." Gil ran naked on the treadmill, his penis flopping around. I looked curiously at the curly black hairs above it.

"Alright, now it's your turn." He stepped off the treadmill and handed me the bottle again. I tried to do as he'd directed, but my dick wouldn't fit. I worried we'd have to break the bottle if I managed to get it in, so I refused to keep playing his perverted game.

Gil sat beside me and leaned to the right. "Okay, stick it here instead," he pointed toward his raised rear end.

"No, why would I do that?"

His penis got a lot bigger.

"Fine, then I'm sticking mine in yours," he pushed me down with his forearm. Why is he doing this? I could barely breathe.

"That hurts. Stop it. You're hurting me. Let's play another game. Stop ..."

The front door creaked open.

"Hola, is anyone home?"

It was Carmen, our housekeeper from Peru. She was married to one of my father's partners.

"Put your clothes on; hurry up. Now! Don't fuck around."

I happily yanked my underwear back on, but that evening, I didn't feel like talking to the tree.

***

"Don't use your teeth, baby. Just your lips. Uh-huh. That's it. That's good, real good." Temple had both hands on the semiconscious girl's head, guiding her back and forth.

My fingernails dug into my palms. I thought of all the horror shows happening in rooms no one sees. How many are never saved because the wicked go uncontested? I retreated to the living room, a storm brewing in my mind. I'd seen enough. I had to get out of there.

Then it hit me that my father had gaslighted me about who he'd wanted to be but never became. Until that moment, I hadn't been able to see it for what it was. The old man was so obsessed with getting even with my mother that he'd let me be tortured before admitting anything happened that didn't fit his designs to win custody of me. But no, it was not a benign rite of passage between boys. It was years of torment and abuse. No, he wasn't restraining my mother to help with her histrionics. He was afraid to let her go. I could've forgiven his failings if he'd been brave when I needed him. He wasn't there for me—but this is my life—my time. Even if I can't save the world from self-destruction, I can still do this. I can stop what's happening to that girl. That's good enough for me.

Another party was underway across the hall, with rap music bumping and a beer keg at the center of attention.

Once the idea came, I couldn't let it go. I edged around the keg and waved to a girl sipping a salt-rimmed margarita. "Who is that guy?" she asked the girl beside her. Boom, boom, boom—it was noisy in the room. I grabbed the phone behind them and tried to form a seal with my hand.

"911, what's your emergency?"

"Oh, um, can you connect me to Officer Elias at the Newark Police Department?"

"Sir, what is your emergency? I'm not your secretary. Call the police if you want to speak with a specific officer."

"Please, I have an emergency, but I can't call them directly. I don't have their number."

There was a brief pause on the line. Rap gave way to disco, and partygoers swiveled their hips, thrusting their hands into the air.

The operator spoke, "I'm connecting you to the police. Next time, call their number directly."

"Newark police, how may I direct your call?"

"Is Officer Elias available?"

"Do you mean Lieutenant Emilio Elias?"

The officer who spoke to my brother and me when I thought I was having a seizure had a new role, but he was the same guy who'd told me that he hated seeing young people mess up their lives with drugs.

"Yes, that's right."

"Hold on."

"Hello, this is Lieutenant Elias."

"Hello, sir; uh, there's something you should know. I live in City Hall apartments, across from unit C11, and there's a guy there named Temple that's got a bunch of drugs he's been giving girls; some of them look about fourteen, and he's making them do sexual stuff."

"Is this a prank call?"

178

"No, but that's funny. You asked me the same thing the last time we spoke. You probably don't remember, but you told me you hate seeing kids doing drugs, and I'm sure that hasn't changed. I promise you this is not a prank. I don't know what Temple's giving them, but after they're doped up, he molests them."

"Did you say he arrests them? It's a little hard to hear you. Can you turn that music off?"

A beefy guy with biceps filling his shirt sleeves looked at me suspiciously.

"I'm sorry, I can't talk much longer. But if you come right now, you'll see for yourself. This guy, Temple, is giving kids drugs and then *molesting* them. There are drugs all over the place. City Hall apartments, unit C11. That's all I can tell you. Please come as quickly as you can."

I hung up and bolted out of the apartment. I made a sharp right and went outside. I didn't want the beefy guy to see me going anywhere near Temple's. I immediately regretted making the call. What if someone finds out it was me? What about the whole scumbag drug-dealing circuit Temple is part of? But what he did to Sam and all those girls who'll be traumatized for life just so he can get off in his closet. No, it's worth the risk. I can still right the wrong.

Then I thought of James. Oh, shit, I didn't want him caught up in a sting if the cops were even coming. I walked around the corner to the sliding glass door at Temple's. James was nearby. I slid it open. When did I call them? Has it already been five minutes? Are they coming?

"Hey, James, come over here for a minute."

"What's up, International? Why don't you step inside? It's a little chilly out there."

Only James and Eva called me that; the Scout suffix had dropped off.

"No, I'm heading home soon, but I want to talk to you about something first. It'll just take a minute."

"All right, you old scallywag, don't get your knickers in a bunch." James stepped outside.

"Hey, let's sit in the Scout."

"Yo, we got a party going on. Lay it on me. Whatcha got?"

"Nah, it's too noisy here. Come on, let's go sit in the Scout."

We returned to the rugged yellow off-roader.

"Have you ever heard of Charles Bukowski? I saw that guy with a tiger tattoo on his neck reading one of his books in front of Jam'n Java. He writes poetry, too. It's not forced or flowery. It's real—there's no apology or pretense. He doesn't bother with easily digestible prose that people gently applaud or try to score any literary awards. He bangs out what the muse tells him, even if it's ten lines about him taking a hot shit in a flophouse. Bukowski's got the word down, man. He can see the color between gray bricks while looking up from a filthy mattress on the floor and find the five seconds of peace that keep you from losing your mind at a bus stop with less than a dollar in your pocket."

"What? You brought me out here to discuss a guy soaking up five seconds of color at a bus stop while he takes a dump?"

"Yeah, those are the moments that define us."

"Whoa, whoa, whoa. What's this? Five-O up in this piece?" James observed.

An unmarked police car had parked in front of Temple's place. This was evident because it was the same make and model as regular, marked police cars. It was further validated when two officers in uniform stealthily approached the sliding glass door. James had left the curtain wide open when we bounced. Bongs, cocaine, blotter sheets, and bleary-eyed meth heads on the floor were all easy to see, even from our perch fifty feet away. James and I shot our seats back flat. I wished the Scout could spark up and get us out of there. I still wanted to redo the last decade, but a trip around the block would've sufficed.

With considerable effort, we raised our seats and watched what was happening. A mix of semiconscious, blissed-out, and highly agitated individuals straddled the line between altered states and the unalterable fact that they were all about to be busted. Less intoxicated partygoers ran as four more police cars arrived. The cops chased after them.

"What the fuck is this?" James asked.

"Maybe the neighbors complained?" I suggested, wishing I'd steered the conversation further from the truth.

"Nah, if it doesn't involve getting drunk or laid, they don't care, but my mother would shed a tear. My sister would capture it in a tiny vial to commemorate the day when the Lord spared me from being locked in the backseat of one of those squad cars. Finally, he watches over me. Who was that author you were telling me about? Buckley? Clearly, our Heavenly Father wants me to read one of his books."

"Charles Bukowski. Check out *The Last Night of the Earth Poems*. I like 'Young in New Orleans' the best." I didn't dare tell him I'd called the police. Like he'd said, as long as he was entertained, did the truth matter?

"I spent some time in Louisiana courting Southern belles and eating fried crocodile. One in particular caught my eye. Her name was Natalie. She was always moping around, listening to The Smiths. Damn, those were dreary jams, but she had such a nice, sweet way about her. It all went down in a small town called Natchitoches at a Christian revival. I have relatives there. You shoulda seen 'em wailing when they laid hands on people under the Big Tent! Some of them took liberties I don't think the Lord woulda been too happy about when they weren't under that tent, but the Lord's always watching, remember that. I would've liked to get to know Natalie biblically, if you know what I mean, but thanks to Morrissey, I only got a couple of kisses," James said.

"I haven't read the whole Bible, but I went to church once. I'd never been inside one and wanted to know what it was like. The sermon wasn't exactly Blues Brothers material, but I liked the wine and crackers they served."

"That wasn't a Sunday snack, my soul-seeking brother—that was Holy Communion."

"Oh, I didn't know that, but I've had bad luck with crackers. I got shot while I was munching on some Ritz Bits. I went to church after I met Jesus, and by then, I loved him. Do you think I'll be okay? I only had one cracker and a sip of wine."

James smirked. "You're supposed to be baptized first, but since you've already had a little one-on-one time with the Lord, he'll probably tack on a hundred push-ups before he lets you through the Pearly Gates."

I laughed, but my mind drifted to deeper questions. If Jesus is the Lord, why did he cry out to God that he'd been forsaken? Aren't they the same person? If I went back in time, I could meet Jesus, the man, but if I follow his law, I'll see him in the afterlife. Will my soul exist for eternity? I cherished the serenity of the Holy Place, and I don't want to go to hell, but... is Heaven boring? I could learn to paint or play the guitar, but after a couple of years, I'd need to do something else. Does time work differently there?

I turned to James for insight, and he listened more intently than before. "During my near-death experience, there was a moment when Jesus put me in a little room, and his voice was reverberating in my head. He did that to show me what life would be like if I wasn't kind. I wasn't in the room long, but even getting shot wasn't as terrifying as that. After I agreed to be kind, Jesus showed me a light and invited me to sit beside him. Then I heard his voice—just like we're talking now—but it had become soothing. That taught me the virtue of following his law and being kind.

"I feel a connection to Moses and Abraham, but Jesus is different. I felt warmth and affection the moment I saw him, and when I sat beside him, the way he spoke and looked at me made me realize he embodies limitless love and compassion. I told my mom about the spiritual visions I had while I was in a coma, and she suggested talking to a rabbi, but I didn't because of all the Christian elements. I told my hospital roommate about my near-death experience, too, but he mostly found it amusing because it was even harder to explain back then. After that, I started reading the Bible and went to church once, but I haven't felt like anyone could help me understand it until I met you."

"I've given you a couple pointers already, but tomorrow we'll get serious. *Eye of the Tiger*. I'll have you doing 100 push-ups in no time."

What would James ask God?

"Whoa, busted!" James celebrated, not commenting further about what I'd said as Temple was perp-walked out in handcuffs. I thought seeing his paymaster carted away would upset him, but he preferred madness over reason. Hanging out with James always taught me something, and I was sure I had more to learn from him, but his love of fanciful stories and the demons he was fighting made it hard to know how much of what he said I could trust.

Temple's head was uncovered, revealing a bald pate that contrasted sharply with the long hair he'd grown around it. I suspected he was hiding something under his cap, but I hadn't fathomed the complexity of his combover. My old man had a combover for a while, but his weave was less elaborate and didn't require a hat to hold in place. As the cops approached their van, Temple's legs gave out, and they had to carry him.

I couldn't judge anyone for hiding their hair loss, having also resorted to concealing mine, starting my sophomore year when a boy poked my head during gym class and announced, "Check it out! Julian's going bald! He's got a big old bald spot on the back of his head!"

"What? I'm not bald! I've still got all my hair." I'd retorted, brushing back my still moderately healthy locks, which had prematurely thinned due to an unpropitious combination of genetics and head trauma.

Luckily, a dodgeball hit him before he could mock me again.

After class that evening, positioning a second mirror behind me, I saw the hairless strip from my scar that had delighted the boy. Since then, I've hid it with a comb and enough hairspray to withstand a hurricane.

***

There were no lights or sirens, but the knock on my front door was unmistakable. A hard, rhythmic pounding rattled the hinges, indicating if I didn't open it immediately, the next sound would be the door flying off its hinges. I didn't bother looking through the peephole. I knew it was the police. I'd avoided the Joneses and gone about my business uneventfully. I suspected Temple's arrest the week before had brought them to my house. How did the police find me? James might have suspected my involvement, but he wasn't one to rat a brother out. My heart raced anyway. My mother had gone out, leaving me with Kevin, though he could take care of himself by now.

Kevin and I liked playing MUDs, also known as multiuser dungeon games. Though MUDs are text-based, their vivid descriptions provide plenty of dimension. I played as an ogre called Splitscreen, carrying an axe I used to chop people in half. Kevin was a dwarf named Triumph, which was a misnomer given that he was already the same height as me. I was always amazed that you could dial a number, listen to the modem squawk, and join thousands of other players guiding their warlocks and wizards around the same digital realm. The pounding started while we were playing one. I opened the door.

"Julian?"

"Yes?"

"May we come in? We need to talk to you about your mother, Sophia." Aside from pounding on the door, the officers were unusually polite. Over their shoulders, I saw gawkers settling in for a show. After all those years of providing such frequent and varied entertainment, we should have charged them a fee.

"Your mother fell into a creek and has hypothermia. Someone heard her splashing behind their house and called us. She's going to be alright, but she needs to stay in the hospital overnight. Are you okay watching your brother until your mother's released?"

"Yes, I can watch him. Where did this happen?" I asked, unsurprised but worried about my mother. The officer explained that she'd fallen into the creek behind the neighborhood beside ours, bordering the train tracks. Sam, James, and I used to cut through it to catch slow-moving trains, ready to ride wherever they went, and for a short time, everything was sublime.

"Where's Mom? Is she okay?" my brother asked after the police left. We'd both witnessed what had happened earlier, and he was equally unsurprised she ended up shivering in a creek.

In her late thirties, my mother began dating a younger man named Tom, perhaps to rebel against the years she felt she'd wasted with my father. His heavy drinking suited her, but his love for Philly nightlife clashed with her responsibilities. I resented being left with my brother while they went out, but I tolerated it since she let me have a driver's license. When Tom left her for someone closer to his age, I hoped she'd drink less, but she didn't.

After drinking enough whiskey to make the ceiling fan whirl for a week, she grabbed her car keys and stumbled to the front door. I got up from the game my brother and I were playing and told her, "You cannot drive like this!"

"I'm going to Tom's. Immunah smack his liddle floozy," she slurred.

"Why? It's over, Mom. That guy's a jerk. You're better off without him."

"I'm goin' there. I'mma talk to Tom. Lemme go!"

"Mom, where are you going?" My brother asked, looking up from the blinking green text on the monitor, where other players were attacking Splitscreen with spears, clubs, and spells while I'd stepped away.

"Kevo, I'll be back," she said. "Iz okay, I'mma be back soon."

"Fine, if you want to chase after that idiot, give me your car keys first."

My mother handed me her keys, and I momentarily felt like I was her father.

She gingerly stepped down the four steps of our front porch, losing her footing on the last one, but managed to grab the railing before falling flat on her face. I let out a short, miserable laugh as she stumbled into the dark—every time I thought the worst days were behind us. I was wrong.

***

"You need help, Mom. You're addicted to alcohol. I'm serious; you know I'm right," I implored once she'd been discharged.

185

"I feel terrible that I put you and your brother through all this. I'm so ashamed. Sometimes I feel like I'm not doing anything right. I've made too many mistakes. It's my fault you got shot."

I walked over and hugged my mom. Her shoulders poked through her thin frame, and her graying hair draped over me. Such a small woman shouldn't drink so much. That eighty-proof shit was eating her alive. We weren't that affectionate, but when we were, there was no clearer sign that she was my mother. If she didn't stop drinking, all our embraces would be lost to the hours that ended too soon. I broke away, and she sat on the floor, weeping inconsolably. I sat beside her. The weight had not been lifted. She did a lot of things right. I don't want her to feel bad. How can I make her understand it's okay to make mistakes? I'd thought about this months ago but hadn't brought it up yet.

"Mom, don't worry about that. I'm fine. It's not your fault I got shot. I never think that. Sometimes, things don't go the way we want, no matter what we do. Of course, I'm not happy I got shot, but I met Mateo and other people who inspired me. When I was in a coma, I had the experience I told you about that I'll be thinking about for the rest of my life. That humbled me, and this should humble you. If you're trying to be a good mom, that's good enough for me, but feeling bad won't help anyone. You need to do something. You need help."

"Okay."

She joined Alcoholics Anonymous the next day.

Chapter 17

I graduated high school with a C average, which disqualified me from direct admission to the University of Delaware. Underachievers like me spent our first two years in the *Parallel Program*. It offered college-level courses. However, our classes were held in drab trailers off-campus rather than the magnificent Greek-themed grounds in Newark, where I used to skateboard. The long commute, uninspiring lectures, and mediocre setting may have been designed to motive us to improve our grades. The program's title reminded me of a line from George Orwell's *Animal Farm*: "All animals are equal, but some animals are more equal than others." After two years, I joined the main student body, diligently taking notes as professors, more satisfied with their station, lectured theatrically.

Meanwhile, my mother stayed sober. Her friends and lifestyle radically changed after joining Alcoholics Anonymous. One night, soon after joining AA, she encouraged me to accompany her to a meeting held in a nearby church. Speaking is optional. Those who choose to speak always begin with, "My name is [blank], and I'm an alcoholic." I looked around as my mother recounted her fateful night falling into the creek and how alcohol had taken over her life and nearly killed her. Various mantras were hung around the room:

"One step at a time." "This too shall pass." "Easy does it."

Though I had no personal experience with addiction, I felt a kinship with the attendees as they recounted the low points in their lives that led them to admit they were "powerless over alcohol." This admission is a plea for help from a Higher Power. The Serenity Prayer, often recited in twelve-step programs, encapsulates this:

"God grant me the serenity to accept the things I cannot change, courage to change the things I can, and wisdom to know the difference."

Twelve-step programs like AA don't claim to cure addiction. They view recovery as a lifelong process. The people at the meeting weren't like those I'd known who believed they were exempt from suffering, like the waiter who mocked me and my fellow patients when I wore my half-moon helmet. I wanted to make him understand the harm he caused. People can change, but sometimes they need a push. I had a complete cutlery set in my kitchen that came to mind.

Alcoholics Anonymous teaches that making amends and forgiveness are essential for sobriety. My mother readily embraced these steps, but I wasn't sure who deserved forgiveness or when I should apologize. I understood my mother's addiction and its consequences, and I held no resentment toward her. I also knew Gil's reasons for tormenting me might have stemmed from his own suffering, but I couldn't forgive him. Is it possible to turn the other cheek in such a cruel world, as Jesus preached? I want to make Gil suffer immeasurably, but I temper that desire to avoid becoming him. Some people should never be forgiven because it only encourages their worst vices. Who should be forgiven? Like the process of recovery, I knew I'd struggle with this dilemma for a lifetime.

After the AA meeting, my mother, a friend she'd met in the program, and I took a trip to nearby Elkton, Maryland. Elkton was more rural than Newark, with abundant farmland, pickup trucks, trout-filled streams, and rolling green fields. But most importantly, it had a truck stop serving food all night.

"You try to stop, but it's so easy, almost comforting, to fall right back into the hole. And the more you fall, the harder it is to get up again. Eventually, you stop giving a fuck and give in to the addiction. If you'll excuse my language," Craig, my mother's friend from AA, explained when I asked how he became an alcoholic as we all sat in a booth at the truck stop.

"Oh, he doesn't care; he's a big boy," my mom said. Her personality shifted after getting sober. She was still my good old ma but more cynical and skeptical. Her sobriety facilitated clearer thinking but didn't clear her conscience, which became evident when I asked, "Was it the same for you, Mom? Kind of fell into it?"

"Fell into what?" she asked.

"You know, all the drinking, coming home and passing out. Do you think it got that bad because it was gradual, so you didn't notice?" I clarified. However, I was not conducting a random survey she could answer casually; I was talking to my mother.

She insisted it wasn't like that for her, and the familiar themes of my father, her mother, and apologies for her parenting arose.

I reassured my mother that her parenting suited me fine as she fiddled with the food on her plate, then joked with Craig to change the subject. However, they served our food on skillets, not plates. The restaurant was called the Iron Skillet and seemed like the perfect place to ride out the fall of civilization, barricaded by tractor-trailers and stocked with enough canned food, hamburger patties, coffee, and buckets of ice cream to weather anything.

As a kid, I spent most of my time on the other side of the truck stop, filled with arcade games and gizmos that I always tried to get my mother to buy. While sitting in the booth, the rustic dishware brought me back to the wood-burning stove in our basement, where I'd sat with my brother and James, unconcerned with anything other than my mother finding his soiled garments. I still hung out with James regularly, but his substance abuse became more apparent after my mother stopped drinking. I'd recently had surgery to relieve a nerve entrapment in my elbow that had made my fingers numb. I was prescribed Vicodin, but an empty bottle rolled out of my glove compartment when I was going to take one.

"I thought you didn't want those," James artfully reasoned as he sat in my truck beside me when I asked him why the bottle was empty.

"Did you not see that it says Julian Weiner on the bottle?"

"I did, but doctors prescribe pills for off-label purposes, too."

"Off-label doesn't mean for James's leisure! And how about you ease up on the narcotics. Especially heroin. When did you start doing that? Was it back at Temple's?"

"Nah, I wasn't into it back then. A guy who lives near my mom's house usually has a stash. He let me snort a couple of lines and it made me right as rain. Just a little pinch, you know. No need to go all *Naked Lunch* on it."

189

"It's a little pinch now, but it won't be long before it's way more than that. I don't want you to end up like your father! I'll help you find another way to chill. We can go bird-watching; don't underestimate our feathered friends' stress-relieving talents."

"You sound a little like my mother, but if you give me binoculars, I'll be peeping into girls' dorm rooms—not looking for toucans. You're tripping on this. I can go months without heroin. I don't need it. But if it's there, yeah, it chills me out, so I have some. The old man? I hate to say it, but he was suicidal. If it wasn't coke, it would've been something else, like a gun or car running in the garage."

"Well, what about that girl, Angie? She OD'd on heroin, and that was not suicide."

"No, with Angie, that was different. She was mainlining it. Remember how her arm was purple with all those red dots?" James ran his fingers up and down his arm to illustrate.

"I remember. She had to have an operation on them, but even after that, she still didn't quit. Joel dated her for a while. Remember him, that guy who sang like Axl Rose?"

"Yeah, he had quite the pipes."

"He shouldn't have quit singing; he was good. If he stuck with it, he'd be a rock star by now, but Joel said Angie was the wild one. She got him to find another guy to screw around with. He tried the threesome thing with her once, but it bugged him out, so they broke up."

"Well, I can't fault her for wanting to sample different pieces of the pie, or in her case, multiple pieces at once."

Early that morning, I parked near the campus mall on Main Street. We'd started drinking coffee at Jimmy's Diner the night before and had two pots. Because of diabetes insipidus, a condition caused by my head injury and marked by the dueling maladies of constant thirst and excessive urination, much of my life is occupied with finding things to drink and places to piss. Pair this problem with our heavy coffee consumption, and I had to go so frequently that I would've been better off pissing my pants.

I was eight years old the first time I went to Jimmy's. A condom dispenser in the bathroom had a picture of the prophylactic with a smile near its bulbous tip. The condom looked like a balloon, so I bought one and started unpacking it in the booth with my mom and Henry, but she plucked it from my hand before I got it out of the wrapper and told me it wasn't a toy. Not long after that, I bought another one, which I inflated. The yucky lubrication on it was yet another reminder to always listen to your mother.

Thinking about threesomes and condom dispensers reminded me of the Triple X Theater, once frequented by randy patrons across the street from us.

"Did you know there used to be an adult movie theater over there?" I asked James, pointing to the stationery store that had replaced it.

"I did not know that, but your enduring memory of the place leads me to believe that's where you were conceived."

"What? People didn't have sex there. They jerked off in raincoats," I said, fairly sure it was not the place of my conception.

"Really? Were there women there, too?" James asked, genuinely intrigued.

"I'm not sure. I never went inside, but the back row would've been the best place to sit. You wouldn't want anyone blasting off behind you," I said, pleased that my triple X seating arrangement observation meant my spatial reasoning may have improved. We burst out laughing. Our delirium from lack of sleep and too much caffeine made everything farcical. Even though I had only coffee, I felt like I'd taken something much stronger.

That made me think of poor old Sam. When I last saw Sam, he'd recently been released from a mental hospital and was back home with his parents. He'd always been unusual, and if anyone I knew would lose their grip on reality, it'd most likely be him. Still, that didn't make it any easier to accept. We talked about the hospital. He didn't like it. He didn't like taking pills and the staff talking to him like he was crazy, though he acknowledged there was some truth to that. I remembered when Sam helped me shake off people's discouraging perceptions after my injury and told him how much I

191

appreciated it. I told him *someone* ratted on Temple, and he was in jail. That made Sam smile for the first time since his psychotic break. I considered telling him someone had killed Temple, but I decided not to since I knew the risks of straying from the truth to get your point across. On my way out, his father, Ted, stopped me. We tacitly avoided talking about Sam.

"How's your mother, Julian?" he asked.

"Good. My mom had a drinking problem, but she's in AA now and hasn't had a sip since starting the program. I'm proud of her."

"That's great to hear. It must've been hard to raise you boys without a man around. But you're the man of the house now, aren't you? You're a big shot." He shifted his weight from one foot to the other, like he was squaring up for a boxing match. I took a step back.

"I don't know about being a big shot, but playtime is definitely over," I said, eager to wrap things up.

"I got a warehouse job at a company called Amazon last month. They sell books. They're based in Seattle but set up shop here because there's no sales tax in Delaware, and they're friendly to corporations. Those cockroach corporations don't give a damn about the working man, but Amazon is new. It's an Internet company. Maybe they'll be different. Eh, what do I know? I operate the packing machines and help keep the shelves stocked. It's a lot better than riding in that garbage truck. Don't get me wrong; I'd have done that for as long as necessary. But this is better. Easier on the bones."

"Why's it called Amazon?"

"The founder, Jeff Bezos, talked about that. He said he wants to sell more than books; eventually, he wants to sell everything."

I still didn't understand why it was called Amazon. Ted saw my face and said, "Well, imagine if all that stuff were floating down the Amazon River, and all you had to do was pluck out what you wanted. Maybe that's why? Like I said, what do I know?" I looked at him, unsure what else to say, and then he added, "They've got stock options too. I don't know if those things will ever be worth a damn. They only seem to help the overpaid suits in the executive suite. You know what I'd like to do to those guys who've never set foot on a factory floor, lobbying for looser labor laws instead of giving us the pension we were promised?" He clenched his fists before releasing them. "Never mind. Fuck 'em. We'll see if Mr. Bezos can cram a bunch of books, TVs, and whatever else he thinks people will buy into the river and make a buck off it. But for now, it's not too bad. Easy on the bones."

I slipped out of my reverie and had to piss again, so I went behind the building, where I was most likely not conceived, and rejoined James in my truck. My ears rang, and my heart was skipping beats.

"I forget coffee is a drug sometimes. You even go through withdrawal if you quit. Is heroin like that?" I asked.

"I don't know anything about that. I just snorted it a couple of times to relax. It's like having a beer. It's not addictive unless you're using a lot."

It sounded self-deceptive, but having never tried heroin myself, I hoped he was right. "I wonder why my mom had to fall to the bottom of that creek before realizing she needed help? I'll have to ask her about it. I see that in you sometimes. Too much is never enough."

"Well, that's because I've got demons inside of me. I'm subhuman. You know that game, *Altered Beast*? It's modeled after me. *'Rise from your grave!'*" James grinned. "I know it's funny because everything is funny, but it bothers me. I worry about it a lot. A couple lines of heroin help me even everything out. It used to be a prescription medicine. That might sound screwy, but it makes sense once you've tried it."

"I know you're not right in the head, but neither am I. Remember what you said about madness? You've got to control it to channel it into something good. I don't think you're subhuman. Well, most of the time I don't. You keep it real; you've got heart. Maybe too much. Maybe I do, too. It's the pain of living. The desperate complication of being nude among all these people."

"Desperate complication?" James chuckled. "I like that. It takes skill to bust out a line like that, International. Hey, by the way, have you seen Eva around? It's been about six months since I saw her."

I smiled, thinking of her, but I hadn't seen Eva for even longer. "No, I haven't seen her around. It'd be great to see her, though. I've got an interview at the University's computer graphics lab on Friday, the one in Recitation Hall with all the Macs. Next semester's about to kick off, so hopefully, if I get it, it won't be too demanding."

"I've been washing dishes at Deer Park. They've got this old dishwasher that splashes food everywhere. You ought to hear that thing groan! Edgar Allan Poe must've designed it himself. You gotta wear a trash bag unless you want to be covered in food your whole shift. The worst thing, though, is the nachos they serve. Building the Pyramids would be easier than scraping cheese off those plates. But I get free food and beer. Well, it's free for me because I help myself, so that's good enough for now."

"What do you do with your arms? Do you poke holes in the bag?"

"Yeah, dude, like a bulletproof vest. It only protects the most valuable assets."

"Have you been using the Internet much? I made a GeoCities website. It was fun to put together, even though it's the least impressive site ever. They started posting our class schedules online and give everyone email accounts now, too."

"Yeah, I like using the Internet. I was researching a couple of things at the place where you're interviewing with the Macs, but I like the computer lab in Smith Hall better; they're more laid-back about using the printers. I haven't made any webpages yet, but I found some cool sites about the occult and Aleister Crowley."

"Who's that?"

"He wrote poetry and founded a religion called Thelema. He summed it up by saying, 'Love is the Law, love Under Will.' Some people thought he was a Satanist, but that's stupid. There's nothing evil about aligning your passion with your purpose. That's what it represents. I'm sure he'd like that line of yours. The desperate complication of—"

"The desperate complication of being nude among all these people."

"That's the juice right there, freshly squeezed—flavor to the last sip. You should change your name to Julian International. Weener, Whiner, whatever ... It's unbefitting of a man with your poetic talents."

His proposition intrigued me. My grandfather had been adopted, so swapping out Weiner wouldn't mark the end of a long lineage, but should I change my last name to International? Julian International? That's too strident. I'm not a celebrity; no one will take me seriously with a name like that. I still need to muddle through life as an ordinary guy.

"Julian International is a little too bold. I could make it my middle name and use Lawrence as my last name. What do you think?"

"Not bad, not bad. After a round of tic-tac-toe, you conjured up a title with style yet tame enough to mix among the bourgeois without fanfare."

Tic-tac-toe. That was about right. My mind and the spaces where cauterized dendrites formed disjointed archipelagos instead of coherent strings of neural circuitry always took detours to string ideas together. Julian International Lawrence. Perfect. That will let me be ordinary or unusual whenever it suits me.

***

The iron dishware clattered as a busboy cleared our table, and the waitress brought our check. I grabbed a handful of salt, pepper, and sugar packets that would make fine additions to the pile of other condiments I had at home. Craig promptly pulled out a few bills and offered to pay for all of us. My mother politely objected, but Craig smiled and waved her off. We thanked him as Ma slid her partially withdrawn wallet back into her purse and snapped it shut.

"It never hurts to save a buck."

Part II – Death

"Hatred, which could destroy so much, never failed to destroy the man who hated, and this was an immutable law."

— James Baldwin, *Notes of a Native Son*

Chapter 18

It was midsummer 1999, my final year of college. Following James's suggestion, I legally changed my name to Julian International Lawrence. James was so elated that I even considered it—he figured out how to complete the paperwork, and I reluctantly agreed. Was I merely swapping one easily derided name for another? I nearly abandoned the switch, but James reminded me what was at stake, and I went through with it: *"Do this, and you'll never forget: life is absurd."*

I gathered all the paperwork James had prepared and went to the Court of Common Pleas. The clerk reviewed my documents and pointed me to the seating area by the bench of the Honorable Justice Goss. After a few questions, I confirmed I wanted to change my name to Julian International Lawrence, and his gavel fell. Just as I began to regret it, a man being led away in handcuffs gave me a reassuring nod and thumbs-up, and I knew I'd made the right decision.

I'd dabbled with computers all my life, and landing a technical support position at the University of Delaware's graphic computing lab was easy. On my first day, a few years prior, a design student at the Mac Lab, or the lab, as we called it, opened a website displaying an assortment of topless women for all to see.

My coworker Albert considered the student's not-safe-for-work navigation. "Now that's what I call Hello, World!" then told him, "I'm glad these sites didn't exist when I was younger. I would've never left the house! But since we're not in your room, you need to shut it down, son."

I admired his c composure. Albert was analytical. He'd type equations into mathematical software, producing cool-looking plots, graphs, and multidimensional matrices that reminded me of the eight-bit video games I used to play with my brother. It amazed me how fast Albert busted that stuff out. My mind wasn't wired that way.

The Internet had evolved from a simple encyclopedia to a space where you could shop, socialize, get a job, and search for songs and videos you'd never seen before. I was hooked, especially after learning that I could shrink the width of a page within my limited field of vision. Every day, more websites launched, and more people visited the lab. Though I worked with technology, I majored in English, the one subject I was good at, to ensure I got a degree. I met my girlfriend, Simone, the previous year at the lab. Simone occasionally helped me with my math and science homework, but she studied graphic design and didn't excel in those subjects either. She'd recently joked, *"I feel like I have to use the parts of my brain you're missing twice as much!"*

It was a friendly tease, but still stung. However, she inspired me to do something I should've done a long time ago: research what the missing parts of my brain were intended to do. Since a large portion of my right hemisphere was damaged, I was most interested in what functions were specific to each half of the brain. Logically, my uncompromised left hemisphere should be dominant. However, according to recent neurological research, the left side of the brain processes logical tasks like square roots and theories of relativity, while the right hemisphere handles subjective thinking. It waxes poetic and ponders philosophy. I excelled in those right-brain subjects, but how was that possible if I'd been shot on the side they required? Had the missing parts of my brain repurposed Pythagoras as Aristotle through neuroplasticity?

The main thing I realized was though I'd overcome many of the limitations attributed to my injury, I was still holding myself back. I'd psyched myself out of things I was perfectly capable of doing, but even after discovering my brain functioned more thoroughly than I'd thought, my GPA remained about 2.0.

***

"The problem is we live in a patriarchal society," Simone asserted after wrapping up her women's studies reading assignment.

"What is that, and why is it a problem?" I asked, turning away from the book report I was writing. We sat at a large circular table I'd grabbed from a neighbor who'd left it on the sidewalk after moving out. Simone had three roommates, but I lived alone, so she spent most of her time at my place, a block from Newark's unassuming Amtrak station, which was little more than a small platform where passengers waited for one of the silver beasts to come screeching to a halt and let them board. I still preferred freight trains and the wooden ties binding their rails. I couldn't imagine day laborers singing the classic, "I've been working on the railroad," while fastening slabs of concrete between commuter tracks.

"The patriarchy is a system run by men, mostly White men," Simone explained. "They think they're entitled to dominate every industry and exclude everyone else from positions of power. Especially women.

"What makes you think it's not a meritocracy and the most capable people make it to the top, whether they're White men or not?"

"Because Western society is built for them. They've always had TV shows with happy White families, politicians incentivized to look out for them, and access to top universities and jobs. It doesn't mean they're racist or don't deserve those opportunities, but they've always had an advantage."

"But wasn't there an equal rights movement? My boss is a woman, and she's well respected."

"That's great, but we can't stop there. I bet she earns less than men in the same role. Hiring a woman just so she can sit next to a bunch of White guys, with a Black man beside her pointing at a dozen squiggly lines on a screen for a corporate photo op, isn't true equality."

"Am I part of the patriarchy? I'm a White man, but I don't think like that."

"Not you specifically, Julian. I'm talking about Whiteness as a social construct."

My response frustrated Simone, and I didn't want her to think I didn't care; I did. My mother said the same biases held her back, but

199

they originated from my grandmother, not men. My mother raised me, and I respect women. I respect Simone. Isn't that enough?

"Let me know what I can do. I don't want you to feel that way."

"Thank you, Julian," she said, embracing me. "But it's not only how I feel. It's the way it is."

"We'll make the world a better place together," I said, scoring a kiss as I remembered my mother admonishing me for indiscriminate benefaction in a world that didn't need me to save it.

***

"I think it's a great idea."

"Yeah, me too. I've been seeing a lot of articles online that say it's a great time to buy a house. Plus, I'm tired of hearing Amtrak trains roaring by my window."

"Okay, Julian. We'll talk to Mr. Michelson and see how much money you can withdraw."

I was sitting with my mother, drinking ginger ale as the musky scent of red and yellow leaves blanketing her backyard filled the air. My brother had started college in Boston, so I'd stopped by to rake the yard and explore the possibility of buying a house. I smiled, remembering when Sam and I pulled our leaf-raking prank on his neighbor and when I used to dive into big piles of leaves with Ben and Seth. My old pals had gone to college out of state, but I'd run into Seth on Main Street a week ago while he was home visiting his parents. He said he was starting an Internet company.

"It's a website that helps you build websites," he explained, sipping a latte at one of Newark's proliferating coffee shops. Lots of things were changing around town. The conference center where I'd worked held jam-packed tech and investor seminars every month, featuring gourmet luncheons and hourly updates on market indices. Vendors filled every store on Main Street, and car dealers made a brisk trade. A couple of guys in suits climbing into a luxury SUV with their foamy drinks was evidence of that. Their towering ride dwarfed my more plebeian pickup.

"Are you going to drop out of school to focus on it? I heard a lot of people are doing that. They're calling them start-ups."

"No way, J. I'm graduating soon, and my parents are paying my tuition. I'm not risking that. It's just a hobby for now."

"Hey, how's Ben doing?" I'd considered sitting down and talking for a while, but seeing him was awkward since we hadn't kept in touch, so I stood there catching up instead.

"Ben's doing real good. He's been helping me. He learned HTML and an animation program called Flash. You work at a computer graphics lab, right? You should study that stuff."

"Yeah, I should. I've been wanting to learn more about making webpages, but I haven't gotten around to it yet. What's your website called?"

"We're calling it CyberCities."

"Doesn't that sound too much like GeoCities? You know, the other site people use to make websites?"

"No, ours will be different. It'll use Flash and start with a C, so you'll see it ahead of GeoCities. That's how search engines work; the results are alphabetical."

"That's clever. Uh, good luck with that. Nice to see you, Seth."

Animation and an alphabetical edge seemed insufficient for a competitive advantage, but lately, anything associated with the Internet attracted investors, so maybe it was. I considered Seth's advice and thought about launching my own Internet company after I could access the remainder of my funds. I kicked the idea around and decided that regardless of what my website did, I'd call it Dotcom.com. When I learned that address was taken, I gave up on the prospect of clever domain name riches.

My mom and I went back inside to rinse our glasses. She'd installed a skylight to brighten up the interior. An empty whiskey bottle with freshly cut flowers poking out of it sat on the windowsill. I was grateful for my mother's sobriety, but I begrudgingly respected that she'd picked whiskey for her poison. The flowers were an intriguing compliment to that. "Mom, why do you have that bottle there? Doesn't it bother you?"

"Oh, Lenny got those flowers for me yesterday, and I had to stick them somewhere. I kept that bottle all this time. I thought, Why not take something terrible and make it beautiful? How else can I make peace with the past?" In this case, an empty bottle was a proper source of optimism.

My mom had little interest in computers until my brother taught her how to listen to Beatles songs and find funny pictures of cats online. She saw Lenny's profile on a dating website, and a few clicks later, she had a new boyfriend.

I visited my mom about twice a month and saw my brother Kevin infrequently. Though we'd continued living at our mom's, our lives diverged after she and Henry divorced. We had separate holidays and family trees. Kevin was six inches taller than me and had a full head of hair like his old man, while mine had already thinned out. Unlike me, he'd gone straight to college without taking a multiyear psychedelic detour.

Whenever we were all together, I got the impression my mother was happier with him. She had fewer mood swings and guilt trips after she got sober, but as my hair fell out, I looked more and more like my dad, which brought back memories she'd rather forget. Few dinners passed without her commenting on how much she liked my brother's haircut or outfit. How big and strong he was. She celebrated Lenny's strength and size as well. *"He lifted that whole sofa by himself!"* It wasn't intentional, making her subtle slights more biting since they showed what she was really thinking. We were undoubtedly bonded as a family, and she wanted the best for us. But I wasn't sure what to make of comments like, *"Your brother still has all his hair. Whatever's going on with yours must've come from your father, but he never let that stop him. He fooled me, didn't he?"*

That's not to say she didn't praise me, but with her eldest son, words of encouragement were more practical than complimentary.

"I'm proud of you for buying a house, Julian. It's a smart investment. Not many people your age accomplish that."

"Thanks, Mom, but I didn't do anything. It's not like I got a job, worked hard, and earned the money."

202

"No, Julian, you earned that money by having to learn to live with your vision and the trauma of being shot when you were only fourteen. Henry went through something similar after going to Vietnam. He never wanted to talk about it, but I know it was hard on him. So don't think it's anything less than something I'm proud of—and you should be proud of yourself, too."

My mom offered to help me hunt for houses, but like she said at the truck stop, I was a big boy now, so I went at it alone. I checked online but only found a local website with a classified section that had broken image links and placeholder text at the top that read, "Create Title Here." I went old school and leafed through the paper's classified section. I shuddered, recalling my days as a paperboy. I screwed that up properly, didn't I? Simone and I toured a duplex near campus listed for $92,000, which we immediately liked. Surrounded by trees and a leafy lawn, the house seemed to grow out of the ground.

"It has good feng shui," Simone said.

Although I'd never heard the term, I understood. There was a positive flow throughout the place. I negotiated with the owner and bought it for $90,000.

When my mother and I visited Mr. Michelson to withdraw funds for the house, he mentioned that the stock market was on a roll and my account had nearly doubled. "I believe this bull market still has room to run. I'd be delighted for you to continue building wealth with stocks, but real estate's a great investment, too." He found the ongoing bull market so delightful he spun around in his high-back leather chair while organizing documents. Seeing him do that in his three-piece suit made me chuckle. It was evening, and the Wilmington cityscape coruscated through his window, reflected like chains of fire in the Delaware River below. The titans of wealth were emblazoned in neon across skyscraper tops: JPMorgan, Merrill Lynch, and Goldman Sachs. Millions, billions, trillions. You could smell money in the air, and there I was, a young man elevated by the Requirements of the Imagination, ready to stake my claim in the new millennium.

He cut me a check, and presenting it to the lawyers in their sartorial power suits at closing was gratifying. I acted real cool about it, though. I lived simply. Even with my rising net worth, I had little desire to change my ways. The brochures from Mr. Michelson's firm showcasing wealthy couples celebrating on a boat off the Gulf of Mexico and reports detailing my holdings felt separate from my life. Those were generic advertisements; they didn't apply to me, but buying a house was different. That was tangible, real. It was proof that money is protection—a castle with high walls.

I no longer needed marked-down meals or hand-me-downs, but I could still live a spartan life if I wanted. Having money doesn't mean you have to spend it. I didn't want to keep up with the Joneses. I wanted them to forget me so I could sit silently. Secure with my millions, unconcerned with all the icons of prosperity they're so eager to display. Go ahead, laugh at me, hate me, my clothes, and my car. I don't care because I only compete against myself.

The only problem is that I wasn't sure how to win.

"I love how you can hear the creek when you open the windows!" Simone cheered, sliding one open as the babbling sounds of water and a cool breeze filled the room. She stood topless in the open air, so enthralled by the splendor of it; she didn't mind that she was shivering. I grinned, remembering how she drew me close beneath our flimsy blanket when it was chilly the night before. I never thought I'd overcome the isolation I felt during my first years of college. I had a couple of friends but not much luck with romance. The easy days of flirting in an abandoned truck were long gone as years of solitude swept over me. I'd imagined conversations with someone I hoped to meet, enjoying small moments—sitting on a brick bench after class, having nowhere to be but with each other. But now I'd overcome it. Safe in our house, I'd overcome those lonely hours.

"I know! It's way better than hearing screaming trains and crappy music coming through the walls," I cheered in agreement with Simone.

The house had three bedrooms and a half-finished basement. My coworker Albert rented a room, and we converted the remaining one into a server workshop. "Knowing how computers communicate is important," he'd said, and he was not wrong.

The living room had two large sofas. Sometimes, I'd wake up and find James crashed out on one. Simone and I always welcomed him. She said it felt like the three of us were family. Albert was less enthused by James's occasional squatting but tolerated it. Albert, being Chinese, was not amused when James asked questions like, "Who writes that voodoo stuff they put in fortune cookies? Is there a school for that?"

"How would I know? I'm an ABC, you idiot! American-born Chinese. I've never been to a fortune cookie factory in China."

"And there's no shame in that, but aren't you curious about your heritage?"

Before one concludes that James was racist, sexist, or a plain old jerk, it's important to understand he was an equal-opportunity offender. I believe James was mixed race, but which races were never clear. He claimed to have ethnicities ranging from Native American to Sicilian. Most people didn't know what to make of James, including the Black man he'd asked to freestyle rap with him on Main Street. The man responded to James' bobbing head and unsteady rhymes with a swift kick to the midsection, ending his unwanted interactions with that demographic. Shifting tactics, he began belting out select verses of "All I Want to Do Is Make Love to You" on crowded trains and buses, ensuring he always had a row of seats to himself. James might have had Tourette's, but his behavior more likely stemmed from frustration with the banality of most people he met or, as Bukowski wrote, feeling alone with everybody.

After I bought the house, James deduced I had more money than my frugal lifestyle suggested. However, I informed him that my modest head injury settlement facilitated the purchase, not a secret Hebrew wealth fund. He alternated between various low-wage jobs and long periods of unemployment.

"Why were you fired?" I'd asked James after his most recent dismissal from Pencader, a university dining hall.

"I almost got canned when they caught me climbing through the dishwasher, but I spun it as a heroic rescue mission to extract a fork that was clogging it. The final straw came when I kneeled before God, who commanded me to offer free sustenance to all who required it."

I rolled my eyes as James continued, "It happened when I was on register duty, and a homeless dude told me he was starving. I figured no one would notice, so I let him eat without paying. Word of my saintly ways must have spread because every hungry mug in the tri-state area soon supped with abandon in the Pencader halls of plenty. They called the cops after a man with a two-foot-long beard left with a shopping cart full of food. They didn't even let me finish my shift."

"Is that really what happened?"

"As I once explained, as long as you were entertained and possibly enlightened, does it matter if I've embellished a couple things?"

"All right, Aesop, feel free to crash on one of the battle stations, but don't try to solve any hunger crises with my refrigerator."

"Of course not, International. That would contradict your miserly Jewish ways."

James likened the duplex to a sturdy old fort, and seeing it camouflaged among the trees, I agreed. Thus, it was fitting to call furnishings like sofas battle stations.

***

After Albert made everyone chow mein, we sat in the living room. His light, zesty cooking was a welcome change from the often saucy, sugar-laden fare found in takeout places.

"This is how it's supposed to taste," he told James, handing him a bowl from the still-sizzling wok. "But if you want to roll with real Sichuan, you cannot fear MSG."

"I understand, brother. I always wonder why those grannies get up in a tizzy when a suey joint adds a dash of MSG to their kung pao, then slathers it with mustard sauce. Crazy old bitches."

206

Albert laughed and retired to the server room. He'd wired the entire house, and even months later, the novelty of working seamlessly between devices remained. A little later, I finished proofreading a report on The Odyssey. James had found my composition and added, "Not only was Odysseus revered by men, but his pimping skills were legendary among the gods. Zeus long desired to bone bitches like Circe, but only Odysseus got his nymph on." I deleted his racy addition, reflecting on its unorthodox use of nymph. Is that a double entendre? Seated across from me, Simone contorted her face. "This is so sick!" she said as an open textbook lay before her. James and I looked up. Our plates were still on the kitchen table. We'd cleared ours, but Simone had not.

"Not to your liking?" Albert had asked.

"Oh, no, it's very good."

"Are you sure? I could make you something else."

"No, it's fine. I just don't want to eat it all. It doesn't mean anything, okay?"

"Oh, yes, of course," Albert said, patting her shoulder to ease any possible offense, unlike James, who might have doubled down on it. But something else was bothering her now.

"What's the matter?" James asked.

She turned the book around and showed us a series of images.

"They disfigured these women's genitals."

The images showed three young women, as she'd described.

"Why did they do that?" I asked, wishing I said something more sympathetic, but I'd never seen such a thing.

"Because it deprives them of pleasure and makes it easier to control them. There's no fucking medical reason. Imagine being a child and having someone slice you up like that." Tears formed in the corner of her eyes.

I thought of my own circumcision as a baby, but clearly, genital mutilation was far worse.

"Some people are so sick, man. It's this crushing idiocy that you can't reason with," I said, recalling how I was ridiculed for the half-moon helmet I had to wear and the scar that showed through my thinning hair. Still, I knew these experiences weren't in the same

207

league as what happened to those girls. They were the lens through which I related to their pain, not a ranking measure to see who suffered more. *"Not you specifically, Julian. I mean Whiteness as a social construct,"* Simone had said, but how can we relate to one another if we're pigeonholed into ideological matryoshka dolls, nested within rigid layers of identity, and told we lack the agency to transcend our bloodlines and past experiences?" It made no difference to me if a White person wore fat-laced sneakers or a woman became president. Where do I fit into all of this?

"Crushing idiocy is right," Albert said, rejoining us. "I learned how to make that chow mein from my grandmother. She owns a Chinese restaurant in New York but almost had to shut it down because some idiot started a rumor that she was putting dogmeat in the food.

James raised his eyebrows.

"No, there was no dogmeat in it, dumbass," Albert said.

"I wouldn't have thought less of you if there was," James said.

Albert couldn't suppress a grin and replied,

"Fortunately, the neighborhood rallied around her, and it blew over. That recipe has probably been in our family for seven generations, and it only took one bigoted rumor to nearly finish it off."

Chapter 19

Glenda, my boss at the Mac Lab, called me into her office. She was in her sixties, slightly overweight, and sported an eighties coiffure. We spoke briefly about staying late to apply a patch to Adobe Illustrator, but what she really wanted to discuss was her recent trip to the Daytona 500. Glenda wasn't the type of person I expected to run the lab. She loved NASCAR, barbecuing ribs, and strapping on leather chaps when she rode on her boyfriend's Harley. Glenda had been with the university since she graduated with a sociology degree around when I was born. Her tenure predated the lab, but she'd kept up with the times. She told me the most important thing in life is to keep learning. Though her degree gave her a keen understanding of the human condition, it played a minor role in her career. That reminded me of James, who navigated life without a lesson plan.

"Isn't it boring watching cars race in circles for five hundred laps?" I asked Glenda.

"It would be boring if you sat there the whole time, but it ain't just racing cars. It's the interviews and trophies. The fans and souvenir shops selling loud and proud memorabilia. And beer—lots of beer. These gatherings show what's on the minds of people who actually make things. Not like us playing with computers or those financial wizards pushing numbers around," she leaned back in her chair and laughed. The wrinkles on her face all seemed to smile, too.

"So, you buy a couple of T-shirts and watch the race?"

"I watched about fifty laps, but it's more fun than you might think. It takes big balls to get into one of those cars and burn down the track. Only inches separate the champs from the graveyard. But the parking lot is the best part—tailgating around pickup trucks, campers, and coolers loaded with ice-cold drinks, baked beans, and potato salad."

"I get it. I've always loved going to the truck stop in Elkton. It's a little slice of life where you can step out of your spaceship and see who else is orbiting the Earth with you. It won't win any culinary awards, but I like it that way. Simple, classic American food. Just add salt, pepper, and a dab of Tabasco sauce, and everything's right with the world."

"Slices of life. I like it. That's what I'm talking about, that's right," she said, then lowered her voice, even though the door to her office was closed.

"There's one more thing they've got goin' on at those races, something you probably won't see at the truck stop. Don't tell your little lady I showed you this. I know she's a feminist—the sensitive type—but Julian, they got some hot bitches there too!" She pulled out a compilation of photographs with fine-looking females in wire-thin bikinis twisting like they were spinning Hula Hoops atop stock cars. Even though photography was quickly going digital, Glenda still loved her photo albums.

"Yeah, I won't be taking her on any dates there," I said with a chuckle.

"It ain't for everyone, but nothing is."

While I enjoyed seeing Simone at work, I felt uneasy whenever guys leaned in close to talk to her or she fell into a fit of laughter when they said something funny. I tried not to be jealous, but these other men always seemed taller, had more hair, or were simply cooler than me. I told James about my feelings, and he warned me, *"The one who needs the most gets the least."*

If one of the ladies in the lab was smiling or joking with me when I assisted her, I sometimes caught Simone sneaking glances at me while pretending to be busy. On those occasions, I laughed a little louder and longer than usual. Attraction often needs a counterpart to awaken it—like a forgotten toy that becomes a child's favorite when a playmate picks it up. I adored Simone and had no designs on anyone else, but I wanted her to remember we had something special. That I was special.

Similar dynamics unfolded at parties, restaurants, and other social settings, where smartly dressed saboteurs roamed freely, eager to compete for Simone's affection with a well-played flirt or roguish grin as they sipped their bourbon neat. The mild anxiety I'd experienced at Temple's place hit harder at parties, where Simone giggled with a glass of wine as I faded into myself. The more boisterous the crowd became, the more I withdrew. She acquiesced whenever I suggested leaving these outings early, but not without grumbling that she was having a good time as we stepped outside and my blood pressure dropped. These anxieties were intensifying, defying my attempts to rein them in. In the meantime, I preferred when it was just the two of us, like that evening when Simone asked to return to the lab because she forgot to print her homework.

***

"Aw man, the building's closed. I have a key to the lab but not the building," I told Simone after angrily tugging on the bolted front doors.

"This stupid class is at 7 a.m. tomorrow. When does the lab open?" Simone asked.

"8 a.m.," I said, frustrated. "Should we go to Kinko's?"

"Do they have Macs there?"

"No, I don't think so." I looked at the trees as if they'd have an answer, then noticed a ground-level window straight ahead was open. Albert had playfully leaped out of it once, so I knew it led into the lab.

"That window's open. We could get in that way." I suggested, even though I had that sinking feeling when I knew something was a bad idea.

"Uh, I don't know. I don't think we're supposed to go through the window. The building's closed, right?"

"Well, Albert jumped out of it once."

Simone laughed. "Why?"

"Someone was playing a *Revenge of the Nerds* clip, which inspired him to act like a goofball."

We stood quietly.

"I guess it's all right. I mean, you work there, and I'm a student. We're allowed in the lab," Simone reasoned.

211

I looked around surreptitiously, not wanting anyone to see us climbing through the window. It was still light, but no one was around. We made our move. Simone couldn't reach the window, so I gave her a boost. I scanned the grounds once more and went in after her. The situation reminded me of sneaking back into my room after a late night with Sam, James, and other derelicts. Simone slid her disk into a computer to print the mock cat food advertisement she'd designed. She avoided fashion layouts, believing they objectified women. The wide-eyed cat she'd chosen for the ad looked bonkers, like Toonces, the Driving Cat from *Saturday Night Live*, crashing off a cliff. I doubted anyone would buy pet food with a cat like that on the bag. In fact, I doubted Simone would be successful with graphic design—she wasn't passionate about it, which showed in her lackluster projects. That was all right; I could take care of us both.

"This stupid printer takes forever to warm up," I grumbled as I stood beside it. The digital readout had displayed "Warming Up" for the past ten minutes. The wax-based colors it used were glossy and smooth but printed very slowly.

Keys jingled in the hallway. It had to be the police. "Fuck, fuck, fuck!" I said, realizing I hadn't looked far enough to my left to compensate for my vision loss when I scanned the grounds. Even after all these years, I sometimes forgot. Sure enough, a university police officer rounded the corner.

"Simone, there's a window in Glenda's office. You can still get out!"

"Wait, what?"

"Just do it!" I hated feeling anxious like this. One choice, one solution. She dashed into Glenda's office, closing the door as the officer approached. The entrance to the lab had a large glass pane, so he'd definitely seen me. I started panicking. What should I say? What if they saw Simone climbing out? I've only made things worse! Well, you've got to roll with it now. I walked to the door and let the officer in. Another officer was close behind him.

"What are you doing in here? We received a complaint about a break-in," the first officer said.

"Broke in? I work here."

"Someone broke in through that window!" The second officer barked, pointing at our illicit point of entry. I'd left it ajar.

"Oh, I got here late, and someone locked the front door, so I had to climb through the window. I have to make sure the printers have ink. I forgot to do that before I left."

"Your ID. Let's see some ID."

Hourly employees like me didn't have staff IDs, so I handed him my student ID. He looked at it disapprovingly, then gave it to his partner, who tossed it on a table without a glance. It was a sterling display of teamwork.

"Your middle name's International? What kind of name is that?" asked the first officer.

"My parents met abroad. That must've inspired them," I said, reciting one of my usual diversions whenever someone questioned it.

"So, you work here?" he confirmed.

"Yes."

"You're not supposed to be here after hours. That's trespassing," the second officer said.

"Working on the printers is easier when no one's around. My boss is fine with it."

"Unlikely," he said. He was quite the conversationalist.

"Is anyone else here?" the first officer questioned.

"No, only me."

"Alright, we've got to take you to the station to clear this up."

I saw my future melting like the wax in that slow-ass printer. Why is it so slow! Then the stupid thing beeped and started printing Simone's presentation. The officers walked over as the pages crawled out. I thought of the movie *No Way Out*, the scene where they're rendering a Polaroid of Kevin Costner, which proves he isn't who he said he was. And there was the goofy cat with its bug eyes. Beneath it was written, Simone Clarke.

"Who's Simone?" The second officer demanded, holding a page between his thumb and forefinger.

"You might not want to touch that before it dries. The ink gets on your skin," I explained.

Sure enough, the officer's fingerprint was on the cat's forehead, leaving a matching imprint on his thumb.

"What the hell?" officer number two grumbled.

The first officer, suppressing a grin, repeated, "Who's Simone?"

"Oh, she's my girlfriend. She's a student here. I was using one of her files to test the printer."

"Where is she? Are you alone or not?"

"It's just me, sir. Can we call my boss? She'll clear this up."

"Fine, but make it quick."

Glenda's home phone number was taped to the phone in her office.

"I need to go to her office to get the number, okay?"

"All right, Meow Mix, let's go," the second officer said. The ad was for a different brand.

I opened the door. The window was shut, and Simone was gone. I dialed Glenda's number.

"Put it on speaker," the second officer demanded.

"Hello," Glenda answered.

"Hey, Glenda. It's Julian."

"Is everything all right, Jul—"

"The first officer interrupted, 'Ma'am, Glenda, are you the manager of this facility? We apprehended Julian Lawrence trespassing in Recitation Hall, room 203, this evening.'"

"I am the director, yes."

"Is Julian employed here?"

"He is."

"Glenda, I was checking the printers. Remember, you said to make sure they have enough ink for class tomorrow?" I interjected.

"Uh, yeah, okay, thanks for doing that, Julian."

The second officer spoke. "Glenda, we received an alert that Julian broke in through a window. Prospective students and their parents are visiting this week. If they see something like that, they'll lose confidence in campus security. We've got a reputation to uphold. Breaking in through a window violates university policy, even if he's permitted to be in the building."

I preferred his one-word replies.

"Julian, did you break the window?" Glenda asked.

"No, it was already open. I climbed through it because the front door was locked."

"Julian illegally crossed the perimeter of the building. He broke in, whether the window was damaged or not."

"What was your name again?" Glenda asked.

"Officer McNealy, ma'am. Badge ID: 8675309," he said it with such zeal I thought he'd salute when he finished speaking.

"Officer McNealy, you're right. That's one of the reasons I value having Julian on my team. He has a disability due to a shooting accident. As we're all aware, the university is an equal opportunity employer that values people for their talents and capabilities irrespective of their differences, a principle I've been proud to uphold throughout my twenty years here. Now, let's get disability services involved. They need to know when any of our, aw shucks, how do they say it nowadays ... when our mobility-challenged members of the community encounter discrimination.

"Ma'am, he broke in through the window. A disability is no excuse for that. The same rules apply to everyone." Officer McNealy insisted.

"He may have come in through the window, but he was only trying to overcome a barrier to his mobility. I'm sure we all agree that Julian is entitled to equal access and opportunity. I'm fascinated by how you've suddenly become a neurologist. That'll help you explain yourself to disability services. Let's conference them in."

The first officer chimed in. "No, no, that won't be necessary. A verbal warning will suffice. Please speak with Mr. Lawrence and explain how this conduct is not, well ... I'm sure you can take it from here. Have a nice evening, ma'am."

"Good night," Glenda said with a hint of sarcasm.

"I'm glad we cleared that up, Julian. If you're done with the printers, we'll lock up and escort you out." Officer Number One said.

215

I told them I was all set, and Officer McNealy shut the incriminating window.

I let out a quick sigh but otherwise restrained my elation.

They escorted me out of the building, and we parted ways. I couldn't wait to tell Simone. I'd never pulled the disability card before, but I understand you have to play the hand you're dealt. As I walked away, the window that had started it all creaked open. Simone peeked out.

"What are you doing in there?"

"I couldn't open the window in Glenda's office. I was under her desk the whole time."

I scanned the area, noting what was on my left side this time.

"It's clear. Let's get out of here."

She slid out the window, and we ran through a vacant parking lot, but we were laughing too hard to get far, so we stopped by a lamppost.

"Damnit," Simone said. "That cop smudged my homework."

I noticed she'd grabbed her freaky kitty print.

"Should we go back and print another copy?" I joked.

"No, I'm probably getting a D in this class anyway. Even my prints without smudges aren't much better."

I was glad I didn't have to tell her.

It was an unusually warm autumn evening, with the sky painted pink. Time rolled by easily as everything felt fashioned to elevate my mood.

"Hey, wanna go to Klondike Kate's? Feel like having a drink?" Simone suggested.

"Uh, do you want to drop off your homework first?"

"Nah, that's okay. A beer bottle stain would probably improve it at this point," Simone said, smiling. A few of her teeth were sharp and angled, making her look like Dracula's bride when she smiled. It was the first thing I'd noticed about her and it made me think she might be the one for me.

Chapter 20

We sat on Klondike Kate's balcony facing Main Street, drinking beers in frosty mugs. They served a typical array of libations and American fare, but the place stood out amid Newark's predominantly colonial architecture. Kate's resembled an old Western saloon, with its heavily lacquered bar, wooden bench seats, and chandeliers. While I enjoyed the ambiance, I couldn't help but imagine a piano in the corner with a grizzled old man playing parlor songs as patrons fired pistols and broke chairs over each other's heads.

"I was so scared those cops were going to find me. Thanks for having my back in there," Simone said after a sip. "You're a good guy. You always try to help people. I remember you telling me about your roommate, Mateo, and how sharing a room with him and being in the hospital made you more compassionate. I see that while you're at work."

She held my hand as she spoke, making me feel foolish for my ostentatious conversations with girls at the lab. But the dumbest part is I doubt she even noticed.

"I'm glad you're not like men I've known who say chivalrous bullshit like, 'I'd die for you. You're my world, baby,' just to have sex with me. They'd die for me but wouldn't meet me the next day for coffee after they got their dick off."

Before Simone, I'd been with only one woman, which happened more by chance than by swindling someone with chivalry. Octavio, a friend from Temple's apartment, had a bungalow in Ocean City, Maryland, steps from the boardwalk. He invited me to visit, so I stopped by before college began and spent a few days walking among beachgoers, soaking in the last days of summer. Octavio and I had lunch, but he got caught up in other things. I didn't see him much after that, which was fine since I wanted to avoid discussing Temple's incarceration. I was never sure if he dealt drugs because, like Temple, Octavio mostly observed and hung out in the back room. He had a girlfriend and never messed around with young chicks. He liked talking about books, too, so he was okay with me. I didn't know his girlfriend's name, and we'd never spoken, but I liked her red lipstick and low-cut blouses.

Octavio played loud music every night. I couldn't sleep at first, but then I imagined I was aboard the atavistic ship I'd revisited on shrooms and drifted off to the familiar sounds of the sea. While swabbing the deck one night, I awoke to someone hoisting my mainsail.

"You don't mind, do you?" I heard someone ask. When I opened my eyes, it was Octavio's girlfriend with her hand down my pants, not the toothless guy gutting fish in a bucket beside me. A welcome sight since, unlike him, she had great lips, hips, breasts, and all the rest. She'd shed clothes and was breathing hard on my neck, awaiting my reply.

"Octavio?" It wasn't the first thing that came to mind, but it's what I said.

"He's fucking someone else."

"Right now?" I said, not quite capturing the mood of Keats, Shelley, or Byron, whom I'd become familiar with thanks to James.

"Yes, in the other room," she purred. I'd heard moaning earlier but had figured it was Octavio and my bedmate. She moved closer and asked, "Do you want to touch me?"

I reached around her hips toward her sumptuous ass. I knew a few sonnets, but I had no clue what to do. I didn't even know her name. I vainly squeezed her butt like I was kneading dough, readying it to rise in the oven, which didn't send waves that fluttered her rudder, so she grabbed my dick and demanded. "Don't touch it unless you're gonna fuck it." Then we set sail.

Although I enjoyed the experience, I was so bugged out after the deed was done that when she stepped into the shower, I burned out of there with a cigarette dangling from my lips, listening to someone complain about the state of the world on talk radio. The sea receded in my rearview mirror, and I never saw either of them again. I thought I'd become a lady's man, but years passed with little more than a dinner date—until Simone ended my isolation.

"Don't worry about those guys, Simone. We're a team. I love you. And I can always blame my brain for any misunderstandings," I said, grinning.

She snorted. "You don't need any cheat sheet. You're plenty smart. I don't know how to do all that stuff at the lab like you do. But Glenda's move was genius. Wait, you weren't offended by that, were you?"

"No, not at all, Glenda's awesome."

I knew Glenda had done what was necessary to help me, and I tried not to be easily offended. I don't want to live life through the lens of a victim or police other people's opinions. The only thing bothering me were the guys who'd slept with her without a second thought. What did they look like? Does she still think about any of them? Simone said sometimes she felt like she had to use the parts of her brain I'm missing twice as much. That didn't offend me either, but it hit me where I'm weak. Yes, I value compassion and believe disabled people deserve some concessions. But I shouldn't have to pull a "shot in the head" card to get me out of every jam. Why did I joke about that? It's not funny—not funny at all. I need to be strong, not self-deprecating, to overcome my insecurities. I have to rid myself of them entirely.

After finishing our beers, I asked Simone, "Do you want to get a snack? The sweet potato fries here are good, or we could look at the menu and see what else they have."

"No," she said, falling silent.

"Hey, I don't mean to dwell on this. I'm trying to understand you, okay? But sometimes you get—you're a little sensitive about food? You know what I mean?"

"Yes," she said and was quiet again.

Her silence made me regret having brought it up. I looked away from the table as streetlights shone upon people milling along the sidewalk.

Simone spoke, "We've talked about your dad before. You know he loved you and all that, but he never did anything about that creepy-ass stepbrother of yours. I know that's affected you, even after he died, but we never talked about my dad and how he messed me up. He's a big part of my passion for women's rights. I want to protect them from men like him. Maybe I should've told you sooner."

"You mentioned your dad is grumpy, and you don't like him, but when your mom visited us, we all had such a good time that it didn't seem worth bringing him up since I've never met him."

"No, I'm not saying you should've. I don't like talking about him, but to understand why I freak out over food sometimes, you need to know what it was like living with my father. He acted like the only reason that we weren't living in a happy Norman Rockwell world was because we were too disobedient to fulfill his impossible ideals. He wanted to come home to a little lady slaving over a hot stove. 'Ooh, what do we have here, honey? The turkey and stuffing look delicious!'

"At dinner, he'd say, 'Are you going to sit there all night staring at it, Simone? What did you say? You've had enough? You have no idea how hard I work to put this food on the table. Simone, honey, you better clear that plate. I'll tell you when you've had enough. Stop that right now! I don't want to see those tears again. One day, you'll have a husband, and you'll never keep him happy if you can't show some gratitude.'

"My sister is two years older than me. She knew how to wave a red cape and get my dad to run by. He never got to her like he did with me. She'd chow down with a big grin, and he'd say what a wonderful daughter she was. But it made me sick to have to clear my plate. Even if I was hungry, I hated being forced to do it. My sister was the smart one. Unfortunately, my mom took the bait, too.

"'Edward, don't talk to her like that. She's only eleven years old. She doesn't need to think about being married.'

"'Debbie, what did I tell you about interrupting me? Crossing me in front of our daughters. Why can't you show me even a little goddamn respect? Look, look, now you've made me angry. It wouldn't have to be this way if you'd just listen!' Then he'd get up with veins poking out of his neck and dig his fingers into her shoulder until his knuckles turned white. She'd gasp with her head low, and he'd sit down, satisfied that order had been restored."

Simone went into a semi-trance as she recounted a depth of trauma I hadn't known about. I saw parallels between the unattainable lifestyle that had burdened James in Simone's story. I had my own challenges, but I never had to deal with that type of dysfunction. I wanted to tell Simone that Gil had not only been cruel but had also molested me as a show of sympathy, but that seemed stupid, like what kids in my Psych Group did to prove who'd suffered the most. Gil got a couple of jabs in, but he never got his dick off, thanks to our housekeeper, Carmen.

"Sometimes I wish I were Godzilla," I said. "How can you reason with some people? You can't! Only Godzilla, shooting lasers out of his eyes, breathing, and farting fire, can school them. You know, to cover both ends, so to speak."

"Farting fire?" Simone asked with a delightful, toothy grin.

"Well, if he had a little wasabi, I'm sure he could bring it out the back."

On the way home, I continued fantasizing about being Godzilla. How would it work? In *Super Mario Brothers*, a game glitch lets you simultaneously be little Mario and his larger, toadstool-augmented, fire-shooting twin. It ought to work like that. Godzilla has scales. I wanted scales. Then I wouldn't have to worry about my hair. Last month I'd joked with Simone about it falling out: "Ah shit, they're fleeing in the rear now, too," but the truth is, I wanted to know what she thought about my thinning hair without seeming concerned.

"Let me see. Yep, it looks like they're taking the lifeboats now. Abandon ship! But seriously, if you don't like how your hair looks, why don't you shave it off? I mean, I don't care. It's up to you."

"I wish I could do that. It's too thick on the sides. It makes the thin spots stand out more, but I've got this scar on my head. Right in the thin area. I'll leave it how it is for now."

"Scar? Scars are badass! No one thinks about that kind of stuff as much as you do. We're always hardest on ourselves. I used to be self-conscious about my teeth, and sometimes people teased me about them, but then I realized I don't care what they think. If anyone tries to bust on my lovely molars now, I give them a big smile, but it seems like the less I care, the less other people do, too."

It's true: self-assurance is a strong defense. Fears always start small—a secret tucked under the shirt, an insecurity hidden beneath your hair—but they grow too big to hide, and the bullies spot them. Point them out. Shout them out until your fears are all that's left of you.

***

Minutes after I arrived at work, Glenda called me to her office. Glenda was usually laissez-faire about lab operations, often leaving things to Albert and me while she wandered campus with her boyfriend, but she could lay down the law when necessary. I didn't expect grave disciplinary action, but she'd earned so much goodwill with me I'd whip myself with a spiked chain if she asked.

"Close the door," Glenda said as I entered her office. I glanced at her desk. We were lucky there was a sheet of wood bolstering the back of it. Otherwise, Simone would've had nowhere to hide.

"I'm so sorry I had to call you last night, Glenda. Thank you. I swear I'll never—"

She raised her finger to shush me and interrupted. "Stop, stop right there. I know you're sorry, but don't be. You're lucky I'm your manager, and I'm not trying to toot my own horn. Lord knows we have enough people who love doing that. What happened last night ... Honestly, I don't care, but luck never lasts. You need to be smart, not lucky. Not everyone will pick you up when you fall. Plenty of people want to punish you for all their pain and kick you when you're down. In fact, that's their favorite time to kick you, but don't give it to them. Don't give them that chance. Do you understand what I'm saying, Julian?"

"Yes, I do. The hardest part of having a disability is that you've already got one arm tied behind your back. Then, some jerk comes along and tries to tie up the other one for a laugh. You helped me so much yesterday. I won't forget it. Thank you for your advice. I shouldn't have been so careless. I'll remember what you said." I

222

nodded vigorously, emphasizing the depth of my gratitude, and turned to leave. I knew I was very fortunate.

"Julian, where are you going? We're not done. I only gave you that pep talk so you wouldn't be too hard on yourself, but there'll be disciplinary action for what you did. It was wrong; no two ways about it."

"Uh, okay. Do you need me to fill out a form or something?"

"Yep, there's something more you need to do." She faced her computer and fiddled with her mouse. I couldn't believe it. Why did she help yesterday only to turn around and be just as officious as those cops? I was still thankful but disappointed. She took her hand off the mouse and, with her back to me, said, "You know what I like about the Internet? It's got every type of music you can imagine: Jazz, piano, rock, and a little country, too."

She's hiding behind her quirky charm to get me to sign something. Have I misunderstood her? Was it always an act? I don't know. Maybe it's legit, and I'm being too hard on her.

"But my favorite thing is the karaoke tracks. They've got the lyrics, too. Well, I guess this Internet thing is pretty cool after all. Have you ever been to a karaoke bar, Julian?"

"Uh, no. Those places always confused me. What do you do there, sing? Like ordinary people sing or something?"

"Or something," Glenda said, opening a file. It was a video of John Denver playing the guitar in front of a mountain range. A track-length timer was counting down. Why is she showing me this? Shit! It's a karaoke track. I know what she's going to do. Should I go out the window? The same one I told Simone about, or I whip myself with chains. Anything would be better than this!

Glenda hit play and started singing 'Thank God I'm a Country Boy,' clapping to the beat without needing to read the lyrics. She stopped midway and faced me.

"Your turn."

"What do you mean? Sing?" I knew that's what she wanted and knew this was coming, but the shock hit me anyway.

She nodded.

"I'm a terrible singer. Women have had their faith in humanity shattered after I sang two verses. You'd only be punishing yourself! Instead, I'll fill out one of those forms we discussed, attesting to my misconduct, and I'll deliver it to the police myself."

"Your turn," she repeated, taking pleasure in my discomfort. I was silent, embarrassed, and on the verge of an anxiety attack.

"What are you, a chicken? Fine, I'll help you get started." She sang the next few verses, and I reluctantly accompanied her, mostly humming the melody. She stopped the music.

"I know what's wrong."

"You do?"

"You've never heard this song before, have you?"

"No, I've heard it. My dad liked country music, but that was a long time ago."

She switched to another website that had the original song. "Listen closely. Once you get that beat in your head, the lyrics come easy."

We listened to Johnny D sing about griddles, fiddles, and easy living on the farm.

"That's pretty good. I ought to listen to more country music."

I unexpectedly missed my dad, even though I also hated him. Country music and fashion were the only things he defended against his wicked bride, BB, wearing bolo ties and jeans on the weekend or playing Willie Nelson to defy her yuppie standards.

On our drives to and from the airport, which bookended my stays out West with him, we listened to country songs between the breathtaking vistas of the San Joaquin Valley, with landscapes ranging from drought-stricken plains to lakes and prairies below vast mountain ranges. My father read everything from *National Review* to *Mother Jones*. He read the Bible, Torah, and Quran. He used to say, *"There's a hardscrabble uncertainty to life, Julian. A mystery we'll never solve by only looking at what we already know. You've got to consider the other side, too."* My father was always searching for clues to solve the Mystery, which I must've inherited from him. I don't know why my father played custody tug-of-war with me or beat my mother until she fell to the floor. I don't know why he was a coward when I needed him or why he did a million other stupid things. But he wasn't all bad. Then, I understood my mother a little more. I understood why she still told stories about burrito-eating contests with my dad and liked flowers in whiskey bottles.

In time with the clapping and guitar, I sang for the sake of my father, whom I'd never forgive but didn't forget had good in him. I saw the griddle. I saw the fiddle and the sun settling low. Once I got going, I felt good about it. I was cured of my shyness. Actually, I can sing ... I can sing! I'm heading to a karaoke bar *tonight*!

Glenda stopped the track and assessed whether I'd learned my lesson. "So Julian, I think we both learned something today, and I hope you'll never do that again."

"I won't. I won't be breaking into any more buildings. That was one of the dumbest things I've ever done."

"No, Julian. Break in every day for all I care. I'm talking about singing. Don't ever sing John Denver or any song again. Where's the pitch? Where's the melody? My ears are ringing, and they never did before. I don't deserve that kind of punishment. I should fire you right now."

The bright lights and adoring fans rushing toward my tour bus faded away.

"There's one more thing. You know I don't like calling attention to myself, so don't get all spun up about it, but I guess it's time to tell you. I'm dying of cancer."

***

That evening, I shared Glenda's crushing news with Albert.

"I wonder what her options are? She should go to Boston. What's that one hospital called? What is it? Oh yeah, Mass General. I heard they're the best. They have all the latest treatments," I said to Albert.

"Glenda said she has colon cancer, right?"

"Yes."

"How long has she had it?"

"I don't know. I didn't want to ask too many questions, but Glenda said she was dying. That's the word she used: dying. But she might've meant it more like she has cancer, and there's still a chance she'll beat it, and we'll all be talking about what a close call it was years from now."

"Hold on, let me search online."

Albert and I sat in his makeshift server room. When we had those chips cranking, it got hot in there, and the electricity bill rose along with the temperature, but I didn't mind. Albert showed me what was happening under the hood of the Internet—the code that converted digits into images, video, and sound. It made the world seem much smaller when his cousin in Shanghai clicked a few keys on her computer, and we could see it shifting pixels on our screen.

"Most people with colon cancer have a good prognosis. How did she look?" Albert asked.

"A little pale, and she's been coughing more, but I never would've guessed she had cancer."

"That must be why Glenda's been taking walks and spending so much time with her boyfriend."

"I wonder how long she's known. I've never heard her complain or feel sorry for herself. There aren't many people like Glenda anymore. People who would rather pick you up than kick you when you're down."

Despite growing gaunt and pale, Glenda continued working until the last few weeks of her life. Soon after I started at the lab, we talked about my near-death experience. She was one of the few people I could talk to about something so hard to believe without judgment.

The last time we spoke, she asked if I believed in the afterlife.

"When I was in the coma, my brain wasn't exactly firing on all cylinders," I said.

"With a bullet in your head, I'd say that's quite an understatement."

"Ha, yeah, I guess so."

"I can't believe the doctor who operated on you knew what to do. It's incredible! I'm sorry to interrupt. Please go on."

"Oh, no worries. When I first came out of my coma, I thought I'd crossed to the other side and come back. My near-death experience was profoundly moving and inspiring, especially meeting Jesus Christ—but during my recovery, I started questioning if any of it was real. I wondered if having the experience was a consequence of surgeons poking my brain and giving me all kinds of medications while I was in a coma. Something I'd heard or seen before might've influenced it as well. For years, I dismissed it as a product of my imagination—until a drug dealer told me that even chemicals have a God-given purpose. His motivations were sinister, but that doesn't mean he was wrong. I've learned some of my most important lessons from people I disagree with, even if it only reinforced my desire to be nothing like them. Regardless of what caused it, that experience changed my life and prompted me to explore life's existential riddles, which I call the Mystery.

"That's a good one—the Mystery! But how can drugs have a God-given purpose?"

"His point was, if God made man, then whatever man produces is a derivative of the abilities God gave us. He tried to twist that to mean it's impossible to stray from God's path, which I disagree with, but I've factored in what he said. I'm sure books and movies influenced parts of what I saw, but I hadn't read the New Testament, so that couldn't have directly inspired what I experienced. After discovering Carl Jung's theory of the collective unconscious, which theorizes that some concepts are inheritable, I realized ideas like redemption and transformation don't only exist in religious texts. For example, my mother isn't Christian. Yet, she goes to AA, where the Christian values of accountability and faith have helped her stay sober.

"The man I saw during my experience looked and spoke as I imagine Jesus would, but the moral principles he taught are found even among those unfamiliar with Christ's teachings, and that suggests archetypal figures can guide us independently of our individual awareness. Still, I'm not implying that Jesus Christ or the divinity of any religious figures are interchangeable. The Christian concept of Salvation involves more than simply being good or praying to any deity that suits you. It requires repentance and faith in Jesus Christ as the Son of God, as revealed through his death and resurrection. I believe there is a world beyond this one where our souls transcend the limits of our mortal coils, but that belief comes more from faith than my near-death experience. I have faith that your soul will flourish far beyond the years we spend on this peculiar planet."

Glenda shifted in her chair, leaning forward and then back again. "Thank you for sharing that with me, Julian, but it was silly of me to ask you about the afterlife. It's not like anyone knows until they get there. But if I see Jesus, I'll tell him you said hello, and don't worry. If John Denver's up there—I won't tell him how you mangled his song."

Glenda passed away two weeks later. We all knew she had cancer, but she still seemed strong. I thought she'd stay with us longer, at least another year, but she was gone. How long had I been talking to a ghost? I wore a light jacket home from work after I heard the news. Gusts of wind billowed my clothes, and I shivered. Why hadn't I worn something warmer? You know why—you thought the sun might approve and hoped the wind would give you a few more weeks before the cold came. No, you should know by now that seasons only bend to our will in fables.

I sat beneath a red maple tree on my front porch as the wind blew its branches toward the end of my street. Dry leaves, curled at the corners, sailed like small boats in the creek across from me. Everything had changed, yet the water remained the same—flowing continuously, undaunted by time.

My thoughts returned to Glenda, and I forgot about the cold. I'd long suspected she was one of those angels I'd been told about—sent to light my way. Who carries the lantern? Who leads us home after our burdens are lifted? Is there more than just a shadow guiding us after we pass on? It's still a mystery to me, but now you know.

Chapter 21

I wonder why they hired that new guy? He's more interested in counting how many people come into the lab than graphic design," Albert said, chuckling as he stood on a chair, fastening a sheet of wood paneling onto the basement wall. Albert and I were about the same height, so I grabbed another chair and hammered on the wall across from him.

Alex Martingale, the new guy, had replaced Glenda at the lab. He was tall and broad-shouldered, with a ruddy complexion and copper-colored hair. His MBA from Stanford undoubtedly influenced his decision to rebrand what had long been the Mac Lab to the Business Center. I was surprised that a campus computer lab could be rebranded. He'd also added several PCs to *"take full advantage of the disruptive power of technology."* It was all rather comical to Albert and me.

The wood paneling had a seventies vibe that brought back boyhood memories. The paneling looked realistic, but it needed to be grainier. It had too many knots spaced evenly apart to cross the uncanny valley of home decor. Yet, if you squinted your eyes and walked back a few feet while considering how much less it cost than the real thing, it was better than the original. With it on the ceiling and walls, plus the hardwood floor, I felt like I was in the tree house I'd always wanted but never had. Though gratifying, it was unrelated to our plan to relocate the servers to the cooler, wood-paneled basement. I didn't feel like renting out the spare room upstairs, so I put some furniture in it and told James he could use it anytime. Still, he preferred crashing on one of the battle stations on the first floor whenever he stopped by, which was becoming less frequent.

Simone had switched majors from Graphic Design to Women's Studies and wasn't around to see Albert and me wearing button-down shirts and dress shoes, as Alex insisted. He was the opposite of Glenda. I didn't even notice if she was there most of the time. Alex got upset if we came in a minute late.

229

"I need you guys to uninstall that Doom game or whatever it's called. I want it removed from every computer. Let's lock them down. We don't want someone coming in here loading up all kinds of garbage, like that Napster program, with those MPPs. We could get sued for that," Alex instructed us.

"Yeah, we don't want to get a virus," I added, so he'd feel like he was masterfully orchestrating our operations. I didn't mention the files he referenced were called MP3, not MPP. The free songs people downloaded on Napster, which uncompensated artists bitterly protested, were a clear sign that the Internet had brought civilization to a crossroads where the past and future diverged, leading us toward triumph or defeat.

"Let's get those Windows machines up and running, too. Having PCs and Macs in the Business Center is going to be slick. I bet that'll attract grad students and business majors. We might see client migration from other labs, too. You can do that, can't you? You know how to get the Macs and PCs to communicate, right?" Albert confirmed we did. Delighted, Alex marched purposefully to his office.

After hours, Albert and I set up the new computers. The surgical nature of feeding various cables through tubes and tight spaces appealed to me. We were rerouting arteries, accelerating neural circuitry, and reshaping the present to make way for the future, which fed from the past in a continuous series of relays, switches, and data packets until it evolved into an irreversible singularity of superintelligence that would destroy us all. In the meantime, it was fun to think about.

The lab, as I still called it, recently got a wireless router. Radio waves fascinate me. Unlike my brother, who understands these things, I wanted a special pair of glasses to see their wavy lines transmitting data through walls and floorboards. I looked around the lab. Rows of keyboards, monitors, computers, cables, and slabs of silicon smaller than my fingernail were executing millions of instructions per second. How did we get here? Sometimes, I see skyscrapers and wonder the same thing. We build bombs and send signals through space, but if you leave someone in the jungle, the best they can do is climb a tree and hope a tiger doesn't eat them.

Graphic design students remained the primary demographic at the lab, and we continued to support all the software and hardware they required. However, our 'clientele,' as Alex referred to everyone at the lab, included a new group: speculators—ranging from my fellow students and visiting scholars to passersby unaffiliated with the university, seeking a respite from the current batch of mediocre sitcoms. They dropped in to check their stock portfolios and the latest market-moving headlines. Instead of downloading games and silly screen savers, they used our Bloomberg terminals and watched CNBC financial news on TVs hung high in the back. The Internet was everywhere, and it was changing everything.

***

"Julian, you'd better come home," Simone implored shortly after lunch the following day as I snuck over to a corner and chatted with her on my cell phone, a bulky contraption I'd recently purchased that stuck out of my pocket but was a far cry from the behemoth Gordon Gekko sported in *Wall Street*.

"Are you okay?"

"It's James. He's sick. I'm not sure what's wrong with him."

"Can he wait a few hours? Alex is a real ball-buster. He won't like me leaving early ... Never mind, I'll figure something out."

I waited outside Alex's office. He was on the phone, using a Bloomberg terminal he treated himself to in his office. A small TV on the wall above it played CNBC. A stock ticker ran continuously along the bottom of the screen during a breaking financial news program. Two talking heads highlighted different points on a chart, showing a crooked line moving steadily upward from left to right. Alex glanced at where I stood and continued talking on the phone without acknowledging me.

231

"Put a buy order in for a hundred shares of TheStreet.com. It just IPO'd," Alex instructed whoever he was speaking with, then typed T-S-C-M into the Bloomberg terminal. A financial summary appeared, similar to what I saw in my investment reports. I usually skimmed through those and tossed them out. However, I always checked my account balance, which was now $334,000.

"Let's see, it's at $20.25 now. Set a limit for $20.75." Alex checked the quote. "Damn, it's already run up to $21. Screw it. Use a market order—I know one of the founders. He's a legend. A real stock market maniac! It's headed to $30 for sure. All right, talk to you later." He put down the phone and waved me in. It was a lazy flip of his wrist like an emperor signaling he needed more grapes.

"Hey, buddy, what's up?" Alex asked.

I shifted the focus from James to Simone, knowing that leaving to help a friend would worsen the lecture that was coming. "Alex, my girlfriend Simone called. Something's wrong with her stomach. I want to go home and check on her. I shouldn't be gone more than an hour. Is that okay?"

Alex rested his chin on his hand and leaned back in his chair. "What? Does she need you to take her temperature? Are you sure this can't wait until after your shift? If we're understaffed, we can't meet our clients' demands. The Provost was here yesterday, and everything was running perfectly. I'm sure she was impressed. If we keep this up, the university might shut down underperforming labs and increase our budget. Life is a competition, Julian. Not everyone gets to win. But if word gets out that our staff is zipping out of here over every little thing, and clients don't receive the prompt service they've come to expect, that'll reflect poorly on us and, more importantly, on our paychecks."

"Oh, I totally agree, but Simone wouldn't call me unless she was really sick. I'll get her some medicine and be right back."

"All right, all right, just mark it on your time sheet."

"Thanks." I turned to leave, but Alex wasn't finished.

"Hey, Julian, by the way, you've got to tuck in your shirt. You look like a slob with it ... Whatever you're doing there with it hanging all over the place."

I hated tucking in my shirt. I hated wearing slacks and hard-soled shoes that made my feet ache while everyone else in the lab dressed casually. Keeping my shirt untucked was a minor act of defiance, letting people know I hadn't chosen to dress this way. When Alex said that, heat flared in my chest, and I curled my fists but quickly regained control of myself and started tucking my shirt in. He laughed, "Whoa, whoa, cowboy! I didn't mean right now. I don't need to see your underwear. Go straighten it out in the bathroom or at home; I don't care. Just get yourself together before you come back. Okay?"

"Okay."

"Listen, Julian, I heard all about what a nice person Glenda was and how she let you guys wear whatever you wanted. You probably could've worked without a shirt at all!" He started laughing at his joke, so I pretended it was funny, too, and smiled. "You might've liked that, but she wasn't helping you. People care about how you look and what you wear. It doesn't matter how we feel about it. That's the way the world works."

Ben said not having a nice car in my driveway hurt my rep; my untucked shirt seemed the same. When Ben told me that, I was more concerned about running into walls than my reputation. Little had changed.

***

"What's going on? Where's James?" I asked Simone as soon as I got home.

"He's upstairs. Julian, he's been doing heroin. I don't know all the details."

I went upstairs. James lay on a twin bed in the spare room. He'd vomited while aiming for the wastebasket but missed, splattering everything around it.

"Simone said something about heroin?" I asked James, picturing the scene earlier: Simone worrying and scolding him: *"Just wait till your father gets home."*

"That's right, International. I started shooting up, but it's not a big deal. I know people have this image of junkies lying in an alley with rotting veins, but it's not like that, and that's not why I'm sick. There was cotton in the needle, and I got cotton fever. That's what made me throw up."

"What do you mean it's not a big deal? It is a big deal. You could overdose. You could get AIDS."

"AIDS," he repeated. "Why do people say AIDS but spell out H-I-V? Why don't they call it hive?" he asked, pronouncing HIV as one word.

"Why are you smiling? This isn't funny. It's dangerous."

"Everything is funny."

"Don't be ridiculous."

"Ridiculousness is underappreciated." James propped himself up on one elbow. "It's the only thing you can trust because it's honest. Ridiculousness has nothing to hide. Everything else is an act."

I pulled up a chair. It was remarkable how James found so many ways to frustrate me, partly because he was absurd and because he was right. James sat up. His lips had a blue tinge, and he was slower than usual, but you wouldn't think he was on drugs if you didn't know him.

"Why do you keep doing this? And now you're shooting up? You said heroin chills you out, but it doesn't seem very chill when you're lying there puking on yourself."

"Why do I do it? When it hits, it's like dipping into a hot bath, and any pain you've ever felt peels away. Pleasure, all the pleasure you deserve. Then I think of ... nothing. My shoulders ease back." He took a deep breath, reliving it. "The sensation moves through me. I lie down, and everything is one—an even tone like a Tibetan bell."

"You know I like messing with people. Maybe I'm a jerk, but mostly, I want them to wake up. Wake the fuck up. All those people sipping cappuccinos and sprinkling paprika on their avocado toast are sleepwalking. It's this sleepy comfort that's so common. The comfort of sneering at those noble savages I let into the dining hall to grab whatever they could before they got taken out like the trash.

They don't know what it's like to be so low that you'd suck your grandma's dick just for the chance to lick the bottom of a trash can. But on the nod, they're out. Not forgotten—erased—just lie back and relax."

"Grandma's dick?"

"Good ole granny big bone."

I smiled even though I wanted to cry and said, "I get where you're going with this. So many people are indifferent to anything besides a basket of lightly toasted bread and a bottle of wine. But that's no reason to destroy yourself with drugs. How long has this been going on? Where have you been doing this? Have you been doing it here?"

"Is that what you're worried about? That little Jamesy will OD or get AIDS in your guest room?"

"No. Well, yes and no. You're like a brother to me, James, and I'll do anything to help you, but this is the real world. I don't want anyone doing drugs here. I barely even drink, man. I just want everything to stay cool—no drama or idiot neighbors calling the police."

"To answer your question, I haven't been doing heroin here, but I regret to inform you that I'll need to shoot up again soon."

"No, you can't do that. You have to quit!"

"Why do you think I'm here? I want to quit, but it's not like Pimp Daddy Odysseus strapping himself to the mast for twenty minutes while the Sirens sing. I gotta ease into it. I shot up enough to get here, not go through withdrawal. I've been doing it at a shooting gallery in South Philly."

"Shooting gallery?" I pictured people in a saloon like Klondike Kate's, sipping sarsaparilla and shooting the chandeliers.

"It's any place where some mug is kind enough to let dope fiends shoot up so we don't gotta nod out on the street."

"How often are you doing this?"

"A few times a day. I have an arrangement with a guy I know from way back. I help him deliver drugs to people, and he pays me in kind, plus a couple of bucks here and there."

"He ... uh, gives you heroin?"

235

"Yes, bwana."

"You seem to be fine with all of this. Don't you think it's a pretty big problem?"

Simone came in before James replied. She'd brought him a can of Dr Pepper, which even had a bendy straw. I appreciated that she wasn't flipping out over James's drug use. Simone never kicked anyone when they were down. I always loved that about her.

"Are you feeling any better?" she asked James.

"In the company of International, how could I not be?"

"Here, I thought this might help your stomach." she handed James the soda.

"My mom gave me this when I had an upset stomach. She told me it's called Dr Pepper because it used to be prescribed by a doctor. I don't know if that's true, but it helps."

James sipped the soda and burped. "Ah, that is nice. Why can't you be a considerate chap like that, International?"

"Oh, I'm sorry, *mon cher ami*. Shall I fetch your slippers and a Cohiba from the humidor?"

We all laughed. "How's your lady studies going? Have you ended women's suffrage yet?" James asked Simone.

"Nice try, James. You're not going to trick me with that. There's no shame in what you're going through. A friend of mine got addicted to heroin, and she went to a free clinic in Wilmington that helped her quit. It's anonymous, with no questions asked. I can take you there if you want to go."

"Thank you kindly, but I'll stick to Dr Pepper for now."

Simone closed the door and went downstairs. Like me, she'd never done heroin but understood James in ways I couldn't. It took me a moment to remember that suffrage meant the right to vote, not suffering. He was a clever one.

I went back to work and told Albert that James had been doing heroin and would be staying with us while he tried to kick it. Albert thanked me for letting him know but said nothing more about my wayward pal. Fortunately, Alex was at a meeting on the other end of campus. Albert explained that it started right after I left, so I was in the clear—I'd been gone longer than I said I would.

236

After work, James and I continued our conversation in the little room upstairs. "I didn't tell you this, but I went to my mom's house last month. She's living in a posh little place called Greenville," James said.

"I know where that is. It's near the children's hospital I was at. They took us on a field trip there once. It was cool. A farmer let us play with some animals in a barn."

"Yep, lots of friendly folks in Greenville. Six-bedroom houses will make you downright neighborly. Representin' in such a prime location. Mama's done well. I even went to Goodwill and bought a suit and tie for the occasion. Parted my hair right down the middle.

"'James?' she said after I knocked on the door. 'How have you been? Come in. Beatrice will be back soon. I'm sure she'll be delighted to see you.' Beatrice is my sister. The one with big tits. I hadn't seen my mom for years, and she acts like I just got home from a horseback ride with Anne of Green Gables."

"Was there horseback riding in that book?"

"You're right. Let's talk about the book, and we'll get to my story later."

"Fine, forget about the gables, but you brought it up."

"My mom and I sat down, and soon, my sister showed up. She did the same thing, acting like I'd returned from an afternoon stroll. They asked what I'd been doing, so I made up a story about working for a big software company with lots of opportunities for advancement because I didn't want to disrupt the jolly time we were having. Then, my sister told me she's studying interior design at Cornell University this fall. 'I love immersing myself in how people interact with space and all the different layouts that make it possible. It's my passion. I don't even care about the money! But I mean, of course, I'm not going to complain that interior designers tend to make very high salaries. What's a girl going to do? Say no to money?' Then they laughed at what I guess was a joke.

"Okay, then my mom starts laying it on really thick. 'It's such a blessing to follow your passion, James. Cornell is very selective, but Bee sent a lovely letter with samples of her layouts and designs.

Naturally, she was accepted. I never had a doubt. One day, I'm sure we'll see your sister decorating homes of the stars on TV!'

"I played along with them until my mom walked me to the door. Then I had to ask. I couldn't let these family history-avoiding pleasantries go on any longer. I said, 'Mom, don't you wonder where I was or why I left? Aren't you a little curious?'

"Then she says, 'James, I called the police and told them you were missing. I tried so many times to help you. What else could I do? But, honey, is that what you would've wanted? For me to go door-to-door asking where my sweet little boy was? You were always so independent. After a month, I decided that if you wanted to come home, you would, and we moved on with our lives.'"

"I don't know everything that happened between you two, but I can see her point of view. What did you expect?"

"Yeah, I should've known it would be like that. I blame myself for going back and expecting anything else. I started walking toward the end of the street to the bus station when I saw Sasha getting out of a Range Rover. She's a Russian chick I dated when I lived there. She looked fit in a tight tennis shirt and skirt. Her hair was cut the way it's been for years, with short bangs in the front. It was like old times seeing that. I looked down at my suit, and even though it was dark brown, I spotted a stain near the collar. I'm sure that gave my mother and sister a good laugh during our failed family reunion. I hid behind a tree, waiting for Sasha to go inside so I could get the hell out of there. Then a dapper lad bounded out of the Rover with a pair of tennis rackets, looking all set for Wimbledon in his Lacoste shirt and matching shorts. I knew the guy. We used to call him The Squire because he'd come galloping in to whisk your woman away for a weekend in the Poconos right after you broke up so she'd have fewer scruples about his short stature and unsolicited self-improvement tips." James had grown several inches taller than me, but his egalitarian insults made me tolerate remarks I might not have from others.

"I didn't know they made shorts. Are you sure they were Lacoste? Could you see the little alligator from the tree? How close were you?"

"International, I will always love you for thinking about that. Yes, I was close enough to see the alligator on his shorts. He brought everything inside, then Sasha returned to the Rover and scooped up a little black poodle. The dog wasn't in a carrying case or anything; it was riding beside them in the car. She carried it like a kid, with its tail wagging, slobbering—that goddamn dog. It had a better life than mine. I decided right then and there that I was shooting up. Snorting dope is like drinking cherry-flavored cough syrup when I need an industrial-strength solution for all that ails me. I've seen people come out of church feeling so righteous and clean. But when they see someone strung out around the corner, they forget all about the good book and stop to stare at them. They see the track marks and say, 'Oh no, how awful! Tiffany, look away. You don't need to see this.' And then they take these careful little steps around that nasty addict, afraid if they wake them up, they'll bite them on the ass or something. Well, I want to be everything those clean freaks hate. *Ut supra, sic infra.*"

"What does that mean?"

"*As Above, so below.* What happens here, all around us, also makes an impression within. Sorrow comes with living and it terrifies us. Everyone sees it but cares more about what their friends will think if they don't raise a glass with them to celebrate someone moving up to the next tax bracket. So, they raise it anyway, wearing the mask as the face behind it fades away, but trust me, boy. They can't silence that scream any more than I can. No, man, it rises through the quiet when you're sitting there smiling as if nothing's wrong with the world until you find yourself down and out. Then the banshee comes, and you'd rather bite your lip off than keep that stupid smirk on your face because none of them will share your pain."

"The way you broke that down, man, that's powerful. Seriously, James, you should be writing all of this down. You could help people who feel the same."

"No, can't you see? I know it's heavy, and so do you, but we're surrounded by people who will twitch in their seats after hearing one word. They'll shout you down. 'There's no place for that in polite society!' That's why I made my way to Philly. Back to the old crew. Oh, those dirty dogs were ready to receive me with a square of concrete, a syringe, and no worries about what comes tomorrow."

"But is hurting yourself the right way to get back at all those sycophants with folded napkins on their knees who will never understand what it means to be free? Don't you remember how good it felt hopping trains? None of this other shit mattered. All we needed was some courage and a bag of beef jerky. The Rowdy Boy life! Don't let those people get you down. Just cool out in this room for a while. All you need is a little sunshine and the sound of the creek, and you'll forget about them."

James looked around the room and said, "It's too cushy to be a battle station, but I'll give it a go."

"Attaboy."

"All right, International. I appreciate everything you're doing for me; I really do, but I gotta cook up again."

"No! We'll help you work through that. We can go to the place Simone was talking about."

"Look, it's an absolute delight jabbering my jaw here, but this is not something you can understand." He was sweating and had started breathing heavily.

"One more shot, then I'll knock it off. I haven't been shooting up that long. I don't need any clinic, okay? But I gotta go steady, real steady."

"All right, whatever. Fine, go ahead if that's what you gotta do."

I was worried about where this was heading. I didn't want James to do drugs at all. I had selfish and unselfish reasons, but I figured if he was going to do it—if he had to do it—this was the place."

"I'm gonna sit on the floor," he said, pulling out his works.

"Wouldn't it be better on the bed?"

"It's too wobbly, but the floor's fine. I don't even need a pillow. You should be thankful I'm not one of those junkies in such a sad state they have to search for a vein until they give up and shoot it in their eye."

James had his works in a Ziploc bag, which reminded me of my mother packing my lunch with a turkey sandwich and juice box. He

240

removed the dusty brown heroin from a smaller bag tied tight with a red rubber band and deftly put a little on a spoon bent back on itself.

"Brother, could you spare one of those cotton swabs you're always sticking in your ears against all common medical advice? A cup of water would be mighty nice as well."

Against all common medical advice, that was rich coming from him. I resigned myself to the lugubrious affair and got him what he wanted. He poured a little water on the powder, which dissolved. A lighter beneath the spoon got it bubbling. Once it cooled, he dropped a blob of cotton into the muddy mix, then slid the syringe through it to draw in the stew.

"It's hard to explain. I always hated getting shots at the doctor's office, but I love this needle. Sliding it in is a pleasurable pain. I feel a kick before the plunger even drops. That might be the best part."

He flicked the syringe to clear out any stubborn bubbles, then slid it into a thick blue vein between his knuckles. I saw what he meant when he exhaled as if he'd taken the last drag of a cigarette. He waited for a small bloom of blood to rise into the elixir to be sure he'd hit the mark, then depressed the plunger. He lazily pulled out the syringe, then slumped down as if he were becoming part of the floor, and my heart sank with him. I froze for a second, but despite what he'd said, I placed a pillow under his head and returned to my chair. Serenaded by the poppy seed lullaby, he turned onto his side, almost smiling. I sat for a minute, wanting to turn the world around, then went downstairs to talk to Simone.

"How's James doing? Is he feeling better?"

"Yeah, but he said he needed to shoot up again."

"What! Why didn't you stop him? Julian, he's addicted to heroin; he's not thinking clearly."

"That's what I thought, too, but I don't know. You should have heard him. As messed up as it is, James seems to know what he's doing."

"Well, is he going to stop?"

"He said he wants to, and you know, let's do everything we can to help him, but a lot of that is up to him."

241

"You sound like you've given up on him. He needs our help."

"I know that, and I haven't given up. See for yourself. Go upstairs and ask James what he wants to do."

Simone trotted upstairs. "Why is he on the floor? James, James, are you okay?" She hurried back downstairs. "Is he supposed to look like that? Is he overdosing?"

I was angry. I didn't want to be, but anger was better than being depressed. Why did James get addicted to heroin, and why was he doing it here? Of course I didn't want that for him or anyone. But I didn't want any more chaos in my life either.

On the one hand, I'd be happy for James to stay with us as long as he wanted. On the other hand, I knew this couldn't go on forever. We agreed that society was full of oblivious hypocrites. Still, there had to be a better way to deal with it than heroin. Simone and I went back upstairs a little while later.

James was back on the bed. He lazily opened and closed his mouth as if he'd just woken up from a nap. I felt like giving him a pacifier, a blanket, and a nice slap in the face.

"He's okay," Simone chirped.

No, he was not okay.

Over the weekend, I helped James through the worst of his withdrawal. A week later, his symptoms eased, but by Monday, he was already back to his old tricks. Albert, James, and I had breakfast while Simone was on campus to attend a talk about third-wave feminism, which the Women's Studies department had sponsored.

"Do they still have opium dens in China?" James asked Albert after swallowing a spoonful of Froot Loops. I'd lost a bet with James that the first word was spelled F-r-u-i-t, not F-r-o-o-t, as he insisted. A trip to the supermarket proved him right. I later learned this is because the product doesn't actually contain any fruit. As I tossed a couple boxes into the cart, I recalled the trouble I had making cereal choices years ago. It hadn't gotten much easier. One way that I avoided the issue was by repeatedly purchasing the same things. It didn't take long for Simone to notice my recurring shopping list and related coping habits, which was among the reasons she'd lamented having to do double brain duty. James retroactively decided his

242

winning bet entitled him to a lifetime supply of Froot Loops. Given the rate he was going, I doubted that would amount to many boxes.

"Yes, James, they do. They even have a members-only opium lounge in the departure terminal when you fly out of Hong Kong," Albert said.

"Really?"

"Absolutely, and for an extra service fee, you can have several Oriental women fan you as you recline with your pipe," Albert wryly replied.

"Dude, you're still clearing that junk from your system and already want to do more?" I shot back at James, turning off his fantasy of stowing away on a container ship bound for the Far East.

"In Xanadu did Kubla Khan, A stately pleasure-dome decree." James maddeningly replied.

"What is up with you, man?" Albert asked.

"It's regrettable. It truly is. Tourette syndrome is my unofficial but likely accurate diagnosis. It hits me like a heat-seeking missile that locks onto the one thing that'll piss people off the most. I want to snap people out of their stupor, but sometimes I don't know why I act stupid other than to tell you I'm crazy. You're a good dude, Bert. Anyone who can quickly conjure up an image of women fanning me in a departure lounge is a good man in my book."

"Since you like books and seem to think the totality of Chinese culture is fortune cookies and opium dens, you should check out the Tao Te Ching. It's a brilliant little book that helps you understand why many things are the opposite of what they appear to be."

"You got a copy?"

"In my room. I'll get it for you."

Albert handed James his copy of the *Tao*. James tucked it into the small sack he kept with him and hit the road soon after the worst of his withdrawal symptoms subsided. I hoped he hadn't gone in search of opiates, but if he was, it was better to be bound for where Alph, the sacred river ran than a warehouse somewhere in Philadelphia.

***

243

I was in Alex's office. He'd converted it into a full-on trading room with financial data streaming on three screens. Years ago, I'd seen a similar setup in Mr. Michelson's office, where he had a small data feed in the corner of his monitor. Alex had long rows of stock quotes flashing red and green as traders bid them up and down. He explained these were real-time quotes, not those amateurish, twenty-minute delayed ones that people in the lab got from Yahoo.

Alex minimized one of the quotation tables and clicked on another application. "I noticed you were away from your desk longer than expected last Friday while I was presenting the university's new timesheet and user access management system. It updates in real time, which is perfect for the Business Center. Welcome to the information age, Julian. I need you to update the nature of your absence in the system's time management module. Let's do it together this time." Alex opened the application. "Make sure you use this drop-down menu to note that it was an unscheduled absence. Going forward, type in the details of every client you serve on this screen with the radio buttons indicating whether the issue's been resolved. We'll have weekly meetings to review your stats. Are we clear, Julian?"

"Yes, that's clear."

It had become clear that I was not "in the clear" as I'd thought when I belatedly returned to the lab. It was irritating that Alex called the lab the Business Center; students had become clients, and he tracked our every move. It was also clear that Albert and I had underestimated him and the relentless march of technology, which evolved in ways that both expanded and limited our freedom.

It's not like I was lazy or had anything to hide. What bothered me was how everything had become so quantified. Glenda recognized that there were rarely eight hours of work, and we didn't need tracking software to pretend there always was. Even though the job had always involved technology, coming into work less than a year ago was like dipping into a friendly swimming hole outside of town. Now every river was dammed, and every drop accounted for. Alex turned any freedom the Internet might have fostered into a means of surveillance and control that could be captured in tidy tables or charts. One thing I did appreciate about him was his eagerness to capitalize on the bull market. Alex didn't require us to log the increasing amount of time Albert, I, and everyone around us spent riding the stock market to riches. It was a once-in-a-lifetime opportunity I was eager to take advantage of, leveraging my money and underutilized mental faculties. I had nothing to prove; it was only a competition against myself.

Chapter 22

Around the middle of 1998, I noticed a growing interest in the stock market. Grad students began checking Nasdaq's closing value on rudimentary websites and talked about trading stocks. I had a stock portfolio for years and thought about it infrequently, but the intrigue did not wane. It simmered until it reached a rolling boil soon after Alex arrived. By then, we were all printing out stock charts along with our schoolwork. A bull market was raging, and everyone in the newly christened Business Center was spinning in their chairs.

Mr. Michelson's first name was Jerry, but I still called him Mr. Michelson in honor of the fourteen-year-old boy I was when we met. I was relieved when I learned I could sell the mutual funds in my portfolio. Damn, those were lame. They were full of old companies like Coca-Cola and Exxon, favored by famous investors like Warren Buffett, who Mr. Michelson often quoted. They were good companies but weren't rocketing higher like Internet stocks. Most of them didn't even have websites. I appreciated the investing principles Mr. Michelson taught me, but they were out of style. No one cared about P/E ratios or diversification anymore. Everyone was focused on a company's potential and the fear of missing out on all the wealth they ever wanted if its stock blasted off before they bought shares.

The first stock I bought was Apple because I worked with their computers and knew people liked them. I'd wanted to call Mr. Michelson for months to get in on the stock market action, especially over the past month when stocks were making new highs every day. Alex succinctly explained the situation: *"Julian, this is a once-in-a-lifetime opportunity. Stocks are headed much higher from here. At the rate everything's lining up with technology, the economy, and the Internet, it'll be too late to get in by the time most people realize how big this is. Zero-sum game, baby."* My account remained in a trust until I turned twenty-five in six months. It was so frustrating—everyone was making a fortune but me. I wanted to dump my dinosaur mutual funds and load up on the hot stocks people were talking about. I still had a long way to go to be on equal footing with the moneymen, unburdened by the world's worries, confined to people with lower account balances like mine. After leaving Alex's office, I called Mr. Michelson to prepare.

"How's it going, Julian? Your graduation's coming up soon, right?"

"That's right, Mr. Michelson; a couple more classes, and I'll be done. It's pretty amazing, isn't it?"

"Congratulations! That's a tremendous achievement. I'm sure your mother is thrilled. How can I help you?"

"If I want to buy a stock, how does that work? Do I need to go to your office? Or can I email you?"

"We don't accept emails. They aren't secure. You can fax us an order or give me a call."

"Okay, thank you."

"Would you like to place a trade now?"

"Oh, can you tell me how that works again?"

"I'll sell one of the ETFs I've purchased to build a tactical position for you.

Did he forget the money's in a trust? Or maybe it's okay to trade as long as I don't make withdrawals? I almost didn't say anything, but I didn't want Mr. Michelson to get into trouble, so I confirmed it was possible.

"If you sell that, um—"

"They're called exchange-traded funds, or ETFs. They're easier to trade than mutual funds."

"If you sell that ETF, can I buy Apple shares right now? I don't need to wait for anything, right?"

"Transactions take three days to settle, but you don't need to worry about that. However, if you want to be more active in managing your money, we should discuss how to value stocks and build a well-diversified portfolio. I know everyone's getting all worked up about these dotcom stocks, but it won't end well if that's all they own. Julian, I recommend familiarizing yourself with

Warren Buffett's strategies to learn more about the type of companies you should buy and hold for the long term."

"I saw him on CNBC. He's pretty old, isn't he? I don't think he understands the Internet. He's smart, but nothing like this has ever happened before."

"This time is different. Those are the most dangerous words in the world of investing. Julian, I was in Japan in the late eighties. Not long before we met. The Nikkei was doubling and tripling, much like we're seeing now. Over a decade later, it's still over fifty percent off its highs. Apple is profitable, unlike most stocks that've been in the news, but it still seems overvalued. I think you're better off with the funds I've got you in, but it's up to you, Julian. Do you want to place the trade?"

I told him that I did, and he purchased the shares. I wasn't sure what to make of that guy. He had a clever quote or statistic for everything. I knew he was looking out for me, but it was my money, and I didn't want him to give me a hard time about making the most of it. It would be better if he kept spinning in that chair like the rest of us.

***

"When the MACD crosses above zero, that's a buy signal, isn't it?"

"Yes, it indicates that a stock is in an uptrend. If you want to be a little more aggressive, set an alert for when the fast line crosses over the slow line. That's an early buy signal, but it has more false positives than a zero-line cross." Albert was discussing some of the more popular technical indicators with a biology professor who'd stopped by the lab to get trade ideas from ClearStation.com, a website we used for charting, analysis, and interacting with other traders. Technical analysis, the graphical study of historical prices, is an essential tool for traders to divine the direction of stocks. The relationships between prices, moving averages, histograms, and volume highlight profitable trends. They were compass points guiding me to greater wealth, like my prized green band, which granted access to the promised land. Our duties extended beyond network and application support to include fielding trading and capital markets queries. It was a new frontier that demanded rigorous analysis and critical thinking skills, which I was pleased to possess.

Alex promoted *"the continual evolution of the Business Center."* In addition to reviewing employee and business center stats, he devoted team meetings to discussing trading tools and concepts. Alex commented, *"All of this comes naturally to me. I have an MBA from Stanford, where they practically invented making money."* His micromanagement irritated me, but I paid close attention. I could build a fortune much faster if I learned the ways of the moneymen. What would Glenda think of the Business Center? I laughed. She'd drag Alex out by the ear and then kick him in the ass.

***

"How did you learn so much about technical analysis? Alex acts like you need an MBA to understand it," I asked Albert as we sat in the basement after work, drinking beer. It was bitterly cold outside, but the servers generated enough heat to kick back on beach chairs in shorts and T-shirts as snow blotted the window.

"They're mostly lines and ratios plotted to track prices over time on a graph. If you want to learn more, check out the tutorials on Clearstation. I've learned a lot on that site," Albert said, then sipped his beer.

I planned to do that tomorrow. I was buzzed, which was enough for me. I'd only been drunk once, and that was when someone spiked the punch at a party in high school. I didn't want to be like my mom had been or James, finding sanctuary in opiates. For me, the Mystery always came first. The existential riddles wouldn't wait for me to sober up to be solved. That doesn't mean I wasn't tempted. Like everyone, I had my share of troubles. I felt sad sometimes. Quite often, actually. Being half-blind got me down the most.

***

In the middle of the fall semester, I bumped into something on my left while walking through a park lined with rows of folding tables. In the absence of sight, I assumed it was a chair and kept going. Two seconds later, I heard a child crying and realized I was wrong. Of course, their father was about twice my height.

"Hey, where the fuck do you think you're going? You slammed into my son!" he snorted as he charged toward me. What I'd thought was the minor annoyance of ramming into an inanimate object escalated into another near-death experience. The boy's mother sat nearby with a basket full of sandwiches, soda cans, and a scowl, matching her husband's growing fury.

"I'm sorry, I'm sorry," I said with my hands raised, signifying that I didn't want to be shot ... again. "I didn't see him. I don't have a left field of vision."

"You don't have a what, motherfucker?"

Homonymous hemianopia is hard to explain, even to someone who isn't about to kill you. I had to summarize the problem quickly if I wanted to stay alive. The boy dusted himself off and asked, "Daddy, why did that man hurt me?" His father's clenched fist was attached to an enormous arm, well suited for the pain he was eager to inflict.

"Someone shot me. I didn't see him. See this scar here? I'm half-blind. I'm sorry," I told him in a single breath. I tousled my hair in the back, where I'd spent all morning concealing the crooked line I wanted him to see.

He examined it and declared, "Watch where you're going next time, fucking faggot." Faggot? I've never cared about anyone's sexuality and find anyone disparaging people over it idiotic, but I didn't have the toolkit required to dismember and reeducate him, so my best option was to keep apologizing. "It was my fault. Sorry," I reiterated, hoping short and simple words would suffice. I began walking away, hoping to de-escalate the situation, but he grabbed my shoulder, ensuring I remained for another round of humiliation.

"Where are your manners, sweetie?" he asked, puckering his lips. "You gonna run back to your little faggot boyfriend without

250

apologizing to my son first? Nathan, come over here." The man released my shoulder and gestured for his son to join him. They faced me like a firing squad. By now, a sizable assembly of picnickers had stopped snacking to gawk without pretense that this was the best thing they'd ever seen.

Nathan stood by his dad and hugged his leg. He wore the same jeans and red flannel shirt as his father. How adorable.

"Nathan, I'm sorry about that, my friend. I didn't mean to knock you down, but I'm glad you're okay." I hadn't intended to say "my friend." It was a little sweetener I spontaneously threw in.

"Nah, Nah, he ain't your friend. Is this guy your friend, Nathan?"

"No, I don't like him. He gave me an owie on my knee."

"Nathan, I can't see well. That's why I bumped into you. But it was my fault, and I hope you're feeling better now."

Their faces looked grotesque, with short, stubby noses, googly eyes, and lips dangling like Mr. Potato Head.

I wanted a chainsaw. Rip the cord, then listen to Papa scream over the buzz of the blade and the smell of gasoline. Cut him at the knee and fell him like a tree:

Look, Nathan, now your dad has an owie on his knee, too! Be a good boy and grab one of those soda cans for me.

The man patted his son on the head. The boy returned to the table and sat by his mother, then reached for a sandwich, having already lost interest in the whole thing—though another, more primitive part of his mind would never forget the satisfaction of seeing his father humiliate the cripple. Big Papa came up to my face. "That wasn't so hard, was it? It's nice to show a little respect, isn't it? Now get the hell out of here."

As I started walking, he gave me an obligatory shove that nearly made me fall on my face. I turned back toward the tables, searching for a sharp utensil to peel out at least one of his eyeballs.

I recalled Mateo propped up on crutches—what had he endured? What had he overcome? I breathed easier, focusing on him.

I wanted to run, but my legs wouldn't cooperate, so I waddled away and found a bench. Whenever conflicts like this occurred, something inside me broke. I worried these things were crucial to

251

my sanity and that I should figure out how to mend them. I frequently had panic attacks, and whenever I did, I obsessively repeated the visual field test Dr. Roshan had taught me.

Seated on the bench, I focused on a pole, raised my index finger, and moved it from the far left across my face. After ten repetitions, I was reassured that my vision hadn't deteriorated since I'd done the same exercise yesterday, and my breathing slowed.

***

I placed my half-empty beer bottle on the table near one of the servers. Albert cracked open another one as a cold wind rattled the window. I sat upright. I don't want to forget my troubles; I want to overcome them, and trading stocks is how I'll do it.

Chapter 23

My defiance of brain damage extended to studying etymology in college. I learned that corporation is derived from the Latin root for "body," which is ironic given that corporations will sever every limb to maximize profits. I shared my observation with Alex, and he agreed it was a savage contradiction but said not to get hung up on it, considering that many of the largest charitable foundations were funded by people who became merciful only after amassing their fortunes. For now, we needed to focus on securing our own wealth.

It bothered me how the stock market often moves independently of economic forces affecting the salaries of people who owned none of the shares we traded long before my Machiavellian observation. However, after considering what Alex said, I realized whatever we produced would be sold to the highest bidder no matter what we did, so I shouldn't get distracted by the working person's plight, and my desire to trade stocks continued unabated. My rising Requirements of the Imagination required me to build a wall so high that brutish motherfuckers like I'd encountered in the park would never get in. I could be merciful later.

Albert, Alex, and I were riding the money tsunami, doing flips at the top of the wave, alongside everyone hoping what we poured into the market would deliver the gold-plated future we desired. In the meantime, we all got a kick from seeing commas added to our net worth as stocks raced higher. Even after my shift, I kept at it. This wasn't out of affection for the lab. The slow speed of my dial-up Internet at home made managing my portfolio impossible. As a result, I spent less time with Simone, but the weekends were enough to let her know how happy I was to be with her.

Once I met my Requirements, we could spend the rest of our lives free from staff reductions, time-tracking apps, mergers, acquisitions, pay cuts, furloughs, and … Thank you for your time. We're still interviewing other candidates, but we'll be in touch.

I explained this to Simone, but she didn't share my excitement when the Nasdaq hit another record high—just below 4000—in the weeks leading up to New Year's Eve. It was hard to understand if you weren't trading stocks. The market seemed to never stop rising, and my confidence grew with it. I was better than the men who fled the morning after they slept with her. I was her constant companion, charting a course by the tradewinds of market forces toward the safe harbor where we'd gather our doubloons like ancient mariners carrying precious cargo past unseen reefs and pitiless pirates, guided by the twinkling lights above. Soon, she'd see it too. I dared to dream, and now the stars spoke to me, though it was a fine line between astronomy and astrology.

Back on Earth, one downer my fellow speculators and I faced in our lofty ambitions was the potential for a global meltdown caused by a computer glitch called Y2K, a numeronym for the year 2000. Nearly every legacy computer system utilized a two-digit date format, meaning that everything from tollbooths to pacemakers might malfunction when the date rolled from 99 to 00, after which these systems might not register 00 as 2000 but another random century like 1700. But I wasn't worried. I'd gained control of my account sooner than anticipated and could cash out if necessary. Nonetheless, my last trade with Mr. Michelson still bothered me. It proved that I needed to be the one in control of my money.

"I'd like to buy fifty shares of S-E-E-K and sell M-S-F-T," I'd requested, providing him the tickers for Infoseek.com and Microsoft. I loved that ticker, SEEK. It didn't influence their fundamentals, of course. It was a good luck charm, but that can be a tiebreaker. Superstition finds its way into the mind of every speculator. No, a cool ticker isn't enough to make a selection, but if two stocks were equal in my estimation, sometimes I'd choose the one with the better ticker.

"That's Infoseek, a dotcom stock, right?" Mr. Michelson asked.

"Yes, that's right. They have a great website." I didn't like his dismissive tone when he said "dotcom", as if profiting from fast-moving stocks was foolish.

"Are you sure you don't want to hold on to Microsoft? It's a solid company and would be less affected by an extended drawdown."

Drawdown. I took note of that word. I wasn't sure what it meant, but I wasn't about to let Mr. Michelson know. I confirmed what I wanted, and he placed the trade. They were both tech stocks, but Microsoft had been around since the seventies—old, like the unsold gems in my grandfather's jewelry box. Infoseek was a search engine site. It was new and moving into markets that everyone was excited about. I was glad I loaded up before it doubled again.

Within minutes, Infoseek fell, and Microsoft rose. Infoseek's chart was perfect. It was marching higher right before I bought it. What happened? Were those old gems in vogue again? The stock market often doesn't move the way you think it will. I'd already learned that. Chart patterns aren't infallible. There are only probabilities that require the nimble mind of a trader to navigate.

Infoseek's failure to launch frustrated me, but figuring out why it fell was a waste of time. If a stock breaks down, you've got to hop on another one, still chugging up that hill. The only thing stopping me from leaving that old locomotive behind is that I'd have to call Mr. Michelson first.

He was right, but I didn't want to hear one of his pearls of wisdom, like, *"It's not timing the market, Julian. It's time in the market."* He'd already mailed me a brochure about the perils of market timing. It highlighted guys like Warren Buffett, who focused on fundamentals and long-term growth. The brochure included a variety of tables, graphs, and footnotes pointing to a panoply of related articles they claimed supported their analysis. Those articles were written by the same last-century moneymen who expected me to be satisfied with chump change until I was eighty and could finally retire with a "statistically probable" pile of money when I was too damn old to enjoy it. I was sure of it. The last page of every brochure featured an old couple smiling shoeless on a far-off Tahitian shore. They never showed photos of guys my age in breezy linen beachwear. That was by design. They were trying to con young men like me into riding a tortoise to the finish line. If I got there too soon, one of them would have to come down. The whole money game is a pyramid. Not much room at the top.

I wouldn't be swayed by their tactics. The skills I'd developed making timely trades and the money from my injury gave me an edge over my peers. I'd reach the summit with a big stack before the future coalesced with the hours ahead when the opportunity to get rich was gone. They'd still be in the wilderness while I was inside, safe from insult, inferiority, and having to defend myself against anyone who wanted to kick me when I was down. I wasn't trading solely for personal gain. I was doing it for everyone I cared about. As soon as I realized my Requirements, they'd all be protected. I would feel no shame. I would feel no pain. I would provide.

No one had the right to talk me out of taking what was mine, including Mr. Michelson. Especially Mr. Michelson. If it weren't for him, I'd already be a millionaire. Online brokerage accounts were gaining popularity. With an online account, you could trade with a few taps on your keyboard. They had dozens of tools and real-time quotes. I could view my holdings on my broker's site but couldn't trade on it. I needed to unlock my money so I could drive the train, and then I'd leave those stodgy codgers with nothing but a blur of steel passing them.

* * *

The university had recently constructed a fitness center next to the lab. Simone and I were stoked when they built it. We were both six cans short of a six-pack and could use some firming up. "It's practically in our backyard," we rejoiced, but after two weeks on the StairMaster, we fell off the wagon. Even the gym was playing CNBC instead of the usual motivational media. It was open later than the lab and was still packed after one of my late-night sessions at work. Someone called my name while I was zipping up my coat. "Yo, J, is that you?"

I didn't recognize him at first—it was Desmond, also known as Minty. "Minty, it's been a long time!" I said, walking his way, ready to shake hands—maybe even embrace. He winced, and I wondered if he'd stopped using that name. However, he greeted me warmly as I approached, so it felt like old times again.

"What've you been up to these days, J? You graduate yet?"

"I got a late start, but I'll be graduating with an English degree soon. I'm also working at the computer lab next door. It's a pretty sweet gig—I spend a lot of time online and see how people use the web. You can make decent money trading stocks if you learn to read charts and know what's happening with technology. I've been doing a little of that, too.

It would be cool if Minty was also into stocks, or even better if he wanted to learn about them. I'll invite him to the lab and teach him how to trade. He'll see I'm no longer some dude who needs people to tilt their exams toward to pass, though with my C average, that might not have been such a bad thing.

"The Internet. Humph. Yeah, everyone's real excited about that, aren't they? That's all they talk about in the computer course I've been taking. I got my business degree last year, but a man's gotta have all the skills he can if he's gonna make it, so I came back for more. You feeling me?"

"Damn right, my man. You'll have your own empire soon. You always had a lot of good ideas. Have you ever thought about starting a dotcom company? I know people who've done well with that. I could introduce you." Yeah, I'll show him a couple of stock charts. How it all works. I'll walk him through it step-by-step. He'll love that. Of course he will. A man's gotta have skills if he's gonna make it.

"My own empire. I like the sound of that, but I don't know about no dotcom. I'm gonna start with something small in my neighborhood, keep it real, you know? I want to work with people I know and rise together. Don't gotta mess with no Bankers if I roll like that. But I appreciate you looking out, J. You take care, man. I gotta be on my way."

Minty took off. He had zero interest in the stock market, and I'd started to sound like Alex. I frowned. I was still trying to save everyone, even if they didn't want my help. But I wanted to help someone. Be good. That was part of my Requirements. But who should I help? My friends and my family, but not Minty. I remembered how we all used to sit at the same lunch table, then merely a wave in the hall, and now he wanted to be on his way. I wish we could've been close like we were, but he had his own Requirements and ways to fill them now. I respected that.

***

As I replayed the conversation on my way home, I couldn't shake the feeling that Minty's comment about 'bankers' was a thinly veiled reference to my being Jewish. We'd bonded over our shared struggle to find a place in a world driven by wealth and status, where prejudice and social pressures often served as barriers. Yet, longstanding tensions between Black and Jewish communities became one of the most formidable obstacles we faced, making us question whether the barriers we fought against would one day stand between us.

In *Notes of a Native Son*, James Baldwin examined the socioeconomic disparities between Black and Jewish communities, which fomented these tensions. Both groups have long histories of facing prejudice and discrimination. Yet, Baldwin noted that instead of uniting over their shared struggles, these collective burdens tend to generate negative synergies and self-defeating hostilities.

Simone focused on another sphere of inequality: the privileges men enjoy under patriarchy, often bolstered by the advantages of Whiteness. But to what extent are we accountable for the groups we're born into? I wanted to define myself through my passion and purpose, not by labels assigned to me—especially after repeatedly being told that Jewish people were excluded from the White race due to their supposed roles in societal problems throughout history. A mode of intolerance that requires reducing millions of people to a recurring set of reprehensible traits. I'm indifferent to how people define themselves, but when you combine the many layers of identity, those matryoshka dolls really begin to bulge.

I'd stopped practicing Judaism once I was in high school and rarely mentioned being Jewish. In addition to no longer practicing the religion, I was tired of confronting the prejudices that have haunted Jewish people for millennia. The semester before I ran into Minty, I took a class on W.E.B. Du Bois's theory of Double Consciousness, describing the conflicted experience of Black Americans. It resonated with me because of my own divided Jewish identity, which I typically hid, fearing it would be used against me. My interest in Double Consciousness grew when I considered the additional fracture my once-unhindered brain and now-disabled one created. I'd wanted to discuss this with Minty instead of the stock market but held back, fearing it would seem like I'd appropriated a concept more relevant to him than me. Ultimately, we drifted apart for reasons unrelated to our relationship—which frustrated me since I never thought I owned the road.

My father said people frequently use victimhood to gain favor or a sense of purpose. Though some seek conflicts or exploit grievances, dismissing all pain as feigned does a disservice to genuine victims. On the other hand, censoring criticism can be equally counterproductive, as Isaac warned when he said accusing people of antisemitism can lead to conspiracy theories and claims of suppressing valid criticism. So, I tried to avoid the term, not wanting to legitimize the unsettling logic used by some who frame accusations of antisemitism as a tactic to suppress the truth—even though I knew that line of reasoning could provide an avenue for outlandish claims to fester. Because opportunities to counter prejudice are lost when they're swiftly met with accusations of intolerance.

By the time I got home, I realized all these factors made me overreact to Minty's comment about 'bankers,' which I'd ironically brought upon myself by trying to impress him with trading jargon and business introductions instead of discussing what I'd wanted out of fear of offending him. It was a lesson I'd learned before: People's perceptions of each other shape their interactions. We have many histories—but the common thread remains: what we see typically reflects our expectations and projections, not the person who stands before us.

***

"I don't understand what these pro-life people are thinking," Simone said as she lay in bed reading the latest issue of *Ms. Magazine*.

"I agree that childbirth is a miracle, but do pro-lifers think they can form a human chain in front of an abortion clinic, and God will take care of the rest? Then they get all sanctimonious when the same women need welfare, or their kids join gangs because they have to work two jobs to take care of them," she lamented.

I sat on the bed beside her and said, "I don't know why people get so worked up over choices other people make that have nothing to do with them. They believe the stronger they feel, the more valid their opinion is. I think emotions are like lightning, and logic is like thunder. I know I've done a lot of things that don't make sense after I think about them."

Simone smiled. "So, what do you think about abortion?"

"I try to avoid hot topics like that because most people have already made up their minds, and the conversation goes off the rails unless you agree."

"You have to have an opinion. You have to take a side, or someone else will choose one for you."

"I agree that childbirth is a miracle, and adoption should be considered if the pregnancy wasn't planned, but getting to that point isn't always straightforward. Some people believe abortion should be illegal and it's evil no matter how soon it's done, but I don't feel that way. I've known women who've had abortions, and none of them are malicious people. Some have kids now and take great care of them. That might not have been possible if they were forced to have children before they were ready. To be honest, I'd struggle with that decision, so I'm glad you're taking birth control!"

Simone sat up, her tone softening. "Yeah, it's easy to judge people dealing with an unplanned pregnancy until you're the one making life-changing decisions, too. You know, I don't care about whatever you've lost from your injury. It only makes what remains more beautiful."

260

We were face-to-face, but I saw myself in a silent film, with a projectionist cranking the reel. Walking, sitting, standing, people strolling along the promenade exchanged pleasantries, but I couldn't hear a word. I didn't know what to do or where to go. What am I doing here? Did the woman with the Doberman say hello or goodbye? I was lost among the blurry faces, but it wasn't a film. It was a waking dream. The sound rushed in. "Gimme a call sometime." "How are you doing?" "See you around." What is it worth? Nothing, because I'll never see them again. At the bottom of the hill, the sea looked the same as the sky. I could've been a cloud riding the wind over interminable highways, snaking through cities too far below to tell where I was going or where I'd been. I snapped back into my body. Are you still with me, dear? There she was, right beside me, Simone. Brick by brick, we'd built our relationship. Our lives were intertwined. It's alchemy, where one plus one begets a trinity, but what once was whole can never be divided without losing a piece.

Later that evening, as the house creaked in the still night, Simone said she couldn't sleep. I offered to read her a bedtime story. She sleepily agreed, and I grabbed *Siddhartha*, one of several books I owned by Hermann Hesse, but I'd inherited this one from my father. The book traces the Buddha's beginnings and must've appealed to him when he was young, before my mother and I were in his life. Before anger had corrupted him.

Simone fell asleep after a few pages. I gazed at her happily as she lay diagonally across the bed, her hair spread behind her. I reflected on her kind words, smiling. She wasn't aware that I'd hotwired my brain for capital gains, and now they were coming quickly. The way she slept left no room for me to lie down. The spare bedroom was a mess, so I headed to the living room and slept on one of the battle stations, but soon after I shut my eyes, my brother-in-arms woke me up when he returned. "In the doghouse again, old sport?" James inquired, manning the other battle station.

"Nah, nothing like that. I just don't want you fighting this war alone, Brigadier."

"As you were, International, as you were."

***

The Nasdaq cleared 4000, and the Zeitgeist whispered, 'Anything is possible.' I'd gained control of my account and was ready to ride it higher into the new millennium.

"Hey, Alex, you got a second?" I asked after waiting five minutes for him to break away from his monitors and open the door.

It was the week of Thanksgiving, and everyone's wallets were fattening up as fast as their waistlines. Another shopping center was under construction near the sold-out luxury condominiums right around the block from it, but that was small-time stuff. Billions were being made overnight. Spend a million every day, and it would still take years to burn through it. Happy days were here.

"What's up, my man?" Alex greeted me with a high-five as I walked in. His mood rose with the market until he almost seemed like the cool boss he clearly wasn't. However, the stock market never superseded his passion for quantifying everything we did in the lab and compiling it into what seemed like numerology to me. Alex rarely discussed his number-crunching ambitions but had once pointed at a spreadsheet and said, "All of these data points will be worth a lot of money someday."

His drive to monetize our clicks and queries still amused me. Still, even when he was in high spirits, I tread carefully because that wasn't Alex's true nature. I often wondered how long the market euphoria would last. Whenever the party ended, so would his high-fives. People frequently debated the market's strength in newscasts and online. Most saw plenty of runway left on our path to greater wealth, but there were also bears taunting everyone with crash predictions, whom I usually blocked. Why listen to those pessimists when even Alan Greenspan, the chairman of the Federal Reserve, couldn't stop the seemingly endless ascent he labeled 'irrational exuberance'?

I knew the rally had to end at some point, and then I expected stocks would hardly move for months like they had when I used to check Hershey's quote in the newspaper. I worried that waiting even a few more weeks to pour everything into the hottest stocks was a big risk. Up, up, up. They were going up now.

I still had all my Hershey's shares in an account my mother held for my brother and me, but I rarely thought about them. Chocolate bars? Why would I care about them? My sights were on a bigger prize. I suspected the funds Mr. Michelson managed weren't in a trust, contrary to what my mother had told me. Why else would I be able to call him and trade with that money? It didn't make sense. It wouldn't be the first time she'd deceived me, believing it was for my own good. If my brother had that money, she would have let him manage it long ago. She had a pension and didn't understand the stock market or how capable I'd become.

"Alex, do you have a minute? It's about something personal, so I can come back later if you're busy."

"Julian, you told me you don't need time off for the holidays. You said you'd be here. That hasn't changed, has it? I've been checking your stats, and you're killin' it. You don't want to end that streak now, do you? There might be some big shots in town, and we all need to shine. We've got to end the year strong, alright? This isn't a good time to take off and sit on Santa's lap." His face flushed, imagining the horror if I weren't in the lab and a single person couldn't get the latest stock quotes.

I smiled uneasily, reminding myself we could high-five all day but would never be friends. "No, nothing like that. I'll be here the whole time. You remember I was injured in a shooting accident, right?"

"Uh, yes, we talked about that."

I stepped into his office. "It has to do with the money I was awarded after my injury. I'm trying to figure out whether it's in a trust."

Now I had his attention. Alex laced his fingers together and leaned forward. "What kind of money are we talking about here, Julian? Seven figures? Seems like you came out okay," he observed, looking me over as if he were a neurologist like the university cop Glenda had berated.

I already regretted this conversation, but there was a solid chance he knew if I could unlock my money sooner than I'd been told. "No, I didn't get that much. We were going to sue the gun manufacturer but settled for a simpler lawsuit."

"All right, so you have this money. Look, you can tell me how much it is or not. I get it. Maybe that's personal, but what exactly do you want?"

"It's okay; I'll tell you. I got $250,000, but I already spent some on a house, a car, and a couple of other things."

"Great, I'm happy for both of us. I guess I won't need to give you a raise anytime soon. That's a relief."

I was glad I didn't tell him how much I'd boosted it. Who knows what kind of idiotic conclusions he'd reach then.

"Uh, well, a raise, of course. That's up to you, but it'd be super helpful if you know how to check if the money's in a trust. If it's not, I could manage it more actively. Oh, by the way, which online brokerage do you use? I heard E-Trade is pretty good."

"They're okay, but I prefer Datek. They have all the same tools the pros use. You can keep track of everything in one place. It's slick. If you want to take a look, I've got it loaded up right here."

I walked over, and he showed me his setup. It was even more insane than the trading tools I'd seen him using only a month ago during one of our team meetings. Alex had an array of windows within windows laid out on his screen, displaying real-time profit and loss percentages, color-coded watchlists, charts, and news alerts, all dancing together. Watching the money ballet was fascinating as we anticipated its next move.

Alex loved talking about the power of all that information, what it measured, and what it meant. He explained how the data guided his decisions, and after a few clicks, he made it span several screens. Alex spoke of new fifty-two-week high alerts, relative strength, convergence, divergence, stochastic indicators, and how he'd taken a class at Stanford with the guy who invented one particular feature. But my attention shifted to the upper left corner of his screen. Due to my vision, I hadn't seen it at first. It showed his total account balance. I wasn't sure. Did he want me to see it? Alex's balance was

$510,000. Mine had ballooned to $605,000. He had less than me! How old is he? Probably in his early forties. Ha! By the time I'm his age, I'll have six million dollars. How much did the president of the university make last year? A few hundred thousand? Well, I've already made more than that this year. All of them, less than me, less than me! Who's the king? I'm the king. King Julian. Alex turned back to face me. I averted my eyes, extinguished the torches, and raised the drawbridge to my castle.

"Figuring out whether it's in a trust should be easy. Check the heading on one of your statements. If you see something like 'on behalf of' or 'for the benefit of' included in the account name, it's in a trust. Otherwise, it's not. Let me know if you need help. I'd be happy to take a look."

He's only happy about his misguided assumption that he has more dough than I do. I thanked him and logged into my account. I didn't see anything resembling what he told me to look for, so I had to wait until I got home and checked the most recent report Mr. Michelson had mailed me. It was right at the top all along. Account name: Julian I. Lawrence Brokerage Account. Account Type: Individual Brokerage. After daydreaming about doubling and tripling my money, my excitement subsided. I was surprised by how quickly my mood changed after confirming the money wasn't in a trust. My mother had lied, but only to protect me, which is what she's supposed to do. Since sobering up, she'd been selfless. The AA program has a role called sponsorship. Sponsors are seasoned recovering alcoholics like her who help people new to the program. These sponsees called her whenever they had a moment of weakness and wanted to drink. Day or night, she always took the call. Sitting patiently for ten minutes or ten days to help them fight their addiction.

Well, soon, I'll put her mind at ease. I'll prove I'm not merely restored but have surpassed who I might have been before my injury. She'll be proud of me. Not because of a house I bought with money that cost me over a quarter of my mind. No, from the money I've made with what remains. I'll show her my account after I make a million dollars. That's what I'll do.

I opened an account at Datek and was on the verge of taking control of my destiny. I could wire the funds without telling Mr. Michelson, but now that I knew no one could stop me, I softened up and thought he should know.

"Hi, Julian. I hope you and your mother are enjoying the holidays. How can I help you? Did you want to place a trade?"

"Thank you, and happy holidays to you too, Mr. Michelson. No, I opened an online brokerage account at Datek. I'd appreciate it if you could send me a check because that's, um, how I'll be managing my money from now on."

After a long pause, he spoke. "Julian, there's a note here in our CRM system. Your mother wanted you to keep your money with me until you're twenty-five. That's coming up soon, but I'd like to continue our relationship beyond that. Why don't you come to my office so we can discuss your plans? If you want to be more aggressive, I can put you in one of the Internet funds we recently launched. They track the Nasdaq closely. Although, as I've said, large caps with robust balance sheets and proven business models will outperform these dotcom companies when valuations inevitably revert to the mean."

After another pause, I spoke. "Mr. Michelson, I know she means well, but whatever my mother told you doesn't matter because it's my money. I've enjoyed working with you. It's nothing, you know; there's no problem with that. But using an online brokerage account will make it easier to trade. That's how everyone does it now. So, would you mind sending me a check?" I said as I made persuasive gestures with my free hand while I held the phone.

"Julian, you have sole discretion over your account, but your mother and I want to see you make the most of it. I've seen people experience liquidity events like yours, an inheritance, or a business deal, and it's worse; it's harder on the mind to never have a large amount of money than to lose what you've had. That's why, as a professional wealth manager and your friend, I suggest you keep working with me."

"Thank you. I appreciate what you're saying, but I've been thinking that I'm going to—well, I'm doing fine on my own. And, of course, if the bull market ends, I can easily close my positions with the online account. You still have my address, right? In Newark?"

"Yes, Julian, I have it, and I'll cut the check for you today if that's what you want, but I'd like to share one more thing with you first. Your account has gained eighty percent since you began actively trading it. In that same period, the Nasdaq has risen eighty-nine percent. You've had the wind at your back, and trust me, it's not a matter of if, but when the market falls, you'll go right down with it because just as a rising tide lifts all boats, an ebbing one sinks them just the same. It's easy to get caught up in the lure of quick riches when a raging bull market is on the cover of every magazine. Those lunatics in the financial media share some of the blame for breathlessly announcing the latest index values at the top of every hour to make you believe that you've got to constantly watch the market or you'll miss out on making millions. They'll play the same game all the way down while indices crash. There's fear; there's panic—if you listen to them, you'll think you have to sell everything five times a day just to stay afloat. Ask yourself, Julian, what are these market commentators doing, screaming in front of wall-size monitors with flashing quotes and smoky skylines? Are they sensationalizing the market or helping you manage your investments?"

"I know what you're saying about people acting melodramatic on TV, but it is exciting. What's wrong with that?"

"Julian, if you got bored with the stock market, they'd be out of a job. But you ought to find it boring. Investing is not supposed to be exciting. Trading and timing the market is very difficult. Yes, some do it successfully, but it's hard—if not impossible—for most people to consistently profit from the approximations and uncertainties of trading. Most market timers underperform the S&P 500, and many lose everything. Forget about trading, and don't worry about missing out. Investing isn't an overnight thrill. It's a long-term reward for patience, discipline, and smart choices over time. I'm not saying you haven't done well with your trades; you have. But if you'd put your money into an index fund, you'd have done even better without needing to make all those trades and take on the risks and tax implications that go with them. Why don't you take a few days to consider what I've said? The market will be closed for Thanksgiving, so you won't miss much by sleeping on it."

I didn't like his little speech. I wanted to part ways as equals, not with him preaching to me while I walked out the door. I politely but firmly repeated my request to close the account and spoke to him for the last time. He was the one who wanted to keep me in a bunch of grandpa funds. The same ones that would keep me waiting another five decades to walk shoeless along the shore. I knew where my money needed to be. I was the reason it had risen so fast. Maybe he could've made more than I had over the past few months, but I'd learned quickly. Once I was directing every one of my dollars, nothing could stop me from making far more than Mr. Michelson ever could, and I'd stroll on those Tahitian shores long before I had a foot in the grave like the people in his brochures.

Chapter 24

It was a perfect Christmas Day. Even as a Jewish kid, I always loved Christmas. Snow blanketed the city, but it was warm enough to walk along the shoveled sidewalks without gloves. Simone's parents were in Florida. I'd finally met her father before they left. He was ten years older than her mother and had aged into a frail old man, no longer the tyrant Simone once described. "Do I have to fill this up, or are you going to help me?" he'd complained when his coffee cup ran dry, but everyone knew he was a shadow of his former self and teasingly put up with him.

"You just sit in your big wooden chair, Daddy. I'll fill it up," Simone snarked. He and I had a short conversation.

"What are you planning to do for work?" her father asked.

"I have an English degree, but I work with computers. I'd like to find a career in technology."

"An English degree! Why did you choose that? Don't you already speak English?" he countered. I wanted to pour that cup of coffee on his head.

I liked going to Main Street on Christmas when everything except Jimmy's Diner and the Chinese takeout place was closed. You could walk in the middle of the road among the wreaths and red ribbons for hours without a single car rolling by. Lo and behold, I'd spotted a lone soul the year before, far from the pews where the miracle was retold. It was James. After laughing that we were the only ones around, my soul brother and I celebrated the birth of Jesus Christ first with a bowl of wonton soup, then a plate of flapjacks. Hallelujah, Praise the Lord.

Albert came from a wealthy family and owned a BMW. However, he'd purchased the car himself. His parents paid for his tuition and occasionally topped up his account, but most of his money came from work, and like me, he loaded that right back into the stock market. The exterior of his car was like any other BMW with a timeless cachet that helped him with the ladies, but it was fifteen years old. The floor had nearly rusted through, and its rear-wheel drivetrain had no traction in the snow despite the cinder blocks Albert put in the trunk to stop it from fishtailing. He was home with his family in New York but left his car keys with me in case the city plowed snow on our street and I had to move it.

"I want to prank this guy, Bill Jones, who lives next door to my mom. He thinks I'm this loser druggie jackass. Let's blow his mind by parking Albert's BMW in front of his house and step out when he's sipping eggnog with the fam. Albert left me the keys, so he's cool with me driving it," I told Simone, leaving out the inconvenient detail that I only had permission to pull it into the driveway.

"I don't know. Who cares what that guy thinks?"

"I know I shouldn't care, but I hate that guy. He was always peeking out his window every time I left the house. He called the cops when I gave his daughter a ride home, which she asked me for!"

"Well, obviously, he lives in a fearful little world that's more of a problem for him than you by now, but if you want to go, let's go. Give me a minute to get dressed."

With my visual deficit, I had no business driving a slip-and-slide sports car in the snow, but it was worth the risk. I puttered over to my old neighborhood and passed the Jones's house twice, but not a creature was stirring, not even sexy Betsy.

"I'm freezing. Forget about that guy. Let's go to your mom's house. I can't even feel my toes," Simone lamented as the weather had chilled and the heater didn't work.

"Okay, one more time around the block. How about a Christmas miracle here? I just need him to peek through the blinds. Don't tell me he only does that when the police are out front."

As we rounded the corner, Simone remarked, "I don't remember anything about punking your neighbor when I was in Christmas pageants. I wouldn't count on divine intervention helping you."

"Well, it's been a while since I read the New Testament, but there's a passage in the Torah where Moses parades a herd of camels in front of his neighbor's shack to score one of his daughters."

"Really?"

"No."

"What is going on in that head of yours?" Simone laughed.

"Many have asked, but no one knows."

Then, not by the grace of God but by chance, Mr. Jones stepped out to get something from his car. I floored it, and we fishtailed wildly, nearly veering onto the sidewalk. I was parallel to Ben and Seth's house. I hoped they were all in the Bahamas, anywhere other than looking out their living room window, watching me try to get even with the Joneses. For a moment, I missed them. Why hadn't we stayed friends? Why hadn't I lived a more normal life like them? Who cares if Ben used to boast about his luxurious Caravan? I did plenty of dumb things, too. We were just kids.

I straightened the car, and we roared down the road as Simone sharply inhaled through clenched teeth. I pulled up even with the Joneses', but when I hit the brakes, we slid another fifteen feet, almost passing my mom's place. That got his attention. He turned as he was heading back inside. "We got him. We got him! Yes!" I was so excited I forgot the little act I'd planned, where I'd open Simone's door and escort her inside. She stepped out of the car, shaking off the cold, and said, "My tits are frozen." It was real ladylike. I paid her little mind as I locked eyes with Mr. Jones. He furtively looked away from me, first at the car and then at Simone. Like a snowman in summer, his jolly grin melted into a frown. Simone took my hand. I smiled, and we stepped carefully through the snow. Mr. Jones remained in the same spot. I gave him a friendly wave and opened the front door.

"Did you get a new car, Julian? What kind of car is that?" I had to shut down my mom's curiosity quick. When she recognized it was a BMW, visions of her brother and the sibling enmity she harbored would resurface and spread to me. I explained it was Albert's ride and we'd only taken it for a spin.

She still had the same kitchen table with pictures of men assembling cars. I recalled my Bar Mitzvah party when we gathered around it to eat treats from a place in New York that may no longer exist. I mapped out its location to avoid bumping into it due to my newfound lack of sight, and we ate pizza, sizzling atop it as the mushrooms glowed. We sat there, drinking kosher grape juice leftover from Hannukah. The whiskey bottle had disappeared from the window. She and Lenny had split up. My mom explained it was a memento she no longer needed.

"What happened? You two seemed happy," I asked.

"Lenny was a recovering alcoholic like me. We had a lot of fun together, but I caught him drinking mouthwash when he was taking a shower. I found out he'd been using the alcohol in it to get drunk for the past month. I felt bad for him, but I had to end it. Nothing is more important to me than staying sober."

"That must have been hard. I respect your strength. My mom lets my dad do whatever he wants," Simone said.

"Maybe it's strength, but I've cried enough for men who don't deserve it. I think it's mostly common sense."

"No, it's not common yet. We still need to fight for equal rights and equal pay."

My mom found this way of thinking annoying. Sure, she liked equal pay but disliked when people got wrapped up in global causes, which she found more sensationalistic than impactful.

"Mm-hmm, thank you for sharing that, Simone," my mother said, pursing her lips.

"Thank you for sharing" is often used in AA meetings. It's said collectively after anyone speaks to support them. However, my mom explained sometimes it has a second meaning: "That was ridiculous. Now sit down and shut up."

"How's the job, Julian?" my mother asked. "Is your boss still giving you grief about what you wear to work?"

"Yeah, there's that, and he loves tracking everything we do, but he's mellowed out. He's happy with how things are going in the stock market."

I was nervous about mentioning the stock market but was confident my mom didn't know I'd ditched Mr. Michelson and was trading on my own. She would've said something by now. I'd brought it up to gauge her reaction, anticipating the day when I showed her my account balance once I'd made a million dollars from trading.

"I wish him luck. One of my coworkers recently quit before her pension even vested. She said she'd hit her numbers like it was the lottery. I don't know. She was probably going to get fired anyway. She was always sneaking off to the staff lounge and messing around with her portfolio. I guess you can get addicted to anything."

***

"Thanks for not saying anything to my mom about me and, you know, the stock market. She obviously doesn't see it like I do," I told Simone as we climbed into the BMW. I still wanted to do a big reveal, but I had to help my mother see trading is a skill, not a reckless gambit for early retirement. I may have seen Mr. Jones peeking out his window, but I didn't care. I'd already defeated him.

"Your mom has an interesting way of looking at things. Do you think she likes me?"

"Yeah, she likes you. She's happy we're living together, but she's not a very touchy-feely person."

"Okay."

"Is it alright if we make a quick stop around the block? My friend Sam lives there. We used to be close, but a combination of drugs and mental illness messed him up. I haven't seen him in years. He might be alright now; I'm not sure. I'd also like to say hi to his dad."

"Sure, let's go."

"I turned the key. The engine popped several times, and the heat kicked on full blast. "Yes! It's working!" Simone said, warming her hands. "I was starting to think I was stuck in a BMW snow globe." It hadn't been much warmer in my mom's house; I didn't mind that she was tight with money, but I would've liked it if she'd been more generous with the heat. I used to turn it up in the evening, and she'd let me thaw out, but visions of a giant gas bill meant her pity never lasted through the night, and a couple hours later, she'd turn it back down.

I parked in front of Sam's house. The station wagon was gone, now replaced by a convertible Mustang. I thought they'd moved, but then I saw the Amazon parking sticker on the rear bumper and knew it was Ted's ride.

"Will you be in there long? Do you mind if I wait here? I'm loving this heat!"

"No, I shouldn't be long, and you being here will give me an excuse to leave if it gets awkward."

I rang their doorbell. Ted saw it was me and opened the door. They'd redecorated. All the furniture was new, and a hardwood floor had replaced the ugly green carpeting I remembered. Behind him, a large television played the classic film *Miracle on 34th Street*.

"Julian, I haven't seen you for a while. What's it been, a couple of years?" He looked over my shoulder. "Nice ride. But you know me—I've always liked American power. The Mustang's been treating me well."

"It sure looks peppier than the wagon. You're still at Amazon, right?" I wasn't sure why he didn't invite me in, but I thought they might have all sat down for a holiday dinner, and I was interrupting, so that was fine.

"That's right. I'm head of logistics for the East Coast division now. I finally cashed out some stock options and took a couple of engineering courses, courtesy of Mr. Bezos. I've done all right."

"Cool. I've been watching their stock. That one analyst, Henry Blodget, thinks Amazon will hit $400. Maybe I should buy some shares." I started smiling, but Ted didn't, so I stopped.

"Yeah, maybe you should, or you could buy some BMW shares, whatever's your pleasure."

"Is Sam here? How's he doing? Can I talk to him?" I wasn't asking for permission but whether it was possible. However, that distinction proved irrelevant.

"Sam. No, he's not here. He had an episode yesterday, so I had to take him to the hospital. They've got him on some meds. He was sleeping when I called. We'll exchange gifts when he's feeling better."

I frowned but was also relieved. I hated feeling that way, but what could I do if Sam was sitting there sedated?

"I'm sorry to hear that. Sam was doing better the last time I saw him."

"He was, but now he's not. That's how it goes with his condition. A psychiatrist we took him to said it was schizophrenia. They've called it other things when they want to be polite but don't get too concerned. I've got great benefits from the job, and he's well cared for. It's a shame, though. Sam wasn't always like that."

"No, he wasn't. I still can't believe it."

"Julian, remember the time I was on the trash truck? Just trying to support my family, and I asked you if Sam was doing drugs. Why didn't you tell me the truth? Don't you think you should have told me?"

The conversation had quickly soured. I glanced at Simone, who probably thought we were having a friendly chat. I tried to turn it back in that direction. "I wanted to tell you ... I should have, but I didn't want Sam to get in trouble. I never thought he'd end up like this. You know I tried to help him, right? I told him not to do LSD or the other drugs that were going around.

Ted slowly shook his head back and forth while I spoke. I couldn't tell if he didn't like what I was saying or if it was more of a "that's a shame" gesture. It brought back memories of all the stupid things that went down in my neighborhood after I was released from the hospital: how people treated me like I was five and my feud with Bill Jones. Did Ted ever talk to him? Did they ever talk about me? The possibility of that pissed me off, so I turned it up a notch.

"You know, since you brought this up, Sam was smoking your weed before he did anything else. That's what got him started. Not me. I never told him to do drugs."

"You're right. I bear some responsibility, but I wish you had told me. Sam might be in a better place if we'd gotten him help sooner."

"I was trying to help him!"

Ted stopped shaking his head. "No, Julian. You were only helping yourself." The old movie played behind him as he shut the door.

"Why were you standing out front so long? Was your friend there?" Simone asked as I drove out of my mother's neighborhood.

"Ah, Sam wasn't home, so we were reminiscing."

Snow had steadily fallen, and I couldn't go more than a block without fishtailing. Taking I-95 would add about fifteen minutes, but they usually plowed it first, so I made my way there. The interstate was plowed but icy. It was a short stretch to the exit, so I didn't sweat it. I drummed on the wheel, fuming. Ted is wrong about me. Wrong, just like Bill Jones was wrong. I've got to show them I'm successful, not the punk kid they think I am.

An eighteen-wheeler cut in front of me, splattering dirty snow. I changed lanes and accelerated to get around it but remained trapped in its blind spot with snow spraying across my windshield. I leaned forward, pressing hard on the gas until I got ahead of the truck, but what should've been a simple lane change turned into an all-out spin. Simone and I screamed. We began rolling backward as the tractor-trailer barreled toward us. The man in the big rig shot me a stare that I thought would be the last thing I ever saw—a flash of light, camels, Christ, Mr. Jones, and don't call it schizophrenia.

He looked more horrified than us, and that was saying something. "We're gonna die!" Simone screamed and had the bright idea to grab my arm, lowering our odds of whatever minuscule chance of survival remained. The Beemer completed its rotation, aided by an ice patch, and we ended up on the shoulder without a scratch. I slowed and came to a complete stop while we caught our breath. The exit was near. Simone and I silently looked at one another, and then I drove to the off-ramp.

***

I had to be at work on New Year's Day in case anything malfunctioned due to Y2K. Stocks had been bucking like broncos, but to the dismay of doomsday cults and survivalists, Y2K had a minimal impact. When the stock market reopened, the Nasdaq hit new highs, lifting my account to over $800,000. With so many stocks doubling, I was disappointed if I didn't make at least $10,000 a day. At this rate, I wasn't just going to be a millionaire—I was going to be a multimillionaire. The way to do it was to cut your losses fast, grabbing the strongest stocks to ride through the choppiness. They were easy to spot; they were going up. Even Barbara Streisand knew that. In an interview, she said, "I'm Taurus the bull, so I react to red. If I see red, I sell my stocks quickly." That seemed obvious, but unlike Barbara and me, most people lacked the speed and agility to grab the green. I was so happy that I'd taken control of my money. Now I could be a bull, too.

"What are stock options?" I asked Albert. With most people gone for the holidays, there wasn't much to do at the lab.

"They're used to build a large position without putting up much cash or to hedge your portfolio. You buy puts to profit from falling prices and calls when you expect prices to rise. But if your timing's off, they'll expire worthless. If you're going to start trading options, I'd suggest keeping your positions small," Albert explained. I asked about options because a trader was raving about them on CNBC, but I'd heard enough. I didn't want to make risky bets on derivatives that I didn't understand when trading stocks was easy. After I hit $2 million, I'd have plenty of time to learn about them and all the other clever trading tricks.

Chapter 25

For a moment, I thought I was having a seizure. Nothing like that had happened in years—not since I'd taken antiepileptic pills a decade ago. I was shocked by how quickly those fears returned. I was still angry with Ted for saying I was only helping myself. I was devastated by what had happened to Sam. What was his problem? He was always flirting with my mom. Maybe something in his marriage isn't working out. That must be it. Only helping myself. Fine. I'll help myself to a boatload of Amazon shares. I'll have more than him when I'm done.

The stock market had been increasingly erratic since New Year's, which I learned is called volatility. Stocks typically trade between support and resistance levels. I loaded up on Amazon after it dropped to a previous support level so I'd profit when it bounced. I bet oldtimers like Warren Buffett didn't even know about those levels, so they missed out.

The volatility made the market swing, and my account balance did the same. I'd approach $900,000, then lose ten to twenty thousand dollars days later, churning my balance below my target. It rattled my nerves, but I pressed on. Nothing was going to stop me from reaching a million.

I had become numb. When I started trading, I couldn't stand losing even a thousand dollars, but soon after that, all those jiggling digits on my screen didn't seem real. Over time, I became so focused on reading charts and reaching a million dollars that it seemed more like I was playing Pac-Man, gobbling up ghosts on the stock exchange, than risking my life savings. However, unlike most stocks I purchased, I knew what Amazon did, which gave me confidence in my hefty position.

Amazon released its earnings report while I was helping an economics professor configure a chart after the market closed. He traded stocks like the rest of us but liked looking at older charts. There are many kinds of stock charts. Some span a hundred years, while others show every second in real-time. Old charts are static images from another era, like maps drawn by cartographers aboard steamships. But real-time charts—ones at the hard right edge—that's where you make money. That's what's happening now. Those charts are mesmerizing, like a charmer drawing a serpent out of a vase. Who were all those other people captured in the movements of the chart—buying, selling, and staring at their screens like me, all of us wondering how high the snake would go?

Today, the professor wanted to compare charts from the years preceding 1929 to the present day. I went to his desk to help. After we set them up, he observed, "There are striking parallels in the parabolic rate of incline between then and now. The bell may soon bend back down if history is any guide." I stepped back to see the whole screen. Both periods had risen sharply. By his estimation, the recent rise could mirror the historic collapse. In the Roaring Twenties, people went to speakeasies and danced to ragtime on gramophones. There were similarities, but they didn't have the Internet.

The professor seemed anxious; he'd probably cash out soon, but people had been calling market tops for months. You would have missed most of the run if you'd listened to any of those nervous Nellies. It takes more than analytical wherewithal to make money in the market. Mental stamina also matters. The professor had one side of the equation, but I had both. Or did I?

When I returned to my desk, something was wrong with my stock ticker. It bugged out sometimes because Datek was always updating it. Once, it was down for three hours in the middle of the day, and I couldn't even get real-time quotes. My account balance was $860,000 before I went to help the professor, but it dropped $70,000 while I was away. The price of Amazon, my only position, had fallen from 81 to 74. I knew big-money players execute large trades after hours that make prices move, but those were typically minor and had never caused an eight percent drop. Something else had happened. A small blue box flashed next to Amazon's ticker. I double-clicked it, and a larger box appeared that said:

Amazon earnings estimate: -$0.04. Actual earnings: -$0.05.

Did that cause the drop? My heart rate spiked, my throat constricted, and my rusting, nearly decade-old Toyota truck, which I'd planned to replace soon, came to mind. But not yet. Not when I was better off putting that money to work in my brokerage account. However, now that I'd lost the value of three trucks, delaying the purchase seemed less prudent than it had a moment ago. I took a few hard, shallow breaths. Amazon's price remained at 74 and wasn't moving. Something must be wrong with this stupid program. I'll reboot the computer and see if that helps. I chuckled, reflecting on how Albert and I always told people to reboot their computers before going to their desks since that solves nearly every computing problem.

Presently, I wanted a reboot to fix my account balance. It took forever. Why is it taking so long! Hurry up! Once the computer rebooted, I restarted the trading application. My balance had fallen further to $788,000. I pictured it going even lower, every dollar dropping into nothingness as I tumbled alongside them. But I don't want to lose money. I want to win. I deserve to win. My chest got tight, and my index finger twitched. Lights flashed, the levee broke, and the pain poured in. Everything was sloping, tilting, diagonal. I was sloshing around inside myself. I shouldn't have rebooted. $790,000 is bad, but $788,000 is worse—unbearable. I sat there panting.

Easy now. Lean back a second. Lean back. Okay, it says Amazon missed earnings by a penny. One penny? How could that make it drop so much? I stared at the screen, willing my balance to rise. It rose to $789,000. Please, please, go up to $790,000. All I need is $790,000. Why I needed $790,000 and not $795,000 or any other value is only logical when filtered through the hyperreal mindset of a speculator who mines every setback for a silver lining. It'll bounce back; it always does. You can't drop out of the race because you hit a speed bump. Think like a winner; master your emotions; picture that big balance, and manifest that million. My field of vision had narrowed even more than usual. Smaller and smaller until all I saw was a little circle of light. In that circle, $790,000 had become more meaningful than pi, rippling in the water like a Fibonacci sequence. Even one dollar less made my big-money plans crumble. In the circle, I was safe. I was sane. I was still going to make a lot of money. Outside of it, my flimsy superstitions failed me, so gimme $790,000; that will take me to a million and beyond.

I checked the Amazon message board, hoping my fellow traders could help me resolve what my whole-number fixation had not. Why had Amazon's stock fallen so far, and what should I do now? But it was a garble of idiocy.

"Short and sweet, baby. Earnings disaster! A tragedy for the longs," one person had posted.

"Everyone knows hedge funds are playing games with the price. It'll be up 10% tomorrow. Buy the dip!"

"I've got my kid's college fund in this stupid stock. What should I tell my wife?"

I clicked on that message and drilled down to read the thread. Someone had replied. "Kiss your wife goodbye, jackass. Amazon is going to zero! All they do is lose money. Total scam!"

FUCK! What did that guy mean by "short and sweet?" "A tragedy for the longs?" Who are the longs? Should I "buy the dip" like that other guy? No, I can't. All my money's in the market. I did a quick scan to make sure I wasn't going blind. My thumb twitched along with my index finger. Everything seized up—broken brain, flailing on the floor. Stop laughing at me! Stop! I can't breathe. I need oxygen. Call an ambulance! *"Mom, Julian was crying when that police officer was here. He never used to cry like that. What happened? What's wrong with him?"* *"Kevin, your brother was shot in the head. Give him time. Try to understand. He's been through a lot."* I'm on a stretcher now. They've strapped me down, rushing me through the crowd. Cardiac arrest. This is how it ends; a burning in my chest. *"We're losing him! I need 1 milligram of adrenaline, stat!"* In and out of consciousness, long lights race overhead. I slowed my breathing. I slowed it down. Slow down. The circle of light expanded. I sat still in my chair.

I looked at my balance: $791,000. Oh, thank God. Good, very good! That's right around the corner from $800,000, and $800,000 is a hop, skip, and jump to one million! I steadied my breathing.

That's it; breathe. Okay. It's okay. You still have plenty of money. Remember when you were in the three hundred thousand dollar range? A million dollars were a million miles away back then. Now you're so close. Did you think your resolve wouldn't be tested? Every war has casualties. Hold them bones! Steady now. Strong. You can do this. As I calmed myself, I became euphoric, which is weird because I still felt worse than when my account was $860,000 but better than when it fell to $788,000. I breathed easily again, my chest felt fine, and the twitching stopped. James, shooting up and then sliding onto the floor came to mind. I was beginning to understand.

I didn't want to pester Albert with more questions about market concepts I didn't understand, such as long and short positions. I scoured the web, but everything I read raised more questions, so I had to ask him for help. It frustrated me that Albert breezed through concepts I struggled with. Though my analytical skills had proven more robust than I'd been led to believe, I knew he'd always be more perspicacious. I'd felt the same about James years ago, but that was limited to how fast I could read. The stakes were higher now. I wasn't beating myself up. Plenty of people who haven't been shot can't even turn on a computer. But once this era of ordinary people like me cashing in on stocks ends, how else can I earn enough to be secure? Enough to be my own master?

I started at the Mac Lab before the Internet became mainstream and computers were less complicated. All the new hires knew how to use *and* program each application. Could I get a job like this again? There'd be a lot more competition, that's for sure.

I'd lived through several recessions, which Henry and Ted explained corporations use as an excuse to lay people off and make way for new technologies and lower-wage employees. Ted was lucky. He landed a sweet new gig at Amazon, but how many will never work a decent job again? How many never find anything at all? If it could happen to them, it can happen to me. Glenda came back to me:

"Plenty of people want to punish you for all their pain and kick you when you're down. In fact, that's their favorite time to kick you, but don't give it to them. Don't give them that chance."

I'd made a lot of money in the market, but the people Glenda had warned me about were always waiting to knock me down. I need more money—much more—to be sure I permanently take all their chances away. Now, right now, these insane stock market gains are my sole shot at evading obsolescence and fleeing the Daily Grind Ted taught Sam and me about that autumn afternoon with all those fallen leaves around us.

How often does a chance like this come around? I need to make enough to last a lifetime now. The risk is missing it. The gamble is whether I'll ever get a second shot if this one, possibly my only one, passes me by.

You can't quit now. It's harder than you thought, but it's almost done, and the whole race will be won. The next century is yours if you get this right. You have some low-level skills that'll keep you employed, but anything other than riding this bull to the finish line leaves you running on a fifty-year treadmill to take one last walk on the beach, then roll into the grave. And that's if you even make it that far without being swapped for the latest thing. The tightness in my chest came back, but I soldiered on. I repeated my self-affirmations. You're almost at a million. You're going to make it. You've got this.

All this was worth mulling over, but the words from Glenda I should have heeded were these: *"Luck never lasts. You need to be smart, not lucky."*

***

Spring was coming soon, but the winter chill hadn't lifted, so Albert fielded my latest stock market queries as we sat beside the servers in the basement.

"I don't know why they call them long and short positions, but when you have a long position, you expect it will rise. Most people stick to the long side. That's all they know about, but you can sell stocks you don't own if you expect they'll fall. That's called selling short. It's funny how you sell a stock to close a long position but buy it to cover a short sale."

"How can you sell a stock that you don't own?"

"You need a margin account to short stock. It lets you borrow money from your broker to collateralize the sale."

I understood, but then I asked him another question that made me understand why people jumped from thirtieth-floor windows during the crash of 1929.

"Can a margin account be used for long positions too?"

"Sure, you can use margin for long and short positions. It goes both ways."

"Knowing how computers communicate is important," he'd said, standing by those same machines, and once again, he was not wrong. It went both ways.

The next day, my Amazon position recovered. I immediately closed it in case it dropped again. Seeing my account balance return to $860,000 was a huge relief, like finding a wallet you'd lost after agonizing over where it was for a week. Reclaiming that cash reminded me I was a winner.

You freaked out over nothing. You've got to chill, man. Chill out. Mental stamina. You can't listen to people like that economics professor predicting a market top with his silly old-time charts. Remember. You've got to grab enough cash to last a lifetime. The pain is worth the prize. You got this.

Now is the time. This is my chance.

Borrowing from my broker with a margin account was perfect. Piling more into every trade would let me lock in my millions before the party ended. I spent the rest of the day figuring out how to open a margin account to magnify my buying power. I couldn't figure out how to do it online, so I had to call my broker, Datek. They told me I needed to fill out a form that couldn't be submitted electronically. The fastest way to get it to them was to fax it. However, the fax machine outside Alex's office made loud squawks and beeping sounds when it sent or received files. It wouldn't have been the end of the world if he saw the form, but then he'd remind me to do

284

personal things on my own time and stomp off to his office. He'd been less chummy since the market had become more volatile.

I stepped into Alex's office and shut the door when the fax machine started buzzing. He spun in his chair and was seconds away from saying, "What the fuck?" But I was prepared with questions about his favorite topic—himself.

"Alex, sorry about the interruption. I've been busy, but I've been wanting to ask you about Stanford, so I thought I'd pop in for a second."

"Oh, yeah?" he said, his face softening as the redness ebbed. He always got that sunburned look whenever anything, even potentially, didn't go his way.

"I graduated recently and was thinking of getting a master's degree at Stanford, like you. Do you have a minute to tell me about being a student there?"

"What's your GPA, man? Did you even take the GRE yet?"

He started turning toward his monitor, already losing interest. I didn't know if the form had finished printing, so I kept the ruse going.

"Uh, not yet. I still need to study for it. I'm in the initial stages of planning. My GPA? It was about 3.0, but I'll include an essay about my injury with my application. That whole experience. That should help me get in. I'd love to go to Stanford. Everyone knows it's the best school."

Actually, I graduated with a C average—a 2.0. The dean gave me one last boot in the pants when he reviewed my grades: "Julian International Lawrence, a two-point-o grade point average. The minimum required to graduate. Let's hope you exert a little more effort in your career. Good luck with that."

Since we worked for the University of Delaware, I started worrying that Alex might find out I inflated my average, but I doubted he'd check.

"Yeah, an essay might help. They've gone soft these days. Anyhow. Stanford—let's just say it was illuminating. It's a cut above. You meet the elite in society—producers, the guys running the show, not the deadbeats begging them for a job. A few guys I know became billionaires. Now, they live in Malibu, flying in their private jets. You know, that should've been me. I worked for a tech start-up before all these people coming to the Business Center even knew what a website was. I should've been more like Jerry Yang. He was there. He saw where this was going and protected his intellectual property. Jerry made sure none of those snakes got a hold of his stake in Yahoo."

He'd gone off on a tangent. All the pages had printed by then, but this was getting interesting.

"Stanford, that's life in the fast lane, but when you're dealing with so many people who are in love with themselves drawn to the Silicon Valley lifestyle—" Alex clenched his jaw. "I don't know if you've got what it takes, Julian. Those guys think they're entitled to everything, even your sweat equity, and will take it all if they can. Whatever, man, I told you the real world can be cutthroat. People are sizing you up every second. That's why you've got to dress for success, and even that might not get you in the door. A lot of times, it's who you know. That's all right. I've got a new plan. I'm not ready to share it with everyone yet, but it won't be much longer until I release it.

"My MBA and a few years of running a business center here in the capital of incorporation ought to be enough to get VC funding from the guys on Sand Hill Road and launch it.

"Julian, if you ever start a business, read up on LLCs, S Corps, and C Corps. That's one thing I've learned more about here than at Stanford. I'm going to structure it right. My name will be at the top of the ticket. No one will fly in a jet fueled by my sweat this time."

"Yeah, who wants to be stuck in first class?" I teased.

"You're a funny guy, aren't you? Don't worry, I'll get that jet, but first class isn't bad for now." He leaned back, ran his hands through his hair, and continued, "No, it's not living like Jerry and his G4, but at least you get to keep the scum out for the price you pay. I love it when they close those curtains. Sure, the seat is great, but I'm paying for something else. I'm paying so I don't have to look at them or listen to their pathetic conversations on the other side of the curtain. I'm paying to be where they can't be. Even if they had the same seats as economy in first class, I'd still pay a premium as long as those curtains stay shut," Alex said, looking straight at me as if I were getting a complete Stanford education with his classist insight.

"Yeah, that makes sense. Everyone's a little too close to each other in economy, but don't you think all those corporate guys make too much money? Shouldn't they give up their jets instead of laying people off when times get tough?"

"You don't get a bigger cut just for showing up to do what you're told. Money drives us, and those jets embody the elevation people who take risks to innovate have earned. Do you think we'd be trading stocks and shopping online if we cut their pay to create socialist subsidies because life isn't fair? No, the Internet would still be a dusty server in the corner of someone's cubicle on K Street. This is something those servant-class crybabies whining about executives being overpaid will never understand. Business is ruthless. The ones who crush inferior competitors deserve the most money because they're the only reason we make any progress. Make no mistake, at least half of that competition comes from the people working beside you. And you know what? I'll say it again: Perception counts more than anything else. That's why you've got to dress the way I've been telling you to."

"Uh, yeah, that makes sense. Thanks for the insight. I'm going to get back to work." I snickered, walking back to my desk, realizing Alex's jet would have seating classes reinstated so he could relish having a royal perch apart from the common folk.

I grabbed the margin account form and returned to my desk. Damn it. I still had to fax it back, which would make the same beeps and squawks. It'd be easier to do once Alex left, but that wouldn't be until after the market closed. I needed that margin account open now, but I had to wait. The form had several questions and checkboxes. The first set evaluated if you were a beginner, intermediate, or advanced, trading the following asset classes:

Options, Futures, Forward currency contracts, Equities, Bonds

I considered checking advanced for all of them to ensure Datek opened my margin account, but I was worried they might call to validate my selections, so I marked everything intermediate.

Next were a series of statements I had to acknowledge reading:

You can lose more than you deposit in a margin account.
We may force the sale of your securities if you cannot meet your margin requirements.
Significant losses may occur in fast-moving markets before you can close your positions.

I'd signed documents with similar scary-sounding language when I'd opened my account, so I acknowledged that I'd read them all without much thought. However, I wasn't sure how you could lose more than you deposited and considered asking Albert about it, but I'd pestered him enough. I filled out the rest of the form and waited in agony for Alex to leave at 6:00 p.m. He noticed I was still at my desk and complimented me on my work ethic, even though all I'd done was sit there waiting for him to leave. I darted to the machine and faxed the form as soon as he was out the door. Activating my margin account capabilities took Datek another two days, during which time the Nasdaq roared 6 percent higher. I'd already be a millionaire if they'd activated it immediately. It was agonizing to wait, but I liked running through imaginary pathways to wealth. Up 4 percent today, 2 percent tomorrow, another 3 percent, and you have cleared a million!

When I started trading, I only discussed it with Alex and Albert. As the market rallied, sites like ClearStation attracted more traders to exchange ideas. While I waited for my margin account to be activated, I spent my free time talking with them online. Most people were clueless, but I also met seasoned pros in the same league as Mr. Michelson as I read different message boards. One guy with the screenname CoolHand earned my respect even though he was short and I was long. He believed the Nasdaq had reached nosebleed levels and was headed for a fall, so he held put options. He'd been saying that for weeks and had been wrong so far, but I respected him because he was methodical. He progressively built his positions rather than jumping in or out with a single shot like me.

Though his strategy was sound, his incremental approach didn't match my objective of deploying every dollar possible while the market ripped higher. Another guy with the screenname Cha0strad3r, who could be crass but was pretty funny, wrote, "PAYDAY CASH ADVANCE. MAX LEVERAGE MY DAWGS. WE GOING TO THE MOON!" I figured he was joking about using a cash advance to make a big bet, but I wasn't sure if max leverage and margin were the same, so I asked him. It would be annoying to fill out another form if they were different.

"Is max leverage the same as margin?" I posted.

"Are you brain dead, dumbass? Don't quit your day job and leave trading to the pros. There are no stupid questions, only stupid people." he replied.

That pissed me off. He must've gone to the same idiot academy as Big Papa in the park. I wrote a lengthy reply explaining that nothing about my brain prevented me from successful trading and that he'd only proven his stupidity with that remark. Then I realized I was inviting further ridicule and deleted it. However, I didn't block my cantankerous comrade since his entertainment value outweighed his offensiveness. Fortunately, someone else answered my question.

"Leverage and margin are one and the same. Max leverage means using your entire balance. But be careful; don't listen to this fool."

I browsed forums unrelated to trading, too, but limited my exposure. Like trading message boards, these communities had heroes and villains, with the loudest voices often the most extreme. Spending too much time engaging with them diminished my faith in humanity. Some users shared media profiling people they despised, paired with the caption: *"Every single time,"* implying that they'd proven these degenerates were repeatedly committing the same offenses—often attributed to their inferior genetics. Reducing entire populations to three words offers an illusion of superiority but doesn't tell the whole story. Concepts I'd learned while trading made me more aware of what they were missing.

During the Second World War, military analysts evaluated the damage on returning planes, believing these areas were the most vulnerable and required reinforcement. They didn't realize these planes were survivors—those hit in critical spots never made it back. This cognitive error, known as Survivorship bias, leads people to draw flawed conclusions based on incomplete evidence. Traders suffer the same bias when they fixate on profitable chart patterns without accounting for other factors influencing their signal strength. Both groups fall prey to selective perspectives, mistaking the partial for the whole. Profilers and their cherry-picked populations get caught in this trap, too.

Stereotypes persist for reasons that could fill volumes, but do the behaviors these profilers point out happen *"every single time,"* or are they suffering from apophenia, seeing connections where none exist—either by ignoring outliers or assigning predictability to randomness? Even brilliant minds like Nobel laureate John Nash fell victim to this flaw. Not every observation is part of a grander scheme. *Sometimes, a cigar is just a cigar.*

The bigger question is, why are some people drawn to absolutes? Why do they cling to them? They paint whomever they oppose in one color, no different than you'd paint a wall—removing its variations and texture. It's easier to hate someone when you obscure what makes them human. I posted a quote from Carl Jung in response to one of the videos they'd posted, hoping they'd consider whether they were being fooled by these fallacies, then closed the page, vowing once more never to return: *'We wish to hear only of unequivocal results, and completely forget that these results can only be brought about when we have ventured into and emerged again from the darkness.'*

My margin account was finally activated. My equity balance remained at $860,000, but a new column showed my total buying power had risen over $3,000,000! I knew I didn't really have that much money, but I loved looking at that huge balance. I started daydreaming about Simone and me on a cruise along the Côte d'Azur, standing on the balcony of our starboard suite as spindrifts played upon the tides. We'd undoubtedly fly first class to get there, but I didn't care if they closed the curtains. I still had love for my brothers and sisters in economy.

"Another cocktail, sir?"

"Yes, and one more olive, please."

"And for the lady?"

"Oh, a ginger ale for me, thanks."

"Your account's gained eighty percent since you began actively trading it. In that same period, the Nasdaq has risen eighty-nine percent."

The more I realized how complex trading was, the more I reflected on Mr. Michelson's advice. I purchased QQQ, an ETF that holds the top 100 Nasdaq stocks. I deployed my $860,000 cash balance plus $140,000 on margin for a cool million in total exposure. I could've borrowed more, but I wasn't sure how it worked, so that was good for now.

After I executed the trade, my account value soared to one million, and a smile shot across my face, even though I knew that included borrowed funds. I scanned the margin section of the site. It displayed -$140,000, which I knew reflected what I'd borrowed, but I didn't like the minus sign. Datek should've kept the margin values positive, so you didn't feel like you were losing money when all you'd done was borrow it. My remaining buying power dropped by more than double what I'd borrowed to $2,700,000. Datek had applied a dynamic ratio to calculate the new total, which I doubted even Albert could decipher. Memories of machines pumping me with medicine and the terror of losing control of my limbs if a bundle of neurons misfired prickled my skin as I questioned the wisdom of using leverage. Don't get your knickers in a bunch, you old scallywag! Your biggest risk is missing out. Understanding the ratio isn't necessary.

QQQ rose 1 percent within the hour—a $10,000 gain! With such straightforward math, stacking up cash was easy to visualize. Stack 'em up. Stack 'em up. At a million, every 1 percent I gained was

$10,000. I'd have to work a thousand hours to earn what I'd made in an hour! I reclined in my seat. *"Another cocktail, sir?"* First class.

The next day, the Nasdaq fell 1 percent. That annoyed me. It always seemed so stupid when the market was volatile. Up one percent, down one percent the next day. Why? What changed in one day? The market remained volatile for the rest of the week but kept marching higher. Once I got comfortable with using margin, I borrowed more. Much more, increasing my exposure to $2,000,000. The Nasdaq shot up 5 percent, and I punched right through a million.

Finally, I was living as a moneyman, fueled by courage and conviction. I'd been tested, forged by fire. Even being shot in the head spurred me on. All the mental and physical pain—the times I thought I couldn't take anymore but persevered—transformed me into a stock market warrior. Now, I could take back everything that'd been taken. All along, there were no random choices. I hadn't seen it before, but *He* was always there. The hand of God, guiding me. Maybe I could even find a way to get my vision back.

Amazing grace, how sweet the sound
That saved a wretch like me.
I once was lost, but now I'm found.
Was blind, but now I see.

I was protected. No amount of insults, arrogance, or misunderstandings could hurt me. All those zeros behind the one were a force field around me. I'd defeated death and genetics, easily ridiculed last names, nosy neighbors, and hand-me-downs. I was set to reclaim my rightful place as the eldest son, the wisest, wealthiest, and most beloved member of the clan.

You couldn't see my wings, but I was flying the whole way home. Before unlocking the front door, I said, "I feel like a million bucks!"

Chapter 26

Engines were roaring in my mind as Cadillacs tumbled from the sky when I stepped inside. "Simone, are you home?"

"I'm upstairs."

I went upstairs to our bedroom, where she was using my computer to check the date of her final exam. I had nothing to hide, so I was happy to share it, but what about her? I checked her laptop's browsing history a couple of times but found nothing suspicious. I worried she was starting something with Drake, whom she spoke of glowingly. He was enrolled in one of her Women's Studies classes. Simone said he did amazing work for women in South America.

I'd seen Drake talking animatedly to Simone and her classmates, who were riveted when he spoke. Simone played with her hair when he came close, which she never did with me. He was tall with long blond hair in a ponytail. Some guys do that to cover bald spots, but Drake had thick hair. To top it off, he had a British accent he exaggerated with excessive enunciation, which I admit sounded cool, but I bet the only reason Drake was in South America was to pick up women under the clever guise of helping them. Things like this—all the things that made me cynical and insecure—made me feel pretty damn good that I'd hit a million dollars. Now I had a million reasons for these worries to go away. I knew money couldn't buy love or a perfect relationship, but it had to help. I was about to test that theory.

"Let me get in there for a second. I want to show you something." I went over to my computer and typed in the web address for Mr. Michelson's firm. The page loaded. I'd subconsciously made a mistake. Despite my success, sometimes I thought Mr. Michelson should be managing my money. The market was up most days, and my growing balance was exhilarating. Still, though down days were rare, losing money—even small amounts—hit hard. The pain of losing outweighed the pleasure of winning. What would the pain be like if I hit a long losing streak? Could I handle that? Mr. Michelson wouldn't have run my account up to a million as quickly as I had, but the market didn't mess with his mind no matter which way it went, so I still thought about him. I retyped the URL and loaded the page for my brokerage account. "Okay, do you want to see something beautiful?"

My balance stood at $1,003,000. The $3,000 seemed small, but I was glad it was there—a cushion keeping those zeros in place to ensure I didn't drop below a million.

Simone came over and witnessed the spectacle shining on my screen. "Oh my God, is that real? So this is what you've been doing all this time?"

"Yes, and I'm not trying to show off at all. This is our money. It doesn't change anything, but it's good to know it's there if we need it. Really good," I said, a grin filling my face.

Simone took a deep breath. "I know that's not your style. Mine either. Showing off expensive things to make you feel superior. But this is amazing! I've never actually seen a million dollars." She had a full-face grin, too.

Many people slave away for the prestige of flaunting flashy brands, unaware they've paid thousands to be walking billboards, while celebrities earn millions to license their smiles so you'll buy the same product which was produced for a dollar—that wasn't my style. "No, I'll never be like that, but I wouldn't mind having a little more fun. Getting out of town sometimes, you know?"

"Exactly. Money shouldn't change anything, but we still need it. I'm not so idealistic that I don't know that. But don't ask me to take another ride to your mom's house in Albert's BMW. That almost killed us!"

"That was a special ops mission, baby. One time only. Speaking of a little fun, how about we take a trip to Washington, DC, right now?"

"Hmm, I'm going to have to say … Yes! I definitely need a break from studying," Simone said with a toothy grin that let me know I'd won. Victory was on the tip of my tongue. Its sweetness swirled through me as all my aspirations happily converged. "But shouldn't we make a hotel reservation? You know, come up with a plan first. We could go tomorrow."

"We could, but don't you remember what we used to say: 'It's not fun unless it's impossible.' Then we'd climb in the truck, drive to a random town, and sleep in the back. Sometimes too much planning takes all the fun out of it."

She thought for a minute. "Let's see if we can stay at my sister's place in Arlington. She has an extra bed. I'll give her a call."

I was grateful for how Simone thought. Even with a million dollars, she was still looking for ways to save money. I wasn't looking for ways to waste it, but after so many years of stressing about it, being judged, and obsessing over it, it was time for a weekend of enjoying it. It would show her the good life we could have—a taste to break up all the ordinary hours waiting for us when we returned. There was that, and I wanted her to forget about guys like Drake.

Simone called her sister, Elizabeth, and she said the bed was ours if we wanted it. We grabbed what we needed and headed for the door as Albert rolled in with his arm around a fit Asian girl. I greeted them and said we were going to DC. Simone did a double take on the way out, checking out his girl. I knew she would tell me about how hot she was in the car. Simone liked doing that sometimes, pointing out hot girls. In response, I started doing the same thing with dudes, calling out good-looking guys when they walked by. I'm not sure what Simone's motivation was, but I did it so she wouldn't think I was insecure. However, I had no reason to do that anymore.

We drove to Elizabeth's place, expecting to stay, but she had three cats, and there was fur everywhere. Our eyes were watering the whole time, so it wasn't long before we said goodbye. Despite their shared upbringing, they had different outlooks. Elizabeth was more lighthearted than Simone. Unlike her little sister, she was unconcerned with inequality or political malfeasance, which I understood. I had a new point of view, too. One with a deeper understanding that making lots of money gave me vitality greater than I'd ever known.

We checked into a hotel in downtown DC. I hadn't planned on staying in a top-tier place, but arriving late in the center of town meant only five-star accommodations were available. Yet it had all worked out the way I wanted, giving Simone and me a proper taste of the comforts we could have now. I shelled out two hundred bucks for the room, and a bellboy escorted us. We'd stuck everything in a single backpack I was carrying, so he entered the room ahead of us and arbitrarily adjusted the furniture and lights. He ambled toward the door, pausing expectantly. I handed him two bucks. Displeased, he replied, "How very generous of you, sir." I'd never been to a hotel with a bellboy before and didn't know much about gratuities. I hoped I didn't see him again.

The room was grand. I'd audited several art history classes Simone had taken, so I recognized a modernist piece by Georgia O'Keeffe on the wall, which made me feel like less of an imposter in a splashy suite. Our room had two king-size beds, a big bathtub, and a glass wall with a smashing view of the Capitol. We started kissing and trying out one of the beds. Simone asked me to close the curtains. I tried to shut them, but they wouldn't budge. I called the front desk, annoyed that a five-star hotel had curtains that wouldn't close. They graciously informed me that a switch on the wall controlled the curtains. I flipped it up, and the curtains made a smooth, satisfying sound as they sealed out the light. I momentarily forgot about Simone as I swished them back and forth.

On our way to breakfast the following morning, Simone and I worried that guests might be wearing tuxedos and gowns but were relieved when we saw everyone was casually dressed. After we ate, a woman with a dusting of chalky white foundation and heavy eyeshadow in a red vest wheeled over a dessert tray, displaying an assortment of bite-size desserts. I took two, which were gone in two bites. Simone politely declined, but the woman pouted playfully, teasing in a gravelly voice, "Are you sure, honey? The strawberry cheesecake is divine. You need to have some fun, girl. How about a little nibble?"

"I said no!" Simone insisted.

"Oh, well, *excuse* me, it looks like someone got up on the wrong side of the bed," the woman said, wheeling the cart away. I snorted, thinking of awful things, like having a catheter in my dick to keep from spitting out my coffee.

We'd arrived late the previous day and hadn't seen the sights. I wanted to go home and study charts to prepare for the week ahead, but we'd only tasted the good life and agreed we should extend our stay. The room was an additional $50 because it was Saturday, but I didn't sweat it.

Later that afternoon, we passed by an Italian restaurant near the White House with small tables draped with white tablecloths beneath red umbrellas. A menu in front featured a selection of Epicurean fare I'd never heard of, written in an elegant font with a conspicuously blank space where the price should have been. One of those places where "if you have to ask the price, you probably can't afford it." I stood, surveying the regal setting. All my life, I'd shied away from pricey meals, fearing well-manicured waitstaff would shoo me away, but that's nonsense. I deserved that fancy grub as much as anyone.

"What do you think of this place?" I asked Simone.

"Nah, I don't feel like sitting around all afternoon. Let's grab some hot dogs and find a bench on the Mall."

It was a typical DC weekend, with tourists and families checking out the usual sights: memorials, monuments, and free museums. I was happy to be there with Simone, as laughter and smiles came easily from a place I thought was lost.

"You were right. Eating simple food outside is better than going to that Italian restaurant. I realized I didn't even want to go there. I just like knowing that I can," I told Simone after we ate, sitting near a group of children on a field trip. I recalled visiting as a kid and being scolded by a guard for trying to climb the statue in the Lincoln Memorial. I didn't even get to touch Abe's foot.

"If you don't want to go there, why does it matter whether you can?"

"Because when I couldn't afford the things other people had, they felt superior—even if I didn't give them the satisfaction of

297

gawking at their luxury cars. Then they'd smirk, calling me a gluttonous Jew if I managed to buy them. There's no way to win except by having the power to live like them and rejecting it."

"But don't they still have power over you if you're not happy unless they know you've chosen to reject them? Why do you care what they think?"

"I don't care, but I had to be sure. If I don't want to buy a fancy car, I know it's not sour grapes now because I'm not weighed down by electric bills or paying off loans. I don't need to purchase another person's product to prove my worth because the Requirements of my Imagination are backed by cash."

"Some of what you said makes sense, but what's a cash-backed imagination? Listen to yourself! You used to laugh at people who talked like that."

"The guy who used to manage my money introduced me to that concept, and it's stuck with me, but you're right. It sounds like something from one of those finance shows I watch all day in the lab."

"That's funny. I thought imagination was free, not something you measure on a balance sheet. How about we grab some Italian ice from that guy over there, or do you want to sit here and dream about sports cars you don't want to buy?"

We laughed and grabbed a couple of cherry-flavored treats. Arlington Cemetery was the last place we went. Visiting hours ended shortly after we arrived, but it was difficult to leave. There were lessons to be learned. I was still listening. Passing through the closing gates, I heard a voice say, "So close to the flame."

I looked back toward the tombstones, jutting from the earth like teeth as storm clouds hung over the treetops. The stories of the fallen ripped through me as the scent of gunpowder lingered from long-abandoned artillery. Freedom had been fought for and won by infantries buried beneath me, their stories contained in tombs, etched on walls with blood and broken stones. Ten thousand years ago, our lineages traced back to people painting on cave walls, writing in signs and symbols that evolved into words capturing our history on a scroll we can never read entirely as we try to make sense of the small span we're alive.

Moments later, rain fell in rhythmic sheets, pitter-pattering on umbrellas. The fading light was phantasmagoric, distorting the graveyard, the Potomac River, and everyone running to their cars, cabs, or down into the metro until it was one big blur. We sheltered at a nearby bus stop. I sat searching for the horizon but saw a single dimension—a wall no one could ascend, bordering the interstitial space where unacted upon ambitions are realized, only to be lost the instant we wake.

I wandered back into the downpour, drenching me to the bone, but I didn't care. I'd become one with the water. It was there, heard without words. In the place where all souls return to the nebulous nature of things, yearning to behold the glory of God once more, I reached out for someone, anyone, but there was only rain. Simone ran to me, possibly afraid I'd gone insane or might disappear in a puddle, and led me back to the bus stop.

"Why did you do that?" she asked.

"Someone spoke to me. I thought it might have been the sky."

"Uh, okay."

The storm soon passed, but we were sopping wet. We hailed a cab, and the driver took us back to our hotel. He didn't notice we'd soaked the seat, but I gave him a big tip anyway. There were no sarcastic quips about my generosity this time.

After a satisfying shower with lavender-scented soap and shampoo, Simone and I hopped into separate beds and chatted about the day. She mentioned the breakfast incident from that morning. "I hate it when people try to force food on me like that. I said no, damn it."

"From the dinner table thing with your dad?"

"Yes, but I didn't tell you about the worst part. I usually forgot about those conversations before I went to bed, but they stayed with my mother."

"Did you ever talk to her about it?"

"No, she didn't have to tell me. My room was next to the kitchen. I saw a light under my door whenever someone opened the refrigerator. I usually ignored it, but one night, I heard someone shuffling around in the refrigerator and got up to see what was happening. My mom was eyeing a tray of chocolate cupcakes we had with dinner, wearing a slip that looked eerie in the dim light. It was one of those nights when I didn't feel like battling with my dad, so I ate one, but plenty was left over. She took out the tray, shook her head, then put it back and left. Twenty minutes later, I heard her outside my room again. I was still awake, so I took another look. My mom was stuffing all the cupcakes in her mouth. I mean like two at a time. The look on her face and all the chocolate on her cheeks. It was such sad misery as if someone else was controlling her arms. I started crying. She finished them all, put the tray in the dishwasher, and went back to bed."

"I hate how old memories haunt us. I'm sorry you and your mom went through that cupcake crap. It's so frustrating. I don't want things from the past to get in the way of the good times we should be having now. We need to take more trips like this to replace those bad experiences with good ones. That's definitely worth spending money on.

Simone sat up in bed. "I know. I don't want some stupid childhood trauma screwing up the rest of my life, either. Sometimes I think I'm over what should be old news by now, but then something like that waitress incident happens, and I realize I'm not over it. I'm glad we got away for the weekend, but I think those memories will always be a part of me."

"So, does that mean we should skip breakfast tomorrow?"

"No, no. Let's go. I can't let some silly hang-up of mine stop us from enjoying ourselves."

"I'm glad to hear that. I was looking forward to having another glass of pineapple juice, but what if that lady pulls her dessert tray routine again?"

"Oh, don't worry. I'll kick it over, then dump your pineapple juice on her."

I pictured the golden juice streaking down her chalky white face and said, "That's right, darling, we'll show them what high society living should be."

***

The Nasdaq was hitting new highs so often that it attracted less media attention. Even CNBC covered other topics to keep us entertained. Tech stocks, particularly smaller ones, were blasting off with rocket fuel, so I switched back to them. By the time the Nasdaq cleared 5000, I was up another $90,000. I considered quitting my job and trading full-time, but even though my salary paled compared to my stock portfolio, it allowed me to keep as much as possible in the market where it could rise to meet my growing Requirements. Rise and rise and rise. I periodically glanced at a ticker running in the corner of my screen during market hours, but when a stock breaks out on insane volume, you've got to click its intraday chart and watch it take off like a space shuttle to experience the hunger for quick cash as every bar stacks on top of another until they form one long line that seems to ascend all the way to heaven. When that happens, you can taste the greed. If I bottled that feeling and sold it, there wouldn't be any more crime because no one would leave their house as long as I kept the drip feed going.

You could post your trades on ClearStation. If you were consistently profitable, people followed you to receive real-time alerts. Over time, I amassed hundreds of followers. When I joked about starting a money management firm, several said they'd be clients if I did.

Around this time, I showed Albert my account balance. I knew it would impress him, but that wasn't my intention. After he gave me a fist bump, I said, "We should start a dotcom company with this money."

He replied, "Yeah, man. If you do, I'm in." But before leaving my side, he added, "It's incredible you've made seven figures, J, but you should consider taking a little off the table. My uncle is a professional poker player. He told me that having a hot hand every time isn't what keeps him in the game. It's money management."

My birthday was in two weeks, and my balance was nearly $1,100,000. If I could reach $1,250,000, that would really impress

301

my mom. That would be all the money I was awarded for my injury, plus another cool million. After that, I figured Albert was right. It'd be time to cash in some chips. Every time my balance rose, my buying power rose with it. I hadn't dared to deploy my entire margin balance, which had grown to over $4,000,000, but the more money I had in the market, the more I could make. I created buy orders for an additional $4,000,000 worth of stock on margin. I paused, standing on the highwire hanging between this moment, what I desired, and the consequences if anything went wrong. Is this too risky? Wouldn't everyone be using the same margin bazooka method if it weren't? My hand rested on the mouse. You can still click cancel. You don't have to do this, Julian. Doing crazy stuff has hurt you before. But what's that sound? Oh yeah, that train's a-comin'. Chugga-chugga-choo-choo! Are we riding these rails or not? I executed my trades five minutes before the closing bell rang. My purchases alone made a few of my stocks tick higher. Wow, I'm a big shot now. During those five minutes, my balance rose by another $5,000. A thousand dollars a minute! The lever on the slot machine was broken. All I had to do was bring a bucket. This is how you win, son! This is how it's done. I spun in my chair. Yo, you know I got the flow. You can call me Monte Carlo.

Now that I'd cleared a million, I figured two million wasn't far off. For all I knew, stocks would run up another year, and I'd make three million dollars. There was no reason to remove the bucket when it was raining gold. On the way home, I fantasized about how the conversation with my mom would go when I unveiled all the money I'd made, which I anticipated doing soon.

"You did this all by yourself, Julian? Made over a million dollars! I'm so proud of you. I've been so worried about you finding a career and being able to take care of yourself since your injury and everything you've been through, but this, this is wonderful. I can stop worrying now."

"Thanks. I'm proud of myself, too! It wasn't easy, Mom. But I had a goal. I had a plan, and I did it—I did it! I'm making a withdrawal next week. I just started researching this, but I want to buy another property, get a stream of passive income going, and let my money work for me. That's how the rich get richer."

Real estate websites had improved since I'd bought my house. Some had as many statistics, charts, and tables as stock trading sites. However, the mapping component was still clunky. I kept the price range tight when I began researching a second property. I was uneasy setting the filter to a quarter of my net worth. Gradually, I raised it even with my account balance, and not long after that, I left it blank. No limit.

Why not dare to dream? When I showed Simone the grand palaces at the upper end of the unfiltered search results, she said, "I wouldn't want such a big house. It'd be a pain to clean and imagine the electric bills." She was right, of course, but soon she liked leaving the filter off, too. "Wow, I've never seen a three-million-dollar house!"

I didn't care about the clunky map on the site or in my mind anymore. I didn't need it. I filled in the missing squares with cash. I never expected to buy any of those enormous houses. Access, opportunity. I'd latched onto the pleasures of possibility, which soon extended into what *could* be possible, fueled by magic math. I still needed to make more money to realize the full extent of my potential, but I could dream in silk pajamas until the kingdom came. I was channeling my future self, the silken self. All I had to do was dream of him, and that's who I'd become. I found no fault in that and let myself envision ever-grander majesties.

I had money now. I no longer needed LSD to see the unseen. My account balance became increasingly irrelevant to my new set of requirements. The Requirements of Insanity. Like my margin balance, insanity had a ratio I couldn't calculate, and I didn't care. I had a dynamic line of credit based on my mood and how high I believed I could run up my account. This reached billions when a dramatic day of market gains made me euphoric. *Double, double, toil and trouble.* Let's mix the medicine. Let it compound until I'm the wealthiest man alive.

***

In market terminology, a gap refers to a literal gap between the previous and current day's price. Institutional traders moving markets via futures contracts during nonpublic trading hours typically create gaps. I'd seen plenty of gaps in the past few months but hadn't thought much about them because stocks mostly gapped up. I liked it when that happened because I'd log on to my brokerage account and make a few thousand dollars before the opening bell rang.

The Nasdaq gapped down 3 percent the day after I made my four-million-dollar margin bet. My tech stocks fell further, dropping 5 percent. When I logged into my account, I saw a crushing loss of $254,000 in bright red in the middle of my screen, which dropped me into the low $800,000 range.

My initial reaction was to sell everything. The thought of repeatedly clicking sell and watching my positions return to the safety of cash was very comforting. However, only institutions can trade in the early hours of the day, so I stared helplessly at the screen. My pores sprang into needles, piercing me with sharp, electric pain like Temple's electrified kitchen countertop. *"Emotions are like lightning,"* I'd told Simone, and they struck me down. I broke out in a cold sweat seconds later and dashed to the bathroom because I thought I might puke. I'd never experienced this level of panic before. Yet, somewhere deep in the primordial machine code of my mind, a chain reaction filled me with fear far beyond the modern necessity of such elevated alarm. I glanced in the mirror. Perhaps the stock market isn't a proving ground for amassing millions. It's a proving ground for all the ways you can experience anxiety.

As squeamishness engulfed me, I remained firmly planted on the toilet seat, fearful that my bladder or bowels might fail me at any moment. Fortunately, I had little for breakfast and sat there shaking instead of expelling anything. These tremors were born from mental anguish unrelated to my head injury. Thoughts, all my thoughts were overflowing ... Why am I shaking this way? I don't want this. I only needed a few more days, and then I was going to take some money out of the market and buy another property. A regular place like everyone else. I wasn't serious about becoming the wealthiest person in the world or having an enormous house with a ridiculous yard I'd never be able to mow. This is my money. My life. Who gave these moneymen permission to steal from me? Fuck you. Give me back what you took. I'm not asking for more than I made. I earned that. All that time. All those dreams—damn, I wish I'd cashed out yesterday.

Whatever was happening to me was more than an involuntary kick after a rubber hammer to the knee. It was a mental malfunction. Spin the wheel again, and any number of aberrations could occur. Centuries ago, Hippocrates may have called my inexplicable agitation a temperamental imbalance. He'd consult his collection of stone tablets and anatomical sketches to determine if I had too little or too much blood, phlegm, or bile. But he'd promptly diagnose me with madness if he saw I'd lost more than the court awarded me in a single trade. Once I calmed down, I returned to my desk. The stock market was still closed to retail traders like me, but my holdings had risen, and I'd recovered $25,000, reducing my loss to $229,000. That brought me back to $861,000, and I began thinking, I've got to hold $860,000. As long as I hold that line, everything will be fine. These numbers, this balance where the roulette ball had stopped, had become the all-knowing, sacred, and benevolent balance of $860,000, floating in a little circle of light.

While my balance teetered around $860,000, something else occurred to me. Why am I down over 20 percent? My leveraged position was $4,000,000, but my equity stake as of yesterday was $1,090,000. If my positions are down 5 percent, I should only be down around $54,000. So, why do I have a massive six-figure hole in my account? What kind of criminal accounting is this? I took out my cell phone and called Datek's technical support. Only two other people were in the lab, checking their portfolios like me.

"Good morning, Datek tech support. Who do I have the pleasure of speaking with today?"

"Hi, my name is Julian Lawrence. I think there's a problem with how you're displaying account balances online. I remember this happening before. Is something wrong with your website?"

After a pause, he said, "No, sir, no system issues have been reported on our end."

"Maybe it's just my account. Something's wrong with my balance. It's not adding up."

"May I have your account number?"

I gave it to him.

"Sir, before we proceed, I need to ask you a few security questions. Phishing attempts have become more common, and these help us quickly verify your identity. What is your mother's maiden name?"

I told him.

"What is your current account balance?"

"Why do you need to know that?"

"Sir, these questions are designed to protect you from anyone improperly gaining access to your account. Please tell me your current balance. An approximate value is fine."

I hated this question. Reading off anything less than seven figures made it impossible to discreetly get my balance back over a million where it belonged. It made me look like I was sliding toward insignificance. Can he see how much I've lost? This guy must think I'm an idiot. I bet he feels sorry for me. Well, he doesn't know me. Even if this turns out to be my fault, I'll call back when I hit new highs and set him straight. "Okay, it was $861,000 last time I looked, but that doesn't make sense. My holdings are only down five percent."

"One moment, sir." There was another pause. I was tempted to refresh my screen but didn't want to make myself sick again.

"Sir, your current net change of negative two hundred fifty-four thousand is valid."

Oh God, it went back down. Hearing him read off all the money I'd lost made me want to puke. Every syllable rumbled through my guts.

He continued, "As of yesterday's close, your account's notional value, which includes your equity and outstanding margin balances, was $5,090,000. Accounting for this and the 5 percent decline in your holdings, the loss of $254,000 is accurate. You may have incorrectly calculated this change based on your $1,090,000 equity balance as of yesterday's close, resulting in a lower estimated loss of $54,500."

"Okay, I see. Everything makes sense now. Thank you." I didn't know what notional value was, but now I understood why my previous calculations were wrong.

"I'm glad I could be of service. Before I let you go, I'd like to point you to the wide variety of educational materials we have available online. The section covering the effects of margin and leverage explains matters related to our call in more detail. Please don't hesitate to call us again if you have any additional questions or concerns."

I hung up. How could I have been so stupid? It should've been obvious that margin isn't a gift from Datek to top up my account. *"As above, so below,"* James said. His definition didn't apply to this situation, yet it encapsulated the problem well. If margin magnifies my profits, it could magnify my losses, too.

I suspected the market would fall further, so I decided to cash out and wait for the right time to load up on stocks again. Then, I'd ride them back up, and it would be like this had never happened.

When the market opened, I closed my positions, relieved I'd cut my losses before stocks fell further. It gave me a masochistic thrill, like wandering through haunted houses, as Sam once explained. Everyone had grim faces throughout the day. No music played, and no one raised their arms triumphantly. That day, the market fell five and a half percent. I felt great. Mentally, I'd recovered. I have a plan. I'm fine.

The next day, the Nasdaq gapped down another 4 percent. Sweet! Everything's an incredible bargain now. When we hit new highs again, I'll make even more money than before. Stack 'em up: $860,000, $1.72 million. Four, five, six million. No limit. Big house! I'll pay someone else to mow the lawn. It won't stay this low for long. Then I checked myself at the door of that gargantuan abode. How do I know how far the market will fall? I recalled how the Delaware Rowdy Boys had no plan other than to hop aboard the train. I'd hopped off, but when should I hop back on? The best thing to do is to trust my instincts. They've served me well many times before. I was in a solid state of mind. This is going to work.

Fewer people were in the lab that day, and Alex complained we were losing customers. Perhaps if he'd stuck to the Mac Lab's original purpose—graphic design—rather than turning it into click-count city, whoever was balancing the budget would have been content that only students and not "our clientele" were using the lab and wouldn't question why we were shelling out thousands of dollars for things like real-time quotes and TVs playing nonstop CNBC.

But that was his problem, not mine. I logged all my work as he desired and didn't worry about which way my "stats" went. All that mattered was getting my money back.

The following day, the market dropped another 2 percent. My instincts and a sober assessment of the latest buy recommendations and price targets in the financial media led me to believe it would be time to reload soon.

A cadre of capital market luminaries asserted their firms were "buying the fear." Then, in a lunchtime interview, the CEO of a prominent investment bank reaffirmed his firm's bullish outlook: "Our research indicates stocks are oversold, and tech valuations have returned to compelling levels given the continued adoption of all things digital. We remain constructive on the sector and have added to our positions throughout the decline."

He reminded us that GDP would continue expanding as technology reshaped every aspect of our lives. "Thousands of businesses still need to get online to remain relevant. Corporate balance sheets are pristine. Consumers can't get enough. High-definition television is coming. Broadband modems are coming. The federal funds rate, discounted cash flows, recession, depression, the dollar, the yen, the pound, the past, present, and future were all priced in forever. Act fast. Buy now while supplies last."

He concluded with his firm's year-end target for the Nasdaq. "6000 by the end of the year."

He must have a room full of market wizards working for him. They wouldn't have interviewed him if he didn't know what he was talking about. He's on my side. We found the weak joints reinforced them and are ready for takeoff again. I made my stock selections and closed the trading program. I didn't want my pores turning into electric needles again. I got this. 6000 by the end of the year. "MY DAWGS, WE GOING TO THE MOON," I said, steeling my resolve. I checked the message boards to kill some time:

"I've hacked into a public database and gained access to a secret list of Jews who've changed their names. We've got a sneaky one here, guys. He changed his name from Julian Lawrence Weiner to Julian International Lawrence. But stay on the lookout—he probably changed it again. They try to be shapeshifters, but we're onto them."

"I've heard of him. Isn't he the heir to the Hebrew International Hot Dog company? I'm telling you, Mossad, the CIA, Mel Brooks, and Julian International—they're all part of the same global cabal. The more you dig, the more you see how connected they are."

"Weener is a hot dog!"

"My sources say Julian and his minions are going to pose as Gentiles and infiltrate our 'We Love to Hate Jews' chat groups. He's part of a global Zionist conspiracy to manipulate our communications into Hebrew. They've developed a nanoparticle they'll put into Hebrew International hot dogs that will make us think we're speaking English when we're actually speaking Hebrew. Since Hebrew is written right to left, everything will be reversed. When we think we're depositing money, we'll be transferring it to them."

"This is 100% confirmed true! I've seen the redacted affidavit. Those Jews have weekly meetings to find new ways to swindle us; watch out when they're being nice; they've always got something else in mind. Before the nano-dog scheme, they were putting aphrodisiacs in pastrami sandwiches to compel you to vote for communists who'll raise our taxes to fund their hedonistic artwork!"

"I know a woman who posed as a sauerkraut delivery person and gained access to their clandestine lab at Hebrew International. She saw them cooking up those nanoparticle dogs—so delectable you'll eat a dozen before you realize you're saying *'Shalom'* and nagging your kids instead of sharing the latest Zionist conspiracy with your friends. She recorded everything. Phase Two involves playing

309

"Hava Nagila" on a loop while they feed us gefilte fish laced with sedatives. While we lethargically dance in circles, they'll triple the money they stole from us in the stock market and have already hatched their next scam before it wears off. I'd show you the video, but it's been wiped from the internet because Jews control it."

"We have to mobilize. Spread the word. Let's come up with some new slogans and then go to college campuses to recruit students under the guise of social justice. As long as we do it in the proper context, we can demand the annihilation of Jews all day without facing any repercussions."

"This sounds like some unkosher Grade-A pickled bullshit. If you're worried about brainwashing, don't eat the hot dogs, but I had one last night and haven't unwittingly said *'Mazel Tov'* to anyone."

"That's how it works! They make you doubt conspiracies about them by convincing you they're too crazy to be true. Once you've eaten the hot dogs, you can't be sure what language you're speaking. I bet they slipped a little Yiddish in there, too. No one would deny that unless they were a *'Meshuggeneh!'*"

"Oh no, he's turned into a Jew!"

"It's a nightmare!"

"Nah, he's always been a Jew, fronting as one of us."

"Ah! He almost had me there, a new low, even for a Jew."

"Every single time."

Ugh, why did I open that site again? On ClearStation, CoolHand simply stated, "Closed puts and took profits. Too much chop to take a side." Okay, that's a good sign. He closed his puts, which means he thinks it's going back up.

Right before the market closed, I opened my trading program. Oh, hell yes! Sweet baby, we're riding to the sky! The market bounced, and my balance climbed back to $960,000. One more day like this, I'll be back over a million, and I can forget all about this unfortunate detour.

Your troubles are behind you. Every dollar gained brings you closer to defeating them. I will defeat the idiot who made fun of my half-moon helmet, my stepbrother, the schoolkids who opened doors

310

just enough so I'd crash into them, and the tech support guy who doubted me. I will defeat them all.

My twenty-fifth birthday had come and gone. That evening, I considered showing my mother my account balance despite it being below a million. No, not yet. Wait a few more days, and then you can wow her with seven figures like you wanted.

***

In the weeks after I showed Simone my million-dollar account balance, we discussed it infrequently. After work, she sometimes asked, "How's your stock market doing?" and I'd reply, "Oh, up and down, but more up than down!" It was cute how she said, *"Your stock market,"* but it also made me sad. I wish the stock market were one big happy bouncing ball the way she made it sound, but it's more complicated than that.

On the jubilant day my balance climbed back to $960,000, I saw no reason to stop taking fantasy tours of multimillion-dollar homes online and continued to do so in the following days. Before the month was over, my balance had fallen below $800,000. I resumed looking at cheaper places and soon stopped altogether.

Everything had gone into free fall. I closed my positions, even though I'd intended to hold them. Moments later, the market made a V-bottom and rocketed to new highs, so I jumped back into the same stocks I'd sold. I felt stupid for not sticking to my plan, but the stock market's head fakes and rug pulls make you second-guess yourself and forget your hard-won lessons. Stocks shot up and down, contrary to what I expected, and then fell further. Relying on my instincts proved as random as cereal selection, and chart patterns had become equally unreliable, but I had to hold on.

I'd swiftly cut the value of a house from my account. I still had the duplex, but over the past year, more students rented houses on my street, and they were often louder than an Amtrak train. "Listening to the sounds of other people against your will is poverty," I grumbled, lying awake past midnight. I should've bought a house on a quieter street where families owned their homes. A place I could pass down through generations: together for the holidays, warmed by the fireplace with home-cooked meals in the kitchen, children running barefoot, and Grandma Simone out back in the garden. A house wouldn't have vanished like my paper profits did. No, you can't let yourself get lost in regret. You need a steady mind to put that money back into your account where it belongs.

My Requirements demanded at least a million dollars, and only the stock market could bring them back. Analyze, visualize, don't give up. There's a way, and you'll find it. Nothing ever stopped you before, and nothing has changed.

I wasn't the only one who'd hopped on one too many broken-down boxcars. Lab attendance fell when stocks resumed their decline. Luxury cars with abandoned leases filled the dealers' lots. Investor conferences were replaced by canned food manufacturer expos and pesticide solution seminars. Businesses closed. People sold their homes and took out loans to replenish their bleeding brokerage accounts. Meanwhile, the Daily Grind reminded us why we needed to win.

The market's gyrations were mirrored in the wide-ranging opinions of analysts. Some predicted the Nasdaq would surge to 7000 next year and that stocks had merely corrected. Others cut that target way down, arguing that the Nasdaq would fall below 1000, far from the 4000 level it was currently at. But I didn't care about next year or the year after that. I wanted to get back to a million this year, this month. Hold on; don't let them take what you've worked so hard for—what you've earned. My moods swung with the market, and hiding the mayhem within me took great discipline.

Chapter 27

Simone and her classmates were studying for their women's studies midterm, but the focus shifted to social justice when Drake recounted his humanitarian work in Guatemala. In addition to Drake and Simone, two other women joined them.

"The lack of opportunities, low wages, and the long hours working in unsafe conditions demanded of these women make me livid! Oh, and don't even get me started on the total lack of childcare. How can they be expected to work in sweatshops and raise their children at the same time? I may have made a small difference in their lives by offering what comfort I could, but there is much more work to be done," Drake recounted.

"I want to fly there right now and fight for those women's civil rights," declared a woman wearing a Che Guevara T-shirt with his name in Rastafarian colors.

"I'm with you, Allison. We'll stage a walkout!" Simone added to their cheers.

The other woman chimed in. "Hey everyone, before you jet around the world, come with me this weekend to help underserved minority groups fill out their voter registration forms and get Internet access. We're privileged that these are easy for us to access, but discriminatory policies have made it so much harder for them. Next week, let's join the protest in New York against oil companies destroying the environment. That's a human rights violation, and it's not okay!"

Simone and her classmates were eager to help, but I found their motivations self-serving as they clamored to be saviors. I detested seeing anyone suffer the indignity of low standards, as I had after my injury. While addressing social and environmental injustices is noble, there had to be less patronizing ways to help people than assuming they need help filling out a form. Doesn't it create more envy than equality when you claim one group is more privileged than another? America is the land of equal opportunity, not equal results. When you fail, the first question you should ask is if it's your fault.

I was in the adjoining room on my laptop, scanning chart patterns, when their social justice itinerary distracted me. Looking at all the lines and levels was exhausting. Few bullish setups appear when stocks are falling, so focus is critical. Otherwise, your eagerness to profit invites apophenia, and like satellites and aircraft masquerading as stars, you'll start seeing patterns that aren't there.

I'd added reviewing stock message boards to my routine. Now that the trend was decidedly down, guys like Cha0strad3r, who'd applauded every new high, switched to reveling in the market's collapse.

"SELL, SELL, SELL! Margin calls and lock limit down cometh. Longs in for a world of pain. My short positions are fattening up with the quickness, like Uncle Herbert mealing on Auntie May's key lime pie after helping himself to a rack of ribs," he wrote. I doubted people like Cha0strad3r owned any stocks. They'd probably lost all their money, and celebrating other people's misery consoled them. Limit down, which he'd mentioned, or its cousin, limit up, halt all trading if the markets move beyond an exchange-mandated amount. Lock limits can last for days when financial markets are highly volatile. No matter how large the loss, knowing that once you close your position, there'll be no more bloodletting is a relief, but with trading halts, there's no way to stop the pain, so you lie awake in an abyss of your own blood until the exchanges reopen. I hadn't experienced lock limits yet, but I had lain awake in suspended agony when market-cratering news dropped on the eve of three-day weekends, which left me locked out of closing my positions for seventy-two hours. Hours I should've spent with Simone instead of telling her, "Maybe later, I've got a lot to do," while I searched for new constellations in the darkest night.

There were two quick taps on the front door. I shut my laptop and went to see who was there.

"Hello, International," James said, standing on my front porch. He had a cut above his right eyebrow, surrounded by dried blood and a yellow bruise. To his right was a Black man, about the same height as him, who looked shorter because his width nearly matched his height. He had a bit of stubble and no discernible neck.

"Your buddy here is in the hole for three hundred fifty dollars. He assured us you'd cover him. Is that right?" Big Boy asked.

The Jaguar parked in my driveway was no longer LX but was in better condition than Albert's BMW, which it blocked. Seeing those two rides together reminded me of when I stood before the foyer at Isaac's estate, admiring his old man's vintage machines. A Hispanic man was behind the wheel.

"Yo, International, you mind taking a ride to the ATM? I didn't want to involve you, but it'll be a short-term loan. I'll even pay you interest," James said.

Simone put saving the world on hold, looked up, and asked, "Is that James?"

"Yes, and he needs to run a quick errand. I'm gonna step out for a minute."

I'd never been a big spender, but now that I was well below a million, I hated spending any money and lived as austerely as possible. I sometimes skipped meals until I could score discounted deli items—the same poor man's supper my mother promoted years ago. This was to compensate for the times Simone suggested an evening out, like having dinner at a trendy new sushi place everyone was talking about. She was never one to waste money, but I'd encouraged her to "live it up a little more" in the weeks before my finances started crumbling. I couldn't abandon these luxuries now, lest she discover I was losing anywhere from $10,000 to $100,000 a day. Sometimes, I made it back—then lost even more.

Avoiding false hope was one of my few trading rules, but I'd begun to bend it by adopting the Sunk Cost Fallacy—clinging to the hope of recovering my losses in the same manner that created them since the burden of accepting that the exponential gains required to even make a small dent in my loses was a bridge too far for me to walk upon. Saving a few dollars gave me hope, backed not by cash but by an alternate self who'd taken different turns. He still wore silk pajamas and didn't need to see prices on the menu. He had ample funds for that—it was a split self I expected to rejoin soon.

I wanted to help James, but I'd have given him a harder time if the possibility of us both being decapitated and hung upside-down from a trestle wasn't more appealing than listening to Simone's study group bat around crises to solve between the bullet points of their exam review.

"I'll pay you back, like I said. It's my bad," James assured me from the backseat of the Jaguar.

I doubted he would, but we had more pressing concerns.

The guy driving was thin, with jaundiced olive skin and a long scratch on his cheek that looked like someone had run a fingernail down his face. Compared to Big Boy, it seemed like only one of them was eating. At the ATM, a few blocks from town, I withdrew $360 since the machine only spat out twenties. I didn't want to give them a dollar more than necessary, but I was eager to get this over with, so I slid the money into my wallet and nervously returned to the car.

Big Boy counted the money and said, "Alright, we good. James, you coming back with us?"

James sat pensively, considering the option; he might have even preferred it.

To the surprise of everyone, including me, I wrapped my hands around his neck, shook him, and declared, "I will fucking kill you right here if you don't come back with me! Do you want to destroy yourself? Well, go ahead, but I didn't pay a stupid ransom to these two for you to head back to a shooting gallery and run up another tab!"

An avalanche of pain had swallowed me—my dwindling fortune, Sam going mad, and James reaching for oblivion piled it high.

I released him, and he said, "Since you asked me so nicely, how can I refuse?"

Big Boy faced me. "These two? What are you talking about? All this money is mine. James and Jose ran up the tab, not me. Uh-uh. You've gone loco *ese*. What do you mean ransom? What do you think? I'm Mel Gibson or something? I don't treat my best customers

316

that way. Oh yeah, I almost forgot; here's your change, ten-dollar bill."

Jose, whom I wasn't sure was still among the living, finally spoke. "Wasn't Mel Gibson the one paying a ransom in that movie? You can't be him. You're not paying anyone."

"Shut the hell up. You know what I mean. Are you trying to say a Black man can't be Mel Gibson? You think I gotta be Danny Glover every time! I'll be Mel Gibson if I damn well please."

"That's a different movie, man."

We exited the vehicle, and they drove away, still debating who could and couldn't be Mel Gibson in this scenario. I thought these were Philly boys since that's where most of Newark's heroin comes from, but the car had a Delaware license plate.

"What did he mean, these two ran up the tab? I thought Big Boy and Jose were going to blindfold us, take us to an abandoned warehouse, and beat us with a pipe. Now I see everyone except me considered that a friendly Sunday drive."

"Because it was a friendly Sunday drive. I said I'd pay you back, and I will ... after Jose pays me back."

"I don't get it. What is going on?"

"Jose lives near my mom's place in Greenville. I've known him since I was a kid. Crazy Cat's been hooked on heroin for a long time. He gets on my nerves, but he's always got smack. The rotund fellow is Maurice. I met him through Jose. He mainly deals drugs to rich kids in Wilmington, but I've also seen him in Philly. It's funny how people think upper-class kids don't do this shit."

"If Jose is so rich, why did you need to tap old International for loot?"

"Jose's father knows he's addicted to heroin. He's sent him to all the best rehabs. Jose's probably been in and out of a dozen clinics. Eventually, his father decided if that won't work, it's better if he shoots up at home with clean needles and dealers who can be discreet, like Maurice."

"Before we get into why you're doing heroin again, I still don't understand what this has to do with me."

317

"I was about to tell you unless you'd like to choke me again. By the way, you used up all your passes doing that. Don't think I'm not still doing push-ups, boy; I'll break your neck."

I kicked the gravel in the parking lot, angry yet relieved that we weren't being beaten with a pipe and screaming for Mel Gibson to save us. "100 push-ups?" I asked.

"What?"

"Remember, *Eye of the Tiger?*"

James grinned, "Oh yeah, I forgot. Life got in the way of that. Didn't it?"

"We better hit the gym before the rest of our lives flash by unless I can do those push-ups with my knees on the mat. You were about to tell me why I handed over a hundred-fifty bucks to our rotund pal, Maurice."

"Drug dealers love giving you shit on credit, even halfway decent ones like Maurice. If you can't cough up some cash, they'll turn you into a little mule, running around doing their dirty work. The only currency required for them to obtain these services is your addiction. Jose usually avoids that rag, but he was low on flow. His dad missed a flight out of Miami and couldn't top up his account. Maurice was cool about it until today when he suggested settling our account by dropping off a few bags in Nicetown, which actually isn't so nice. That's when I thought you could help a brother out, but like I said, I will pay you back."

When we returned to the house, Albert was alone. He asked James if he'd finished reading the *Tao Te Ching*, the little book he'd given him.

"I did. The main thing I learned from it is that less is more."

We all sat down to discuss it.

"That's not a bad take, James. It's a little oversimplified, but not bad. I'm glad you read it," Albert said.

"Me too. I'm about to bust out some samurai skills now."

"Wrong country, James. Another thing you should learn from the *Tao* is to quit while you're ahead."

"What do you like about it?" I asked Albert.

"Chinaman use little book to find big inspiration for fortune cookie business."

We all laughed as he beat James at his own game.

"I like it because, with simple language, it reveals the forces that shape the universe—like the water shaping stones across the street as sticks break in the current, but the grass bends and survives while shade and sunlight sustain life along the banks. The *Tao* is nameless and formless yet flows through everything. These concepts can even help with trading by teaching us to find balance."

"How does that help you with trading?" I asked, with growing interest in what I could learn from his little book.

"Like James said, sometimes we accomplish more with less effort. That's why I recently sold my stocks and took a break from trading. Too many hedge funds and computer algorithms are exploiting fear-induced market dislocations to find a good trade right now."

Learning that one of the smartest guys I knew had sidelined himself from the market sent chills through me. Did I have any rules left that I hadn't broken? Where were the guardrails to keep me from driving off a cliff? If only I'd sold when I had over a million dollars! Why? Nope, no point in showing my mom now.

Later, I sat with James in the spare bedroom upstairs. "I should read that *Tao* book. I haven't told you about this, but I've been taking a beating in the stock market lately."

"What did you expect? You heard what Albert said. Nowadays, it's mostly computers on the other side of every trade. You can get lucky for a while, but even John Henry died battling the steam drill."

"Well, then, I need a little more luck. I was raking in cash before and still have some nice gains from trading. But nothing I've done lately seems to work. I see other traders who've got it down. They're still making money. I'll be alright. I just need to tweak my method and trade more like them, that's all. It's funny, though. I was trying to get back to my high-water mark, but now I'm happy if I end the day with a small loss. When I first ran my account up to where it is now, I was so happy, but returning to it after being so much higher has the opposite effect. Everything is backward. I was thinking heroin addiction is the same."

"Yeah, I see where you're coming from, but with heroin, if you stop for a while, you get some of the old feelings back the next time you do it. When I was at Jose's house, we tried to quit. I wanted to quit, but after three days of going through withdrawal, we decided we'd been clean long enough to get back into it and called Maurice to hook us up with a fat bag of junk. That's addict logic for you."

"Is that why you've got that thing above your eye, and he had that scratch on his face?"

"Indeed, emblems from the ravages of withdrawal."

"I can't say I'm happy to hear that, but at least you're not depressed. I'm definitely feeling down. I've gone through these phases before. All these up-and-down market swings. I always managed to get back in the zone, but it's different this time."

I did not mean that as Mr. Michelson had warned me when he spoke of the dangers in those words. I meant it was different for me, not the stock market. The difference was that now I knew it was not different at all. The Internet opened many avenues for wealth creation but did not make profitless companies worth hundreds of billions of dollars. I had more realistic expectations now. Filling my Requirements with a million dollars would have to wait. Yes, I still wanted all that money back, but first, I needed to boost my account by $100,000, or $50,000. The truth is, the dollar amount didn't matter. I only knew that I couldn't quit now. Not while I was losing. Not when I only needed a few more winning trades to feel on top again. After that, I could work on getting my million back.

"Where'd you learn that bit about trading against computers like Albert was talking about?"

"I know you haven't seen me around much lately, and whenever you do, I've been coming off a bender, but I do more than shoot up heroin and read Chinese philosophy. I learned about those market algo tricks in an article about mathematicians gaming the market. I'm sure they appreciate you handing over your cash. However, I threw in the line about John Henry myself."

I cracked a knuckle on my chin and reflected on his observations, which I knew were true but still could not accept. Trading had shifted from easy money to a game with long odds, like the big glass box with a crane where you put in some change and try to claw out one of those precious little bears that seem so easy to grab. Sometimes they are, and sometimes you've barely got one by its little white tag. There's a slim shot at success, but that's all you've got, so you hang on, hang on. I thought it was all so simple: move a couple of coins around, and millions would be mine, but now I was clinging to a tag hanging on the edge of a hook.

I was down to $550,000, which was still a good chunk of change, but I felt dead broke because I was losing money instead of making it. How long would this losing streak last? If I quit, I'll never get my money back, but if I don't, I might lose more. How much more? Oh God ...

"Mom, I lost a lot of money. Yes, all right, yes, it's all ... gone. I know, I know, I should've kept it with Mr. Michelson, okay? Don't you think I know that! I'm not stupid!"

Lost in the fractured light.

What am I doing? I should've bought a new truck or put an actual Porsche in the garage! Anything would've been better than believing that catching falling knives wouldn't leave a pool of blood where my future had been.

Stop. You can't think like that. Mama doesn't know about the money rolling in and out of your account. No one does. Why don't you quit now and hold on to what you still have? How much are you willing to lose?

All of it.

Why? Because until I saw a zero balance, I clung to the hope of reclaiming my losses. All mathematical probabilities indicated I wouldn't see a million dollars again anytime soon, which would've convinced me to cash out if I hadn't found other ways to fool myself into feeling good. Even though I was far below the former heights I'd known, I could still be a winner by lowering the bar. However, it was a watered-down victory that turned winning into mere maintenance. I'd lost a lot, but I shook it off. Losses hurt even in the deepest fog, but they were from another lifetime. That was someone else. It was still possible to live the life I wanted if I focused on the future and left those old bones behind. I knew I needed profits, but they'd only come if I held myself together long enough to see those gains again.

James kept his word and repaid me with interest a few days later. I'd have been happy for him to keep the money if it meant he would stop doing drugs, but until then, I didn't want to hook him up with a clean, well-lit place to indulge himself, so I accepted it. I wanted him to understand using heroin comes at a price. I wanted him to quit. I wasn't the only one unhappy with James for keeping one foot in Xanadu. Albert told me when his girlfriend Lisa came over and saw James strung out on the sofa, she'd almost dumped him. That reminded me of the sleepwalkers James despised. Still, I understood how distressing it was to see him in the throes of addiction. Albert politely suggested I do something about the battle stations doubling as a shooting gallery.

***

"What's going on with you? It seems like you're not even trying to quit anymore," I asked James as we walked beside the creek. The road alongside it extended several miles, but not far from my house, a trail most locals knew about led to a waterfall where we continued talking.

James skipped a stone and said, "No, I'm not trying to quit. That's the truth. I'm the type of guy who needs something that lets me shut off my mind for a while, even if it kills me. I'm sick of pretending I can fit in with all these proper citizens. It's not just a drug; it's a rejection of everything they are. Locked in the square; locked out of life."

The area by the waterfall was idyllic—trees bent over the slow-moving current, water bugs creating rings as they skated on the surface.

"That reminds me of something I heard during my near-death experience: *'Examine the universe within yourself. Is it as vast as the one around you?'*"

"*Ut supra, sic infra.*" James observed, watching the water ripple.

Yes, that was similar to what I said. The collective unconscious. Patterns repeating. *The Tao is nameless and formless yet flows through everything.* I'd heard variations of that before, too. Was it all part of a greater truth? A sign from God? How will I ever know if it's *him*?

I skipped a stone into the bubbling water at the base of the waterfall and said, "The square is an illusion of security if you stay inside it for too long. There's as much risk in keeping the world out as letting it in because nothing's certain in our lives. All we can do is try to tilt the odds in our favor. Every decision is a bet, whether we know it or not. Are we safe from the storm or caught in a hurricane? The square has no style or romance. Nothing crazy will happen to you there, and life isn't worth living unless you color outside the lines. Most people hide behind safe societal choices: go to college and get a job. Get a good performance review, and they'll give you another gram of cocaine to keep you comfortable in your cage or a shock if you step outside it. They say it's best to dress like the rest. Run counter to the crowd, and your reward will be ridicule. Sometimes, I want to be like them, but their mediocrity crushes those called to ascend where no lamp has yet been lit."

"Well, well, let's get on with it."

We laughed as he fittingly quoted *No Exit* amid our existential angst.

"Look, I've blown a lot of cash, but I've still got enough to help you. I want to help you, but I'm out of ideas here. Isn't there a clinic or somewhere you can go? I'll check in with you, and we'll both take methadone. Then, we'll go to New Orleans and find your girl, Natalie. Maybe she doesn't listen to The Smiths anymore."

"My cousin down south told me Natalie got married. Someone smarter than me figured out how to get more than a kiss from her. I bet she still likes The Smiths, though."

James sat on a rock, listening to the current and the creatures in the trees, and then said, "Two who flew over the cuckoo's nest—I like that. Being locked up in a loony bin together strikes me as a fitting fate for us, but it's not what I want. Let me know if you get tired of me nodding out on the battle stations. I have other places I can go. Don't worry about me."

***

After my conversations with Albert and James, plus the stress of sawtooth charts chopping up my trades, I was on the verge of cashing out. Then, the market rallied, recovering 20 percent of its losses. Before that, I'd fallen to $450,000. The rally only brought me back to $540,000 but raised my confidence enough to angle for a big win. $540,000? All I need to do is double that. A nice easy double, and I'll be back over a million! Fuck math! Fuck probability! I'm singing; I'm dancing. I can hear the drums.

It didn't take long for my dreams of a fast lane back to fortune to veer off course as I fell with the market to the upper $400,000 range. By then, I was so deep underwater that I had no idea how far I was from the surface. I was back to wanting to stay fully invested until I felt like a winner again—until I could breathe from up high again.

The more I lost, the more I understood that the pain of losses outweighed the pleasure of profits. I needed an impossible number of winning trades to overcome the agony of losing. I often jolted awake at 2:00 a.m., face-first with the oncoming truck again. I'd entered a realm of inescapable calamity as my anxiety shifted inward.

My borrowing limit shrank with my account value, but I still had enough to capitalize on occasional rallies. Though far from my former highs, even modest profits motivated me to keep trading despite my dwindling odds of success. I thought these rallies were reviving me, but every losing streak tore my mind in ways that were harder to mend. The market had shifted from bull to matador, as nimble as a blade slicing through my body.

Amid the crash, the day came when I exceeded my margin loan limit. A warning I hadn't seen before appeared when I logged in: a yellow banner with a red triangle informed me of a margin call and that I had to raise $20,000 or my positions would be liquidated. I didn't want to sell a single share more than necessary to get rid of the warning. Not now, not while everything was falling. Every share I sold at a loss pushed me further from the finish line. I refreshed the screen, hoping it would resolve itself, but the negative balance grew by another $3000, and the warning seemed to be a deeper shade of red.

I considered taking a $23,000 cash advance on my credit card. However, I was still sane enough to stop myself from swapping one financial problem for another. I kept selling shares until the warning went away. I was starting to hate these stupid stocks. Who cares if they sell pet food, microchips, or Swiss cheese! Just give me my money back, and I promise I'll never trade again.

With fewer winning trades, I needed another way to stay positive while I tried to recoup my losses. So I created a new screenname, Splitscreen, a throwback to when I'd wielded a big blade to eviscerate my foes while playing MUDs. Undercover as Splitscreen, I pretended that I had taken a credit card cash advance. "Fully loaded with a credit card cash advance, homies! Screw those FICO tabulating chumps. I'm about to make a mint!" I posted. One guy responded, "Wow, me too. We're gonna be rich." Another lady despondently wrote, "I borrowed money from my father but already lost half of it. Next time the market rallies, I'm selling everything. I have to at least break even." A more sensible trader chastised us. "What are you idiots thinking? No one knows how far the market will fall, and it sure as hell doesn't care about helping you get your money back!

And it did fall. Some days it fell a little. Some days it fell a lot. Fall and fall and fall. The chart would've been beautiful if we could've turned it upside down. The closing bell no longer stopped the ticker in my mind. I couldn't relax, whether stocks were moving or not. In my Rowdy Boy days, I clung to boxcars and barreled down hills on a little piece of plywood. Now, I feared numbers flashing on a screen.

During the stomach-churning crash, exploring ways to recoup my losses with my alter ego was helpful. I enjoyed reading reactions to my posts and imagining potentialities. I slipped out of my skin and walked through walls, becoming a green blob again, reconstituted in Cartesian products of identity in a multiverse of me, untethered from reality. I doubt even God would've recognized me. Sometimes, I considered selling short to profit as the market fell, but I didn't want to get cut down by one of its furious rebounds. Still, the idea of climbing back to a million while the market plummeted was appealing—double revenge. I could build my wall as I watched my enemies fall. Fall and fall and fall. Since I wasn't comfortable selling short, I drafted my surrogate self. I retrofitted Splitscreen as a short seller, deploying him to the battlefield to tease longs about their losses, even though we were aboard the same sinking ship. The water's fine; jump right in.

"I'm short and strong, sucker longs! Sleeping till noon while your stocks get roasted. Keep trying to pump, 'cause I'm making bank while everything dumps." Another troll kept the ill thread going, "Ooh baby, ooh, so sweet watching bulls get roasted. Gonna lick 'dem bones off the grill and stash that cash while I watch you fry." Trolling posts like this got instant feedback. The more flamboyantly offensive, the more people replied. Soon, a big troll posse formed, all claiming they, too, were short and feeling great satisfaction watching Longs suffer as we profited from their pain. As I thought of new ways to take pleasure from their pain, someone traced my posting history and exposed my deceit, noting that I'd claimed to use a cash advance to boost my long positions but now was profiting from the short side. Thus, I had to dishonorably discharge Splitscreen and make another avatar. All in all, this second self provided gut-busting, vengeful relief from the unfunny state of my mind and the market that made it that way.

I could rewrite history, casting myself as a victor—or as a fair-weather friend of the demented with a palindrome tongue—take on a sadistic role, basking in schadenfreude over the losers.

This escalated to the point where I'd created four different identities to concurrently troll long and short traders on the message boards without being called out as a con. I had them agreeing, debating, and insulting each other like puppets in a one-man show. Sometimes, I forgot who was who, posted something out of character, and had to dishonorably discharge multiple avatars in a single day, creating new identities to continue the charade. Spending time away from the market was a welcome respite as I became less obsessed with its movements, flying upside-down in my bulletproof biplane behind enemy lines. However, this was a cold comfort, as my money remained in the stock market, still very much affected by it. One afternoon, while engaged in my message board shenanigans, Alex tapped me on the shoulder and asked to speak with me in his office. I was instantly alarmed that he'd used his proliferating suite of surveillance applications to observe my unhinged antics and wished I'd never started this lunacy. His red face inflamed my anxiety to the point that I was about to preemptively confess, but he spoke first and spared me from self-incrimination.

Chapter 28

I was in Alex's office discussing recent changes to our Bloomberg license, not my motley group of message board avatars as I'd feared.

"Julian, why did you tell Bloomberg we wanted a business license?" Alex asked. His face was almost as red as my margin call warning.

"One of their sales guys called last week and suggested that. He said it had more features and was free, so I let him switch our license. Shouldn't we have a business license at a business center?" I shrugged. He always flipped out over nothing.

"It's a business center at a fucking university!"

"What's the difference?" I meant to say it forcefully but spoke closer to a whisper.

"What's the difference? I'm glad you asked. I'll show you." Alex gripped my chair and, in one forceful motion, slammed it flush into his desk. I suppressed a groan as my sternum hit the lip, and my face nearly struck his monitor. I felt like a sack of broken bones as if I'd been in a car accident. I couldn't move my arms.

He read the email, which I scooted back to see, "Mr. Martingale, Congratulations on upgrading to a business license, which provides faster downloads and enhanced data analytics. After your 30-day free trial concludes, an additional $20,000 annual fee per machine will be billed as a single payment. Thank you again for being a valued Bloomberg customer."

"An additional $20,000 per machine. Now, do you see the difference? That salesman played you for a fucking fool, Julian. Free trial. I would've seen right through that. You should've checked with me. You're not the decision-maker here, and since you can't even follow simple directions, you never will be."

"He said it was free, not a free trial. Can't you switch back to the previous license?" I gripped my chair, fearing I'd faint.

"No, that's your responsibility now, and you better hope they'll change it, or you'll have to tell accounting we need another $60,000 to upgrade our machines. Good luck keeping your job after that. Great work, Julian." Alex slowly clapped as if he were in a box seat at a lavish affair.

"Alright, I'll talk to Bloomberg." Everything was going against me: the stock market, Alex, Big Papa in the park, and now this idiot from Bloomberg who conned me. Chainsaw—a cut at the knees is too kind. Line 'em up and rip the cord. I'll lop off their heads in a single stroke, pick them up, and then ...

"Julian, why are there heads on pikes in the front yard?" Simone would ask.

"Baby, that's what happens to people who go to war with me. If it bothers you, I'll put them out back."

"Let's go! Why are you sitting there? This is your top priority. Forget everything else, and from now on, I want to review all your emails before you send them. Don't click send unless I say you can. Is that clear? Are we clear?"

I tried to reply, but even though I was seething inside and wielding two chainsaws, I couldn't speak ... Then the grass grew tall around me, swaying as a hot Saharan wind tousled my thinning hair. I was back where I never wanted to be, grazing with the gazelles, a lion's jaws tight around my neck. He knows I won't counter him. I can't. Though my heart still beat, my soul had departed.

I licked my lips and mumbled in agreement, which Alex took as affirmative but expressed how I felt about lopping off his head.

Given I'd done nothing that merited being slammed into his desk, Alex pivoted to disaster control as the red faded from his face. His shoulders eased.

"Hey, buddy, look. I guess I was a little abrupt with you earlier. You know I'm not upset with you, though, right? I should've told you what I've been developing sooner, and we could have avoided this. I've modeled the Business Center after the start-up I was involved in at Stanford. But the people I was working with ... how they structured the corporation ..." Alex squinted his eyes. "Long story short, I thought they were my partners, but as soon as they had enough capital to launch it, they cut me out.

"We made solutions for the human asset management market. I know that's not as sexy as trading stocks, but there's massive revenue potential there. My partners scored a couple of million after I was out, but soon they'll pay for swindling me. I've created a superior application suite that makes managing these assets simple, effective, and highly profitable, so they better start looking for another line of work. I've named my solution, Business 2.0, EBD—Every Bit of Data, to showcase it properly. I know I got a little hot there, but I'm not upset with you. You've been coming around, Julian. Your clothes still need help, but you have consistently strong stats and have done a great job learning all the major market concepts. After I show you how EBD works, you'll see why we can't afford any more setbacks like your ill-conceived business license swap."

I nodded robotically, and he shared his fabulous plan.

Alex walked me through a PowerPoint presentation. Although his slide deck utilized standard shapes and templates, it held traces of ingenuity and foresight, facilitating the dark future he championed throughout it. "Many corporations have hundreds of thousands of people on their payroll, each with tedious personal needs and an inflated sense of self-worth. Sure, you can throw them a pizza party to raise morale or hand out a couple of perks tailored to whatever cultural cross-section of society they think makes them matter, but with all the orthodontist appointments, funerals, weddings, divorces, childcare costs, and mortgages—they're a burden. A company won't grow if it wastes too much time on the concerns of low-level employees—tinkering with spreadsheets and turning wrenches. They must be reduced to icons in a folder, sorted by salary and productivity stats until they can be replaced by automation or artificial intelligence.

"This slide demonstrates how the C-level team can use whatever metrics they see fit to categorize, slice, pivot, and then display their entire organization on a single chart. The data can be filtered down further, allowing them to easily exclude less profitable lines of business from consideration. See how that slice disappeared, and I've recalculated the total as if it were never there?

"When EBD onboards staff, it assigns each employee a series of numbers, eliminating the need for additional personal identifying data throughout the system. With just the first three digits, management is equipped to execute tasks including, but not limited to, hiring, firing, promoting, demoting, and sending company-wide emails that appear inspiring and benevolent while discreetly absolving themselves of liabilities in a few clicks. The senior executives' tasks are even more streamlined. For example, say they want to make a corporate donation to one of those uppity philanthropic outfits with their tear-jerking documentaries of oil-covered waterfowl and refugees carrying sad little sacks past bombed-out buildings on their backs to present an air of social responsibility to the media. Double-click, done. Then, they can spend the rest of the day fulfilling their core duty, counting the cash.

"My role here, leading the Business Center, is temporary. I'm better than this. EBD is worth billions. Managing employees is just one use case, Julian. It has tremendous commercial potential, too. With the data I've gathered, marketing firms worldwide can categorize prospects so efficiently that they'll know what people want to buy before they do. I was planning to offer you and Albert a spot on the team I'm assembling to bring EBD to market. We can discuss an equity stake, too. However, due to recent economic stress, I've accelerated the time to market. A venture capital firm is interested in first-round funding, but I haven't secured it yet, so we need to be mindful of how we present ourselves to the broader educational community.

"Business 2.0, EBD, will be ready to release in a few months, but I'm still gathering data for the proof of concept, so we can't afford any more mistakes, understand? The university could shut this down. They don't understand that surrendering our privacy, even our most intimate fears and desires, every time we go online is an inevitable byproduct of the ascension—the commodification of information itself—so we might as well make a lot of money from it. But they will, Julian. Everyone will, and they'll pay handsomely for data people freely give to me, which will generate returns that will be the envy of the world. Let's work together as a team to resolve this business license misunderstanding. Let me know when you're ready to email Bloomberg. I'll swing by and take a look, and we should be back in business. All right? Does that sound good?"

I said, "Yes," with a voice that seemed to emanate from somewhere else and returned to my desk, where I slumped in my chair, staring at the monitor. You'll always be that guy people push around in the park. No! I'm gonna break down Alex's door and beat the hell out of him. I don't care how big he is; I'll pummel his ass into the ground. Now you'll show me some respect, won't you, boy! … I let out the breath I hadn't realized I was holding in. How am I supposed to know if the lab has become a place of commerce, education, or whatever unholy blend of both he's envisioned? How can I do my job while I'm chained to his cockamamie plan, which I can't understand but don't dare derail? Hop on, hop off. Hire, fire, sell short. Click to complete your order. The economics professor came over and asked if I could help configure a chart using data from the 1970s. I said, "No," without turning from my screen. Nonplussed, he asked Albert for assistance. I mindlessly opened and closed Adobe Photoshop, remembering when Glenda ran the lab before the clown in her office took over, making it his launchpad for status and the spoils of corporate dominance.

"Hey, Julian, what's going on? What happened in Alex's office? I thought I heard yelling," Albert asked after helping the professor. I lifted my right hand to acknowledge him without turning my head. I still couldn't lift my arms. They were straps of rubber, bloodless, useless. I wanted to say something but couldn't.

Albert sat down beside me. "Julian, don't worry about that guy. Whatever he's wound up about is an illusion only he cares about."

Albert's saner perspective was refreshing. I took a deep breath and explained the Bloomberg debacle, leaving out Alex's promise of a stake in Business 2.0, EBD. Albert helped me draft an email to persuade Bloomberg to reinstate our original license agreement. I hated that I needed Alex's approval to send it. Walking out right then and there crossed my mind. I don't need this job … but I have to climb back. I was wrong to lower my expectations. I can still get back to a million. I did it once. I can do it again. It's still required. Now more than ever! Now is the time. This is my chance. Though my salary was meager, it covered my expenses and, most importantly, allowed me to keep the money I had left in the stock market so that Simone and I had a fighting chance to push back the barbarians and build our wall, our city, our escape.

I got Alex, and he came to my desk. Now he was the laid-back version of himself—yet another fair-weather friend of the demented. "Nicely done. You've covered all the bases. That ought to do it. Fire that off and let me know what they say."

I sent the email, and Bloomberg reinstated our original license within the hour. A part of me wished they hadn't. I was willing to immolate myself as long as Alex was incinerated with me. I was about to forward their response to him, but I hesitated. Should he review it first? He said to check with him before clicking send, but that doesn't make sense. I didn't add anything, and it was going directly to him. I felt like I was five years old, scolded for running down the hall. I showed Albert Bloomberg's response. "Should I forward this to Alex?"

"Yeah, of course, send it. Are you sure you're okay?"

"Maybe not," I admitted, forwarding the email. After our shift, we walked home together.

"The flow of Chi energy is foundational to Taoism," he told me.

"Oh yeah?" I replied as I sank into the ground, waiting for my chin to hit the dirt.

"You've seen the yin-yang symbol, right? You know, that double paisley circle with two smaller circles inside them?"

"Yes, I've seen it."

"That's a symbol for harmonizing duality, which can be achieved by balancing Chi. We're typically unaware of our Chi until it's out of alignment. It's not hard to see that's how you're feeling now, twisted."

I nodded.

"There are ways to get Chi back into alignment. Tai Chi is the most common. I'm sure you've seen people in the park doing slow-motion shadowboxing. That's Tai Chi."

"I used to know a guy who did that, but it was only to pick up chicks."

"Mockery won't lead you to the Tao," Albert said.

I stopped walking and busted out some silly moves, pretending to do Temple's nitwitsu. Though I was messing around, I started feeling better. Albert laughed.

"I'm not sure what that was. Let me show you how it's done." Unlike me, Albert knew the way and demonstrated the proper technique. I matched his movements, breathing at the same rate, and rejoined the living with my soul reclaimed. Albert sat on a bench, and I followed suit. He closed his eyes and interlaced his fingers, forming a triangle with his hands. "Listen for the color of the sky. Look for the sound of the hummingbird's wings, Grasshopper," Albert said, pretending we were in an episode of *Kung Fu*. He smiled at the corners of his mouth and then sat calmly, meditating. I tried to do the same, but the first thing that came to mind was Alex. *"You look like a slob."*

No, you're a fucking slob. Great work, slob! My eyes burned. I opened them. Albert was still meditating. I closed my eyes again. I didn't see a golden light or an eternal oasis, but I realized my stress in social settings could be related to Chi. I recognized Taoism as part of the Mystery and vowed to explore it and Chi energy further. We sat for a few minutes, then headed home. At the front door, he said, "Chi energy seeks clear channels. How you were feeling before happens when your Chi is blocked. Sometimes, you've got to break through that blockage, but less aggressive options usually exist. Either way, don't let that twisted feeling hold you back. Get up, have tea, paint, go for a walk. Just as still water harbors the deadliest pathogens, an idle mind and body cause the most damage."

In that moment, I loved Albert. His help shifting my perspective undid enough of the day's trauma for me to stand without shaking.

That Friday, my visions of morning Tai Chi sessions with Albert, followed by hours of Taoist discussion over tea, vanished when he delivered bad news.

"Hey, J, I'm moving in with Lisa next week. I know it's short notice, but you can keep my security deposit."

I didn't know Albert well when he moved in, so a security deposit seemed prudent, but now I hardly wanted to charge him rent.

"Are you sure? You could both live here, and I wouldn't raise the rent."

"Oh, thank you very much, Julian. I appreciate that, but it makes more sense for me to move in with her. She has a place off campus near I-95, where I'll need to be after I graduate anyway."

"All right, but don't worry about the short notice. I'll give you your security deposit back."

"Okay, thanks."

"I'm sorry, but I have to ask. Is it James? I know having him here has been ... unusual. I've known him for a long time and don't want to turn my back on him. I'm aware it can't stay like this forever."

Albert sighed and said, "Well, I've grown to like the guy more than when I first met him. I respect what you and Simone are doing to help him, which is so kind of you both, but yeah, James has gotten involved in things I'm not comfortable with. I didn't want to say anything, but I've seen him hanging out with people selling drugs at parties. I'm not here to tell you how to live your life, Julian. I'm only sharing this because you asked, and I was planning to move in with Lisa soon anyway. But if James doesn't commit to overcoming his addiction soon, it's going to hurt everyone trying to help him, too."

"Thanks for being honest. Even if you're not living here, please feel free to stop by anytime."

Albert moved out as planned.

***

James, Simone, and I had breakfast at Jimmy's Diner the weekend after Albert had moved out.

"I thought Jewish people weren't supposed to eat pork," Simone teased as my plate of eggs, toast, and bacon arrived.

James poured a generous helping of sugar into his coffee and responded on my behalf. "You know, Simone, bacon wasn't around when Moses received the Ten Commandments, but I bet our heavenly father would've permitted it if this salty, greasy goodness existed back then."

We all laughed, and I said, "You know, I'm just following in the footsteps of my forefathers. They must have noticed the Lord's bacon omission at some point because there's a Yiddish word for it: *Treyf*. It literally means flesh torn by beasts. Most Jewish people associate it with food that's not kosher, but they still like to nibble on it."

"I think there was bacon around the time of Moses," Simone corrected.

"In that case, don't mind if I do," James said, snagging the two strips of bacon off my plate, which gave us another laugh and James indigestion later.

Our coffee was refilled as customers came and went. It felt like we could sit there forever. I thought of the scene in Star Wars where the gang is trapped in a giant trash compactor. Death hadn't defeated them, no matter how close it came. They were undefeated until the compactor crushed them. The only problem was that the crush was coming. Time was coming for them, but the crush could've been avoided if time stopped. Time is a tangible thing, made of matter and relative to energy at the speed of light squared. There should be an algorithm to reverse time like hedge funds use to manipulate the market. But no one knows those numbers, and we can't reverse time for the living or the dead. I knew it was true but didn't want to believe it.

I was happy that evening—perhaps Albert was wrong? The good old days were coming back. I felt alright. I closed my eyes and fell asleep: a single key, two, then three, as the maestro gleefully passed his misery onto me with clanging keys. But everything has faded now. It's far away; the edges are decayed. Long shadows leap like flames, contorting into crooked fingers and pointed noses. I am afraid—I run down halls and stairs leading into walls. I spin around; I want to go back the way I came, but the floor curls back into itself, an ouroboros. "Julian, get in there," the piano man cajoles. "You're small; you'll fit." I know he's lying, but I climb into the trash compactor anyway. He turns it on. It doubles as a dryer now. Tumbling and tumbling as hot metal breaks my bones and burns me. When I opened my eyes, I knew the nightmares had won again.

***

"What's up with the spot above your right eye?" I asked James about the thin, crooked line along his brow as he helped himself to Simone's leftover food in the refrigerator. I had some, too, since he'd already eaten too much for it to go unnoticed.

"Oh, I Krazy-Glued it," James explained. I figured it was from a withdrawal attempt and let it go. Then I noticed his arm. It had turned yellow from too many spikes in his veins. I had the same problem once, but that was from an IV drip while I was in a coma.

"How about your arm? Do you need anything for that?" I said, pointing at the bruises.

"Nah, that happened before. It'll clear up."

"This isn't good, James."

"It's not as bad as you think."

Due to minor construction at the lab the following week, I didn't have to be at work until noon. I slept in and woke up feeling better than I had in a while, but when I went to grab a stack of twenty-dollar bills I'd left on my desk, it was gone. I asked Simone if she knew what had happened.

"I had a hundred dollars on my desk, but it's missing; do you know what happened?"

"No. What was it for?

"I sold those bikes that've been in the shed since I bought the house. I was going to deposit it today."

"You don't think that—"

"It had to be him."

She lowered her gaze.

"No, it's fine, James. I'm going to install an ATM in the living room. Making you scrounge around for change whenever you need a hit was selfish of me," I said, confronting him when he returned moments later and matter-of-factly acknowledged what I already knew after I stopped him from making a beeline to slide a needle into his arm upstairs. I missed the days when James at least pretended he wasn't addicted to heroin. I wasn't angry at him. I was angry about what was happening. I wanted to toss his addiction into the rippling water across the street and never see it again.

"It's not called a hit; it's called cooking up. You don't understand the cravings—you can't. If it wasn't for that cash, I would've bitten through a bolted door to score some dope, so don't take it so personally."

His arm was still yellow, though his eye was healing.

"At least your eye is getting better."

"Junkies' surgical skills are underappreciated."

"That makes me think of the hole in my head."

"Your trepanation? What made you think of that?" James asked. Given his vast knowledge of the occult and many extraordinary things, he knew the medical term for where the pellet left a hole in my skull. I felt my brain pulsing whenever I touched it, just as I'd regrettably told Hazel once. I generally avoided touching it.

"Trepanning goes way back. Some theories about it make sense, but most don't. Gluing yourself together made me think of that and surgery in the Middle Ages."

"Some say trepanation enlightens you."

"I can confirm that falls into the nonsensical category." I sighed and said, "I understand you don't want to go to a rehab clinic, but at least see a doctor for your arm. Don't worry about the money, okay? I've never had cravings like yours, but I know what it's like to want something so badly you'd bite through a lock to get it. I'm not mad. I'm concerned. I'd rather spend my money helping you quit than keep throwing it away in the stock market. But we've got to do something soon—like today when I get back from work."

"We don't have to wait. It's better if I bounce. I'll leave right now."

"You know it's not like that! But what do you expect? I can't sit here and watch you destroy yourself."

"It's alright, International. I agree with you. It's not fair to you or Simone. I've got other places I can go."

"Where? With Jose?"

"Maybe."

"Forget it. Forget I said anything. Wait until I get back from work. We'll figure something out."

"There's no solution we can put in a pretty little box! You're right. I said you're right, and now we're gonna do something about it. Want to know why I'm leaving? It has nothing to do with you. We're cool, International. We're cool. It's the desperate complication of being nude among all these people."

It was the most beautiful and awful thing I'd ever heard. I don't know what I meant when I said it, but James did—better than I had. Simone was still around when James casually departed. He thanked us for our hospitality but insisted he really must be going. With a smile, James explained that there were unseen empires he wanted to explore and then moseyed out the door. Simone was more upset when he left than I expected as if she'd never see him again. She was right. Ten days later, James died.

Chapter 29

I found out shortly after James died—two weeks after I'd last seen him. Though I was no longer a student, I continued attending art history classes after work, sitting quietly in the back since I wasn't enrolled. I loved all the colors and concepts but often closed my eyes and listened to professors gushing about Frida Kahlo, Basquiat, and Caravaggio. Simone had graduated and often snuck into lectures with me when she wasn't looking for a job. One night, when I'd gone alone, someone called my name after class.

"International?"

Only two people called me that: James and ... "Eva?"

"Yeah, it's me. How are you?"

Her short, spiky hair dyed black made her pale skin look porcelain, and those pouty lips were impossibly crimson. I recalled how they parted like a blooming rose and her hot breath on my hands that chilly night in the International Scout. She stepped back and twirled playfully in her jade-green dress as the world blurred. I wanted to kiss the very air she breathed. Where was time? Gone. Two planets, elliptical, two figures in motion, moving as one. I never liked dancing, but in that instant, I understood its elegance. Slowly spinning together, one arm around her, the other holding her wrist.

Simone and I had our ups and downs, but I loved her. My attraction to Eva didn't contradict that. Hazel, Eva, and Simone were all in my heart. But now, right now ... Eva was knocking at the door. Why was this feeling so strong? Eva and I shared one caress and talked a few times after that. One thing was clear: she'd blossomed well beyond the fifteen-year-old girl I'd considered kissing. The worst part was that I sensed she shared the attraction. But I'd changed too. Luckily, I was wearing a baseball cap. I didn't want her to see the continental drift—the islands of mottled hair surrounded by widening swaths of scalp. If I had more time, I could explain my hair, face, and scars. If I had more time, I could explain every imperfection.

"Oh, hi! I'm doing well. I've been working at that computer lab across the street for almost four years now," I said, pointing, leaving out anything about it being a business center. "I graduated recently, but I still like going to art history classes and letting the stories sweep me away."

"You were always a dreamer, International."

"Yes, but I'm not the only one. What've you been up to, Eva?"

"I'm in my second year of school. I wandered around for a while, working at thrift stores and record shops. I always liked vintage stuff. But I knew that was never gonna last. Gotta grow up sometime, right? Now I'm a psych major, but honestly, I don't even know what I'm going to do with that!" she said, which made me adore her more. Stop it. Politely say goodbye and walk away.

"Guess what? I changed my middle name to International—for real. I went to court and did it." I showed her my driver's license.

"No way! So cool! Remember, I gave you that name. When did you do that?"

"Of course, I remember. I did it a couple of years ago. James talked me into it. Did you two keep in touch? Did you ever talk to him?"

"Sometimes, but mostly a wave when he was passing by. I liked him, but he was so ... difficult to understand, you know?"

"Yeah," I said, chuckling. "I'm sure James would agree."

"It's so awful how the police found him. I wonder what happened. I heard about it two days ago."

"Found him where? What are you talking about? What happened?" I knew James wasn't destined to live to a ripe old age, but I figured he'd been busted for a petty crime, walking around in his underwear, shouting spirited epithets at anyone he deemed needed an insult.

"They found James in a river ten miles outside Philly."

"Wait ... in which river? What was he doing, swimming?"

"International, he's dead. When they found him, he was already dead."

I could not ... keep ... steady, this second, that second, unraveling. I stretched into a long, empty scroll rolling downhill. No muscles or bones; loose guts; two-dimensional; flipping around like a busted TV.

"They did an autopsy. It was a drug overdose. The police don't know how James got into the river. It took them a couple of days to identify him."

"How do you know this? Are you sure it was him?" It helped to speak, to say something. It stopped me from toppling over.

"We had a few of the same friends. Some of us used to hang out at Temple's apartment. God, that guy was so creepy! Our friend Matt sent me a link to an article about the police finding him in a river. It was James. I'm sure." She wiped a tear from her eye. I wanted to cry but couldn't. I'm sure we felt the same pain, but ever since the day James slumped against the wall after shooting up, a part of him was gone, and that's when my grieving for him began. I still loved James, but after that, he was no longer the guy I knew—running from the dogs or poring over the Kabbalah until the sun rose.

"Can you send me the link? I had no idea that this ... that James ... that James died. I saw him a few weeks ago at my house. I thought he was in Wilmington. He explained it to me—him and the drugs. I know he had a terrible addiction, but he was way more than that. I mean, you knew him. You know what I'm saying. Somehow, this all seems inevitable, but that doesn't make accepting it any easier. He was looking for a way to ease the pain of living from the first day I met him, but he also knew how to make the hard times a little easier. There were days I might not have gotten through if he hadn't shown me how to celebrate the absurdity of living."

"I heard James got into heroin. I already know four people who overdosed, so I'm not surprised; just sad about what happened to him, but I know exactly what you're saying. I'll always remember James the way he was before he started doing drugs. I'll send the link to you as soon as I get home. Give me your email. It's nice to see you, though. I wish I had better news. I'm sorry. I thought you already knew. He loved talking about all the crazy stuff you did together. 'International, that's my man! Only guy I know, just as crazy as me.' It always cracked me up when he said that. Oh, and that one guy? The guy with freckles—he was kinda chubby?

"Sam."

"James told me stories about you and Sam hopping trains with him, hanging out in the woods, smoking cigars. Did y'all really do that stuff?"

"Yes, we did," I said with a bitter smile. I gave Eva my email, which she stuck in her purse. It looked like it was from a thrift shop, which made me think of the old days—what was and could've been.

"Hey, I gotta go. Here, let me give you my number. We ought to hang out sometime."

We embraced. Eva fit into my arms flawlessly. I felt her close to me, even after she walked away. I stood, wanting to know: Why do the good times go so soon? James lived, he died, and all that remains is fenced in today. In my mind's eye, I'm pulling into the park. There he is, sprawled out in the back of my truck, two tabs on his tongue, existential, outrageous, leaping from roof to roof across heavy freight. No one else taught me as much, made me so mad, made me wonder and understand there is something we cannot tame within us all. I loved him, and now he was gone, glorious in a flash of light, but, like everyone, chained to the passing of time with no way to frame it. Everything is ephemeral because all unfixed prints go back to gray, then black.

I told Simone what happened the moment I got home. Tears streamed down her cheeks; my eyes stayed dry. When was the last time I cried? About three weeks after our trip to DC. When my big money plans started unraveling. I spent years thinking about how great my life would be once I had a fat wallet, and then it was gone quicker than it had come. This miserable day made me see the depth of my self-deception. Now is not the time. This is not my chance. One million dollars? It hadn't fulfilled the Requirements of anything. No, I'd only seen the glory to know the pain of losing it. And now, even the death of my beloved friend left me apathetic. I wanted to grieve with Simone as any normal person would, but it seemed like I was on the wrong flight, flying away from everyone.

"We should have done more to help him! What else matters if you can't be there for the people you love? I can't believe I won't see him again. How could James be dead?" Simone wailed.

I told her I was hurting too but disagreed that we could have done more. James didn't want our help. He wanted peace, which we couldn't provide. Maybe he'd found it in his final resting place. Simone and I lay close that evening, taking comfort in each other to overcome the pain we shared. I steadied my breathing, focusing on harmony and balance—death comes for everyone. We are one with the water. It was tough, but we'd get through it together.

***

"I doubt we'll ever meet a guy like him again," Albert said with a sad grin when I told him James had died. "I wish he'd found another path. Under all that obnoxiousness, James had a lot to offer the world. I'm here for you. Let me know if you want to talk anytime." I appreciated that. We could discuss the books James introduced me to and the splendor he saw in things no one else noticed. Those were good memories, but the best thing about him was the hidden stories he uncovered, like when he saw an old Italian man struggling to water flowers in front of his gelato shop. James lifted the can from his hands and finished the job for him. Afterward, we sat on the patio out back, sipping double espressos and listening wide-eyed to tales of his mafioso-laced childhood in Boston's North End.

The old man reminisced about his first gelato shop—meeting Whitey Bulger, being questioned by the FBI, and explaining that the sweet treat was all he had to offer the gangster. As he spoke, we were transported to another time, before the liver spots and bony hands—back to when he was a handsome young man, riding a bicycle over to the waterfront where he'd call Maria from a red phone booth, 'Meet me at 10 p.m. on Battery Street, near the cobblestone cul-de-sac. That's right, where the marigolds grow. Don't worry. I'll be there.'

There were many things I could say about James, but I had no words to share. No anecdote could bring back the man who made the memories—the lies, the truth, the excess, and the understanding that even with all the ugliness, beauty and joy prevail.

***

"I'd like to take some time off. A close friend of mine died. Simone and I both knew him," I explained to Alex in his office.

"I'm sorry to hear that. Was he your age? If you don't mind me asking, what happened?"

"It was a heroin overdose. His name is James. He was twenty-three. He didn't use to do that kind of stuff, just the last few years." I added, not wanting Alex to reduce James to an addict with his legs sticking out of an alley.

"That's tough. I keep seeing articles about kids overdosing on heroin. Some of them are barely teenagers. I'm sorry about your friend, but it makes you wonder, where are the parents? What do they expect if they don't provide structure in their children's lives? I blame the public school system, too. So much garbage they're teaching kids these days."

"It does make me wonder. I wish I had the answers," I said, wanting to keep our conversation as short as possible before it took any horrible detours.

"All right, let's see here ... They've got something online about this. Have a seat. Let me take a look." Alex searched within the university intranet until he found a document titled "University of Delaware Employee Sickness and Bereavement Leave Policy." He scanned the document, scrolling up and down, looking for a line, a paragraph, or a bullet point to tell him what to do. He sighed several times as he read. I almost felt sorry for the guy having to work so hard. If only it were all laid out in one of his single-page charts, he could've resolved the matter with a few clicks.

I was relieved there'd been no more Bloomberg-type incidents. I didn't want to think or feel. I only wanted to make it through the day without any more pain. That morning, my account had fallen below $400,000. I sold everything before going into Alex's office. I avoided looking at any charts or market indexes. I could spare no distractions as I forced my fingers to do what my mind refused. It was hard to shake the nagging feeling that I was being suckered into selling right before the market rebounded. I still wanted to make money but recognized that I couldn't treat the market like a punching bag swinging back at me after every blow. I needed to be meticulous, like CoolHand. He understood avoiding hard hits matters as much as landing them.

But I had not been like CoolHand. What I'd done was random; reckless. It wasn't nimble trading executed with an agile mind or the Lord guiding me. It only worked while money rained down, and all we had to do was grab it. My hubris blinded me from seeing the sky had returned to reclaim its millions from everyone foolish enough to believe the wind only blew one way, even though every dollar we'd wanted to double was blowing out the door. I had a choice to make. Wait for the sky to give me my money back or stash the cash I had left before it took the rest. I had no way of knowing which way the wind would blow. All I knew was I needed to halt my failing mental state. I closed my positions. My last and greatest trade.

Alex finished yo-yoing with the document and concluded, "There's nothing here about time off for friends. I could've given you a week if it were your parents or a sibling." I wanted to smack him. Did there have to be policies and rules for everything?

He liked those rules when they suited him. When they didn't, what he'd insisted was an incubator for his soon-to-be billions—where we day-traded in pursuit of endless riches while he counted every click—flipped into a humble educational institution so send someone else the bill.

"I'll tell you what. Why don't you take the rest of the day off? I'll let you mark it as a scheduled absence, but I'll need to see you back here tomorrow. Rules are rules, buddy. We all have to live by them." How nice that we were buddies again.

It was early Thursday. I had the rest of the day to wander around and process my emotions, then all I had to do was get through Friday, and I'd have the weekend to reflect on James's life with

346

Simone. On Saturday, we could go to Middle Run Valley to trek across low-slung bridges beneath the mossy trees, or better yet, stop by Milburn Orchards on aptly named Appleton Road and walk among the ripening red apples that would be sweeter when pumpkins about ready to burst were beside them in October. Near the orchard was a farmhouse with a big red barn, home to sheep, cows, and chickens clucking in their coop. I thought of that because of what James and I did with Sunrise when Simone and I were first dating. Sunrise was a stray cat Simone found near her house with orange fur, which inspired the name. Sadly, Sunrise soon entered the sunset of her life. She became sickly and puked all over the place. To make matters worse, one of Simone's roommates had a labrador who never tired of barking at her as she hid beneath the bed.

One day, when James was with me, we found Simone crying in her bedroom, cradling sickly Sunrise; she couldn't bring herself to euthanize the cat. I wasn't sure which of them was a sadder sight. James said he knew a place to take our pukey orange pal where she could live the rest of her life in peace. Simone brightened, we grabbed Sunrise, and James guided me to the farmhouse. Sunrise puffed up her fur, hissing the whole way there atop my headrest. We parked outside the gate. Cats were gathered by the barn, munching on a big pile of chow. I scanned the area for the owner, but Sunrise bolted toward the farmhouse before I spotted them. I'd never seen her go five feet without puking, so I stopped and watched Sunrise run, her fur shining like the Golden Gate. Looking beyond the farmhouse, past the crops and waddling ducks, out yonder, James said, "That's a miracle. It may be a minor revelation, but I see the signs. We have walked with the Lord. Whether you're a kitten or a lion, His love for us remains." James saw the power of the Lord in many weird and wonderful ways. I only wish he'd seen more of it in himself. That evening, Simone declared the three of us were family.

It sucked that all the money I'd piled up was swept away when everyone rushed for the exit much faster than we'd come through the door. The fact that my net worth took a round trip instead of leaving a gaping hole in my brokerage account, like many who completely blew their stacks, was a minor consolation until a nagging voice cut me down again. The whole thing was an unfortunate oversight. You know as well as we do that you were never meant to be a millionaire. We've relieved you of that burden. The moneymen have put everything back where it belongs—with us. We appreciate your business, but it's high time you accepted that you'll never be worthy of what we have because even when you win, you lose.

The voice broke through any illusion of relief I'd cooked up, and all my agony hit me again. Why didn't I sell when I was over a million! You can make decent money trading if you know how to read stock charts. Thank you, Mom. I'm proud of myself, too. It's nice to have a little extra, isn't it, Simone? How very generous of you, sir—utter buffoonery.

Simone came home soon after me, delaying my sentencing. Stupidity was the verdict. Now, what must the punishment be? I put my arms around her, but Eva filled my thoughts. I tried to block her out, but my mind wouldn't cooperate as I dealt with James's death. We sat on opposing battle stations.

"I have to tell you something," Simone said, with her hands clasped between her legs. No one says, "I have to tell you something," unless it's something you don't want to hear. "I had sex with someone else."

The depth of my unhappiness shook me. I'd suspected this for a while but never thought it would happen. I told myself these fears were only insecurities. Insecurities that Simone washed away with every kiss, every laugh, and every night she came home to me. The touch on my shoulder and the stupid song we couldn't stop singing— all the happiness we shared in the hours that were over now. The happiness. Gone.

"Who was it! That phony English McMuffin motherfucker, Drake? I knew it. I knew this was going to happen."

"Drake Evans? The guy in my third-wave feminism class? Julian, he's gay."

I shot up from my seat. "No, he isn't. He's lying. I know all about guys like Drake. Everything's a big show for the score."

She stood up. "You'd better tell Drake's boyfriend, who was French-kissing him outside class. No, I had sex with James."

"What do you mean, James? James, who died? Is that who you mean?"

"Yes."

I slumped down, unhappiness hanging from my face. It made me even sadder to picture myself looking so glum.

Simone spoke. "It happened the week before James left. He was feeling really bad about his addiction, his family, and the way his whole life was going. I don't think he talked to you about some of those things. I knew there was some attraction, but I never expected anything like this since I always felt like we were family. I wanted to comfort him. I ran my fingers through his hair and—"

"Well, we aren't family, and I guess he wasn't my friend either. It looks like I can't trust anybody."

"He was your friend. What we did ... I don't know how to explain it ... We were both hurting. I thought it'd be a moment of tenderness—something that'd help us through it. It became more than that, but it wasn't like this big romance we planned to keep secret from you."

"Was it just that one time?"

"Well, it was that one day, but two times."

"What! Why did you do it twice?" I was turning to rubber again. Tai Chi wasn't made for this. Where is my big stack of money! I'm nothing without it. I need it—all of it!

"That's not the point! For months now, whenever we rented a movie or were about to go for a walk, you'd say, 'Hey, sorry, can we do this another time? I gotta check on some things. Shouldn't be long.' Then you'd run over to your computer and spend all night looking at those charts. How do you think that made me feel, sitting alone in the dark? Once or twice, okay. But it started happening— all the time. How long did you expect me to wait for you to wake up!"

What could I say? She was right, but she wasn't finished. "And you're always coming home late. We hardly have sex or talk for more than five minutes. I didn't want this to happen, but here we are. I'm not attracted to you anymore. I love you, but—"

"Not attracted to me? I've been doing this stock market shit for us—so we can be free from everyone who'll treat us like trash if we don't have enough money. But I ended up staring at a screen all night, watching it get shredded instead. I tried so hard to get it back. I wanted to spend more time with you, but I've been drowning, drowning, drowning. You don't know the price I paid; how hard it is some nights. I can't breathe. I wake up with my mind filled with numbers, patterns, and all these horrible, unsolvable equations. Sometimes, I can't even close my eyes. That's why it's been this way."

"But who else will help us? Your dad? My mom? Your Women's Studies degree? All that save-the-world bullshit you talk about? You know most of those people don't want your help. Your friends need injustice to have an identity. If inequality, racism, or whatever grievance they're outraged about didn't exist, they wouldn't be able to run around feeling superior to everyone happy with their lives.

"'You do not have to fully humanize your black characters by dehumanizing the white ones.' Do you know who said that? James Baldwin and it applies to everyone. You create more problems than you solve when you elevate a group of people by putting another one down. Who wins when everyone is angry and divided? You say I have to take a side? No, I refuse to wear my opinion like a brand name. There are no easy answers. How about some humility? Where's the common ground? So you want to save the world? Well, what about our relationship? Why would you leave after I've done so much to make you want to stay?"

We caught our breath. I looked out the window of our unhappy home. The screen door was broken again.

"You're right about some of my friends; maybe me too, okay? Sometimes we're only heroes in our minds. But seriously, do you think I believe if a skinny White girl like me marches into a Black neighborhood with voter registration forms, everyone will rush out of their houses singing, Hallelujah, we're saved, Simone is here!

"Like Thoreau said, sometimes people lend themselves to the wrong they condemn. Some causes are corrupted or become cults, but that doesn't mean I should stop fighting for what I know is right, even if some people fighting alongside me are idiots, doing it for all the wrong reasons."

Simone surprised me. I thought her activism was misguided, but who was I to judge? I'd been fighting for our future, but what if we didn't have one? She had a purpose. Without her, what was mine? My anger over what happened with her and James shifted from the center of my attention. In the early days of dating Simone, I'd kissed a girl I knew from high school behind a bar. She probably had too much to drink and forgot about me within the hour. It was stupid, and I regretted it, but that wasn't me anymore. I had to think ahead. I didn't want to be alone. I hardly had any friends. And with my hair falling out, I'd never find another girl. They don't dream of guys like me. She needs to stay. I'm all out of chances. I don't care; hurt me again. Please don't go.

"I didn't know you were going through all that mental stuff with your stock market. You made it sound like it was helping you break free from the people who'd used their big money to put you down. Didn't you say you were only competing against yourself? Can't you see the only way to win is to be happy with who you are? Anyone who treats you like trash is trash. Let the karmic scales deal with them. You know I was never with you for money, and it's not about your stupid hair before you get all hung up on that. I love you for your selflessness and your wild ideas. It's never been about anything else. Think about it. If you can't let go of whatever you're doing with those stock charts for a few minutes and sit down to dinner with me, I don't know. That's crazy! I might not make much money with a women's studies degree or save the world, but I'll always have time for the people I love."

"I keep thinking about you having sex with James. I see you together, close like we're supposed to be ... I hate you both, but I don't want to; I know that won't help anything."

"I was wrong to do that. But blame me, not James. He was in a terrible place, physically and mentally. I thought I knew how to help him, but I didn't. Who knows, maybe I made him feel worse."

"No, you always had his back, even at his lowest points. No matter what I think about the shit you just told me, I'll always admire you for that, but does this mean we're breaking up? Why should we? I still love you."

"Julian, I love you too, and I'm sorry to be cold, but sometimes love isn't enough. We have to make a choice right now. We can say nasty things we don't mean or accept that our relationship is over and hold on to what we still have."

"I understand if you're attracted to other people. I've felt the same, but what are we going to do—have sex with everyone who looks good? You can't do that if you want to build something. Love requires sacrifice. I don't want to be with other girls. I still want to be with you. Why are you acting like it's already over? Don't you even want to try?"

"Julian, I'm sorry. I can't. I know it's hard, but we have to move on."

I reflected on my encounter with Eva—that rush—I had to admit it had faded with Simone. I didn't want it to matter, but it did. My relationship with Simone had been over for a while now.

That night, we slept in separate beds. Around two in the morning, she climbed into mine, and we embraced. But the more tightly I held her, the further away she felt because it was the last time. Tomorrow will come, and the days will blend together. I'll wish I'd found the words to make her stay, even though there were none left to say. Then everything will stop as I crumble in the rain and hail, wearing down the stone man. I'll scatter in that lonely field as I return to dust. You'll see me in the sunbeams, drifting over foothills full of wildflowers, luring the bees, where boys play, and old men fade away.

Chapter 30

I wanted to get back into stocks. The way I saw it, cycling through my gains and losses amid the market fluctuations was simply the cost of learning to trade. Simone had moved in with her sister. With what I'd learned and no distractions, I was ready to trade like a pro. No random bets or putting everything into a single stock this time. Rules, patience, and diversification. Now I knew what to do. I was on the verge of getting back in the game after the Nasdaq plunged another 10 percent. It's such a steal now. I can't believe so many stocks selling for hundreds of dollars are less than half of that now. Everything's on sale! I'll make another million, two million—maybe more!

The feeling faded as sadness over my sudden loss of James and Simone turned into full-fledged depression while I rehashed the immutable past. You invested all that money and time in the stock market and still lost what you wanted most. Great work, Julian. Simone shouldn't have slept with James, but what did you expect? You had your head so far up your ass—even when you were together, she was alone—and she was right. You could have done more to help James. Blowing up over a hundred bucks was stupid. You pushed him away. But it wasn't the money; it was the desperation, the addiction. That's what I hated. I shouldn't have given him such a hard time. You could've tried to get him to do less. No, it doesn't work like that, and what if he died shooting up in the house? How can you think like that? Why are you so selfish? But it's true. He should have gone to a clinic. How many times did I tell him? How many times! Those counselors went to school for this. They knew how to help him—not me. It's not my fault!

Beyond my isolation, the depths of madness the market had taken me wore on my mind. My desire to speculate on stocks dwindled when I considered the mental instability I'd experienced. Who was that guy infatuated with the stock market? I was sick of tickers, breaking news, and intraday charts. Four million on margin.

All-in on a single stock. How could I have been so insane? Go outside, sit on any corner, and no one will give you a dime. But even when I blew through hundreds of thousands of dollars a day, I didn't appreciate that losing money is always easier than making it. My luck had already run out by the time I realized luck was the sole reason I was winning. Who was responsible? The mainstream media? Alex? My parents? No, pointing fingers at anyone else is the same as the lights and sounds of the pachinko. If you turn off the bells and whistles, there are only the thuds and thumps of the simple machine. Pull the lever and release. That's me, falling unceremoniously toward my inevitable end.

I had no answers, so I let the crazy show fall to the floor. But now what? Back on the treadmill? Productivity stats? Counting, clicking, and faces blurring by. Is this my life? Is this it? Trivial things began to sadden me. One morning, I missed a loop when I fastened my belt. It was empty—a wasteland. I almost couldn't make it to the lab.

Albert invited me to hang out with him and Lisa, but I'd look at my thinning hair and all those dollars down the drain, and it was clear I belonged at the bottom of Alex's company chart. No, Lisa wasn't interested in what I said, nor were her friends. Anything I said would be infelicitous. Better not to say anything at all. Things with Alex went swimmingly. My newfound docility pleased him. When he asked me to do something, I did it right away. He called me buddy and praised my performance stats every week.

I avoided my mom like I avoided everyone else. *"Julian, are you okay? You hardly said anything at dinner. Maybe you should talk to a therapist. I know a good one. He's very understanding. It feels like you're talking to a friend."* That's the sort of thing she'd say. Plus, she had a new boyfriend named Dale. He'd retired from a federal job with a full pension and was always happy, which made me want to punch him in the face. He'd say, *"Good things happen to good people,"* and other platitudes unworthy of repeating. The last time I saw them, we all went to 7-Eleven, which I used to enjoy. But as we walked down candy aisles and around coffee machines, Dale whistled along with the two tones of the door chime, oblivious to how stupid he sounded. "Bing-bong, bing-bong." Dale was too high on life to realize what a fool he was.

Sitting with my mom before I left cheered me up a little. The old bird was still all right.

"So, are you feeling any better about Simone? Are you dating anyone else?"

"No, Mom, I'm not dating anyone, okay? You'll be the first to know. Simone and I are doing okay as friends. She got an internship at the urban development office in Washington, DC. It's funny; that doesn't have much to do with her degree, but she likes it."

"How's she going to save the world doing that?" my mom said. She was trying to cheer me up, but it annoyed me.

"Why do you believe, 'We can't save the world?' Do you think it's not worth saving or that we shouldn't help anyone?"

Dale was in the other room watching a football game. He had the decency not to drink around my mother but acted like a drunk anyway. "Let's see some offense. Run the ball!"

I considered offering him a refreshing bottle of mouthwash.

"Most people talking about saving the world are in it for the attention and excitement of being part of what's happening. That's what we called performance art in the sixties—a happening—and that's what saving the world is. A big show," my mom said. "They carry signs protesting whatever the latest headlines tell them to be upset about. It could be landmines blowing off children's legs or misleading labels on a pack of tofu. It's horrific. It's irrelevant. It's whatever outrage they've sanctioned to sell advertisements and get politicians more votes."

"I bet one day there'll be a website where people post pictures of themselves protesting. They'll measure their success by how many people click on the photo," I suggested, thinking Alex would be into that.

"That sounds ridiculous, but ever since this dotcom thing started, I've seen a lot of things I'd never believe, but counting how many times someone clicks on a picture seems boring. They'd need something else that shows how many people liked the picture. How about a thumbs-up?"

We laughed at the idea. People counting how many thumbs-ups they got? Who would want to do that?

"But back to your question: Should we help other people? Yes, and that starts with helping someone help themselves.

"Look, I'm no saint, and I'm not saying there aren't causes worth supporting. But do you know how many people I've helped in AA? As many as necessary. No one else seems to care that their family won't talk to them, they lost their job, and they hate themselves for being a drunk, but I get them away from that bottle. Sometimes, all it takes is letting them know they're not alone. These people need my help, not global catastrophes that I didn't start and have no idea how to resolve. The ones trying to save the world force us to shut down our lives so they can shout about something that won't be solved by blocking the road. They demand we sacrifice our freedom to fight fascism and fail to see their hypocrisy when they insist they're saving the world.

"We can't win every war. Who you choose to fight for determines who gets left behind. No one made them the ambassadors of benevolence. I'll fight my own fights, thank you. Because they don't care about the unglamorous problems people have. They don't have the guts. They've got no interest in the real dirt, where there's no one shouting, no crowds or cameras around. Just you, fighting for someone that the world has left behind."

I admired how much she'd changed but didn't say anything. I didn't want to hear her say, *"Aw, thank you, Julian. That's so sweet."*

The City of Newark was repairing the road near my house. They made a ton of noise and left all the manholes open so no one could drive down the street. It pissed me off. A gray cloud hung over everything, even in the middle of the day. Gray was glued to my mind. I thought about the future website my mother and I joked about where you could count how many people gave your photo a thumbs-up. What would they call it? How about MyFace.com?

I was being too cynical. Even with my dim view of humanity, I doubted such a website would ever exist. It was weird that I never thought about traveling to the future. No, the future had nothing for me, and neither did the present. You could've given me a million dollars, and I would've dumped it in one of the open manholes on my street. But make no mistake: I would've preferred to have a million dollars and experience ennui as a rich man rather than a penniless one. I still wanted revenge and protection. But I was too depressed to do anything about it. Just as I was wrestling with the paradox of not caring about money while knowing I'd be better off having plenty of it, I thought I should go back in time by jumping into one of the open manholes. Why not? Nothing else makes sense. I'd recently caught myself saying aloud, "I can't live like this." I said it then and had been saying it throughout the day. I stood in front of a manhole and considered jumping. Hello, is anybody down there? They left those covers off for you. It's a sign. The one you've been waiting for.

Jump. You can leave this body and all of its incontrovertible pain behind. One little leap will erase the past and transport you back to the beginning. It'll be even sweeter the second time around. No, that's crazy; I laughed. Or is it? You're only saying it's crazy because you think that's what people should say. You've lost more than you'll ever gain. Restarting the clock is the only way to be whole again. Is this really happening? Am I alive—or a zombie with delusions filling my head? Who am I? I walked away, mumbling, "The mental state, the mental state," unsure if I was the one speaking, and went home.

That night, I couldn't sleep at all. My legs kicked, and I spun in bed. It was impossible to lie still. The impulses kicking my legs and twisting my torso swam to my mind, reconceptualizing every horror I harbored in the gossamer etchings of my psyche. My dreams, memories, and reality blurred as the night wore on.

Burn your hand. It's a game; you'll like it. Try not to pull away. There's a lighter in the drawer downstairs. Go get it. Flick the flame. Do it for five seconds. That's nothing. Come on! Fear is fun. Don't be a baby. You don't have to burn your palm. Burn your fingers instead.

No, I'm not doing that. Why would I hurt myself?

No problem. Just a game. Just a game, Julian. Forget about the fire. Stick a knife up your nose instead. Use a skinny blade. It only

357

hurts at first. Once it's past the bone, it slides. It'll feel good. Pain and pleasure are the same. Stop crying. I thought you were a big boy. Push it all the way into your brain.

Pacing around, I quieted the wicked voices, then went downstairs.

I did Tai Chi in the basement. It relaxed me, but I was still agitated. The servers were gone, but I liked being surrounded by the wood paneling. All that wood on the walls, ceiling, and floor. Wait. What's happening? Something's wrong … My skin feels so hot. I'm pinned inside myself, inside myself, inside myself. The room is shrinking. It's a wooden box, a coffin. I'm being buried alive. I need air! Where's the window? My ears are ringing. It's Loud, it's too loud! I've got to get out of here. This can't be real. I can't do this. Not even for five more seconds! I gritted my teeth with my head in my hands.

Calm down. You're in control. Don't let those demons fool you. Turn their shadows around. One day, you'll talk about all of this anxiety. What a freakshow that was, huh? Thousands of people will come to hear you speak. They'll love you. It took courage to say that. What an inspiration, they'll say.

I sat on the floor, unable to sit still, but had begun feeling better. It's okay. It's over. You're in the same room you've been in a thousand times. But as soon as I shut down one nonsensical stream of consciousness, another replaced it.

No, no, no. You're boring; no personality. You're annoying. No one wants to listen to you. You'll be broke soon. You're bleeding money. You can't stop time. Spend, spend, spend. The hours will spin like seconds. Without the stock market, we'll bleed you dry; with the stock market, we'll bleed you dry. If you leave your job, you'll never get another. You're running out of money. Get back to work! Sweep the floor. You missed a spot. Over there—the ashes of yourself in the corner.

I rubbed my eyes and saw spots bleeding into different shapes and patterns like I'd seen on shrooms. I must've reactivated them, and now I'll be stuck seeing like this. How am I going to survive? Don't do this to me. Please, haven't I suffered enough? I tried to

358

stand, but none of my nerves were working. Something is really, really wrong. The ceiling is on the floor. I'm going to fall through the wall. The ringing's too loud. Why is this happening to me? Turn it off! The crush is coming. It's coming for me. I'm going insane. Insane, insane. I gotta get out of here. Enough!

I know what's happening. I know who you are, and you will not go unpunished. I can be an animal. I can let go of my limits. I have no limits! Why are you grinning? Do you still think it's funny? Will you think it's funny when I tear the flesh off your face? I tore a sheet of plywood off the wall. … limb by limb. Chop, chop, and your body is broken. You don't get to pin me down and take whatever you want without me coming back at you a hundred times harder! I'll chew your fingers off and bite through every bone. Go on. Scream! Scream like you're being raped by the devil in the same room where you learned to do somersaults on the carpet a week ago.

Scream as long as you want, loud as you can, but it won't change a thing because you'll never be the same. Not after this is taken, this essential part of you, sacred part of you. The innocence that made it easy for the little boy to laugh. Something inside him isn't clean anymore. The dirty little boy. Dirty on the plane, dirty when he gets home; don't let anybody know. Why would you do that to a child? No, don't tell me. Don't say a word. I've locked the door; now listen. I will teach you. I will show you, you will see, and you will feel it when I rearrange what remains of you with a serrated blade. Please understand that your screams are intoxicating, oh, so very satisfying as I rip out your eyes like you ripped out the lie that I'd ever be anything but totally fucked up.

After I put my boot through the back of your head, I'll rejoice while you gurgle on the blood bubbling from the hole where a person used to be. Ha-ha, you won't be grinning anymore! I reached out. I held my hands up. Hold me, hold me, lift me from the water. Let me in, and let me be weary. Nothing lost, nothing gained; pull me up. Help me up; get me on my feet again. I touched one of the cinderblocks I'd exposed and left a bloody print. Specks of light. Light through the window. The light. Calm down. You're in control.

I did a field of vision test. It's okay. Your vision is the same. It feels good to breathe. Breathe. I'm so glad that's over.

I went back upstairs to bed.

"Hominy Hubbity." "Hominy Hubbity."

Who's saying that? What does it mean?

"Hominy Hubbity. Hominy Hubbity," a voice said teasingly.

I know what that is. The words I used in the hospital when I tried to pronounce homonymous hemianopia. Did I really get shot in the head? Why? It should've happened to one of those tall, handsome guys with great hair. They have such easy lives.

You're lying in bed. The creek is outside the window. Focus on the sound. Relax your body and your mind will follow. I wish James and Simone were still around. What about Eva? Did she want to talk to me? I don't need much. A quick conversation, or five minutes with the woman I had sex with at the beach. I should've gotten to know her better. No, she was annoying. I laughed. You're too far gone for them anyway. Alone, always alone. I slept for two hours.

I started having more panic attacks, filled with nightmares I carried into the waking world until I collapsed into a stunted sleep. My anguish had been mutating into madness for a long time. Losing all that money must've made my mind revolt against me. All the times I thought I'd been revived, I was dying. All the times I kept the pain inside, the pressure built until all the pieces of my tortured life shot through me like a bullet in the brain.

Once I quit trading, I thought everything would return to how it was before I endured the pain of unwinding my spectacular gains. But now I knew the pain had made me descend through an ocean of unhappiness to the burial ground of bad memories I thought I'd laid to rest. I doubted any amount of psychotherapy, medication, or Tai Chi would help. It was all too tangled and deeply rooted for me to free myself. I needed something big to reboot my brain. One day, looking in the mirror at my zigzagging hairline and the bald spots behind it, I decided it was finally time to shave it off. A symbolic cleanse, as Simone had suggested. What about my scar? Even a glance at it had my classmates reeling in malevolent delight, but those were schoolyard taunts they only pulled off because my hair made the scar stick out.

Remove the hair, and the scar will blend in—plus, you can't make it look any worse. I ran an electric shaver over my head, jumped into the shower, and smiled at the dramatic improvement in my steamy reflection. You can't have a receding hairline with no hair. You hardly look bald anymore. Let's go out and put it to the test. You better go right now before you lose your nerve. Let the mental cleansing begin.

The first few times I passed someone on my way into town, I reflexively covered my scar. I became less self-conscious as I got used to the summer rays shining on my head. I liked what I saw in parked car windows—the close crop made me look youthful, one might even say—handsome! I should've done this years ago. On Main Street, where more people were about, I might've seen a few people staring at me, but like Simone said, if I didn't care about a couple minor imperfections, neither would they.

I went to Scott's Ice Cream for a celebratory scoop of chocolate and sat on a bench out front, enjoying myself. I ran my fingers across the remaining stubble on my scalp. Finally free. No more hats or clever angulations of hair trying to conceal what isn't there. Mid-lick, I saw a reflection in a parked car. Not mine. Inside Scott's, a girl with a cup of strawberry ice cream whose spoon had fallen to the floor pointed at me, sobbing because of the monster she'd seen. Her father scooped her up and hurried outside, shielding her eyes. He glared at me. How dare you! I just about died with the cone in my hand.

The scar on my head begins above my right ear, runs along the side, and down the back of my head. I was so fixated on my receding hairline that I forgot to check how the back of my head looked before leaving my house. I chucked my ice cream cone and hurried home without further incident until I reached the edge of campus, where a Jeep full of frat boys had stopped at a red light.

One of them leaned out of the open frame and said, "Hey, Frankenstein, when did they let you out of Transylvania?"

Students seated on the grass closed their books and searched for the subject of his inquiry. "Whereabouts may I spy this freakish delight?" someone asked. "Wasn't Frankenstein the doctor, not the monster? What's all this ballyhoo about?" another questioned.

Across the street, way up high, a pair of gargoyles shrieked from their perch atop the stone church steeple. A cauldron of bats burst through the stained-glass window in the center of its wall, soaring above me. Two broke away and descended, circling close—a mother and her child. The pup flapped its little wings, trembling.

"What's wrong with its head, Mama? It's so ugly. I'm scared."

"Careful, Jeremy. *Es ist der Jude!* And this one is even more deformed than most—it's missing part of its brain, and with that enormous nose, I'm surprised it hasn't suffocated from the stench of its own filth. Don't get too close; they often carry diseases."

"Shouldn't it be in a cage? I think it wants to bite me."

"It was much safer when these Ashkenazi goblins were forced to wear yellow armbands as punishment for poisoning the masses with deadly vaccines and pushing genetically modified crops as part of a Russian psyop. That made it easier to avoid them." In a flurry of panicked flaps, they rejoined their brethren above.

The gargoyles burst from their stone prisons and the remnants fell like meteorites. Large pieces cracked the sidewalk, one shattering a car's sunroof. They shook off the remaining rubble, revealing gray skin, porcine nostrils, and wide-pointed ears. "Liberation!" The larger one rejoiced, spreading its massive wings. It faced me from afar. "Look at it! The scar is a minor offense. Disgusting! Even from up here, I see it rotting inside."

"Yes, but it can take our place. Observe. The segmented abdomen of a roach is less repulsive than that thing. It's positively apotropaic," his smaller companion noted as he grinned, baring sharp incisors. Finally, free from the witch's curse, the bats and beasts departed, unappreciative of their vile liberator. At last, their prophesied replacement had arrived.

The light changed, and I ran after my frat boy foes, intending to leap on the Jeep and drag one of them off with me. Even if we both died, it would be worth it.

"Look at him go. That ain't Frankenstein. It's Quasimodo!" A second frat boy rejoiced. He was so elated by the cohort of deformed Gothic creatures he could associate me with that he swung on the frame, shouting, "Woo-hoo! Woo-hoo!" As they peeled around the corner, I was disappointed when he slid back into his seat. I hoped he'd be thrown from the vehicle and run over several times.

A girl on a Vespa swerved around me as I darted across the street to grab a crumpled newspaper tumbling along the curb. I pressed the pages against my head and tried to stop the bleeding.

At home, I took a small mirror Simone left behind into the bathroom. A ghastly sight was seen when I positioned it behind me. My thinning hair had concealed the puffy, pink, scary-looking scar much more than I realized.

The remaining problem was going to work. Alex didn't let us wear hats, and he wasn't one to make compassionate exceptions. I was so upset I thought about quitting, but it was never a serious consideration. There was a chance I'd trade stocks again, and the emerging theme of my mental illness eventually rendering me unemployable made me want to spend as little of my savings as possible. As long as I kept my meager paychecks coming in, I could hold on to what I still had, which helped me stay sane, so there would be no quitting over this.

I'd seen some eyeshadow beside the mirror Simone left behind. I clumsily disguised my scar with it. You could tell something wasn't right, but it looked more like a crooked brown line on the back of my head than the work of Dr. Frankenstein, which was good enough to show up for work.

"Now that you told me, I can tell it's a scar, but if you hadn't said anything, I'd think you got a bad haircut and were using makeup to even it out," Albert consoled me after I showed him my occipital artistry.

"Thanks, that's what I thought too, but Bert, people on Main Street were having a jolly old time busting on me before I had a chance to cover it up, and a little girl started crying when she saw my scar."

"What! Are you for real? Did she really start crying?"

"She did, and her dad wasn't happy either. It's infuriating when people get riled up over things like that."

"Ah, don't let them get you down, Julian. It's not that bad. Some people have no hands. Imagine how they feel."

"I get what you're saying, but that doesn't help. I saw kids who had it way worse than me in the hospital. I know I have a lot to be thankful for, but I never feel better because someone else has it worse. That only makes me more depressed."

"Well, there's a cheery lad. I'm going to run that security patch on the PCs. I'll catch up with you later."

Alex immediately wanted an explanation. "What's going on back there? Is that lipstick on your head?"

"No, it's something else that I used to cover the scar on my head. I cut my hair too short. Trust me. It looks better this way."

He sat flustered, probably wishing a policy existed for reprimanding me. "All right, fine, but go to a barber next time. You need to look more professional. Julian, you need to grow up, okay? This is silly stuff. How many times do I have to tell you? Nice clothes and being well groomed. It costs a little more, but it pays big dividends."

By the following week, my hair had grown enough to require less concealment. But plenty of the scar remained exposed, so I continued using the eyeshadow to cover it.

It started raining during my lunch break, so I cut it short and returned to the lab. The first thing I had to do was clear a paper jam in the color printer. The task was so complex a nuclear physicist would struggle with it. I freed the crumpled paper by practically standing on my head and partially disassembling the printer. I accidentally struck someone with my left arm when I stood up. In the past, my first instinct would've been to apologize. That was typically easier than explaining why I couldn't see them. Instead, I remained silent and turned to see who I'd collided with.

A woman cradled the breast I'd apparently elbowed, as if it were a small child I'd slapped, compiling a list of all the reasons I disgusted her. I'd overheard her drama-filled conversations about hot guys, celebrities, who she was dating, and who she broke up with was dating. She glared, expecting me to grovel, but instead, I said, "I didn't see you there. The printer's working if you'd like to use it."

I ignored her scowl and returned to my desk. When I looked up, she was still in the same spot, waiting for an apology, which wasn't coming. A brief stare-down ensued, and she walked away. Fuck her. She can't imagine what it's like to be forced to repeatedly explain yourself to dimwitted idiots furious over something as simple as standing up. I'm done with that. She should apologize to me. When I got home, I noticed the eyeshadow had run down my neck in thick streaks like bulging black veins due to the rain. So that's what was behind her long leer. She was upset that Quasimodo, with bulging veins in his neck, had elbowed her. At least she had something new to gossip about.

***

"Julian, I need to see you in my office," Alex messaged me the next day using the chat plug-in included in the latest release of our employee tracking software. Despite all of my troubles, I continued working diligently. He probably wants to talk to me about a promotion or that EBD thing he's working on. I strongly preferred the former but wasn't about to refuse extra cash. Either way, things were turning around for old International. I had a big grin when I opened his door. However, a woman in her fifties with short white hair and a dour face beside him made it clear no accolades or equity stakes were coming. I said goodbye to Mr. Happy Face and took a seat.

The woman spoke. "Julian, I'm Gwen, head of Human Resources for University Computing Services. I'm here because you've been accused of sexual harassment. I need to record your explanation of the incident before it's reviewed by the board."

"I was accused? Me? Julian Lawrence?" I asked, confused, pointing at myself. Whatever happened, the way she presented it was formulaic as if the resolution to being a pervert was the same as baking a cake.

"Yes, Julian. Last night, Alicia Wilson informed us you struck her breast. After that, you were, in her words, 'studying her.' I hope you realize looking at someone suggestively is also considered sexual harassment at the university."

I nodded, wanting to quickly clear my name with the obvious explanation of my visual impairment.

"She was very upset, Julian, and it's my responsibility to ensure the university provides an environment free of threats and hostility."

"I didn't strike her anywhere. I was fixing the printer and accidentally bumped into Alicia when I turned because I don't have a left field of vision. I didn't even know she was there."

"Okay, but why were you staring at her? Did you at least apologize for hitting her?"

"That's not what happened. I can't help it. My brain is damaged in the back, here in the visual cortex." I turned to Alex as I pointed, which only muddled what I was trying to tell Gwen. "Alex, you know what I'm talking about. Did you tell her? It's obvious what happened. My vision. It was a misunderstanding."

Alex shook his head. "Julian, I can't comment. I'm not permitted to disclose your medical history."

I turned back to Gwen. "Can't you look at my medical record? Then you'll see what I'm talking about."

"Julian, I'm here to gather information, not assign blame or punishment. As Alex said, we can't view your medical records unless the board decides to launch an official investigation."

I wasn't sure if being called Quasimodo or prosecuted for an inadvertent elbow jab was worse. What about my pain? What would Gwen have to say about Gil? What he'd done to me was a hundred times worse than this trumped-up charge for something I didn't intend and couldn't prevent. I was being shot again, like I'd told Ann in our Psych Group when Jonathan's mother threatened me. But when I got shot, I had a cool roommate, a gym to work out in, and a medical team taking care of me. Now, they wanted me to surrender my last shred of dignity. It made me want to smash their heads together like a pair of empty coconuts ...

... I wanted them to know what it's like when the windows inside you shatter, and then the mirror shows a foreigner, not who you used to be ...

"This is bullshit! I didn't do anything to anyone. Look at my employee record. Everything I'm telling you is in there. You shouldn't be attacking me. I'm the victim here."

"Julian! Please comport yourself. You haven't been charged with anything yet. The board will review your testimony, then determine if filing an official complaint is necessary."

"Why would you file a complaint? I didn't see her. I barely tapped her with my elbow. Why would I sexually assault someone with my elbow? It doesn't make sense."

"Julian, Alicia came into my office crying. She said you struck her forcefully. It doesn't matter if you use your hand or elbow. Let's move on and record your response to her leering accusation."

"First of all, it was her leering at me, but whenever I look at someone, I have to look at them like this." I demonstrated my oblique line of sight. "Because I can't see a person's entire face unless I look at them from an angle. She might have mistaken that for something it's not. Like I told you, I don't have a left field of view due to an injury I had a long time ago. Another thing is I used some makeup to cover a scar I've got on the back of my head. See?" I said, showing Gwen my poorly camouflaged scar, though the same defense hadn't helped with the guy in the park. "A little later, I realized the stuff I put on my head was running down my neck because it got messed up in the rain. Alicia might've thought I looked weird, so maybe that upset her too. I don't know."

"Alicia didn't say anything about your appearance. Julian, I've explained that I can't include information about any disabilities you may have today. Healthcare accountability laws prohibit us from receiving privileged medical information outside the proper channels. Please continue without sharing any such privileged information."

Alex sat at his desk with his back to us, opening and closing spreadsheets, pretending he was hard at work. But I knew he was following the whole fiasco.

"Okay, I'm going to try this one more time. I was fixing the printer. When I got up, I accidentally hit Alicia with my elbow. I went back to my desk. She hadn't moved from where we collided, and I glanced at her, wondering why. Later, I realized the makeup I'd applied to my head was dripping down my neck, which might've also upset her."

"Perfect!" Gwen chirped. She made some notes and concluded, "That's all we need for now. As the case proceeds, you may continue with your duties here, but I want you to stay at least ten feet away from Alicia until you hear from me again. We take this very seriously, so please be mindful of her personal space."

"I'd like to stay a thousand miles away from her, but what if I don't see her coming? She's the one who should stay away from me."

"Yes, I can see you're angry about this. I'll be sure to mention that to the board."

Gwen neatly filed a few documents and notes she'd taken in a folder and left. Before shutting the door, she turned and studied me, perhaps cycling through gothic characters to associate me with.

"Why didn't you tell her about my injury, Alex? All these flimsy rules never stopped Glenda." I demanded after Gwen left.

"Julian, I can't discuss that with anyone like she told you. But if I were you and got myself in a jam like this, I'd get a lawyer. That's what I'd do."

"Got myself in a jam? I didn't do anything."

"Lawyer," he repeated.

I returned to my desk but left work early, even though I knew our lovely surveillance applications were tracking every second of my life. I was worried I'd crack up when I started repeating, "No, you're a slob! Grow up! You're a slob!"

That night, I called my mom and recounted the unjust elbow jab tribunal with Gwen.

"You should sue the university!" she suggested. The thought had crossed my mind, but extricating myself from Alicia's bogus accusation was more pressing. "Julian, be careful what you say to that woman; her job is to protect the university, not you. I doubt she's interested in your side of the story."

"The whole thing is ridiculous. Who gets off on elbowing someone?"

"I know, but that's not what you should focus on. Eventually, they'll have to consider your injury. Why don't you get a letter from Dr. Roshan?"

"Even if he writes me a letter, I need to hire a lawyer to send it to that lady, Gwen. She and Alex kept plugging their ears whenever I tried to explain anything related to my injury. You know those healthcare laws that are supposed to prevent discrimination against people with disabilities? They're backfiring on me." The irony of the inverse outcome when Glenda freed me from the clutches of the university cops did not escape me.

"What a mess."

"Yep."

"Don't overthink it. You did nothing wrong. Let me know if you need my help."

Talking to my mom cheered me up for about five minutes, and then I sank deeper into despair. The worst part was that I'd squandered so much money and had to fight these spurious allegations without a mountain of cash to make them disappear. I wanted to retry the case against Jonathan, the boy who shot me. Guilty! Guilty! I'd shout. They hadn't adequately appraised the damage or appreciated how hard it would be. I should've gotten so much more. I deserved a hundred million dollars.

I made an appointment to get a letter from Dr. Roshan. He was fully booked for the rest of the month, but his secretary said I could drop by for a brief visit next week. Whaddya gotta do to get an appointment around here—get shot in the head? I jested after I got off the phone. I need this like a hole in my head. I didn't laugh that time.

Working at the lab with these accusations hanging over me was agonizing. Albert aided me by looking after students and the remaining stock market wizards seated near Alicia. Despite another day of bad news on CNBC, I ignored the market's fits and everything else. Why should I care?

Chapter 31

Before my appointment with Dr. Roshan, I wrote my own letter. A suicide note. The only thing troubling me about checking out early was how it would affect my mother. After all those years of sobriety, I didn't want her tipping the bottle back again. But we live our lives alone, and I was the one waking up every night at 3:00 a.m., afraid I was going blind, even though it was too dark to see anything. The pain was supernatural—bigger and heavier than me, yet I carried it. I carried it.

I got my thoughts out and clicked save. However, I didn't print it. I was still debating whether to make it look like an accident—finishing what fate had already started in 1989. I planned to lie on the tracks so my old friend—a freight train—could send me on my way. I'd felt suicidal over hair loss, loneliness, and the loss of people I loved, but those were mere inconveniences compared to what I was going through now. As the plague doctor neared, I didn't care if the beak-faced bastard sterilized the blade as long as he cut out the pain from the skull-shaped cage bonded to my brain.

I was lost, adrift between anger and isolation. Furious that I'd blown so much money and was exiled into a world where the double-click assassins knew me by a few digits. If I wasn't grateful for my shot at making a dollar for every million they got, they'd gladly hire someone else to count, click, and categorize. Here, we gladly build castles for the aristocracy, content as long as our aspirations to rise above servitude are satiated by recycled hallucinations flashed upon our eyes, so we can vicariously live the lie we want through actors, models, dictators, and politicians on yachts with massive phallic bows and helipads—all sashaying like the Rockettes somewhere off the coast of Mallorca while sipping mangosteen and lime mojitos with mint leaves swirling in the glass. Everything was synthetic, designed to distract me as I sold myself to buy things I didn't need but was told I couldn't live without.

I heard people talking, but there was static between us. They took comfort in the shared drudgery of Mondays—busy, busy bees. Watching these apparatchiks buzzing in their hive of prefabricated pleasures made me want to stab myself and lie bleeding to shock them out of the comfort they took in their imprisonment, as long as no one broke out before the Daily Grind stole equal shares of their lives. Cheer up, Julian. Smile. No one likes a gloomy guy. Frowning man is bad. Happy, frowning, smiling, sad. Frowning man is bad. What a terrible attitude! If you'd smile, you wouldn't feel sad.

Too much had gone wrong to find humor in the pain of living anymore. Misery had trampled me, leaving a broken man, bitter about the nasty scar slapped across his skull and the agony it created, which I'd been a fool, believing I could escape.

All that remained was a warped simulacrum of myself, conjoined to my withering soul, disappointed it was taking so long to die. Why would anyone want to be around me? Well, James would, but he's dead. Anyone else would see my sorrow and run away before it contaminated their happy, structured lives. I didn't want to go to Dr. Roshan's office either. What will he think when he finds out why I need the letter? He'll think I'm pathetic like so many others do. It's time that I accept they're right. I wish he could've written a different letter addressing what everyone who's known me for long ends up asking: "What is going on in your head?" No one else was qualified.

**

Sleepless again. Is anything my comatose buddies told me true? No, God didn't talk to you; that was nothing but a trippy edition of Sunday school. No different than satellites masquerading as stars. They should've let me die. Everything they said is unfit for the world I know.

The following day, I put a small handwritten note in my pocket with the filename and location where I'd saved my suicide note. I titled it "DesperateComplication.doc," but I didn't specify what it was. That gave me a little wiggle room in case I changed my mind.

371

What a modern way to die! As the burden of living lifted, these absurdities brought me joy again.

I went to Jimmy's Diner and had a cup of coffee. It made little sense, but I declined when the waiter offered to refill it because I didn't want to wet myself after I died due to my diabetes insipidus. Everything was eerily beautiful. I mean everything, even the naked bulbs in the diner that made me see spots when I looked away. A man with white hair and a tweed vest walked by, puffing on a wooden pipe, smoke curled in the air. That's what awaits me. Heaped into the grave, I'll be transmogrified, returned to the elements. I saw the world clearly because I could end it all today, and there'd be no more aching through this life. No more hating everything, including myself.

Watching the man puff on his pipe made me want a cigar. I decided to get one and head to the graveyard around the corner from Klondike Kate's. If I had the nerve, I'd burn through it, then lie on the nearby train tracks. I doubted I could do it, but I'd done many things I thought I couldn't, so maybe I could.

It was temperate, undemanding weather outside. I walked between worlds in a dreamless state, indistinguishable from nonexistence. On a side street nearby, I went into a drugstore and waited in line to buy a ninety-nine-cent stogie they kept behind the checkout counter. I hadn't splurged on anything in a long time, and there was no reason to start now. It was the middle of the day, and a single register was open with a long line of people. It was stuffy in the store, and I was anxious to get out of there. Why don't they open another register instead of lounging in the back? I eased that out of my mind. Stay calm. This is the end of it all. Stay in this comfortable space. But I couldn't hold on to the feeling. Why is it taking so long? I've got an appointment with Death that I don't want to delay.

I loosened my collar and looked around impatiently. I considered leaving, but I'd clawed my way this far. If I was burning up among the pills, facial cleansers, and discounted toiletries, they deserved to wait and feel the burn, too. Not much longer now; be patient. It was Saturday. It pissed me off how everyone ended up shopping at the same time on weekends, like cattle culled for slaughter. Should I have chosen a weekday to die? But then I'd have to take off from work and listen to Alex whine about punctuality if I didn't kill myself at the appointed time. *"Coming in five minutes late may not seem like much, Julian, but it creates imbalances that leave our clients feeling unappreciated. Make sure you use the proper drop-down menu to note that it was an unscheduled suicide attempt."*

Should I quit my job and then kill myself? No, it won't be satisfying unless I can disrupt the stupid Business Center when I die. This is not how a suicidal person is supposed to think. You've got to let go of everything. I stood behind an obese woman in a motorized wheelchair who was next in line and visibly perspiring from whatever ventilation malfunction was tilting the thermostat to the right. A wire basket fastened to the front of her wheelchair was filled with junk food: potato chips, candy bars, and cheese-flavored crackers, lying beneath two glass cola bottles that hung precariously close to the edge. She'd already peeled open one of the bags, helping herself to a few chips as she puttered around the store. Why is she eating that crap? She wouldn't be so fat if she wasn't. Look at her. I wiped my forehead and glared at the flesh hanging from her sweaty arms. She can barely lift those flabby arms.

A tall, blond man in a cowboy hat behind me spoke in a loud, slow Southern drawl on his cell phone. "Now it ain't no big thang. Yes, Sally, I'll help Jake with the winch after I auction Bobby's Bronco, like I told ya. It's gonna be fine. They got them nice wheels kids like nowadays. Yep, yep, that's right. Loaded it onto the trailer first thing this mornin'."

Auction? Hello, have you heard of the Internet? Sell it online, dumbass. When's the last time this idiot left the farm? Who needs people like him?

Finally, the line inched forward, and the wheelchair fatty approached the cashier. It took the lady forever to use the little joystick on her wheelchair to get close enough to dump her crap on the counter.

"Can I help you, ma'am?" a stocking clerk solicited, trying to appease everyone grumbling in the growing line.

"No, I can take care of myself. Gimme a sec, okay?"

Oh! Now Fatty's getting pissed. What right does she have to be angry? What the hell is wrong with her? It's her fault she's in that wheelchair. Shoveling that garbage in her face. God, why do I keep seeing people with self-inflicted problems everywhere? Think your life is tough, Fatty? Try being shot in the head. I was on the verge of saying something to her. She needs to be more considerate. Can't she see we're waiting? The woman grabbed a cola bottle but couldn't reach the counter, tipping it over with her half-eaten bag of potato chips. The bottle broke, and soda poured out as potato chips floated atop the puddle like water lilies in a dark lagoon.

The woman sobbed, "I'm sorry. I'm so stupid, I can't do anything right. Oh! Oh no, I dropped a buncha chips, too." Her gaze remained fixed on the ground. The clerk ran off to get a mop. The woman's eyes were hound dog red.

"Can we get a little help here? People are waiting. Is someone going to open another register?" a woman with a slim figure wearing a tight red jogging suit behind the cowboy complained, her pleading face glistening with beads of perspiration. She was right. They needed to move the wheelchair out of the way and keep things moving. I was glad someone had finally spoken up.

The cowboy stepped out of line and strode toward the woman. No one could deny that his swagger was genuine in his boots and jeans with a big buckle on the belt. "Ma'am, why do I see tears in them beautiful brown eyes? Go on and dry them eyes. I'm gonna take care of you. Tell me what you need. Another bottle of soda? Them chips look like they must've lost their crisp, too. Mmm, that ain't gonna taste right. How about another bag? You like that barbecue, huh? Okay, I bet they got some more."

He rested his hand on her wheelchair as he spoke, and she clasped her hands over his. "Oh, thank you; that is so sweet. You're such a sweet, sweet man. But it's my fault. I know I've made a fool of myself again. How about I move aside? I don't want to trouble everyone waiting behind me," she said in a warbly pitch. What he said wouldn't have much weight if it were me, but with his Southern diction, these words he did deliver.

"No, ma'am. Your mama didn't make no fool. Come on now, we all clumsy sometimes. Last night, I dropped a couple pots we was gonna use for a big family dinner in pig shit. Woo wee! I was piping mad. But me and my girls went straight to Taco Bell, and it worked out all right. Now you want another soda bottle and them chips we talked about?"

"That would be lovely. Thank you so much. You're an angel—just an angel," she said, looking up at him as we stood red-faced, silence settling over the line.

"Angel! Ho ho! My wife surely don't agree with that! Now, don't go nowhere. I'll be right back. Take it easy now, alright. You ain't got nothin' to worry about."

No one spoke as the man trotted away and returned with a soda bottle and chips. The city toppled over—a vast desert remained.

Cruelty empties out the good in us. I'm so ashamed. That's what I did, and that's what you'll do. It's faith. All you gotta do is believe. Kindness is created when we are one body. How do I raise my soul? I won't forget. Watch where you're going next time! I'll be kind. I promise. When the bond is broken. O God! Tears welled in my eyes, and my soul wept. I prided myself on nonconformity and know the pain of people putting you down. Yet, when I had the chance to step out of line and help someone feel a shred of dignity, I didn't heed the call. I forgot all about cigars and suicide and ran out of the store. "Please, don't leave me," I pleaded with the one who broke the world, then collapsed five feet from the front door, where I prayed to be free of all the pain that made the hardships I'd faced insurmountable. I had no doubt *this* was what I Required.

"Are you all right? Sir, are you okay?" The people gathered around me asked as I lay unsure how to answer. I dusted myself off and left them wondering, What possessed that boy? I might've said, "I am ashamed," but these words would not satisfy *him*, so I left them unspoken and continued toward the graveyard, where I sat upon a fallen tree beside the railroad tracks and tried to find the faith to carry on. I found no solace in the finite world when I Required the boundless glory of God in my hour of frailty.

The small cemetery was quiet. It was nice to hear the wind rustling hedges and branches instead of people wailing about waiting in line. I walked past the tombstones to get my Chi flowing, and it's possible to reach the same conclusions I have with many spiritual perspectives because all signs point to this. Strolling through the graveyard with all its gentle ghosts, I dissected the past, sifting through my memories to piece together the roots of my failing mental state. The truth eludes us when everyone sees the killer who fits their presumptions—*with a slim sword for a stick.*

I'll never know whether Alicia's allegations were motivated by fear or prejudice based on my appearance. Still, I couldn't understand why she'd be distraught over what I knew was an accident. I dismissed her side of the story until the day's events made me recognize that my selective perspective had blinded me despite knowing that dangers lurk when we neglect what lies beyond our field of view—and I should consider other perspectives, including hers. I reveled in the confidence my rising stocks created as cash-filled fantasies bolstered the man I wanted to be. But my dreams defaulted when I lost my winnings, and the fantasies I'd relished collapsed, too.

The trauma and insecurities I'd buried behind my winnings resurfaced as my account balance crumbled. My heart could not heal, filled with parasitic hate that thrived on the faults I found in others while I neglected the restorative power of kindness, as I'd witnessed in the cowboy's selfless act toward the woman in a wheelchair. I no longer resented the tribulations of people ridiculing me or that Alicia had misconstrued our collision. *"Pain purifies,"* James once told me, and his death made its meaning clear to me. We cannot have compassion without pain, nor can we have grace without mercy. I wasn't sure if my soul was worth saving until I saw the Lord blesses those who use their afflictions to help others with kindness and compassion.

This wisdom is hard won because love and hate are interlaced like a Möbius strip, defying easy explanation. How can we love one another if your joy requires my pain? If you reach out, but I walk away? If every form of love and hate were written on a single scroll, no one could read it all.

I've seen pictures of Charles Bukowski sitting half-naked on his sofa, blinds down, empty beer bottles and cans covering half the floor, with a one-eyed cat stretched out behind him, both with Cheshire smiles. His scarred face was fitting—battered but always defiant. He'd probably hate that line about him, which only makes me love him more. He knew how to compost the filth we leave behind, turning the detritus of human folly into something beautiful. His epitaph, *'Don't Try,'* reminds me of *Wu Wei*—effortless action—a concept from the *Tao*. Many have tried to explain what his epitaph means, even though their effort contradicts it. So, *don't try.*"

Bukowski found the color between the grey bricks. Sometimes, I see them; sometimes, I only see grey. He famously observed, *"We're all going to die, all of us, what a circus! That alone should make us love each other, but it doesn't. We are terrorized and flattened by trivialities, eaten up by nothing."* Life is often senseless and cruel. Yet, I will seize the opportunities God grants me to serve. We can counter life's harsh realities by recognizing that kindness overcomes them, fostering deeper connections through love and friendship, where new possibilities are born.

I remember when there was less righteous indignation and fewer people making a spectacle of things that offended them. I may have imagined those Golden Days, but they're attainable if we reject hateful mythologies based on what divides us and embrace what we share. These ruminations conveyed that the Mystery lies in the search, presence, and experience of love and beauty. The Mystery is unsolvable because life is the pleasure of solving it.

Chapter 32

Over a decade had passed since I last saw Dr. Roshan, but his office was in the same location. He had more awards for excellence and less hair on his head, as did I. I'd written a letter requesting changes to my workspace to accommodate my vision loss, which I asked him to sign. This served the dual purpose of my fabrication and the real reason I needed the letter.

As we talked, I looked around Dr. Roshan's office. Pictures of India, anatomical diagrams, framed neuroscience articles, and photos of him with former patients—including me—lined the walls. What a long time ago that was!

We shook hands. On my way out, I asked him one last lighthearted question.

"Dr. Roshan, people often wonder why I'm strange and ask what's happening in my head. I never know how to answer, but if anyone can explain, it's you. Can I give them your number next time they ask?"

"Sure, you can, but if they're doubting you after everything you've overcome and accomplished, they should call me and have their head examined. Though I'll charge them double for wasting my time," Dr. Roshan said.

We laughed. I was almost out the door when he called me back.

"Julian, would you kindly come over here for a moment? I want to look at your scar, the area along the back."

As he studied my scar, I explained, "I usually keep my hair longer to hide it, but I wanted to see how it looked with a crew cut. The scar stuck out more than I expected, but I've accepted that, and I'm eternally grateful you saved my life."

Dr. Roshan pinched the skin along my scar, prodding it in a few places. He clicked his tongue and commented, "This wasn't my cleanest cut, but we didn't have much time for perfection, did we? If you're interested, I know a hair restoration surgeon who could revise it and make it much smaller. He works in this building. Do you have another thirty minutes? We can stop by his office if he's free."

"What! Really? That would be incredible."

He called the other doctor, and we proceeded to his office.

The other surgeon, Dr. Tillman, examined my scar with a scope, wiggling it along the back, then said, "You have excellent laxity, perfect for a scar revision. I just had a cancellation for an appointment two weeks from now. It will be a brief outpatient procedure, but you'll need someone to drive you home. We can do it then if that works for you."

"Yes! By the way, how much will this cost?"

"It'll be pro bono, no charge. How about you give me a hundred bucks for the supplies, and we'll call it even?" Dr. Roshan shot him a disapproving look. Dr. Tillman chuckled and added, "Julian, this will be easy for me, so forget about the supplies. I'll do it free of charge."

"Wow! Thanks, Doc. And while we're at it, could you do something about my hairline? I mean, you're already going to be in the vicinity, right?

"Don't push your luck, Julian," Dr. Roshan said.

***

Dr. Roshan hadn't charged for the letter, but hiring a lawyer for a boilerplate response was unacceptable. Knowing full well that a hyphenated French name projected unassailable legal authority, I settled the matter by designating Jean-Baptiste Clamence, the loquacious judge-penitent from *The Fall*, as my attorney. I included the address and phone number of the Newark Police Department because if these attestations didn't satisfy "the board," they could send me to jail for all I cared. I researched how to craft such legal letters, found a sample online, and made the appropriate modifications, which took care of that. *"Well, I guess this Internet thing is pretty cool after all."* At the lab, I added legal-looking letterhead from the law firm of the Litigious Legalese Group, then added a silhouette of the Statue of Liberty. I printed two copies and placed them in separate envelopes. It was a damn good forgery. I should have majored in graphic design. I gave one to Alex, went to the HR office, and gave Gwen the other. I was nervous they'd bust me, but the worst they could do was fire me, and my days at the Business Center were numbered anyway.

***

Gwen emailed me two days later, requesting I call her. She thanked me for my patience and informed me the board had expedited my review. I was cleared of all charges. In her concluding remarks, she noted though I could freely move about, it was advisable to give Alicia some space. I suggested sharing my extenuating circumstances with Alicia so she'd understand why I hadn't seen her when we collided, but Gwen politely objected.

"Julian, I appreciate the suggestion, but it falls outside our conflict resolution guidelines. Once again, thank you for your patience and understanding throughout the process, which, I remind you, we've put in place to protect all relevant parties in a dispute."

Well, you can't say I didn't try.

Alicia was three rows to my right. She periodically shot angry glances at me, but I didn't care. I was tired of being angry. I was also tired of color printers, billion-dollar data points, and stock charts. When the day began, I thought I'd wait until I found a new job before calling it quits, but the thought of walking out became too strong to suppress. Now is the time. This is my chance. I printed a letter tendering my resignation and prepared to move on to the next phase of my life after giving it to Alex. I put a lot of thought into it.

I quit.

Sincerely,

J International.

I walked into Alex's office with the letter in hand as he fiddled with a merry-go-round of red quotes flashing in his trading application. On TV, an exuberant analyst chronicled up-to-the-minute news about the market's continued crash, with stock photos of stressed-out floor traders and plummeting red line graphs. The same analyst cheered the market's ascent with equal enthusiasm. I was intrigued that they made a living as a fair-weather friend of the demented instead of doing it in online forums for free. Duplicity! What a lucrative enterprise! It doubled their returns. I wanted to sneak a peek at Alex's latest balance but figured that wasn't what mentally stable people did, so I ignored the impulse.

Alex faced me and said, "Hey, buddy, I just heard the good news. You must be relieved! How about this market, huh? Can you believe the Nasdaq is down over sixty percent? This has got to be the buying opportunity of a lifetime. I don't know about you, but I'm doubling down."

Standing there, I reflected on how worthless he thought I was when he slammed me into his desk, and I'd become too weak to retaliate. It was no longer an act—I didn't care about his account balance or whether stocks were going up or down. I would've liked it if Alex were remorseful as I walked away, but he'd have a new buddy in a few weeks with whom he'd share his grand designs, so I accepted that he'd always be a jackass and didn't need an apology.

"Yeah, I don't know about that. I'm in cash. By the way, I'm quitting. I've explained everything in this letter."

Alex read the letter and threw it into the air melodramatically. He grimaced as his face flushed like an invisible sun had burned him.

"I quit? What, do you think this is a joke?"

"No joke. I was about to head out unless you have something to say." I risked him launching from his chair and swinging at me, but I wouldn't sit there and take it if he made a move. Chi seeks the level. I'd punch him in the neck, headbutt him with my titanium threaded skull, bite off a finger, take a few deep breaths, then pour some green tea, which I'd stir with the finger I'd bitten off. Mmm, it pairs well with the grassy notes of the tea. Do I detect a hint of lemon, too? Wonderful. I'd place my nose centimeters above the cup and take in its heady fragrance. The bloody finger would add a touch of bitterness—it's too bold for the average consumer, but there's a market for this. I'm sure of it. Chop, chop. There'd be no limp-limbed beatdowns today. Still, I hoped there was a better way.

"This is totally unprofessional, but what else should I expect from you, J International ..." He scoffed, which I found highly satisfying.

"You're right. I'm not cut out for this. I don't know what I'm going to do, but I won't spend another minute with you. I'm done listening to you whine whenever your billion-dollar proof-of-concept fantasy of whatever you think the lab is supposed to be doesn't work out. There's no reason for you to be such a dick. There doesn't always have to be an angle to get ahead as if life were a zero-sum game. Though it's true that not everyone gets to win, and it's your turn to lose. People don't need a database quantifying everything they do; they don't need a spider's web of statistics to know what's right. You could have been kind. That's what people need: respect. A simple hello. It's free, easy, and will get you where you want to be far more expeditiously than everything else you're doing. Go on and tidy up your slide presentation and click on those tickers. Still, you'll never have true wealth because you're too busy thinking about yourself."

Before shutting the door, I tossed the damp tea bag in his wastebasket and looked down at the red-faced gazelle. Its dark, unblinking eyes were fixed upon me as it lay motionless in the grass, not even trying to right itself with those little stick legs. It clung to life, but its soul had departed. I'd done it for sport. I wasn't planning to eat until I could snag some discounts after 7:00 p.m.

Chapter 33

My mother arrived shortly after Dr. Tillman had finished excising my scar. My head was throbbing, and the skin was tender where he'd fastened staples. Still, a scar revision is a hell of a lot easier than having brain surgery. My mom said hello to Dr. Roshan. We both thanked Dr. Tillman and got into her car—a new Honda Accord—a new beginning for both of us.

"Let's have a look," my mother requested. I tilted my head. Dr. Tillman held up a mirror when he was finished, but my head was too bloody to see it clearly. "Oh, Julian, it looks wonderful! It's barely visible, just a little line. It's such a big improvement!"

"I'm glad there's a little left to remind me I'm still in the club."

"What club?"

I laughed. "I'll tell you when I figure that out."

I stayed at my mom's house after the surgery. When we got home, I checked out Dr. Tillman's work. A warm rush came over me when I saw a thin white line beneath the staples. However, after the joy faded, I acknowledged that patching up my appearance hadn't fixed every problem. I'd evaded suicide, but I still yearned for another version of myself and wasn't satisfied with my life.

In retrospect, my time in the market was little more than drifting with the tide as the sky drenched us with dollars, only to take them back like droplets condensing on the other side of the glass. Outside the hours I spent raiding tombs and absconding with booby-trapped treasures, alongside the moneymen and my fair-weather friends, my life seemed the same. What difference does it make if I live or die? Aside from defying death and disfigurement, do I have the courage to do something more worthwhile?

After soldiering through a helping of microwaveable quiche and an unpalatable dish my mother had made with hints of unintended but likely harmless fermentation, we talked at the kitchen table with images of auto workers.

"Mom, when you were an alcoholic, did you ever think about time travel?"

"Well, Julian, I'm still an alcoholic and always will be. Because even after a decade, just one night out with drinking buddies at the bar. One drink—that's all it takes to fall back into the hole. I'm not saying you can't climb out again, but it's better not to fall in the first place. I'm sorry; what was the other thing you said?"

"Have you ever wished you could time travel? Sometimes, I want to go back to the eighties, right before I got shot."

"Yes, I've thought about that—going back and living my life again, sobering up the times I was ashamed of how drunk I was. But then I wondered how I'd clean up that mess without affecting the rest. What if I lost the things I loved when I changed what I wish I hadn't done?"

"Why not do both?" I asked. "Keep the good times and get rid of the bad ones."

"I'm sure you've seen time travel movies where they fix one thing, break something else, and create a new set of problems. I wouldn't want to erase the experiences I regret if it meant not having you and your brother. You'll never understand the joy of giving birth. I'd fall in that creek a hundred times as long as I got to have that." She paused to wipe away a tear. "Nothing needs to be changed. I accept what brought me here. It's better to learn from the past and live in the present."

"Yeah. That makes sense. It's kind of embarrassing, but I often have these time-travel fantasies, even though I know there's no going back. I've thought about what you said before—how changing one thing can change everything. I always assumed that the fate I altered would be better. But, like you said, there's no guarantee of that."

"Why would you be ashamed of that?"

"No, not ashamed, embarrassed. They're different."

"How?"

"Embarrassment is wanting to disappear after you do something stupid. Like in fourth grade when I forgot the notes to my saxophone solo and tried to hide."

"I remember that! You knocked over all the drums and cymbals, then everyone stopped playing. They even shined the spotlight on you! I'm sorry, I shouldn't laugh, but you looked adorable."

"I'm glad one of us enjoyed it. I quit playing the saxophone after that. But shame, shame is when you want people to suffer because you're in pain. Why should anyone feel good when I'm hurting? Why should I help you when no one's helped me? What about me?"

"I stick my neck out for nobody," my mom said, quoting *Casablanca*.

"I realized this after an incident in a drugstore; a lady in a wheelchair needed my help checking out. She didn't ask me directly, but I'd already refused. It wasn't a conscious decision, but it was a decision because that's who I'd become: someone who hates anyone who needs help and wastes my time. Then this cowboy saunters out and—"

I started bawling, my face flat against the Model T mechanics, my tears rusting their machines.

"What is it, Julian? What's wrong? Why are you crying?"

I sniffled and wiped my face. "It's the story I'm trying to tell you—what happened in the store. The cowboy—um, he was wearing a cowboy hat; that's why I've been calling him that—he did what I should have done. It was so easy to help that woman, but I didn't. That's not me, you know? Not after what I've been through." I paused to get a grip on myself.

"The cowboy stepped out of line while everyone else stood there, annoyed with the woman. He didn't simply put her stuff on the counter; he gave her the dignity everyone deserves and put us all to shame for what we should have done. I should have helped that woman, but now I understand how we destroy ourselves through hate and become what we oppose. That is the hypocrisy of hate." She nodded.

"There are so many things I'm angry about, but hate has never resolved them." I laughed as some of the weight of my life lifted. "Nothing infuriates our enemies more than our success, but our greatest achievements are made through love. God was with that man; through His mercy, he was blessed. I saw it when he spoke to the woman in the wheelchair, and now I believe that cruelty is the only thing that's shameful."

"Wow, Julian, I never thought of you as the religious type!"

"I haven't been to any religious services since my Bar Mitzvah. I believe in God, but I've had many sources of inspiration that influence my faith in the mysterious forces that shape the universe."

"I support whatever spiritual path you prefer, but what if you steal from someone? Isn't that shameful, too?"

"We're not going to extract the Ten Commandments from this one experience. There are many things we shouldn't do, but nothing ever made me feel worse than standing in that man's shadow. That was shame. Kindness leads us into the light; without it, the shadow is all we'll ever know."

"What about when I used to go out drinking and leave with your brother? And that one time when I was too drunk to drive, and you took my car keys? I might have run over someone if you hadn't stopped me. I'm still ashamed of that."

"Yes, someone could have been hurt, but they weren't because we've always helped each other. You have a disease. You got help and have helped so many other people. That's a story of redemption. There's nothing shameful about it."

"Interesting. That's a great way to look at it. People at my AA meetings would like that. Mind if I share it with them?"

"Sure, if you think it'll be helpful, but don't share my cymbal-crashing story, okay?"

After saying goodnight to my mom and going to bed, I started reminiscing about Hazel, transported back to my teens. That might have been inspired by hanging out in my old milieu, where I'd tried to summon the courage to call girls in instead of staring at the phone, debating if rejection or romance awaited me. That was before the Internet, chat programs, or cell phones existed. If you were dating someone, short of being together, all you could do was stare at the ceiling with the phone cord wrapped around your wrist, wondering why the silly things you said to each other had so much power over you. After I asked Hazel to the formal, we shared more kisses, but I liked most when we'd talk for hours on the phone. I don't remember much of what we said, but I remember how happy I was to hear her voice and that she felt the same. Nothing can replace the innocent hours we lost when my life was forever changed. It was painful, but many of the sweetest things are. As Henry said about the double rainbow, some moments elude picture frames, cherished for what they could've been.

The Nasdaq continued its descent, plummeting over 80 percent from its March 2000 peak before hitting bottom in October 2002. It then took another thirteen years to surpass its dotcom peak. It was one of the worst stock market crashes in history. Six months after quitting, Albert called and let me know that Alex had committed suicide. I hadn't known he had a wife and child. By the time I quit, he'd lost most of his money and was doubling down on the same mistakes that'd made his ship take on water before. The final straw came when a ransomware attack hit the lab. The attack originated from a phishing link that Alex clicked. Albert told him to report the breach to the head of information technology immediately, but that's not what Alex did. He tried to frame Albert, but the IT team quickly discovered the truth using the tracking software Alex had championed to produce a detailed report that indisputably incriminated him. By the end of the day, they'd locked Alex's login, disabled his keycard, and escorted him out of the building. Alex began beating his wife, who subsequently filed for divorce and left with their child. His life spiraled from there, and he hanged himself in an apartment he'd rented.

I was glad Alex was gone, though I pitied his brutal end and felt no joy in his demise. I saw similarities between his belief that mercy could be postponed until our wealth was secured and my mother beseeching me that I couldn't help anyone if I was broke. Yet, her actions proved that kindness should never be delayed. The time to be kind is always now. While I appreciate aspects of most problematic people in my life, I've chosen not to forgive them— holding fast to how I've finessed my way around those fools to avoid perpetuating the pain they tried to pin on me.

Don't be cruel; don't fight your demons on the stock exchange. Choose love over hate. Now what? I had a good amount of dough left, but I needed to do something more than lounge around as my savings dwindled. Even though Alex was gone, I wasn't interested in returning to the lab. My mom suggested volunteering at the children's hospital until I figured out my next step. She explained that Ataru, who'd helped me pass math, had been a volunteer. *"Ko-rek-tu."* He tutored to keep busy when he wasn't with his daughter, who was being treated there for leukemia.

I registered to tutor at the children's hospital. They were thrilled to see me but didn't specify what subject I'd be teaching, which made me wonder whether I was up to the task. My mom called a few days before I began and said she'd received the latest report on the assets she held for my brother and me, including my Hershey shares, which my grandmother purchased when I was born. The $500 investment had grown by 7,667 percent: $500 × 76.67 = $38,335. No, not $1,000,000, but pretty damn good for a single $500 purchase with dividends reinvested and no speculating or debates with fair-weather friends along the way. A solid case for less is more. On the way to the hospital, I stopped by the farmhouse to see if I could find Sunrise. A big dog barked at me behind the fence bordering the barn, so I couldn't get close enough to check if she was there. But I like to think Sunrise was sitting on the porch, nice and fat, with kittens of her own. Then she'd hiss at that dumb old dog, and it'd scamper off behind the barn, where it would lie in the grass beside the waddling ducks.

Before getting started, I met the director and other volunteers. They provided complimentary meals, so we had lunch beforehand. Volunteering is its own reward, but free food? It pains me to think of all the stale deli meals I could have skipped.

I asked the hospital staff if they knew where my old room was, half expecting to see Mateo with his cup of maté there, but they didn't know. Someday, I'll find him in Uruguay and try to lift myself over puddles with his crutches. After the formalities, it was time to work. They brought me to a classroom and introduced me to the boy I'd be tutoring. He was eleven years old and had been in a car accident that required the Jaws of Life to extract him. The crash damaged his prefrontal cortex and led to the amputation of his leg.

A bag at his side collected urine. Trust me, kid, you don't wanna yank on that.

His name was Michael, and he had trouble speaking. His parents bombarded me with questions, frustrated that their son's recovery was going slower than expected. I wanted to reassure them, but I could only say we each have our own journey. The hospital staff escorted them out, leaving just Michael and me. That's when it hit me—I shouldn't have come here. My chest tightened as I started pacing. Should I jump out the window? This was a mistake. How can I help him when I can barely manage my own problems? I'm not a teacher. They didn't even tell me what he's supposed to learn. I can't do this. The final boss entered the arena and hit me from the left, where I hadn't seen him coming. You're weak; you're a coward. Go grill me a steak. I like 'em rare, and grab me some booze. Any kind, I don't care. Step aside. Let a real man help this boy. I looked around, frantic. I needed to find someone—anyone who could help him. Please help us.

I thought of all the sides I'd seen—those who wanted to bury me in their misery and those who carried me when I was lost in a labyrinth of my own tears. Who will we be? If I free myself from fear through the courage that kindness keeps for us, I can carry the ones who need me. I stood and approached Michael. I wasn't wearing cowboy boots, but no one could deny my swagger was genuine. I smiled, and so did he.

Who will help *him*? I will.

Julian Lawrence

CT scan	MRI

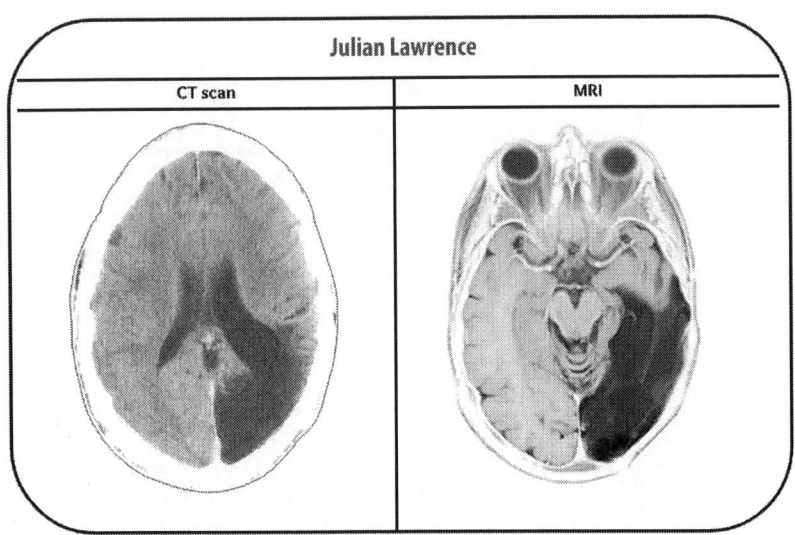

Acknowledgments

Thank you to everyone who provided editorial support.

Disclaimer and Copyright

While characters in this story are derived from a combination of people I've known, their names and identifying characteristics were changed to respect their privacy. Any full name matching a person, alive or deceased, is coincidental. Because of their contextual presence in the story, there are brief, unattributed references to the works of William Shakespeare (Macbeth), Samuel Coleridge (Kubla Khan), T. S. Eliot (The Love Song of J. Alfred Prufrock), John Lennon (Imagine), Carl Douglas (Kung Fu Fighting), and Tommy Tutone (Jenny). Most capitalized and italicized words in this book were used according to editorial and stylistic guidelines and have no additional significance.

The quote, "God does not require us to succeed. He only requires that you try," is often attributed to Mother Teresa. Some sources claim she never said this. However, the potentially apocryphal origin of the quote makes it fitting for Part I, given the characters Julian and Mateo's uncertainty about religious figures and beliefs. "A slim sword for a stick," mentioned in Chapter 31, is a quote from Ryunosuke Akutagawa's book A Fool's Life. The text also references Rashomon by the same author. General information and background research was done using Wikipedia.

Though I independently created the line, "The Mystery is unsolvable because life itself is the pleasure of solving it," at the end of Chapter 31, it resembles a quote from Søren Kierkegaard: "Life is not a problem to be solved, but a reality to be experienced." I believe many paths lead us to the same truth.

"There is a sky above the sky" is a message I received while comatose. Many years later, I learned a similar phrase is used in a Chinese proverb, loosely translated as, "There are people beyond these people, outside of sky there is sky." The shared usage of this phrase is entirely coincidental.

Some characters, such as James, speak indignantly about people I never met, namely his mother. I've recorded their unverified opinions, which may be biased and inaccurate. Their opinions are not my own.

Some characters are a combination of individuals, and the dates of some events occurred at a time and place different than those portrayed in the memoir. This memoir chronicles the first twenty-five years of my life. While many views and beliefs I developed during this period remain, others have evolved and less closely reflect who I am today. Please learn from my mistakes, but don't repeat them. Hopefully, they make for educational and entertaining reading, but in no way are endorsements to copy them, particularly hopping on trains.

I wrote and edited this memoir with assistance from my human editor. Several months after its completion, generative AI tools like ChatGPT and Google Gemini became available. I then used these as a third set of eyes for tasks similar to those performed by my editor and me—such as verifying grammar, checking facts, ensuring coherent sentence structure, and validating the accuracy of various fallacies discussed in the text.

Cover design by Lizbe Coetzee Copyright © 2024 J International

ISBN: 978-0-9847879-4-4 eBook
ISBN: 978-0-9847879-6-8 paperback

Author contact: jinternational@manzanitallc.info

Made in the USA
Columbia, SC
22 January 2025

52238819R00236